The Rhetoric of Character in Children's Literature

Maria Nikolajeva

The Scarecrow Press, Inc.
Lanham, Maryland, and Oxford

In memoriam Astrid Lindgren

SCARECROW PRESS, INC.

Published in the United States of America
by Scarecrow Press, Inc.
A wholly owned subsidiary of
The Rowman & Littlefield Publishing Group, Inc.
4501 Forbes Boulevard, Suite 200, Lanham, Maryland 20706
www.scarecrowpress.com

PO Box 317
Oxford
OX2 9RU, UK

British Library Cataloguing in Publication Information Available

The hardback edition of this book was catalogued by the Library of Congress as
follows:
Nikolajeva, Maria, 1952–
    The rhetoric of character in children's literature / Maria Nikolajeva.
       p. cm.
    Includes bibliographical references (p.) and index.
     1. Children's literature—History and criticism. 2. Characters and
    characteristics in literature. I. Title.

PN1009.5.C43 N55 2002
809'.927—dc21

2002019952

0-8108-4886-4 (pbk : alk. paper)

~

Contents

Acknowledgments

This book is the first result of a large-scale research project on "Children's Literature and Narrative Theory" financed by Stockholm University. During my three-year research grant, I was able to devote my whole attention to the theory of characters, which is almost an unheard of luxury for a scholar in the humanities. I feel privileged by having been given this opportunity and would like to extend my thanks to the Department of Comparative Literature at Stockholm University for supporting this project, especially given the fact that the alternative proposal was August Strindberg.

The idea for the specific examination of literary characters in children's literature was prompted by the members of the research project "Children's Literature: Pure and Applied" at Åbo Akademi University, Finland. While the initial inspiration came mainly from Mia Österlund and Kaisu Rattyä, during the later stages of my work, Maria Lassén-Seger's investigation of transgressional characters provided many valuable thoughts.

The book was researched and written during my two years as a visiting professor at San Diego State University (SDSU) in California. I would like to extend my thanks to Alida Allison for initiating this enterprise; to Carey Wall, the chair of the Department of English and Comparative Literature at SDSU, for providing this opportunity; and to all colleagues at SDSU for the stimulating intellectual climate. Nobody is forgotten, but I must emphasize weekly lunchtime conversations with Mary Galbraith as an indispensable part of my scholarly process, as well as Carole Scott's ever-inspiring skepticism.

Roberta Seelinger Trites has been especially important during this time, with her unfailing confidence and support. Apart from this personal inspiration, I received many helpful comments on my research during the seminar she invited me to give at Illinois State University.

I received several opportunities to present parts of my research at the University of Turku and the Åbo Akademi University, Finland; the Danish Center for Children's Literature, Denmark; and the conference on Modern Critical Approaches to Children's Literature at Middle Tennessee State University, Murfeesboro.

I am indebted to Judith Plotz for soliciting an essay on work in children's fiction (appearing in *The Lion & the Unicorn*), which has become incorporated into chapter 10.

Great thanks to Lydia Williams, who managed elegantly to change hats from being a demanding and helpful colleague to shaping my text into proper English idiom.

Finally, thanks to my husband Staffan Skott, who once again showed patience and understanding during my long and boring explications on intersubjectivity and psychonarration.

INTRODUCTION

~

Why a Theory of Character?

I wrote this book in response to recurrent experiences as a university teacher of children's literature. Before I became aware of the problem, I, like so many of my colleagues, favored examination topics such as "Discuss characterization in . . . ." What we got back were dull, descriptive essays, even though we naturally wanted something other than a rendering of what characters do in the story or even an evaluation of the ideas they represent. However, the fault was ours: we failed to offer our students adequate tools for analyzing the artistic means used for characterization.

The issue of characters seems to be so self-evident that few studies of children's literature have paid any attention to it. We may find some basic concepts in textbooks, and we often see children's book reviews mentioning something to the effect that "characterization is strong and vivid." However, there is no clear understanding of what exactly "characterization" includes. Scholars do not agree about the nature and function of characters in literature for children, nor has theoretical research been done on characterization in children's fiction. Little established terminology exists for discussing characters and characterization. No theoretical work compares characters in general fiction and characters in fiction for children.

Among the many questions that teachers put to schoolchildren when discussing literary texts, I find two particularly illuminating: "Who is the main character of the story?" and "Who do you like best in the story?" (Less sophisticated versions include "Who would you like to be friends with?"; more sophisticated: "With whom do you identify?") When teachers ask such questions, they obviously assume them to be simple and self-evident, but on closer consideration they would probably have problems, as do my students—many of them future teachers—determining the main character in *Little Women* or *The Lion, the Witch and the Wardrobe*. Moreover, the assumption that as readers we necessarily must identify with some character in the story we are reading has been seriously questioned by contemporary literary theory. Children's writers have successfully subverted identification by creating a variety of repulsive, unpleasant characters with whom no normal human being would want to identify. The problem of subjectivity in literature, which has recently become a key issue in general criticism, has so far not reached the attention of children's literature scholars, with few exceptions (e.g., McCallum 1999). These are just two very elementary examples of the complexity of this seemingly simple matter.

Unfortunately, there is no option, as there has been in some other areas of children's literature research, to borrow concepts and analytical tools from general criticism. The theory of character is only marginally more developed in general literary studies. Searching the subject "character and characteristics in literature" in the Library of Congress on-line catalog, I found 427 items, 95 percent of which fall roughly under one of three categories: (1) "who is who in literature," including who is who in Shakespeare, Dickens, Jane Austen, and so on; (2) writers' manuals ("how to create a plausible character"); and (3) critical studies of particular writers or works. In the third category, the majority of studies focus on the question of *what* or *who* the characters are or, at best, what they represent, rather than on *how* they are constructed and revealed for the reader. In children's literature research, Gillian Avery's (1965, 1975) studies of nineteenth- and early twentieth-century heroes and heroines in children's fiction are a very good example.

Many titles are misleading in this respect. For instance, *Life Made Real: Characterization in the Novel since Proust and Joyce* by Thomas F. Petruso (1991), a brilliant study of what characters are, hardly addresses any theoretical aspects of characterization. Mary Doyle Springer's (1978) promising title *A Rhetoric of Literary Character* has the subtitle *Some Women of Henry James*, which corresponds better to the contents of the study. The titles of some studies of children's fiction are equally deceptive; for instance Raymond Jones's (1997) *Characters in Children's Literature* is an annotated index, while Margery Hourihan's (1997) *Deconstructing the Hero* is a marvelous feminist study of ideology in traditional children's literature.

Paradoxically, the most rewarding theoretical discussions on character are to be found in general studies of narrative, not specifically focused on character. These range from the standard *Aspects of the Novel* by E. M. Forster (1927) to one of the most recent contributions to the field, the second edition of *Narratology* by Mieke Bal (1997). However, far from all theoretical works on narrative pay attention to character. Such a milestone in contemporary theory of the novel as Wayne C. Booth's (1961) *The Rhetoric of Fiction* does not discuss character or characterization at all. In *The Nature of Narrative*, Robert Scholes and Robert Kellogg (1966), striving to go beyond the examination of the novel and to build bridges between ancient or medieval and postmodern literature in terms of narrative structure, have provided valuable insights into characterization. In fact, most of this illuminating study is about character, even the chapters devoted to plot, point of view, and meaning. Scholes and Kellogg maintain that "characters are the primary vehicles for revealing meaning in narrative" (104). Yet, while some valuable observations are made in the chapter on character in narrative (160–206), they have long been surpassed by more recent studies, especially in the area of depicting the characters' inner life. Also the chapter on point of view feels outdated, given the expanding nature of narrative studies in the last quarter of the twentieth century.

The ever-increasing number of writer's manuals on character do not, of course, represent any scholarly rigor; however, given the general lack of sources, they should not be neglected (see Card 1988; Cowden 2000; Edelstein 1999; Hood 1998; Kress 1998; Lauther 1998; Swain 1990). Although, for obvious reasons, not based on any theoretical ground, they do suggest the vast scope of artistic devices available for writers in creating characters. These include descriptions, dialogue, background, psychologically plausible personality traits, professions and hobbies, relationships, involving characters in a plot, using setting for characterization, and so on.

The dilemma for a children's literature scholar is that it is almost impossible to extrapolate the results of general narratological studies to children's fiction. One very good example is that many genres discussed in studies of narrative are not relevant for children's fiction, such as the courtesy novel, fabliaux (Martin 1986, 31), sacred myth, epic, legend, allegory, confession, or satire (Scholes and Kellogg 1966, 3). With very few exceptions, such as Roald Dahl, children's literature does not employ the grotesque. According to conventional genre definitions, all children's literature can be labeled as bildungsroman. The nature of children's literature presupposes a different set of rules both for the authors' creation of characters and for the readers' understanding of them.

A number of studies, often of surveys, discuss concrete types or characters in children's or young adult fiction: the portrayal of Afro-Americans (MacCann 1998), homosexual characters (Cuseo 1992; Day 2000), immigrants (McCoy 2000), people with disabilities (Robinson 1992), and so on.

An ongoing interdisciplinary research project examines the representation of grandparents in children's fiction (see also McElroe 1999). However, all these studies, once again, are focused on *what* rather than *how*.

Some basic concepts, for instance, from Forster's *Aspects of the Novel*, such as the binarity "flat and round" characters, have been used in assessing characters in children's fiction by Rebecca Lukens (1990) and Joanne Golden (1990). However, it is mainly contemporary narrative theory (Seymor Chatman, Shlomith Rimmon-Kenan, Mieke Bal, Thomas Docherty) that provides new workable tools for approaching characters, while some studies on mental representation and point of view (Dorrit Cohn, Ann Banfield) have opened new horizons.

While many general questions concerning literary characters will certainly be pertinent to children's fiction, its specific poetics present some additional challenges. Characters in children's fiction are not necessarily less complex, but they must be comprehensible for young readers. More commonly than in the mainstream, they serve as ideological (or rather educational) vehicles. Furthermore, child characters are by definition dynamic, under development; they have not accomplished their psychological maturation yet. All these factors, and many others, imply that characters in children's fiction are in several respects constructed differently than in general fiction.

What basic questions comprise a theory of literary character? The most profound point of departure should be the ontological status of characters: are we to view them as real people, with psychologically credible features, or merely as textual constructions? Literary theory from Aristotle to the present day offers diverse answers to this question. The difference between *Homo sapiens* and *Homo fictus* (Forster's terms, adopted by later scholars) is especially relevant in children's literature research, since children, as unsophisticated readers, have an even stronger tendency than adult readers to interpret characters as real, living people and judge them accordingly. As readers, we can understand literary characters better than we can ever understand real people; characters are transparent in a way real people can never be. In children's fiction, the assumption is that writers can represent the experience of child characters more easily than they can represent adult characters, which has gained children's fiction the reputation of being "simple"—a position I have strongly interrogated in my previous research.

We must further consider the fact that the role of characters in fiction varies between historical epochs and between genres. In children's fiction, the function of characters is closely connected with overall didactic purposes: characters are supposed to provide models and statute examples. This results in such specific features of children's fiction as the use of collective protagonists, a device that enables writers to show a variety of human traits without employing too much complexity in characterization.

The second basic question in the theory of character concerns how literary characters are revealed to readers and what devices and strategies are used by authors in the creation of characters: external description, internal representation, direct and indirect speech, narrator's comments, actions and reactions, and so on. In this area, the most interesting dilemmas originate from the very essence of children's fiction: a narrative that is told by an adult to and about a young person. The discrepancy among the cognitive levels of the author, the narrator, the character, and the implied reader creates a wide scope of possibilities that seldom occur in general fiction. In fact, most narratological studies point out texts such as *What Maisie Knew* and *The Sound and the Fury* as exceptional examples of depicting preverbal and nonverbal conditions (a child or a mentally disabled person), while this discordance between the author and the character is a rule rather than an exception in children's fiction.

My book thus has two purposes: to investigate the ontological and epistemological aspects of characters in children's fiction, and to pinpoint the principal differences between characterization in children's fiction and in general fiction. It has also been my ambition to offer consistent and easy-to-use terminology for discussing characters and characterization. The division of my study into two parts, "Ontology and Typology of Character" and "Epistemology of Character," reflects an attempt to distinguish between two separate sets of issues, which are regularly confused in general studies and in textbooks in literature. On the one hand, we have characters on the story level: their place in the narrative, their mutual importance, the degree of integrity they represent, the values they express, and so on. These questions may be summarized as "What are literary characters?" (cf. the common definition of story: "what is being told"). On the other hand, we have characters on the discourse level—characterization: how characters are constructed by authors and how readers reconstruct them from the texts (the common definition of discourse: "how it is being told"). Although story and discourse, and, subsequently, the appearance of characters on story and discourse levels, are naturally interdependent, I find the distinction crucial.

The structure of my chapters varies considerably depending on the content. Some are more theory focused, with brief examples, while others go more deeply into individual texts. This structure is intentional. It reflects my aim to cover the vast area I am exploring and at the same time pay particular attention to those parts of it I find the most essential and exciting, and least examined by previous research. At an early stage of my examination, I gave up the idea of being comprehensive, since the theory of character is obviously a lifetime of work for a large team of scholars.

In its theoretical framework, this study is deliberately and consciously eclectic. No single critical theory has provided a universal view of character; I focus instead on particular aspects. I have incorporated ideas from Russian formalism and French structuralism, Anglophone new criticism, Frye-inspired mythical criticism, Jungian criticism, feminist criticism, reader-response theory, speech act theory, and not least contemporary narratology. None of these theories is employed in its entirety; rather, I have chosen to appropriate concepts and theoretical stances that seemed to suit my specific needs in addressing a particular issue.

My study presupposes that the reader is somewhat familiar with contemporary narratological terminology. My basic sources are the works of Genette, Chatman, Prince, Rimmon-Kenan, and Bal. For a brief introduction to the terminology and its specific connotations in children's fiction, I recommend Joanne Golden's *The Narrative Symbol in Childhood Literature* and my own book, *Introduction to the Theory of Children's Literature* (or, for those who read Swedish, its Swedish-language counterpart *Barnbokens byggklossar*).

PART ONE

ONTOLOGY AND TYPOLOGY
OF CHARACTER

CHAPTER ONE

~

Approaches to Literary Characters

The various theoretical approaches to literary characters have oscillated between two extremes: characters as mere agents in the plot and characters as complete psychological existents. I have no intention of discussing this question in detail here since it has been adequately covered in several studies, most consistently perhaps in Seymor Chatman's (1978, 107–38) *Story and Discourse,* in which he goes through theories of character from Aristotle to postmodernism. However, I will reiterate a few central points, filling in the development of criticism after Chatman as well as some essential omissions in his study. In the first place, I will try to place these general arguments in connection with children's fiction. I will begin, though, by considering the place of the character among the agents of narrative communication.

The Character's Place in the Narrative

In Chatman's (1978, 151) scheme for narrative communication, the character is conspicuously absent:

Implied author → narrator → narratee → implied reader

Chatman's schema does not include the focalizing character, or focalizer, separately from the narrator, which is a decisive distinction for Mieke Bal (Bal 1997, 19*ff.*). Adapting this schema to include the character's place in the communicative chain, I would suggest:

Implied author → narrator → character-narrator → focalizer → (focalized) character → character-narratee → narratee → implied reader

3

Let us consider all possible relationships between these agencies, in which characters are involved.

Real Author—Character. Although the issue is less important for a text-oriented critic like myself, it still deserves mentioning. It may be essential in several types of narratives—for instance, (1) autobiography, in which the character is (or, rather, is assumed to be) identical with the author; (2) authentic diary, presenting the same relationship, except that the author is synchronized with the character; and (3) biography or hagiography, in which the author does not entirely "invent" the character but is assumed to present a credible portrait based on facts. In children's literature, biography and autobiography are, in the majority of cases, used for educational and didactic purposes, the authors choosing their own or other people's lives as a model, more rarely as a cautionary tale. Since I am, in the present study, not interested in nonfiction for children, I see no point in discussing this any further; however, both genres present a number of challenges in their character construction (see, e.g., Lathey 1999).

Implied Author—Character. Since the implied author is responsible for the ideology of the text—that is, the views and opinions expressed in it explicitly or implicitly—the relationship between the implied author and the character is of overall importance. In a mainstream novel, a character can serve as the author's mouthpiece. The implied author of a children's novel is an adult, while the protagonist is a child. The author's views cannot thus be directly expressed through the child character without the narrative assuming an unnatural tone. A possible solution is to use an adult secondary character who will provide the desired opinions and counterbalance the child character's "false" beliefs and assumptions.

Narrator—Character. In my argument, I share the opinion of those critics who maintain that *all* narratives by definition have a narrator, even though it may be covert rather than overt. In a mainstream novel, there may or may not be substantial gaps between the narrator and the character; that is, the narrator may be omniscient or focalize one or several characters; the narrator may have equal knowledge and experience with the characters or be superior to them. In a children's novel, the narrative agency is an adult, while the protagonist is a child. Several strategies may circumvent the problem. The adult narrative voice may adopt the child's level and pretend to be a child. The result is often a rather unnatural tone ("single address," in Barbara Wall's [1991] classification). The narrator may judge the child from his superior position,[1] communicating with the implied adult coreader over the child character's head ("double address"). Finally, he may cross-write child and adult ("dual address"; "equal address")—that is, share the child's perspective without losing his adult authority and experience (see some essays in Beckett 1999). Internal focalization is the foremost device to achieve this effect.

Character-narrator. Implies a first-person narrator who is also a character in his own narrative, or *homodiegetic*, in Gérard Genette's (1980) terminology. In a mainstream novel, this narrative mode seldom creates a problem. In a children's novel, once again the very fact that the character is a child with limited life experience and limited vocabulary restricts the scope of events, actions, insights, and emotions that can be treated.

Several options are possible. One is to use a retrospective (extradiegetic) narrator: an adult telling the story of his or her childhood. Another one, which is very rare in children's fiction, is an adult intradiegetic narrator, telling the story of a child. The narrator is thus not autodiegetic (not the protagonist of the story) but rather an observer, sometimes called witness-narrator, similar to Dr. Watson in *Sherlock Holmes* or Nick Carraway in *The Great Gatsby*. The example I can provide from children's literature is Lloyd Alexander's *Vesper* novels, told by the young protagonist's adult guardian. The narrator is thus limited to an exclusively external rendering of the events, which suits the adventurous structure of the novels well. The third, and most widely adopted, option is to use a genuine child perspective, an autodiegetic child narrator, making his inexperience and naïveté the primary narrative device. This character-narrator is by definition naive and unreliable, since the child lacks knowledge, experience, stable views and opinions, the capacity for self-evaluation and self-reflection, and so on. In mainstream fiction, this device involves using an outsider or a mentally retarded person (e.g., in *Forrest Gump*) as a narrator.

Focalizer—Focalized Character. The difference between the narrator (the agency whose voice we hear) and the focalizer (the agency through whose eyes and/or mind we experience the events) is of overall importance both for Gérard Genette and Mieke Bal. In children's literature it is especially pertinent, since it emphasizes the discrepancy between the (adult) voice and the child point of view. I find it significant that Bal (1997, 23, 31–32) illustrates a number of her statements about narrators and focalizers with children's books. On the other hand, we should distinguish between the focalizing character (the one who sees) and the focalized character (the one who is seen).

One of the most radical aspects in Genette's theory is the elimination of difference between personal (first-person) and impersonal (third-person) narration. An impersonal narrator focalizes another character, a personal narrator focalizes himself, either synchronically or retrospectively. For our interest in character, the difference between the narrator, the focalizer, and the focalized character is more important than between the personal and impersonal narration.

Narratee—Character. The notion of narratee has been introduced in Chatman's communication model mainly for the sake of symmetry, even though, unlike narrators, narratees are seldom overt in literary texts. A child character listening to a story—for instance, Christopher Robin in the outer frame of *Winnie-the-Pooh*—is a good example. Bastian in the first part of *The Neverending Story* is a narratee, while in the second part he becomes the sole protagonist. In *Dance on My Grave*, the narratee of Hal's written account is the social worker, Miss Atkins. Covert in the beginning of the novel, she is repeatedly evoked toward the end.

Character—Narratee. A covert narratee may be evoked in a children's story by an address, such as Kipling's "Oh my Best Beloved!" in *Just So Stories*. Such a narratee is obviously not a character in the story.

Character—Implied Reader. The implied reader is roughly defined in reader-response theory as the real authors' idea of their audience as inscribed in the texts. In other words, the implied reader is an abstract receiver assumed to have the capacity to assess the text, including the characters. In the mainstream, we can clearly see that the implied reader of Joyce's *Ulysses* is different from that of a supermarket novel, or, historically, the implied reader of *Gulliver's Travels* was assumed to have certain knowledge of Swift's contemporary England that present-day real readers may lack. The implied readers of *Ulysses* are supposed to be able to penetrate the complexity of the novel's three main characters; the implied readers of a supermarket novel are supposed to be satisfied by its superficial and stereotypical characterization since they are not seeking deep psychological portrayals; the contemporary implied readers of *Gulliver's Travels* were supposed to recognize the real people whom Swift depicts in a satirical manner. Similarly, in a children's novel, characters are constructed so that they can be understood by the implied readers; for instance, they think, behave, and speak the way the implied readers are assumed to think, behave, and speak. Implied readers of children's fiction have age, gender, level of education, cultural background, and so on, which all affect the character construction. It is not seldom that writers misjudge their audience. Writers may declare that they write for boys and girls between ten and twelve, while the implied readers of the novels may have to be slightly older and more mature to understand the character, or the character's experiences will only appeal to girls, or the particular settings and events of the novel presuppose a certain knowledge of the British public school system in the nineteenth century, or the intertextual links address a reader with substantial reading habits. All this does not necessarily prevent real readers from enjoying a text that postulates a different implied reader.

Real Reader—Character. Although empirical research lies beyond the scope of my interest, some very general remarks can be made. Young readers usually have stronger empathy with literary characters, mainly because they perceive them as "real" (an example of naive reading). Sophisticated readers can detach themselves from the narrative and appreciate a story with unattractive, repulsive, morally depraved, evil, and criminal protagonists (*American Psycho* or *Neuromancer*). Young readers normally lack this ability; when there is no clearly indicated subject position in the narrative, they may feel frustrated and confused. On the contrary, young readers seldom have problems identifying with anthropomorphic animal or toy characters as long as these hold the disempowered subject positions similar to their own (therefore, mice, bunnies, and kittens are more popular in children's fiction than tigers and other aggressive carnivores).

For a young reader, an age difference of two years may feel significant. While as adult readers, we seldom have problems reading about characters who are significantly younger or older than we are, for child readers a difference in age between themselves and the characters may create insurmountable barriers. Empirical research shows that children prefer to read about characters of their own age or some years older. As far as gender preferences are concerned, it is maintained that boys normally like to read stories about boys, while girls make no distinction.

I have no doubts about the truth of these statements; however, I believe that such preferences have more to do with plots than with the gender of characters. Male readers are, in our society, conditioned to prefer "masculine" plots (dynamic, linear, action oriented), which seldom have female protagonists. Female readers prefer or are conditioned to prefer "feminine" plots (circular, character oriented, psychological), which may have both male and female protagonists. In fact, young adult novels are mostly read by preteen or younger teenage girls, regardless of whether they have male or female protagonists.

Mimetic and Semiotic Approaches to Characters

As I noted earlier, the central question in discussion of literary characters is whether they should be perceived (and subsequently analyzed) as real, living people or as purely textual constructions. The two polarities have been described in terms of open versus closed (Chatman 1978), mimetic versus semiotic (Rimmon-Kenan 1983), mimetic versus nonmimetic (Docherty 1983), or mimetic versus thematic (Phelan 1989). The concept of mimetic characters—or rather a mimetic view of character—is based on a mimetic view of fiction at large—that is, of fiction being a direct reflection ("mimesis" = imitation) or representation of reality. A semiotic or thematic approach presupposes that characters, like all other textual elements, are made of words alone and have no referents in the real world. A mimetic approach treats characters as individuals; a semiotic approach treats them as linguistic entities. A scholar's task may vary between the interpretation of characters (in psychological or ideological terms) and an analysis of character construction (in narratological terms).

While the first task, with mimetic orientation, has been widely applied to adult as well as children's novels, the second has been seriously neglected. One of the most influential studies of literary character, W. J. Harvey's (1965) *Character and the Novel,* takes a firm mimetic approach. Thomas Docherty (1983, x–xiii) is quite critical of Harvey's study because it ignores the vast scope of characters outside the realistic tradition. Since nonrealistic genres comprise a considerable part of children's fiction, we would limit our understanding of character by applying only mimetic approaches.

Let us consider the consequences of the two approaches, also paying special attention to their relevance for children's literature. A mimetic character is assumed to "mean" or "represent" something. To take some of the more radical examples, for a Marxist critic, characters are representatives of their class; for a feminist critic, they are representatives of their gender; and so on. Mimetic characters allow and sometimes require that we go outside the text and construct the character from our own experiences. We can explain their behavior by their social origins, ethnicity, gender, culture, and upbringing (about which we may or may not know anything from the text). In children's novels, we also expect child characters to behave consistently with what we know from child psychology about their cognitive level, emotional (in)stability, and so on.

The danger of the mimetic approach to characters is that we can easily ascribe to them features that the author had no intention of providing, merely because "girls always like gossip," "boys are naughty," "schoolteachers are insensitive," and so on. We can further ascribe to them backgrounds not found in the text, merely on the basis of our experience. Driven to the absurd, this approach results in the type of questions ridiculed in the famous essay title "How Many Children Had Lady Macbeth?" (Knights 1965). In children's literature, we can, for instance, ask how Tom Sawyer has been affected by whether he has had measles or whether Heidi was nursed by her mother or by a wet nurse.[2]

It is equally dangerous, and in my opinion illegitimate, to ascribe to literary characters traits extrapolated from real people, which is easily done when novels contain at least some autobiographical elements. For instance, although there are obvious similarities between Jo March and the author of *Little Women*, I would not be prepared to search for motivations behind Jo's behavior in Louisa M. Alcott's biography.

It is sometimes too easy to speculate about characters and claim that someone is evil because his mother was unkind to him when he was a child. It is equally easy—and common—to read a literary character using schemata from child psychology and even clinical psychiatry, thus treating characters as medical "cases."[3] While such studies may throw some light on our understanding of human nature as illustrated by literary characters, they seldom go beyond speculations. Indeed, literary characters do not necessarily have to behave the way real people do, and they do not necessarily follow the prescribed behavioristic patterns or the observed course of mental disturbances. Even when authors are familiar with developmental psychology, they are not obliged to construct their characters in consistency with it.

Let me exemplify my argument. How shall we judge Edmund's behavior in *The Lion, the Witch and the Wardrobe*? The writer gives us some hints about his having attended a wrong kind of school to excuse his choosing the wrong side in the battle of good and evil. We can speculate about his being a middle child, perhaps neglected in favor of his older brother and younger sister. We may think of dozens of reasons why Edmund needs to take revenge on his siblings. We may suggest that he is suffering from separation trauma or from extensive fear of air raids, from which the children have been evacuated. We can interpret his falling for the White Witch's charms as an indication of his dependence on his mother and his immediate dislike of Aslan as a prime case of Oedipus complex. We can discuss his personality from different angles, dwelling on a child's natural vanity and desire for attention, or on the effects of poor nutrition at his boarding school—a well-known fact about British schoolboys in that era. In doing all this, we need to step outside the text and apply our knowledge of human nature, of child psychology, and of British history and social culture. On the other hand, we may simply state that the plot demands a traitor and that Edmund's behavior is not motivated by his psychological properties but exclusively by the textual conditions. This would be an example of the semiotic, or nonmimetic, approach. Naturally, we should remember that literary characters are, by definition, more semiotic than real people, since they are part of a design. Assuming that characters are closed textual constructions (semiotic entities), we extract the essential traits of the characters exclusively from their sayings and doings in the text. We can state that they have no existence outside the text, so if nothing is said about a character's background, then this background has never existed. Since we do not know anything about Edmund's parents, we have no reason to speculate about his relationship with them.

Only with a mimetic approach can we discuss characters as "plausible" and "implausible." In *Stuart Little*, the little mouse's origin is a textual mystery: he is somehow born to completely ordinary parents. In the recent film version, a mimetic interpretation is applied: Stuart is not the natural son but an adopted one. In a semiotic approach, the question of Stuart's origin is irrelevant. Without having done any empirical research, I would maintain that young readers are in this case much more open to semiotic interpretations than some adults, including the makers of the film version.

I find it worth mentioning that in some studies of character, no distinction is made between mimetic and nonmimetic (semiotic, thematic) characters, and mimetic and nonmimetic *approaches* to character. The difference is, however, of overall importance. I do not believe that characters have intrinsic qualities of being mimetic or nonmimetic. Robert Scholes and Robert Kellogg (1966) suggest that the "connection between the fictional world and the real can be either *representative* or *illustrative*" (84; italics in the original). The former is mimetic; the latter, semiotic. The former duplicates reality by imitation; the latter suggests an aspect of reality. The former appeals to reason and encourages searching for a meaning; the latter appeals to senses and defies meaning. For instance, such characters as the villain and the hero may be seen as having either psychological properties of evil and heroism, respectively; or they may be viewed as purely aesthetic types (Scholes and Kellogg 1966, 99).

The problem with Scholes and Kellogg's (1966, 102) examination of characters is that they view characters as *being* representative or illustrative, social or aesthetic, rather than discuss the two polarized approaches to them. In fact, depending on a scholar's general attitude toward literature and the chosen direction of criticism, one and the same character may be treated as either representative or illustrative, either as a social type or as an aesthetic function, and both approaches are naturally equally legitimate. It seems, however, that within children's literature criticism, there is a very strong tendency toward treating characters as mimetic and representative.

Baruch Hochman (1985, 49) argues in his study of character that a single approach is not possible, since authors' attitudes toward characters change throughout history, as do general views on human beings. I find this observation especially relevant for children's literature, since the changing views on childhood affect the way characters are presented.

Character as Actor: From Aristotle to Structuralism

For Aristotle, characters are subordinate to the plot; their function in a literary work is merely to perform actions. Aristotle distinguishes between *pratton* (actor or agent) and *ethos* (psychological figure, personality), maintaining that agents are indispensable in a literary work, while psychological characters are optional. The only traits allowed to actors are "noble" or "base"; all other human features are not essential for the plot. This theory, primitive as it may seem to us today, has obviously been used as the underlying principle for traditional children's fiction, in which characters' actions are more important than their psychological features.

Within formalist and structural theory, developed 2,300 years after Aristotle, characters are also treated merely as agents who perform certain actions and therefore have no psychological features whatsoever.[4] It may also be said that characters have certain fixed roles. In Vladimir Propp's (1968) study of the magic tale, *Morphology of the Folktale*, seven such roles are identified: the hero, the false hero (who parallels the hero but fails to perform the task), princess (object of the quest; not necessarily royal and not necessarily female), dispatcher, donor, helper, and villain. Since children's literature historically grew out of folklore, most of these roles are to be found in children's fiction. In *The Lion, the Witch and the Wardrobe*, the four children are a collective hero (possibly with Edmund as the false hero), the White Witch is the villain, Aslan is the dispatcher, the Beavers are the helpers, Father Christmas a donor, while summer and peace in Narnia are the achieved object of the quest. In *Tom Sawyer*, Tom is the hero, Injun Joe his opponent, Huck Finn his helper, Becky the princess to be rescued, and so on.

A further evolution of the seven-character scheme, developed by A. J. Greimas (1983), has resulted in the *actantial model*. The agents in this

SENDER → OBJECT → RECEIVER

↑

HELPER → SUBJECT ← ANTAGONIST

model are called *actants;* they perform actions. It is essential to distinguish between an actant and an *actor,* the latter being a concrete figure in a plot. The collective character in children's fiction consists of several actors but is one and the same actant. The four children in *The Lion, the Witch and the Wardrobe* have the same function in the plot, and together they are one actant. All Taran's companions in the Prydain Chronicles are the same actant; they fulfill the helper function. Bal (1997, 32) speaks of a collective actant.

All structural models describe the characters in relation to the plot and only superficially how they relate to each other. This does not allow a deeper analysis of the characters' traits or "inner life." Therefore, such models have been successfully applied both to folktales and formulaic fiction (crime novels, mystery, adventure, horror, romance). A structural approach to formulaic fiction, presented by John G. Cawelti (1976, 91), singles out four roles in a detective story: the victim, the criminal, the detective, and those threatened by the crime but incapable of solving it. These roles correspond to Propp's characters of princess, villain, hero, and false hero. They can also be pressed into the actantial model. However, as Chatman (1978, 112) correctly notes, formal approaches are seldom applied to contemporary psychological novels, in which critics as well as readers are normally more interested, for instance, in why the characters behave the way they do. This is acknowledged in Tzvetan Todorov's (1977, 66) *The Poetics of Prose,* in which he makes a fundamental distinction between plot-oriented and character-oriented narratives. I find this distinction crucial for any further discussion of character in children's fiction.

Traditional children's fiction is unmistakably plot oriented. It is commonly believed that young readers are more interested in plot than in characters, as compared with adult readers. Since myths and folktales are conditioned by plot, operating with flat and static characters, early children's books, imitating folk narratives, also concentrated on the plot, mainly exploring characters to clarify the morals of the story. The first adaptations of adult fiction into children's stories (*Robinson Crusoe, Gulliver's Travels*) usually cut away most of the character development and focused on the plot, sometimes reinforcing this element more than the original. When Chatman (1978, 131) claims that functional or actantial theory of character is "inadequate," he presumably means that it is inadequate for analyzing complex contemporary characters in character-oriented narratives.

The vast majority of children's books are plot oriented. This includes not only formulaic fiction but also novels of quality. It would be meaningless to analyze Dorothy in *The Wizard of Oz* in psychological terms, since she only has one feature: she is good. She is, by contrast, highly motivated in her behavior by the objective of the plot: to return home. The functional or actantial model would be more than adequate to describe the characters in *The Wizard of Oz*. There has, however, been a notable shift in Western children's fiction, beginning in the 1960s, toward a more profound interest in character, toward psychological, character-oriented children's novels. In many contemporary novels for children, we observe a disintegration of the plot in its traditional meaning; nothing really "happens." There is no beginning or end in the usual sense, no logical development toward a climax and denouement; the story may seem to be arbitrarily cut from the character's life, or is even more often a mosaic of bits arbitrarily glued together (see further Nikolajeva 1998a). On the other hand, the examination of the character is usually much more intense.

The ratio between plot and character cannot, of course, be viewed as an absolute criterion of literary quality, but we tend to evaluate contemporary children's fiction by characterization rather than by plot. This corresponds to the trends in general literary criticism. Tzvetan Todorov notices the development of contemporary literature toward character-oriented narratives, even though he himself mainly analyzes plot-oriented, apsychological narratives, such as *Decameron* and *Arabian Nights*. Alongside Todorov, Roland Barthes (1974) in *S/Z* takes a step away from the rigid structuralist approach to character, allowing literary characters a certain degree of psychological personality as part of the narrative structure.

Character as a Psychological Existence:
From Henry James to Harold Bloom

The cornerstone of Henry James's theory of fiction is his statement on the interconnection of character and action, best expressed by his much quoted passage from *The Theory of Fiction* (1884/1972): "What is character but the determination of incident? What is incident but the illustration of character?" (37). He thus rejects the common division of fiction into novels of incident (or plot oriented, in Todorov's terminology) and novels of character (character oriented). Despite this, throughout his theoretical works James pays substantially more attention to character than to any other textual aspect. In fact, the prior quotation continues, "What is either a picture or a novel that is *not* of character?" (37; James's emphasis). Character is thus for James the focus of fiction, and all other elements of the text, such as plot, setting, subject, and style, are subordinate to character. Moreover, in his assessment of plot and action, James gives priority to internal events and actions, which are by definition character bound; his own novels are the best illustrations of this principle.

James distinguishes between characters—fully developed psychological existents—and figures, or types, which may illustrate actions or situations but are not as artistically sophisticated as characters. For him, the psychological dimensions of literary characters are the foremost criteria of merit, and characters lacking psychological depth are artistic failures.

The well-known study by A. C. Bradley (1904), *Shakespearean Tragedy*, treats characters in Shakespeare's plays as if they were living people, assembling their personalities from psychological traits that are partly explicit in the texts, partly implicit and determined by our knowledge or understanding of human nature. Bradley ascribes to characters a high degree of motivation, searching behind their actions and reactions certain psychological properties rather than the author's design. He also ascribes to them moral qualities based on their actions, seeking a psychological explanation for those. Thus, he finds the origins of Edmund's envy in *King Lear* in the fact that he is an illegitimate son, providing excuses for the character's evil behavior (cf. my argument earlier on another Edmund, of *The Lion, the Witch and the Wardrobe*). He further makes a distinction in degree of evil between Regan and Goneril, yet stating that, as females, these characters are evil by nature!

Almost a century later, Harold Bloom (1998) was to take another view of Shakespearean characters in *Shakespeare: The Invention of the Human*. Bloom's illuminating view of the psychological characters as a relatively late invention in the history of Western literature brings in the question of when psychological characters appear in children's literature, when the human being of children's books was "invented." I will address this question in detail in the next chapter. At this point I can suggest that since children's literature is a considerably later phenomenon than general literature (two to three hundred years compared with many thousands), we may assume that psychological characters do not appear in children's books until quite recently. In fact, I would roughly estimate their emergence as occurring in the last fifty years. This also accounts for the predominantly mimetic attitude toward characters in children's literature.

The Author and the Character:
Expressive Approaches

The Romantic tradition regards the literary text, including characters, as the expression of the author's mind (see, e.g., Abrams 1953). The biographical approach to fiction, dominant in literary criticism during the nineteenth century, views characters as mouthpieces, the bearers of the authors' ideas. This approach is seldom discussed in contemporary criticism, perhaps because it is considered obsolete. It has, however, been revived in two radically different theoretical directions: the psychoanalytical and the sociohistorical. A psychoanalytically oriented biographer views characters as projections of the author's psyche and treats the character's problems as direct reflections of the author's problems. It is fairly common to search for the origins of some famous characters of children's literature, such as Peter Pan or the Little Prince, in their authors' childhood traumas (Franz 1981; Rose 1984; Wullschläger 1995). While these studies may throw some light on the authors, using their literary work as confessional testimony, I normally do not find that parallels with authors' lives add significantly to our understanding of characters. However, this approach should certainly not be neglected.

The other approach has resulted in considerably more serious theoretical stances. Its foremost proponent is none other than Mikhail Bakhtin, whose work on literary character is probably the least known of his many overwhelming theories. Bakhtin's early fragments, which most certainly were intended as part of his more comprehensive theory of the novel, have only recently been introduced into Western criticism. Of these, his unfinished long essay "Author and Hero in Aesthetic Activity," written in the 1920s, is of a special relevance for my study (Bakhtin 1990). However, one of the best-known works by Bakhtin (1984), *Problems of Dostoyevsky's Poetics*, introduces some of his major notions about literary characters being the author's mouthpieces in a dialogical, polyphone chorus of views and opinions. Thus, for Bakhtin characters are deliberately constructed by the author to express his views, and therefore they have little to do with human nature or psychology.

Although Bakhtin was by no means a Marxist, this is not far from the Marxist notion of characters as bearers of the ideology of their social class, or feminist views of characters as bearers of the ideology of their gender. Little as this may seem to have to do with children's literature, we notice obvious parallels with the approach of certain children's literature critics who view children's texts as educational and ideological vehicles, and the characters therefore as bearers of "right" or "wrong" values. In traditional children's literature, we often meet adults who provide young readers with clear-cut morals and therefore function exclusively as mouthpieces for the author's didactic views. One of the best examples is perhaps the cricket in *Pinocchio*, treated in criticism as "the voice of conscience" (see Zipes 1997, 61–87).

The Character and the Reader:
Reader-Response Approaches

Reader-response criticism presupposes that the reader constructs the character, alongside all other elements of the text. This view is to be found in studies by Wolfgang Iser, Stanley Fish, and Umberto Eco, to name only a few (for an overview of reader-response theories, see Rimmon-Kenan 1983, 117–29). One of the most profound of the few available studies of literary characters, *Character in Literature* by Baruch Hochman (1985, 32), claims that the impact on the reader is the most essential function of the character.

There is otherwise little in reader-response criticism that is focused specifically on character, so I will have to explicate this position by inference. Chatman speaks repeatedly about characters being assembled and interpreted by the audience; Hochman speaks about readers "retrieving" characters from texts. It is argued that readers relate the information they get about characters partly to their experience of real life, partly to their previous reading; in this respect, each individual reader's previous experience is decisive for the interpretation of character. Iser's central concept of textual gaps suggests that, first, the text may deliberately leave certain character traits unspecified, to be filled by the reader; second, that concrete readers will fill these gaps differently.

I share Umberto Eco's and Jonathan Culler's more restricted view of implied readers as compared with Iser's, which presupposes some inherent features of the text itself that guides (or manipulates) the reader to adopt a certain interpretation. In children's fiction, such guidance or manipulation is generally stronger than in the mainstream. A children's author will probably be more explicit about characters' traits, behavior, and motivation; the author's construction of the implied reader is more conscious and deliberate. This makes reader-response theory in some respect more pertinent to children's fiction.

Many semiotic-oriented theoreticians have questioned readers' emotional responses to characters. For instance, do we as readers feel truly sorry for Desdemona or Anna Karenina? Without having proof in empirical research, I would once again venture to state that young readers feel stronger empathy with literary characters and that children's writers appeal to the readers' feelings in a more immediate way.

Furthermore, for children's fiction, we may find it necessary to identify some types of implied (inscribed, encoded, ideal, hypothetical, model, virtual[5]) readers that would "retrieve" characters differently. First, we should distinguish between primary audience (children) and secondary audience (adult mediators). A children's text does not necessarily have adults as its implied coreader (although in practice it is almost impossible to avoid); therefore, the demands we as adults put on characters in terms of unity, consistency, or complexity are not relevant for the primary implied reader.

Second, we should distinguish between sophisticated and unsophisticated readers (competent/incompetent in Eco's terms, informed/uninformed in Fish's), who do not necessarily coincide with the categories of primary and secondary readers. An unsophisticated reader, following the plot and focusing on events, will perhaps miss most of the clues given in texts concerning the personality of the characters and may not find them important. Understanding characters is part of literary competence, in Eco's meaning, and a competent reader will know how to retrieve a complex character from a number of features presented in the text.

Third, there is a difference between synchronic and diachronic readers (or, in H. R. Jauss's [1982] terms, a shift in horizon of expectations). Mark Twain's or Louisa M. Alcott's contemporaries understood their characters differently than we do today. Some radical contemporary reevaluations of characters are based on changes in expectations and values, not least reevaluations of gender and race. Similarly, speaking of located versus dislocated readers, we acknowledge that a Swedish or Bulgarian or Chinese reader will each have a slightly—or sometimes substantially—different understanding of an American character compared with an American reader. Making use of Fish's concept of interpretative communities, we can say that each community will have a slightly different understanding of characters in any given novel.

Denigration of Character: From New Criticism to Poststructuralism

The drive to reduce characters to the level of purely textual constructions is a natural consequence of the development of contemporary mainstream fiction (see Hochman 1983). In certain texts, notably the French *roman nouveau*, characters indeed lack psychological features. French novelists and theoreticians of literature (Alain Robbe-Grillet, Nathalie Sarraute) deny characters any substantial importance in contemporary literature. American New Criticism has been especially hard on character. Postmodern views of literature and art have taken the defamation of character further still. The aesthetic of postmodernism strongly interrogates the stability and unity of the individual, thus claiming that literary characters as psychological entities are impossible and unnecessary.[6] The fallacy of such critical directions in their attitude toward character seems to be that they depart from a limited scope of literary works that indeed render characters insignificant; based on those, the conclusion is drawn that characters are subordinate in fiction at large. According to Thomas Petruso, the characters of Proust and Joyce, as well as those of a number of later twentieth-century writers, such as Faulkner, are in the first place projections of their authors and second "vehicle[s] of our perception of the fictional world" (Petruso 1991, 88). Already in the title *Reading (Absent) Character*, Thomas Docherty (1983) declares his position in character theory.

One of the most radical reevaluations of character is presented in a study by the Swedish scholar Lars-Åke Skalin (1991), *Character and Perspective*, which focuses on characters in August Strindberg's novels but also offers a solid theoretical argument. While Docherty's premises for a changed view of character is based on the change in the aesthetics of character as such in contemporary fiction, Skalin calls for a semiotic approach to character in general, denying also characters in classic literature any psychological dimensions.

For a children's literature scholar, such radical positions present serious challenges. Children's fiction has so far not created characters similar to Proust's Marcel or Joyce's Stephen Dedalus, not because children's literature is inferior but simply because the theme of both Proust and Joyce, artistic self-realization, is not relevant for a character of children's fiction. The self-reflexivity of contemporary mainstream characters can never become a prominent feature of children's fiction, since a self-reflexive child character would, in most cases, be psychologically implausible. The development of characterization in the mainstream Western novel "since Proust and Joyce," for instance, as presented by Petruso (1991), does not indicate that children's literature is lagging behind but rather that it runs parallel to the mainstream. In offering a theory of characters in children's fiction, we cannot therefore directly apply models available in the mainstream criticism, since the study objects themselves present a significant difference.

After examining a variety of attitudes to literary characters, I naturally feel obliged to take a scholarly position of my own. Although I definitely lean toward the semiotic end of the spectrum, I agree with Seymor Chatman (1978, 119*ff.*) when he states that a reasonable approach is something between these two polarities. However, I do not share Chatman's desire to reconcile the two views, since I find them fundamentally incompatible. Rather, I would adhere to Shlomith Rimmon-Kenan's (1983, 35–36) line of argument. The preference of one or the other has to do with a more general attitude to art; a mimetic approach will inevitably result in treating characters as psychological existents, while a semiotic approach will suggest regarding them as textual constructions. In certain types of narrative, as suggested earlier, characters might be more prominent and thus more psychologically motivated, while in others they will be subordinated to actions and therefore reduced to elements of the plot design.

Finally, the view of character depends on the level of reading and interpretation. An unsophisticated reader may follow the plot of *Mio, My Son* or *Bridge to Terabithia*, without paying attention to the psychological subtleties of the characters; a sophisticated reader will, in the same texts, concentrate on the characters and put higher demands on their mimetic qualities. Neither view is "better" or more "correct," and the concepts of open and closed, or mimetic and semiotic, characters should not be apprehended as evaluative.

In children's literature scholarship, a long-enduring bias toward mimetic interpretations of characters calls for special scrutiny of the concepts. I find it of overall importance to remind ourselves and our students that literary characters are indeed constructions, fictitious figures and not actual human beings, that they have no will of their own and do not have to behave in consistency with real psychological patterns. It is therefore advisable to avoid analyzing them as if they were human beings, claiming, for instance, "He does this or that because he wants . . . ." Instead, we may put the question why the writer has chosen to let the character act in a certain way, even though the writer may have succeeded in creating a psychologically plausible character. On the other hand, as suggested earlier, unsophisticated readers tend to concentrate on plot rather than character. A great number of children's literature critics and scholars question contemporary children's novels (as well as some classics, such as *Anne of Green Gables*) on the basis of their "lack of plot" and their focus on characters and relationships. Conversely, too much formulaic fiction (*Nancy Drew* and *The Famous Five* series; *Sweet Valley* and *Goosebumps*) has been accused of deficiency in characterization and subsequently in artistic merits, without acknowledging the textuality of characters as part of the genre specifics. These common attitudes call for a deeper understanding of the status of character in a narrative.

The Ontological Status of Fictive Characters

Baruch Hochman's (1985, 13–27) study *Character in Literature* provides an excellent survey of opinions about the ontological status of characters, including the difference between characters and real people. One of the early critics to address this issue was E. M. Forster (1927) in his lectures *Aspects of the Novel*. His term *Homo fictus* as opposed to *Homo sapiens* has been adopted by many critics. In real life, Forster argues, we have remarkably limited possibilities for knowing anything about other people and their background, unless being told about it; or about their thoughts and feelings. Conversely, in literature, we are frequently allowed to learn everything about a character, right down to the tiniest detail.

Hochman (1985, 59) develops Forster's statements, noting that in order to "retrieve" characters from texts, we connect them to our experience of real people, yet they are not identical in their ontology. Hochman does not reject Forster's views but corrects them slightly. Literary characters do not exist: we cannot interact with them physically or mentally; we cannot interfere with their actions. For instance, we cannot stop Othello from strangling Desdemona (60). A parallel example from children's literature would be that we cannot warn Jess in *Bridge to Terabithia* against going to the Smithsonian with his teacher when we sense that something will happen to Leslie in his absence.

Literary characters are like dead people, "written" once and for all. We can only respond to them. They lack the unity, complexity, and coherence of real people. They have no background other than that provided by the text. However, unlike the case of real people, in literature we can obtain all relevant information about characters, and authors can arrange this information into coherence. We may not know everything about any given character, but we know all we need to know. "Literature . . . has a capacity to charge relatively limited quantities of information with a sense of significance and to consolidate them into patterns of meaning" (Hochman 1985, 70). We make constructs on the basis of limited information, just as we do with real people. Yet, real people are opaque, while literary characters are transparent. They have motives and values that we can take part of. Characters are more structured than real people. They are connected to the overall structure of the text within which they appear. An important observation is that in fiction only central characters are complex and coherent, while peripheral characters seldom show any complexity. In real life, all people are presumably equally coherent. Yet we certainly know more about the people in real life who are closest to us ("central"), while peripheral characters in our lives may feel quite one-dimensional. Literature is, in this respect, constructed similarly to life.

The ontological status of characters presents some specific challenges in children's fiction because they act within nonmimetic modes considerably more often than in the mainstream. A critic who presumably is not very well familiar with children's fiction makes the following observation:

> A fiction is realistic if it describes characters with a combination of properties that would not be strange or out of place if exemplified in individuals in the real world. More interesting, it affords an explanation of our response to certain forms of allegorical, fantasy or science fiction writing. How is it, for example, that a novel such as George Orwell's *Animal Farm* can strike us as "realistic" or "true to life," when ostensibly it describes a world radically different from our own, one in which farmyard animals speak, think, and reason exactly like human beings? Many children's stories present the same problem. (Lamarque 1996, 38)

As often as not, characters in children's fiction are animals (or even inanimate objects) rather than human beings. Even when they are human beings, they appear in fantastic settings and situations, which eliminate the imperative background information. The Swedish critic Staffan Bergsten (1978) points out, "Characters in realistic stories are normally supplied with a past: they have parents, have had a childhood, grow up and develop. The figures of myth and fairy-tale, however, most often step out of nothing. They simply *are*" (27). Bergsten uses this statement as a starting point for his discussion of Mary Poppins, one of the many characters in children's fiction who appear from nowhere and disappear mysteriously in the end.

For a human character, we fill the gaps in the characters' backgrounds with our previous experience. We assume that they once had parents, that they were born and then grew up to their present state, and so on. In a novel such as *Winnie-the-Pooh*, any similar questions are eliminated by the premises of the narrative. The characters have no background, even though Piglet claims to have a grandfather called Trespassers W., and Owl claims to have an Uncle Robert, whose portrait he has on the wall. However, the toys have no past. This is, in fact, a marvelous illustration of the concept of the inherently "closed" character. We do not know and cannot know anything about the character apart from what we can read from the text. When first Kanga and Baby Roo, and later Tigger, "arrive" in the forest, we do not ask where they come from and what they were doing before. On a metafictive level, we may assume that the boy Christopher Robin gets new toys for his birthday or for Christmas. In the fictive world of the forest, they simply "arrive"; and the boy-ruler dismisses the question posed by his subjects, just as an insensitive parent may dismiss a question from a child about the "arrival" of a new sibling:

> When Pooh asked Christopher Robin, "How did they come here?" Christopher Robin said, "In the Usual Way, if you know what I mean, Pooh," and Pooh, who didn't, said "Oh!" (81)

The problem is, however, more complicated for Christopher Robin himself. Although it is never mentioned explicitly in the text, we know that at the end of the second book he is being sent away to a boarding school; that is, in judging the "human" character Christopher Robin, we make inferences based on our extratextual experience.

There seems to be a difference between genres in providing the characters' background. In adventure stories, the background is often of no importance. Thus, we know that Tom Sawyer is an orphan, brought up by his mother's sister, and also that Sid is his younger half-brother. However, we do not know anything about Tom's parents. How long have they been dead, since Tom does not seem to have any memory of them or feel any grief? Did Tom and Sid have the same mother and different fathers; or did Tom's mother die at childbirth, whereupon his father remarried to beget Sid, and in this case what happened to this second wife? Has the father left the family to seek his fortune elsewhere, like Huck Finn's? These questions (e.g., cf. "How many children had Lady Macbeth?") are insignificant because the parents have no function in the plot other than being absent, and since the novel is plot oriented, the character is not burdened by identity crises arising from his orphaned status. On the contrary, in a predominantly character-oriented domestic novel, such as *Heidi* or *Anne of Green Gables*, the background of the protagonist is carefully accounted for, since it is essential for the character's quest for self.

Here are some assumptions about literary characters, based on our experience of real life:

- They have been born. This is true in most cases, unless the origin of the character is extraordinary. For instance, Thumbelina appears from a flower, and the title character of *Konrad* appears from a tin can. The extraordinary origin is an essential part of the plot.
- They have parents, even though the parents may be unknown. Unless we are told that the character has been conceived through artificial insemination or egg donation, we assume that they were conceived in the usual way. However, once again, the origin of "supernatural" characters is unclear. Did the Little Prince ever have a mother and father? Where do toys come from?
- They have had a childhood. Unless we are told anything specific about the childhood of an adult character (unhappy, idyllic, large

family, single parent, only child, wartime misery), we assume the childhood to have been "average." In children's fiction, childhood is not the characters' past but their present. However, the same rules apply: unless we are told about any unusual facts in the child's earlier years, we assume them to have been average.

- They have attended school. At least in our Western society and in contemporary literature, we assume that characters have received some education. We would expect a character who is a college professor to have a Ph.D. and a company president to have a degree in business, a pilot to have a certificate, and a judge to have graduated from a law school, and we are likely to be told if there is any remarkable deviation. For child characters, their age will immediately reveal their level of education, whether it is essential for the plot or not. A ten-year-old character who cannot read must have a very good reason for this disability. A child who never attends school (such as Johnny in *Johnny My Friend*) is perceived as exceptional.
- An adult character will be expected to have at least some sexual experience, whether or not this is essential for the plot. If this is not the case, we will be told so and probably also given an explanation. Certain circumstances may account for the lack of sexual practice—for instance, if the character is a Catholic priest. Unless stated otherwise, we will also assume characters to be heterosexual. Married characters will be assumed to be having or to have had sex, and if they have sexual problems these will most likely be part of the plot. Child characters are assumed to have no sexual experience, and if they for some reason have experience (e.g., if they have been sexually abused) we will be told so.
- The characters are mortal and will die one day (unless we are given a good reason otherwise, as in *Peter Pan*). They will get burned if touched by a red-hot poker; they will bleed if cut by a knife; they cannot survive falling from a tenth-floor window; they cannot stay under water for more than a short time or fly. Every departure from these premises must have some form of explanation, usually dictated by the genre.

Such are the basic assumptions that we as readers have in our minds when constructing the complex portrait of people we read about. These assumptions build up the "default value"; to assume anything else we must be told so, as I have shown. To these, we must also add our knowledge of the characters' social and historical background, which may have shaped their personality. Any unusual experience that is necessary to understand the character's present position or state of mind has to be presented in the narrative, explicitly or implicitly; everything else is fruitless speculation. We cannot claim that Regan is mean toward her father, King Lear, because she is suffering from premenstrual syndrome, and we cannot claim that Tom Sawyer is naughty because his father was an alcoholic and his mother had loose habits. In these cases, the difference between mimetic dimensions and mimetic functions (Phelan 1989, 11) is crucial.

The Problem of Fictionality

I have already suggested that children's literature criticism leans toward mimetic understanding of characters. I shall not try to decide which was the first, the chicken or the egg—that is, whether teachers and librarians have observed that young readers in fact view literary characters as "real" or whether adult mediators have imposed this attitude on children. Children's authors testify that young readers often inquire whether the events described in books have actually happened and whether the characters are portrayed from real people.

Distinguishing between fiction and reality is indeed one of many problems that young readers (and sometimes even adult readers) encounter when reading novels. However, unlike documentary or journalism, fiction is not a direct rendering of reality but an artistic transformation of it. In *Fictional Worlds*, Thomas Pavel (1986) brings forward some essential questions of fictionality. Thus, he wonders whether Natasha in *War and Peace* is less real than Napoleon (16). A parallel in children's fiction would be the question whether Caesar in *The Story of the Amulet* is more real than the four child characters. Caesar and Napoleon are historical figures, while Natasha or Nesbit's Anthea and Cyril are fictional. But is their status within the fictional world of the novel any different? Based on speech-act theory, Pavel's (1986, 11–42) study shows that all fictional characters are nothing but words, without any actual referents in reality. Most studies of fictionality share this view (see Lamarque 1996). Many critics stress the conventionality of the reader's understanding of character, "the fictional contract" (Price 1983, 1–23). Furthermore, the majority of children's novels do not present any actual historical figures, and if they do, it is of less importance. Our appreciation of literary texts seldom suffers if we do not recognize real people behind the figures in *Alice in Wonderland* or if we do not know that Christopher Robin really existed. In fact, Christopher Robin the character does not resemble the real Christopher Milne too much. The charming boy with curls wearing a tunic is purely fictional.

Since part of the traditional aesthetics of children's literature is, for didactic purposes, to pretend that texts reflect a reality and that characters are psychologically credible, it is of overall importance to take fictionality into consideration when discussing the characters' ontological status. Contemporary texts can destroy the illusion of reality in fiction, for instance, by means of metafictional devices.

Notes

1. Throughout the present study, I am using the masculine personal pronoun to refer to characters as well as the narrator unless the gender is clearly feminine; the preference is a matter of convenience and has no further implications.

2. It is interesting how some film versions seem to feel obliged to provide a background to explain a character's behavior. As I am writing this, *The Grinch* has just started playing in American theaters. To compensate for the meager plot of the book, the filmmakers have supplied a background story of the Grinch being abandoned as a baby, which ostensibly has made him mean and grumpy.

3. Some favorite gurus in such studies include Erik Erikson, Melanie Klein, and D. W. Winnicott.

4. Critics of Russian formalists, especially of Propp, are seldom aware that formalism, and later semiotics, were principally a means of escaping the superimposed ideological bias in official literary criticism. By concentrating on the form, Soviet scholars could avoid discussions of plots and characters in terms of ideological correctness, not least Marxist concepts of class struggle.

5. Reader-response scholars argue for a subtle difference between these terms, which is of no relevance for my purpose. See Booth 1961; Iser 1974, 1978; Culler 1975; Eco 1979; Suleiman 1980; Fish 1982; and for children's fiction, Chambers 1985.

6. For an excellent critical overview of postmodern approaches to character, see Petruso (1991, 3–38), a chapter sarcastically titled "Babies in the Bathwater."

CHAPTER TWO

~

From Hero to Character

Northrop Frye's Displacement of Myth and the Typology of Characters

In his treatment of literature as the displacement of myth, Northrop Frye (1957, 33–34) discerns five consecutive stages:

1. Myth: presents characters as being superior to both humans and the laws of nature (gods)
2. Romance: presents characters as being partially superior, idealized humans who are superior to other humans but inferior to gods (semi-gods)
3. High mimetic narrative: presents humans who are superior to other humans (heroes) but not the laws of nature (e.g., not immortal)
4. Low mimetic narrative: presents humans who are neither superior nor inferior to other humans
5. Ironic narrative: presents characters who are inferior to other characters, such as children, the mentally disabled, animals, and so on

By this definition, all characters in children's fiction would appear at the ironic stage, since they naturally lack experience and knowledge and are therefore inferior to adults. However, even a brief glance at a number of classical and contemporary children's novels demonstrates that this is not the case. Characters in children's novels are empowered in a variety of manners and operate on all the displacement levels.

The peculiarity (and perhaps weakness) of Frye's model is that his categories can be applied diachronically as well as synchronically. In other words, on the one hand the five stages reflect the historical development of world (= Western) literature; on the other hand, the various modes of representation coexist within any given period. (They can even coexist within one and the same text, as the different levels of interpretation, but this is of no relevance for the present argument.)

According to Frye, contemporary Western literature has reached the ironic stage, at which most of the characters we meet in novels are weak, disillusioned men and women. This is only true of quality literature, since most formulaic fiction operates within the romantic mode (which in Frye's terminology includes romance, adventure, fantasy, etc.), and at least some contemporary adult fiction still uses mimetic modes. Furthermore, Frye's model does not presuppose linear development but is formed as a cycle, which means that after the ironic stage, a new mythic stage can be expected. We see this clearly in such late twentieth-century literary trends as "magical realism." We can also view the concept of myth in a broader sense, including modern myths—for instance, as treated by Marina Warner (1994b) in *Managing Monsters: Six Myths of Our Times*.

Children's literature is historically a recent form of fiction.[1] Its emergence in the eighteenth to nineteenth centuries coincides with the establishment of realism (mimetic modes) in the mainstream; therefore, it seems, Frye's five stages coexist more frequently in the children's literature than in the mainstream of any given period. In contemporary Western children's fiction, we meet characters from all Frye's modes, perhaps with the exception of the purely mythical. Like all theoretical tools, the categories are abstractions and cannot always be directly applied to any existing character. A collection of essays, edited by Victor Brombert (1969), *The Hero in Literature*, plots the changing notion of heroism and our attitudes to literary character from ancient times to our days. Although none of the contributors make use of Frye's terminology, the emerging typology of character more or less coincides with Frye's, going from mythical hero through romantic, epic hero toward contemporary "bourgeois" and intellectual hero. Many of the observations in these essays are also pertinent to children's fiction.

It is essential to understand that Frye's categories are not evaluative, neither historically nor typologically. As Scholes and Kellogg (1966) point out, "[t]he inward life is assumed but not presented in primitive narrative literature. . . . This inscrutability of characters, their opaqueness, is neither a defect nor a limitation. It is simply a characteristic" (166). In ascribing contemporary psychological characters higher artistic quality than the epic hero, we commit a serious aesthetic fallacy.

The Mythic Hero and Children's Fiction

Myth as such is absent in the history of Western children's literature. Unlike literature, myth is based on the belief of the myth bearers; when this belief disappears, the myth ceases to be a myth (see Frye 1963). Since children's literature emerges long after Western civilization had lost its traditional mythical belief, this stage is not represented in children's fiction. Mythic heroes have been studied extensively from a variety of viewpoints (see Miller 2000). The most important mythic figure is the cultural hero, who teaches his people to use fire, to hunt, and to cultivate land. These stories were not relevant—as living narratives, essential for survival—for young readers at the time children's literature became a separate artistic form. If we treat Judeo-Christian belief as myth, we can naturally say that Bible stories retold for children are mythical children's narratives. This corresponds to the mythical stories of archaic people, which were told indiscriminately to children and adults. In certain cultures, mythical stories are still very prominent as instructional narratives for young people. However, most of the classic myths, such as the Greek, Celtic, native American, African, and so on, are in the Western world retold for children who have no direct belief in them—myth has been displaced and instead functions as romance.

In his study *The Hero with a Thousand Faces*, Joseph Campbell (1949) presents an analysis of what he calls the *monomyth*, the universal mythical pattern we find in the vast majority of narratives. The movement of the monomyth is separation—initiation—return (Campbell 1968, 30), which corresponds exactly to the "basic plot" of children's fiction, identified as home—away—homecoming (Edström 1980; Nodelman 1992). While Campbell's work is perhaps more useful for dealing with the structure of the story, as an excellent complement to Propp's fairy-tale schema, we can use Campbell's description of the mythical hero to contemplate which traits of this hero have been inherited by the characters of children's fiction. Naturally, Campbell's model is not uncontroversial in its overtly psychoanalytical orientation and must, therefore, be applied with some caution. Yet it helps us see clearly the similarities between myth and children's fiction.

The hero in Campbell's model is a young male going through a rite of passage. In this respect, all children's literature is similar to the monomyth, and all characters in children's fiction are a further development of the mythical hero. Like the mythical hero, the child character must depart from the ordinary situation in order for there to be a plot. In children's novels, a popular device for achieving physical dislocation is to send the characters away for summer vacations (*Five Children and It*), because of illness in the family (*Tom's Midnight Garden*), or because of some danger (air raids in *The Lion, the Witch and the Wardrobe*). The characters will then receive a message about their special task and acquire help that, depending on the genre, is either natural or supernatural. The young protagonist should not be left without assistance, since only then can life lessons be taught. However, the helper cannot be one of the parents; usually it is either a complete stranger or, occasionally, a grandparent (see further chapter 6).

As the next step, the character must cross some form of threshold. In fantasy novels, the threshold is tangible, as the character is transported into a different world. However, this plot element is present in some form in all narratives. Rarely, if ever, in children's fiction is the painful and sometimes rather graphic dismembering or annihilation of the mythical hero presented. This element is in children's fiction either omitted or transferred to a secondary character, presumably to spare young readers the horrors of empathic identification with the hero's suffering. However, we do see some remnants of ancient stories—for instance, when Little Red Riding Hood is devoured by the wolf.

The mythical hero is subjected to a series of trials, as is the character of children's fiction. Once again, the trials and tasks are more tangible in romantic modes (fantasy, adventure). In mimetic modes, they assume symbolic forms—for instance, the quest for identity. One might argue that the central episode of Campbell's schema—the hero's meeting the goddess—is not present in children's fiction, presumably because the purpose of such an encounter is marriage, involving initiation into sexuality. We must, however, remember that the original myth is displaced in fiction and that in children's fiction, censorial filters may be imposed on the narrative. Many child characters do indeed meet either a friend or an opponent of the opposite sex who initiates a turning point in the protagonist's life (Hugo in the *Hugo and Josephine* series; Leslie in *Bridge to Terabithia;* Johnny in *Johnny My Friend*). Campbell mentions the figure of the goddess-temptress, an evil figure seducing the hero; we encounter this figure, for instance, as the Snow Queen in Andersen's fairy tale or the White Witch in *The Lion, the Witch and the Wardrobe*. According to Campbell, the goddess in myth represents the hero's mother, and by marrying—mastering, conquering—her, the hero replaces his father in the universal hierarchy. While such an interpretation may seem repulsive in connection with children's fiction, the transformation of the pattern can be traced in many novels. Also the next stage in Campbell's schema, atonement with the father, is something we frequently find in children's novels (Jess's reconciliation with his father in *Bridge to Terabithia*). The hero's triumph is almost indispensable, as is the following reward.

In addition, like the mythical hero and unlike most characters of adult fiction, the child character returns to the point of departure, sometimes through flight and rescue, and often crossing the return threshold to ordinary life. There is also a promise of further adventure; that is, as long as children remain children, they can cross the boundaries between the ordinary and the magical world (Wendy in *Peter Pan* can go to the Neverland until she grows up; Lucy in the Narnia Chronicles can return to Narnia until she becomes too old for it).

This very brief comparison between Campbell's description of myth and some basic patterns of children's fiction demonstrates that although myth as such may not be a part of children's fiction, the mythical hero is a major source of inspiration for all children's writers (see also Stephens and McCallum 1998).

The Romantic Hero

The romantic hero, superior to ordinary human beings, is one of the most common character types in children's fiction. We meet this type primarily in fairy tales and fantasy, in which the child is empowered by being able to travel through space and time, by possessing magical objects or by being assisted by magical helpers.

In fairy tales retold for children, characters are usually empowered in a way that makes them superior to other human beings. They are endowed with magical agents enabling them to be transported in space, metamorphose into animals or other, presumably better, human beings (e.g., Cinderella's transformation from ashes to diamonds). However, fairy-tale heroes normally have helpers possessing stronger powers than themselves, without whom they would not be able to achieve their goals. If fairy-tale protagonists are semigods, their helpers are gods. Ultimately, this reflects the power relationship between children and adults in society.

With few exceptions, fairy tales have always been regarded as suitable for children, apparently because fairy-tale protagonists, like children, grow from being the underdog to being strong and independent. Another essential trait of fairy-tale heroes is their lack of complexity, which is considered appropriate for young readers from a didactic viewpoint. Fairy-tale heroes know no nuances; they are 100 percent heroic—they never doubt, never fear, never despair. In fact, they are very seldom individualized. If described at all, they possess a standard set of traits: they are brave, clever, kind, beautiful, and so on. Of course, the exact content of these traits may change with time and culture; the behavior of fairy-tale tricksters, for instance, is often considered highly immoral in contemporary Western societies. However, the fairy-tale hero or heroine, the oppressed youngest brother or sister, empowered by magical means, is decidedly the origin of the contemporary character in the children's novel, in not only fantasy but everyday stories as well (see my treatment of some characters in Canadian children's fiction: Nikolajeva 1994).

In contemporary literature, romantic heroes are widely represented in formulaic fiction, such as crime, adventure, thriller, and romance. The foremost scholar of formulaic fiction, John G. Cawelti (1976), points out that "the protagonists of formulaic literature are typically better or more fortunate in some ways than ourselves. They are heroes who have the strength and courage to overcome great dangers, lovers who find perfectly suited partners, inquirers of exceptional brilliance who discover hidden truths, or good, sympathetic people whose difficulties are resolved by some superior figure" (18). Cawelti also maintains that formulaic protagonists are not intended to be identified with but rather to confirm "an idealized self-image" (18).

The romantic hero of children's fiction has, like the fairy-tale and the formulaic hero, a standard set of traits, such as strength, courage, devotion, and so on. Although the origin of this type is unmistakably the classic epic hero (Gilgamesh, Hercules, Odysseus, Sigurth, Roland), the premise for the romantic child hero is the idealization of childhood during the Romantic era. It is based on the belief in the child as innocent and therefore capable of conquering evil. Although this ideal child is now being interrogated by some critics (see some of the essays in McGavran 1999), it affects the ways in which child heroes are still constructed in certain text types today.

In the previous section, I have already shown how mythic patterns are displaced on the romantic level. The most important difference, which allows reiteration, is the return to the initial order, the disempowerment of the hero, the reestablishment of adult authority. The mythic hero kills his father and usurps his place, which would be highly improper in a children's book. From magical journeys to alternative worlds or histories, the child hero is brought back to the ordinary, sometimes being explicitly stripped of the attributes of previous power (most tangibly seen in the transformation of the kings and queens of Narnia back to children at the end of *The Lion, the Witch and the Wardrobe*). The magical object is irretrievably lost or loses its magical power (*The Story of the Amulet*), the magical helper is removed (*Mary Poppins*), and the character once again stands alone without assistance, no longer a hero. Thus, in many children's fantasy novels, the characters become displaced yet further away from myth, onto low mimetic and ironic levels. This would appear not to be the case of high fantasy, such as the Prydain Chronicles, which at first glance follow meticulously Campbell's myth model. However, at the end of the five-novel cycle, Taran is left without magical assistance as all magic forces leave Prydain, which thus suddenly transforms from a mythic realm into ordinary Britain.

Contemporary authors, even though they may lean heavily on myth, will inevitably deconstruct it in some way. Ursula Le Guin, for instance, felt obliged to take her heroes through such a deconstruction in *Tehanu* (Hourihan 1997, 225–33). Only in formulaic fiction can purely romantic characters still exist today. Interestingly enough, while the romantic hero has been such a prominent source of influence for children's fiction, the romantic heroine, the object of the hero's desires (see Rabine 1985), is a conspicuously absent figure. Presumably the nature of relationships between hero and heroine in a romance is irrelevant for the young characters of children's fiction. While some children's novels certainly depict romantic friendships, portraying characters such as Becky Thatcher, there is no correspondence in children's literature to the great romantic heroines of the mainstream such as Isolde, Manon Lescaut, or Madame de Rênal.

The tremendous success of the Harry Potter novels may be partially ascribed to the fortunate attempt to reintroduce the romantic character into children's fiction. The character of Harry Potter has all the necessary components of the romantic hero. There are mystical circumstances around his birth and infant years, and he is displaced and oppressed until suddenly, on his eleventh birthday—the common age of initiation—he is given unlimited power. He has a whole group of gurus and supporters and an infinitely evil and powerful opponent. However, his innocence and his intrinsic benevolence make him superior to the evil—adult—powers.

Yet, Harry Potter is a child of his time, of the twenty-first century. He appears as a reaction to a long chain of ironic characters, showing ambiguity in their concepts of good and evil, gender transgression, and other tokens of the postmodern aesthetics. Harry Potter is a very straightforward hero. We know what to expect from him. After decades of parody, metafiction, frame breaking, and other postmodern games, it may feel liberating for the readers to know where to place their sympathies and antipathies. Of course, it is conceivable that Harry will eventually go over to the dark side. But such a development would almost feel trivial today, especially in the wake of *Star Wars—The First Episode*.

After so many antiheroes in children's as well as adult literature, a hero is welcome. However, Harry's appeal is that he is not a hero of the Superman caliber, but an ordinary clumsy and bespectacled boy. A boy who turns out to have magical powers yet receives most praise for his sporting achievements. A boy who is disobedient and curious, who is not at all brilliant in school but quite average. A boy who has friends and enemies, who needs to eat and sleep, and who, in book 4, is at long last awakening to the charms and mysteries of the opposite gender. Harry Potter is at once human and nonhuman, with the same emotions we all know: longing for Mom and Dad, loneliness, insecurity, curiosity about his identity and origin. In this respect, he differs from the traditional romantic hero, devoid of any such sentiments. Thus, Harry is repeatedly taken down to the mimetic and ironic levels, only to be elevated to hero status again at the moment of decisive struggle.

High Mimetic Characters

High mimetic characters are humans who are superior to other humans in terms of, for instance, bravery, wisdom, patriotism, and so on. The famous story of the Spartan boy who hides a fox cub under his shirt is a typical example of a high mimetic narrative. Although not originally intended for young readers exclusively, it has been reprinted in many children's primers. High mimetic narratives for children emerged almost simultaneously with the early retold fairy tales. They were mainly of two types: hagiographies (lives of saints) and plutarchs (lives of important historical and political figures). In the United States, biographies of presidents published for children have always been popular, and in France there are dozens of books about Joan of Arc. In Victorian children's fiction, we also find an abundance of child martyrs. In some countries (e.g., the former Soviet Union), these genres—modified into lives of revolutionaries and war heroes—were prominent as late as in the 1970s. In China they still constitute the majority of children's fiction.

The function of high mimetic narratives is educational, whether they address children or adults. As observed earlier, high mimetic characters are superior to other human beings, including the reader. This implies that high mimetic characters are supposed to serve as models not only for the other characters in the story but for the readers as well. In children's fiction, such characters are used for educational and didactic purposes. In the following subsections, I will provide some examples of high mimetic character types.

Allegorical and Emblematic Characters

Allegory is a rhetorical figure that enables the author to present characters and events simultaneously on a literal level and on another, transferred level. Allegorical characters may represent either abstract ideas and values (allegory of ideas) or other real or fictional figures (historical or political allegory). Allegorical characters are the extreme form of what Scholes and Kellogg (1966) call illustrative, who "do not mainly represent sociological or psychological types. They illustrate philosophical and theological positions" (100; see also on allegory 105–59).

The most frequently used example of allegory of ideas in mainstream literature is *Pilgrim's Progress*; a very good example of a political allegory is *Animal Farm*. Very few contemporary children's novels are intentionally written as allegories, and allegorical characters seem to belong in the past (there are exceptions, such as *Terrible Things: An Allegory of the Holocaust*). Since allegory is by definition a didactic literary form, contemporary children's authors, who tend to avoid didacticism, seldom choose purely allegorical characters for their work. I will, however, show some examples of allegorical interpretation of children's novels, in which the allegorical level is, significantly, only one dimension of the text. Just as it is possible to read *Animal Farm* without discerning the allegorical depiction of early Soviet history, it is likely that most young readers will ignore the potential allegorical interpretations of some children's novels unless these are brought to their attention. Such an attitude partly depends on the fact that contemporary readers in general are not trained in allegorical reading.[2]

The most obvious examples of allegorical figures in children's fiction are to be found in the Narnia Chronicles, which some critics reduce to being exclusively a Christian allegory (Sammonds 1979, 1988; Schakel 1979). We can clearly interpret Aslan as Jesus and the White Witch (or Jadis, as she is called in *The Magician's Nephew*) as Satan, while the remaining characters must be squeezed into various supporting roles. The disadvantage of this interpretation is that it centralizes the godlike figure, whose subjectivity is beyond young readers' grasp, which seriously questions the status of this novel as children's fiction.

One of my students has suggested the following allegorical reading of *The Lion, the Witch and the Wardrobe*. Having noticed the year of publication, she interpreted the story as a depiction of World War II, with Narnia as Europe, the White Witch as Hitler, and the four children as the four Allied Forces: Britain, France, the United States, and the Soviet Union. The role of Aslan was not quite clear in this interpretation, but the attempt was aimed at reading the novel as a very straightforward historical allegory. Once again, young readers will most likely miss this dimension. However, both allegorical readings without doubt point at the complexity of the text.

Another famous—or perhaps rather infamous—allegorical interpretation of a children's novel is the reading of *The Wizard of Oz* as a social allegory. The Scarecrow represents the farmers; the Tin Woodman the factory workers; the Cowardly Lion the Populist Democrat candidate of 1896 and 1900, William Jennings Bryan. The Wicked Witch of the East, who has enslaved the Munchkin people and is killed by Dorothy's house, is the inhuman industrialization in the East Coast states. The Wicked Witch of the West is the malevolent force of nature bringing drought, which Dorothy eventually kills by means of water. Dorothy's silver shoes are connected with the silver issue (free coinage of silver in addition to the U.S. gold standard). Most of the events of the novel are interpreted as direct allegorical representation of real events and issues (Littlefield 1964).[3]

Even though such interpretations are fully legitimate, it is highly unlikely that young readers will ever make similar observations. These examples show that although allegorical characters may indeed be discovered on certain interpretative levels in children's novels, these levels are habitually overlooked by young readers. Moreover, while C. S. Lewis's allegory was obviously intentional, the intentionality of Baum's story is quite dubious and is rather "in the mind of the beholder."

Another didactic characterization device is the use of emblematic characters. Emblematics are part of the Baroque tradition in art and literature employing personified virtues and vices and other human traits. Unlike allegory, which demands substantial decoding on the part of the reader, emblems are permanent conventional signs (the cross as an emblem for faith). Verbal—that is, literary—emblems usually occur in the form of transparent character names that immediately signal the most prominent— often the only—trait of the character. Emblematic characters were quite frequent in early didactic children's literature. In *Water Babies*, we find two emblematic characters Mrs. Doasyoubedoneby and Mrs. Bedonebyasyoudo. A Swedish comic strip that ran in a children's magazine from the 1920s to the 1960s featured two characters, Miss Save and Miss Waste, whose traits are quite obvious from their names. In contemporary children's fiction, the use of emblematics for characterization is primarily ironic, even though this irony may be wasted on young readers. *The Wind in the Moon* has several emblematic characters, notably the governess Miss Serendip. *Charlie and the Chocolate Factory* portrays the negative characters emblematically as, for instance, the glutton Augustus Gloop and television-addicted Mike Teavee. In *The Phantom Tollbooth*, we encounter princesses Rhyme and Reason and many other emblematic figures. All these characters are flat, possessing one main trait that is clearly expressed by their names. Both allegorical and emblematic characters are based on the premise that they "represent" something—that is, a mimetic approach to fiction.

Characters as Ideological Vehicles

In the vast majority of traditional children's literature, child characters are used as models for young readers. They are virtuous beyond measure, good and kind, pious, obedient, and humble. In many cases, as we read these texts today, the characters seem either ridiculous (*Little Goody Two-Shoes*), which definitely was not the author's intention, or hopelessly sentimental (*Jessica's First Prayer*). There are naturally exceptions, such as Diamond in *At the Back of the North Wind*. However, the purpose of all such characters is to set a good example for the reader; therefore, the positive traits of the characters are amplified beyond natural proportions. *Struwwelpeter* with its negative examples has exactly the same function, only in reverse.

More modern examples of the use of characters as models can be easily found in the literature of the former Soviet Union: young war heroes and revolutionaries, vigilant scouts who reveal spies and saboteurs, boys who save other children or adults from drowning or fire, children who assist the country by collecting recyclable materials, and so on. These heroes have no other traits than being heroic. Notably, one of the official, highly praised young heroes of the Soviet ideology was a boy who denounced his own father as the enemy of the regime: such actions were highly encouraged at the time of the Great Terror during the 1930s. Interestingly enough, after the fall of communism, such heroes immediately gave way to a flood of Russian Orthodox saints and martyrs in books for children.

Another clearly didactic use of characters is as mouthpieces for the authors' ideas and opinions. Here, however, an interesting difference can be noted between children's fiction and the mainstream. Young readers are supposed to empathize with young protagonists and thus learn lessons together with them. This implies that the protagonists themselves cannot be used as mouthpieces, but rather wisdom must necessarily come from a secondary character, whether an adult or a child. Indeed we see a variety of such mouthpiece figures who explain, preach, and warn, seldom leaving the readers room for further contemplation. One would assume that such novels for children belong to the past, but one of the recent international bestsellers, mysteriously crossing over from children's fiction to mainstream, *Sophie's World*, employs such a didactic adult mouthpiece character.

Low Mimetic Characters

Low mimetic narratives present ordinary children in ordinary situations: domestic stories, school stories, and so on. Although "realistic" characters seemingly have existed in children's fiction from the beginning, I would argue that characters appearing on the low mimetic level—neither superior nor inferior to other characters—are a relatively recent development. If we consider the protagonists of some classic novels for children, we discover that they are portrayed as anything but ordinary. The four March sisters in *Little Women* are exceedingly virtuous and become still more so as they go through their self-imposed "pilgrimage." Tom Sawyer finds sufficient treasure to ensure him of a pleasurable future in the adult world. Anne of Green Gables becomes a brilliant student and is eventually described as quite good-looking. Cedric Errol in *Little Lord Fauntleroy* is nauseatingly blameless, in addition to inheriting great wealth. I could continue this enumeration for a long while.

We can probably regard Laura in the *Little House* series as an early low mimetic character who is ordinary in every respect. Modern low mimetic characters appear on a larger scale in Western children's literature after World War II as a result of major changes in society, rapid urbanization, changes in family structure, as well as the achievements of child psychology. Low mimetic characters allow the most natural subject position for contemporary young readers: they are not freed from the obligation to attend school by eternal summer holidays; they are not extremely lucky to be in the right place at the right time to have exciting adventures; they are not exceedingly bright, or brave, or handsome; they do not marry princes or millionaires; and they do not find treasures that will allow them to live happily ever after.

Ironic Characters

It has taken children's fiction a long time to venture into the ironic mode and depict characters who are weaker, physically and spiritually, than their peers, in addition to being inferior to their parents and other adults. Unlike fairy-tale heroes, these characters are not empowered at the end of the story. At best, they remain the same; at worst they perish, incapable of coping with surrounding reality.

We have recently witnessed a radical change in the narrative perspective of children's novels whereby the didactic, authoritative narrator is supplanted by character focalization. This enables some contemporary authors to portray the world through the eyes of a naive and inexperienced child. In this field, children's authors have a wider scope of expressive means than their colleagues in the mainstream, who have to employ, for instance, mentally disturbed characters to achieve the same effect. While most narratologists are limited in exemplification of the totally naive perspective to

Benjy from *The Sound and the Fury*, children's literature scholars can easily enumerate several dozen children's novels using the same device. An excellent example is Ramona Quimby. On her first day of school, Ramona has to learn "a puzzling song about 'the dawnzer lee light,' which Ramona did not understand because she did not know what a dawnzer was. 'Oh, say, can you see by the dawnzer lee light,' sang Miss Binney, and Ramona decided that a dawnzer was another word for a lamp" (*Ramona the Pest*, 21). Apparently, the character's confusion is based in her ignorance and naïveté. The readers are supposed to recognize the words, which gives them superiority over the character. However, if for some reason they do not, the situation leaves them as helpless and puzzled as Ramona.

Low mimetic and ironic characters are the first ones historically and the only ones typologically that presuppose and allow a portrayal of internal life. Therefore, we are most likely to find such characters in contemporary psychological novels for children. If, according to Harold Bloom, a psychological human being was invented by Shakespeare, in children's literature it was invented collaboratively by such authors as Katherine Paterson, Patricia MacLachlan, Beverly Cleary, Maria Gripe, Nina Bawden, and Michelle Magorian.

It is not always possible and still less fruitful to draw a definite boundary between low mimetic and ironic characters in children's fiction. As pointed out in the beginning of this chapter, all child characters are by definition ironic—that is, inferior to their surroundings and, by extension, to the readers. However, in children's fiction, the readers may be just as inexperienced and disempowered as the ironic character. In other words, young readers may find themselves at the same level as the character. Although we as adult readers may see the young protagonist's faults and mistakes, a young reader may fail to do so. Contemporary writers have developed means of drawing the readers' attention to the ironic status of their characters, and I will discuss a few of these.

Detachment and Alienation
In traditional fiction, children as well as adult readers are expected to identify and empathize with at least one character, to adopt a subject position coinciding with a character's. One of the main premises of postmodern aesthetics is the subversion of subjectivity, which is often achieved by making the protagonist repulsive in some way: physically unattractive, morally depraved, a criminal, or even an inhuman monster. Two extreme examples of this strategy, often combined with graphic, naturalistic descriptions of violence, are *American Psycho* and *Neuromancer*. Although violence has

started to make its way into juvenile fiction, most children's writers still erect a clear barrier concerning what can and cannot be described in a novel addressed to young readers.

Some contemporary characters in children's fiction efficiently alienate the reader by being unpleasant and thus offering no clear-cut subject position. While Mary Lennox in *The Secret Garden*, repeatedly described by the author as "disagreeable" in the beginning, quickly gains the reader's sympathy, being an orphan and exposed to the adults' indifference; a character staying unpleasant throughout the story may leave the reader concerned and even frustrated. Vinnie's father in *Flip-Flop Girl* is dead, and since her little brother has taken the worst damage of his death, Vinnie feels neglected. The situation may seem similar to that of Mary Lennox; however, while Mary makes the most of it and improves, morally, physically, and mentally, Vinnie is consistently presented as exceedingly nasty, not to say destructive. Her self-pity leads her to maltreat her little brother (it is primarily her fault that he has become autistic), to isolate herself from her well-intentioned mother and grandmother, and to have preconceived opinions about Lupe, the only classmate who tries to be friendly. Vinnie's competition with Lupe over a male teacher's attention only adds to her hostility. Finally, this rivalry makes her vandalize the teacher's car. Here, the narrative device of filter—shifting the reader's point of view away from the character's—enables the reader to dissociate from the focalizing character. Filter is used to amplify the estrangement effect, which normally means that the focalizing character is alien in some way: obnoxious, physically or mentally disabled, an immigrant, an animal, or a monster. Without going to the furthest extreme, the author tries the strategy of making Vinnie just annoying enough to interrogate the readers' inevitable subjectivity.

The use of alienating characters in children's fiction is problematic, and some authors do not manage to be consistent in their creation. Stanley in *Holes* starts as a typical ironic character: he is obese, not particularly likable, and even though we are told that he is innocent of the crime of which he is accused and punished, the way he is described provokes alienation rather than empathy in the reader. He is also presented in an oppressed position: literally deprived of his freedom in a labor camp, humiliated and abused. Halfway through the novel, Stanley develops more heroic, high mimetic traits as he risks his own life to save a friend; and in the end he finds a treasure ensuring him and his family a carefree life ever after. This sudden elevation of the character to the romantic mode is not only implausible but incompatible with the ironic outset of the novel. Presumably, it is the author's tribute to the conventions of children's fiction, demanding a happy ending.

Metafictive Character

The prefix *meta-* in the postmodern terminology refers to *framing* (also called *embedding*)—that is, the deliberate construction of the narrative on more than one diegetic level. Patricia Waugh (1984) includes fantasy among metafictive devices. In this case, all characters traveling between the real and the fantastic world, or, in time-shift plots, between two real worlds by some fantastic means, must be counted as metafictive. Fantasy is a much more conspicuous frame-breaking element in mainstream fiction than in children's fiction. Therefore, I do not see any point in discussing one of the most common narrative devices in children's fiction, the magical journey, as metafiction. Instead, I will reserve the notion of a metafictive character for those who in some way transgress the frame boundaries of the narrative—for instance, by appearing on different diegetic levels or even by being aware of the existence of other levels. True, fantasy with its explicit heterotopia allows for endless metafictional options (see Petzold 1999). Bastian in *The Neverending Story* enters the fictional world he is reading about. Too-ticki of the Moomin novels sometimes seems to be watching the events from another narrative level, and Snufkin is aware of being inside an adventure story. Christopher Robin is a metafictive character in the sense that he appears on two different diegetic levels. However, we do not actually see him pass from one level to another; the passage is implicit, the metafiction covert. (For more examples of metafiction in children's novels see Nikolajeva 1996, chap. 7.) None of these characters really leave the reader puzzled, since the character's ability to break the diegetic frames is apprehended as part of the fantasy convention.

In a novel written apparently in a mimetic mode, metafictive characters create a sense of uneasiness, since the reader is left uncertain as to their ontological status. Hal in *Dance on My Grave* comments, "I have become my own character" (221). Ditto in *Breaktime* exists on two diegetic levels: the frame story and his own first-person narrative. Moreover, at the end of the novel, not merely the credibility of Ditto's narrative but the very existence of the character himself is questioned. Ditto is perhaps the closest juvenile fiction has come so far to the concept of a canceled character—that is, a character totally lacking any psychological features whatsoever, exclusively a textual construction, consisting of words. Canceled characters are no longer possible to discuss in terms of personal integrity. Some critics have pointed out that Sarah in *The French Lieutenant's Woman* has no mimetic function in the story; she does not "represent" anything. By introducing a character like that, the author breaks the illusion of mimetic reality. We can perhaps say something similar about Johnny in *Johnny My*

Friend. Johnny is a catalyst initiating a change in the protagonist, without being affected. Such characters are unusual in children's fiction, since children's writers most often wish, probably for didactic purposes, to offer their readers a psychologically acceptable identification object.

Myths of Individualism and Children's Fiction

Critics have recurrently maintained that children's fiction differs from mainstream in terms of themes and characters, although no concrete examples have been offered to provide evidence. I have argued elsewhere (Nikolajeva 1998b) that contemporary juvenile fiction has broken all previous taboos as far as themes and subjects are concerned. Considering characters, we can perhaps still claim that certain types of character are highly unusual and will perhaps never become common in children's fiction, not as result of taboos but because of the nature and aesthetics of children's literature.

In his study *Myths of Modern Individualism*, Ian Watt (1996) discusses several major archetypal characters that have inspired Western writers during the last five hundred years. He starts with Faust, a character seemingly as far away from children's fiction as possible. The various versions of the Faust legend present the character from a slightly different moral angle, but in any case Faust fails because of the choice he makes. As adult readers, we can regard Faust as a victim or as a villain in his own drama; young readers, who have not yet established clear moral values, will have problems relating to this character. There are, however, several contemporary children's novels that make use of the Faust motif—for instance, *The Satanic Mill* by Ottfried Preussler and *Tim Thaler, or The Sold Laughter* by James Krüss (notably, both authors are German—that is, strongly connected with Goethe's Faust tradition). The difference between Preussler's and Krüss's characters, on the one hand, and the various representations of Faust, on the other, is that child characters are allowed to triumph over evil powers. They find a way to escape the contract with the devil, mainly thanks to their childlike innocence, in accordance with the traditional Romantic view of childhood. Thus, although children's literature can in principle utilize the Faust character, it is always substantially modified to suit the general aesthetic of children's literature.

Watt's next example is Don Quixote, who, like Faust, is a failure, but not because of his egocentric disposition but because he is born in the wrong time and wrong society. Don Quixote is an ironic character in Frye's terms: he is inferior to his environment since he knows and understands less than any other character in his vicinity. One might then conclude that Don Quixote is by definition the prototype of any child character. However, ironic characters in modern children's literature are, as pointed out earlier, usually empowered at least temporarily. Generally, child characters develop toward knowledge, experience, and maturity, even though this process may not be explicitly shown in any given text. While Don Quixote must surrender to the societal norms and will never be given another chance, a child character, even if disempowered by the end of the novel, has the potential to recapture the power position allowed during the temporal empowerment.

Watt's third figure under scrutiny is Don Juan, the least likely character in children's fiction, for several reasons. First, the nature of Don Juan's exploits is beyond the scope of a child reader's experience. This does not imply that a Don Juan plot is necessarily tabooed in a children's novel; it is simply irrelevant for the age range in which children's fiction characters appear. Second, Don Juan's behavior is highly immoral even if we translate it into forms more appropriate for young readers. Several scholars have pointed out the parallel between sexuality in general fiction and food in fiction for children. Gluttony and greed are common motifs in traditional children's literature, inevitably followed by punishment, although rarely as ultimate as the one imposed on Don Juan. The radical difference is, however, that a greedy child, who stuffs himself with food and is punished by stomach ache, does no harm to other people, unlike the destructive and unscrupulous Don Juan. We can once again see this as an adaptation to the conventions of children's literature: a child character cannot be allowed to be evil and depraved; the misdeeds only affect the child himself and teach him a lesson.

These three examples show that the superficially impossible characters from adult literature can indeed appear in children's fiction on certain conditions—namely, provided that the defeat is either wholly turned into victory or at least is significantly less profound. Children are as yet not fully developed individuals, and their temporary misfortunes do not indicate the irreversible downfall of Faust, Don Quixote, or Don Juan—hence, the generally acknowledged aesthetic feature of children's literature as being hopeful and optimistic.

The fourth archetypal figure of modern literature that Watt discusses is Robinson Crusoe, and here we see a striking difference between this character and the previous three, in the way children's literature appropriates them. Robinson is one of the most prolific sources of children's literature, since this figure propagates liberation from parents, independence, individual development, and the spirit of enterprise. The novel is based on the same basic plot many scholars have observed in children's literature: home (safe, but boring)—away (exciting, but dangerous)—return home. It empowers the character in an extraordinary situation, allowing degrees of growth and maturation more tangible and more profound than would be possible under normal conditions. Unlike Faust and Don Juan, Robinson Crusoe not only has been subject to numerous adaptations for young readers but has provided inspiration for a whole genre of Robinsonnade, focused on survival and resulting in children's novels as different as *Hatchet* and *Slake's Limbo*.

Watt views the four archetypes in his study as expressions of modern society's attitudes toward individual freedom and integrity as opposed to the ancient and medieval focus on man as part of a community. Childhood is supposed to be a collective experience. It is then not surprising that children's fiction draws extensively on the myths of antiquity, the childhood of Western humanity, in the first place, the quest figure of Odysseus. Does this mean that children's fiction has not yet reached the phase of "modern individualism" that Ian Watt discusses in his book? Rather, as I see it, Odysseus and Robinson Crusoe are much more universal for the psychological and ethical issues of humanity and therefore pertinent to children's as well as adult literature.

To Watt's three characters who are less relevant to children's fiction I could add, for instance, the Wandering Jew and Hamlet. Yet, we can certainly find parallels to the Wandering Jew (with its variation the Flying Dutchman) in children's novels about characters who cannot or do not want to grow up, such as Peter Pan and Tuck Everlasting (see Nikolajeva 2000, chap. 4). Diana Wynne Jones makes use of the archetype in *The Homeward Bounders*, in which the child character is allowed to break the curse, releasing Prometheus, Ahasuerus, and the Flying Dutchman from their eternal torture. As to Hamlet, we see the character archetype clearly in the movie *The Lion King*, in which the child naturally is allowed to triumph. Some other archetypal figures that may have inspired children's authors are Kaspar Hauser, transformed in the numerous stories of feral children (Mowgli being the most famous), or Dracula, the source of the vast trend of vampire novels.

Not surprisingly, all Watt's characters are male. If we try to recall great Western myths that have inspired female characters, we might perhaps count Joan of Arc as the model for contemporary juvenile novels about girls in disguise; otherwise our sources are extremely limited. Personally I am not convinced by attempts to squeeze female characters into Campbellian male mythical patterns (Pearson and Pope 1981). We must turn to contemporary

feminist criticism to discern recurrent patterns in creating female characters—for instance, "the madwoman in the attic" (Gilbert and Gubar 1977).

Female Archetypes and Children's Fiction

Annis Pratt's (1981) *Archetypal Patterns in Women's Fiction* can be regarded
as a feminist reply to Campbell's overtly masculine analysis of a hero.
Unlike Campbell's universal hero, the figures of women's fiction—historically a later phenomenon in human culture—are characters appearing on
mimetic and ironic levels. It is hypothetically possible to put a female character in a mythical or romantic narrative, but this will be a simple gender
permutation, creating a "hero in drag" (Paul 1990; see also Nikolajeva 2000,
147–49).

Since most of Pratt's patterns are clearly connected with sexuality and
eroticism, direct parallels can seldom be drawn between her categories and
the female characters we find in children's fiction. Her study is focused on
the female novel of development, a narrative type not really relevant for
children's fiction. The characters discussed in Pratt's book are adolescent
girls and adult women. Children's fiction is "pregendered" in the sense that
in the majority of children's novels, protagonists are gender-neutral—that
is, more or less interchangeable in terms of gender. However, just as I have
"translated" some masculine patterns into their correspondence in children's fiction, I will try to do the same with some of Pratt's observations. For
instance, the green-world archetype, an adolescent girl who lives close to
nature, is one of the most common female protagonists in children's fiction.
In the adult novels Pratt discusses, the mature woman looks back to her
green-world time, cherishing "a memory to which she returns for renewal"
(Pratt 1981, 17). While this recuperating memory is merely hypothetical in
children's fiction, the green world itself and its "green-world lover" can be
found in a great number of children's novels with female heroines. Wendy
is one of these heroines, escaping into her green world away from both
urban civilization and her parents' oppression. Wendy indeed returns to her
green world in her memories as an adult. Heidi, Mary Lennox, and Ronia
the robber's daughter are further examples of the green-world heroines.

The rape trauma that Pratt discusses next (Persephone, Daphne) would
seem irrelevant for children's fiction, unless we treat it very broadly. The
father–daughter conflict, based on the father's oppression, is central in, for
instance, *Ronia the Robber's Daughter*. In young adult fiction, it has become
a prominent motif, including incestuous rape.

The growing-up grotesque archetype implies meeting the incompatibility of personal freedom and societal demands by going into depression or seclusion. As Pratt observes, in literature boys grow, while girls shrink (Pratt 1981, 30). This shrinking has also been described in terms of abjection, a girl's feeling of aversion toward her own body as it develops into a young woman's:

> She hadn't had a new dress since they sold the sheep four years ago. Since then, her body had begun to make those strange changes to womanhood that exasperated her. Why couldn't she be as thin and straight as a boy? Why couldn't she have been a boy? Perhaps, then, her father would not have had to leave. With an older son to help, maybe he could have made a living for them on the hill farm. (*Lyddie* 22)

The tomboy archetype in children's fiction is an excellent example of abjection. Rather than accept their own femininity, heroines such as Jo March and Anne Shirley suppress it by manifesting nonfeminine behavior. Both characters have to subdue their hot tempers, incompatible with feminine norms; Anne is also literally silenced as she abandons her imaginative, poetic language. Cross-dressing is another way of denying one's body and gender. In contemporary novels, the grotesque archetype can be stretched quite far, since young women's unwomanly manners are tolerated slightly more than in Jo March's days. Louise in *Jacob Have I Loved* suppresses her femininity to distance herself from her pretty and talented twin sister. She is also trying, as does Lyddie in the preceding quote, to fulfill her father's secret desire for a son. Louise dresses carelessly, has a male occupation, fishing, and on the face of it makes no attempts to grow up as a "normal" woman. This is her survival strategy, and the author deliberately describes her as unattractive (among other things, with an ugly scar from chicken pox), the way she apprehends herself. A much younger Paterson heroine, Gilly Hopkins, employs a similar survival strategy by being deliberately nasty.

Marriage as archetypal enclosure is often imminent or hinted at in girls' fiction. In novels for younger children we encounter pretend marriage—for instance, between Wendy and Peter (explicit) or between Ronia and Birk (implicit). Otherwise, rather than the woman's submissiveness to her husband, in children's novels we see the girl's submissiveness to the father. Among possible strategies in marriage Pratt finds complicity or insanity, the latter hardly acceptable in a children's novel. We may find a parallel of the equal-marriage novel in cross-gender friendship on equal rights or sometimes with the girl being stronger—for instance, in *The Secret Garden* or once again in *Ronia the Robber's Daughter*. Otherwise, in the nonmarital or premarital relationships between men and women Pratt singles out punishment for transgressing sexual norms and puzzlement based on the discrepancy between natural desires and "unnatural" social expectation. Both patterns can be easily translated into corresponding situations in relationships between genders in children's fiction.

As to love and friendship between women, we see numerous examples of this in classic girls' novels, such as *Little Women* or *Anne of Green Gables*, without necessarily ascribing to the relationship a lesbian connotation (cf. Trites 1998). It was much more common and acceptable in the past for women to have a romantic friendship, like Anne and Diana's; and the fact that Jo expresses a wish to marry Meg to keep her in the family is in no way an indication of her lesbian preferences. In contemporary young adult fiction, however, the lesbian novel is becoming a noticeable subgenre (Day 2000; see also the special issue of *ChLAQ* 1998, no. 3).

The archetype of singleness and solitude is only possible in children's literature on certain conditions. For instance, Pippi Longstocking can be allowed to live on her own since she possesses a carnivalesque trait—exceptional strength—and is further empowered by an endless supply of money. Another solitary female character, Momo, has similar supernatural powers. A solitary child character can thus only appear on a mythic or romantic level. In fact, these figures represent Pratt's archetype of single women and witchcraft (see my interpretation of Pippi as a witch in Nikolajeva 2000, 112–18). Even though a character may not directly possess any magical powers, her isolation and otherness will necessarily make her surroundings apprehend her as a witch—for instance, Loella in *Papa Pellerin's Daughter*. A "realistic" young heroine trying to survive on her own often fails, like Johnny in *Johnny My Friend*.

In children's literature, the heroine's single status is not a final decision, and cannot be. Loella is eventually retrieved from her voluntary isolation and placed in an orphanage, something that Pippi can avoid because of her supernatural powers. Jo March would like to remain single and pursue her writing, but she has to comply with the norms of her society. Lyddie can decide that she will wait to marry until she has finished her education, but in the loosely connected *Jip: His Story*, we meet Lyddie happily married, in an equal-marriage archetype, conceivable in 1996 when the novel was written, but hardly at the time portrayed. According to most surveys, female schoolteachers in the nineteenth-century United States were fired as soon as they got married. Lyddie and Luke's marriage is therefore an anachronism, expressing the author's wishful thinking.

Single women and sex, which Pratt also discusses, are definitely irrele-

vant in children's fiction. "Old maids" can, for obvious reasons, not be protagonists but otherwise are frequent characters, such as Aunt Polly in *Tom
Sawyer* or Aunt Josephine in *Anne of Green Gables*.

Pratt's final discussion on the novels of rebirth and transformation, with
a strong Jungian flavor, does not in my opinion differ substantially from
Campbell's model. However, Pratt points out that one of the strategies for
successful individuation for female characters is androgyny, which we see
clearly in a growing number of contemporary novels (see Österlund 2000),
especially if we treat this concept broadly, including social androgyny as
opposed to biological.

One final remark I would like to add is that in children's fiction, girls are
doubly oppressed: as women and as children. This implies that in a children's novel, a female character's development is more universal than in the
mainstream, where the femininity is overt and explicit. Not least, girls' fiction is historically a relatively recent genre; therefore, masculine patterns
are "default values" in children's fiction, as in many other fields. Paradoxically enough, the contemporary ironic character of children's fiction has
inherited significantly more traits of the female archetypes, as drafted by
Pratt, than those of Campbell's hero with a thousand faces.

Concluding Remarks

Viewing the characters' ontological status from a historical perspective, we
can clearly see that contemporary characters tend to become more like "real
people," appearing on low mimetic and ironic levels. Our shifting criteria
for "plausible" characters depend on several factors—for instance, on our
growing knowledge of human nature (which young children normally lack);
on our changing values of human virtues and vices; and finally on the variety of human behavior. Examples of real heroes are today found only in formulaic fiction. Even when child characters are temporarily elevated to high
mimetic and romantic levels, they are subsequently brought back to ordinary life, and romantic heroes are deconstructed in a variety of ways (see
Hourihan 1997). Contemporary characters are not meant as examples for
young readers to admire, but as equal subjectivities. The opposite trend,
prominent in contemporary mainstream postmodern fiction, which makes
characters increasingly resemble empty verbal constructions, is as yet
extremely rare in children's fiction.

Another question to put in connection with the development from hero
to character is the adult authors' capacity to adopt a child subject position.
It would be reasonable to assume that adult writers would feel most com-

fortable writing from their own superior position, presenting child characters as inferior physically, morally, spiritually, in terms of knowledge, experience, economy, and societal power. However, even a very brief glance at
a number of children's novels reveals that the ironic mode is the most complex and demanding. On the other hand, the romantic mode allows adults
to empower the child, thus creating an illusion for the character and the
reader that such empowerment is indeed possible. On the high mimetic
level, adult writers can use characters to provide young readers with examples and ideals. Which endeavor is to be regarded the most successful
depends exclusively on the purpose the authors have when writing for children. The development from hero to character in children's fiction is thus
not a simple linear process. It reveals the attitude toward childhood and
toward children's reading at any given moment in any given society.

Subjectivity is further an essential question in children's literature. In
mythic, romantic, and high mimetic modes, subjectivity is outside the text
and, moreover, frequently connected with an adult narrative agency. Subjectivity in low mimetic and ironic modes is inside the text and therefore
usually connected with a child character. Thus, we may observe the development from outside to inside subjectivity as a process parallel to the development from hero to character. The question of the subject position
becomes of overall importance when we face the necessity to determine
who is the protagonist, the issue of the next chapter.

Notes

1. This is not a universal opinion among children's literature scholars; see, for instance, Gillian Adams's studies of medieval children's literature (Adams 1998). It
is, however, my firm belief that it is futile to speak about children's literature before
the emergence of childhood as a social category, which occurs in Western culture
during the Enlightenment and Romanticism. See Ariès 1962; Zornado 2000.

2. Compare the four levels of reading of the Bible or of Dante's *Divina Comme-
dia:* literal, allegorical, tropological, and anagogic, of which most readers of today
will only choose one or two. In fact, the printing history of Eve Bunting's book mentioned earlier confirms my thesis. It was first published in 1980 as *Terrible Things* by
Harper & Row; the subtitle, manipulating the readers' allegorical interpretation,
was added in the 1989 reprint by the Jewish Publication Society in Philadelphia.

3. I am indebted to Roberta Seelinger Trites for bringing this article to my attention.

CHAPTER THREE

~

In Search of the Protagonist

Why are we interested in knowing who the protagonist of a children's novel might be? In the majority of cases the answer seems so obvious that the question itself is ridiculous. Most unsophisticated readers never encounter the problem of deciding who the protagonist is. Unfortunately, many schoolteachers encourage this unreflecting attitude in their students, by asking the simple question "Who is the main character of the story?" and feel satisfied with a straightforward answer rather than putting the whole problem under scrutiny. The question of the protagonist brings forward not only the complexity of characterization but also the complexity of texts.

Main characters, or protagonists, are, by definition, those who stand in the center of the story and around whom the story rotates. Despite this very obvious principle, it is not always easy to decide who is the main character in a story. Let us consider several criteria that enable us to identify the protagonist of a children's novel.

The Title Character

A good criterion is, of course, that the protagonist is the character mentioned in the title, the title character. This is a criterion applicable to children's as well as mainstream literature. The title character can be mentioned by name only: *Emma* or *Heidi*; or by first and last name: *Robinson Crusoe, David Copperfield, Jane Eyre, Mary Poppins,* or *Cassie Binegar.* The name can also have an attribute, appellation, or epithet: *Anne of Green Gables, Harriet the Spy, Ramona the Pest, A Bear Called Paddington,* or *Ronia the Robber's Daughter*; alternatively, the attribute may stand in its own right: *The Little Princess* or *The Hobbit.* Furthermore, the title can mention the

49

name together with the setting: *Alice in Wonderland, Pippi in the South Seas* (cf. the classic title *Iphigenia in Tauris*). It can mention the character having adventures, thus also indicating the genre: *Gulliver's Travels, The Adventures of Tom Sawyer,* or *Emil's Pranks.* It can mention the name together with the central object or image of the story: *Harry Potter and the Goblet of Fire.*

In all these cases, the title character is without any doubt the protagonist. However, it is not always so obvious. The title *Tuck Everlasting* contains the name of an important but definitely secondary character. The title character of *Sarah, Plain and Tall* is not the protagonist. Comparing the titles *The Wizard of Earthsea* and *The Wizard of Oz,* we discover that while the first title indeed indicates the protagonist, Ged, the second novel's protagonist is not the title character. Similarly, comparing *Charlie and the Chocolate Factory* and *The Lion, the Witch and the Wardrobe,* we see that while Charlie is the protagonist, neither the lion nor the witch are. Superficially, the title *The Little Prince* has the same relationship to its protagonist as *The Little Princess.* However, while Sarah Crewe is undoubtedly the protagonist of *The Little Princess,* the case of *The Little Prince* is more ambivalent. While most unsophisticated readers would unproblematically suggest the Little Prince as the protagonist, a deeper investigation of the structure and meaning of the text would inevitably lead to the conclusion that the novel is about the adult pilot, who is also the narrator of the story, while the prince is his nostalgic image of lost childhood.

Winnie-the-Pooh seems a very straightforward case of a title character. However, while all unsophisticated readers would unanimously proclaim the toy bear to be the protagonist, most critics agree that the story is actually about Christopher Robin, and the further interpretation of the toys depends on the point of departure one takes (see Sale 1978, 17; Kuznets 1994, 34, 47–53). The title *Charlotte's Web* makes Charlotte the spider the protagonist, while is it more natural to give this role to Wilbur the pig. In the Swedish translation, this ambiguity has been "corrected" by changing the title to "Fantastic Wilbur," which, among other things, shifts the gender emphasis. Thus, in many cases it is a matter of interpretation of the whole text that decides whether the title character is also the protagonist. *Moominpappa at Sea* may suggest reading this late Moomin novel as the father's story, and occasionally it has been read this way. However, if we read the whole Moomin suite as the narrative about the little child's path to maturity, there is no reason to abandon Moomintroll as the main character simply because the title tells us to do so. By comparison, *Exploits of Moominpappa,* a prequel of the suite, definitely has the father as protagonist.

The appellation in the title *Flip-Flop Girl* refers to Lupe, while the protagonist is without doubt Vinnie. *Agnes Cecilia* featured in the title is a personal name, but the protagonist's name is Nora, while Agnes Cecilia is the name of another character she is looking for. The title is ambiguous; Nora encounters a woman called Agnes and a girl called Cecilia, but not until the very end of the story does she find the one she has been searching for.

Tom's Midnight Garden draws our attention to the protagonist who is a boy. A more sophisticated reading reveals that Tom's ghostly experiences in the garden may be the result of Mrs. Bartholomew's memories of her childhood and that she is the true protagonist. Naturally, all these arguments may seem too subtle to be taken into consideration at all; however, the examples show the complexity of the initially very simple question of title characters. Titles appear lucid on one level of the text, but complicated and ambivalent on the others.

Furthermore, we may be coaxed into believing that the title character is also the protagonist. While *Peter Pan in Kensington Gardens* certainly presents the title character as the protagonist, in *Peter Pan and Wendy* the situation is more complicated. After a closer look at *Peter Pan, Mary Poppins,* or *Pippi Longstocking,* we notice that the title characters are not protagonists. Rather, they are catalysts that initiate the story and bring excitement (or sometimes conflict) into the lives of real protagonists. In the first chapter of *Mary Poppins,* the title character is presented through the eyes of the two astonished children, and her way of talking, her behavior (e.g., flying or sliding up the banisters), and her magical ability to produce a variety of objects from an empty bag clearly mark her as "the other." At the end of this chapter, we are allowed a glimpse of the other characters' emotions: "everybody . . . was glad of Mary Poppins' arrival. Mr. Banks was glad. . . . Mrs. Banks was glad. . . . Mrs. Brill and Ellen were glad. . . . Robertson Ay was glad" (21). We are, however, never allowed to enter Mary Poppins's mind: "But nobody ever knew what Mary Poppins felt about it, for Mary Poppins never told anybody anything" (21). Throughout the three novels, Mary Poppins's role is that of a helper (in Propp's sense) rather than a hero. She brings adventure into the lives of two ordinary children, allowing them to encounter all kinds of exciting people and visit magical landscapes. In most cases, she promptly denies that any of the wonderful events have taken place at all. I would therefore definitely claim that Mary Poppins is not the protagonist of the novels featuring her name in the title.

What shall we do about titles that have two names? The title *Lottie and Lisa* is the translation of the German *Das doppelte Lottchen* (Double Lottie), and both of the twins are equally important. The novel *Hugo and Josephine* is a sequel to the novel called *Josephine,* in which we correctly assume that the title character is the protagonist. When the second character is introduced in the title, we believe that this additional character plays a role equal to that of Josephine, especially as his name stands first (this may be a matter of rhythm, though). However, Josephine continues to be the protagonist not only of *Hugo and Josephine* but also of the third novel in the trilogy, titled *Hugo.* The additional character, Hugo, has the role of a helper and guide, who assists Josephine on her identity quest. The titles of the sequels are—perhaps deliberately—misleading.

Some famous titles include a group of characters: *The Railway Children, The Children of Green Knowe,* or *The Children of the Noisy Village.* They may even give us the exact number of characters—for instance, *Five Children and It, The Famous Five,* or *The Secret Seven.* A collective appellation is possible: *The Treasure Seekers* or *The Borrowers.* The title *Little Women* alludes to the four characters of the novel but also offers an evaluation (perhaps *little* meaning "immature" or even "insignificant"). In the Swedish translation, the title *The Children of Green Knowe* has become "Tolly and His Friends"; that is, the accent has been shifted toward one of the characters. Moreover, the original title most probably does not allude to the protagonist, Tolly, but to the three children he meets during his time-shift experiences, Toby, Alexander, and Linnet. The connotation of the title *The Children of Green Knowe* is thus different from that of *The Children of the Noisy Village,* the latter directly pointing at the central group of characters. In *The Borrowers,* the child, Arietty, is emphasized by the author; she is more important and more interesting than her parents.

I will come back to the fascinating problem of collective protagonists in children's fiction in the next chapter. At this point I will confine myself to stating that the criterion of the title character is good for a start, but not completely reliable. The same is true of characters depicted on the cover. Some covers of *Heidi* and *Anne of Green Gables* portray the girls who are the protagonists, just as *Tom Sawyer* and *Emil's Pranks* feature the boy protagonists. However, the covers of *Mary Poppins, The Little Prince,* and *Pippi Longstocking* show the characters who, as I have just argued, are not necessarily the protagonists. These covers manipulate us to adopt a certain interpretation, since we assume that the cover character must be the protagonist. This manipulation impedes a more sophisticated interpretation, I suggest.

Finally, many titles of children's novels do not feature any character, focusing instead on the central image of the story (*The Subtle Knife*), the setting (*Treasure Island*), the issue (*Homecoming*), or the plot (*The Dark Is Rising*). Such titles give us no help in deciding on the protagonist and can even be misleading. According to the author, even many adult coreaders were puzzled by the title *Jacob Have I Loved*, since there is no character in the novel named Jacob (Paterson 1995). It is, however, clearly explained in the novel where the quotation comes from and what it implies.

"In Order of Appearance . . ."

If we made a random choice among the books most often mentioned in general studies of children's fiction and thus perceived as "children's literary canon," we would probably discover that half of the books start by presenting the protagonist, in some way or other, already in the opening sentences, while the rest do not, and may even establish ambiguity of some kind. On the other hand, the delayed presentation of the protagonist may create suspense: "If you want to find Cherry Tree Lane all you have to do is ask the Policeman at the crossroads" (*Mary Poppins*). The presentation of the setting precedes the presentation of the protagonist. This is in fact a very common way of opening a novel: "It had been a great house once, with farms and fields, money and jewels—with tenants and squires and men-at-arms" (*The House of Arden*).

The most common opening formula of a fairy tale is "Once upon a time there was . . . ." It is this opening that the author of *Pinocchio* alludes to:

Once upon a time there was . . .
"A king!" my little readers will say straight away. No, children, you are mistaken.
Once upon a time there was a piece of wood.

This is a marvelous metafictive play with the readers' expectations; moreover, their true expectations of the formula to introduce the protagonist do not fail, since the piece of wood will eventually turn out to be the protagonist.

In fairy tales, however, it is more likely that the formula will introduce the hero's parents, royal or common, than the hero himself. Novels for children break this convention more often than they follow it, presenting the protagonist by the formula "Once upon a time, many years ago—when our grandfathers were little children—there was a doctor" (*Doctor Dolittle*). On the other hand, *Thumbelina* starts more traditionally as "Once upon a time there was a woman who wanted a little child of her own," whereupon the woman is abandoned almost at once and the story is wholly focused on the tiny girl. In fact, this is what often happens in fairy tales, which start with a childless royal couple wishing for a child or expecting one (Snow White, Rapunzel, Donkey-Skin). Once the child is born, the parents can be easily disposed of and often are. *Ronia the Robber's Daughter* adheres to the traditional pattern of the hero's wonderful birth; however, the novel introduces the protagonist in the very first sentence: "On the night that Ronia was born a thunderstorm was racing over the mountains." Unlike the fairy tale, Ronia's parents do not disappear; on the contrary, they are very central in the novel's conflict.

We tend to assume that the person first introduced in a story is its protagonist. When a book starts with "Alice was beginning to get very tired . . . ," there are indeed strong reasons to believe that the story will be about a girl called Alice. The assumption is amplified by the title and perhaps by a picture of a girl on the cover. The beginning "A little boy was sitting in the corner of a railway carriage looking out at the rain" (*The Children of Green Knowe*) makes us, quite correctly, assume that this boy will be the protagonist. The opening of *Peter Rabbit* may seem to deviate from the pattern: "Once upon a time there were four little rabbits." However, Peter is almost immediately singled out as the main character, by contrasting: "Flopsy, Mopsy, and Cottontail, who were good little bunnies, went down the lane to gather blackberries/But Peter, who was very naughty . . . ." The fact that Peter is also the title character supports our apprehension.

The Prince and the Pauper begins, "In the ancient city of London, on a certain autumn day in the second quarter of the sixteenth century, a boy was born to a poor family of the name of Canty, who did not want him" (9). The boy, Tom Canty, is one of the two title characters, and the second one, Edward Tudor, is introduced in the next sentence: "On the same day another English child was born to a rich family of the name of Tudor, who did want him. All England wanted him" (9). Since the title mentions both boys, we have no help from the title deciding on the protagonist. The prince stands first in the title, but Tom is introduced first in the narrative. The two boys are equally important to the story.

The novel titled *Tom's Midnight Garden* starts, "If, standing alone on the back doorstep, Tom allowed himself to weep tears, they were tears of anger." Together with the title, the beginning makes us apprehend Tom as the protagonist, although, as I have mentioned, another, more subtle interpretation is possible. A novel that does not indicate a title character, *The Wind in the Willows*, starts, "The Mole had been working very hard all the morning, spring-cleaning his little house." There are several characters in the book who may equally be perceived as the protagonist. In fact, many readers would certainly suggest Toad as the protagonist, since he is without doubt the most colorful character in the novel. However, having been introduced to Mole first, and perceiving the first scenes of the Riverbank through Mole's eyes, we may have a strong reason to single out Mole as the protagonist.

The presentation of the protagonist can be deliberately delayed, as in the following case, to create a humorous effect:

> These two very old people are the father and mother of Mr. Bucket. Their names are Grandpa Joe and Grandma Josephine.
> And these two very old people are the father and mother of Mrs. Bucket. Their names are Grandpa George and Grandma Georgina.
> This is Mr. Bucket.
> This is Mrs. Bucket.
> Mr. and Mrs. Bucket have a small boy whose name is Charlie Bucket.
> This is Charlie. (*Charlie and the Chocolate Factory*, 11–13)

From the title we expect Charlie to be the protagonist. In the first sentences he is provided with a pedigree, before he makes his own appearance. This is in fact similar to the presentation in *Karlson on the Roof*:

> In a perfectly ordinary house in a perfectly ordinary street in Stockholm lives a perfectly ordinary family called Sanderson. They have a perfectly ordinary father and a perfectly ordinary mother and three perfectly ordinary children, Sebastian, Barbara and Midge. (1)

In *Anne of Green Gables*, it takes a long time before we meet Anne, the protagonist. In the first chapter, Marilla, her future foster mother, discusses with a neighbor what kind of a boy she and Matthew have decided to get. This amplifies the shock when they get Anne instead. A similar device is used in *Heidi:* in the first chapter we mostly hear Dete's voice giving us the background for Heidi's arrival in the mountains. A much more recent novel also plays with the readers' expectations in a similar manner: *Harry Potter and the Philosopher's Stone* starts by introducing the Dursley family, who play a very peripheral role in the plot, while the protagonist is first mentioned briefly halfway down the first page ("The Dursleys knew that the Potters had a small son") and does not come properly into focus until the next chapter. However, since his name appears in the title, we have no doubts about Harry being the main character.

Perry Nodelman (1985b) devotes a whole article to the opening of *Charlotte's Web:* "Where's Papa going with that ax?" I find the opening chapter the greatest failure of this novel. The concern Fern feels toward the little pig and the care she shows him create a strong empathic bond between her and the reader. When the narrative perspective abandons the girl and focuses on the pig, the spider, and other animals, the initial expectations are betrayed. In fact, the real child and her emotional needs are profoundly ignored in this novel, and the main issue—the inevitability of death—is treated, as I see it, totally unsatisfactorily from the human point of view. If the novel had been consistently built up on the animal level, we would have been able to read it as a metaphor or allegory of human life. However, the initial chapter creates a human dimension, which, although dropped later, makes the resolution of the Wilbur-centered plot merely underscore Fern's unresolved anxieties.

"All children, except one, grow up" is the opening line of *Peter Pan*. If we become curious about this unique child, our curiosity will not be satisfied until the fifth page. The opening paragraph continues as "They soon know that they will grow up, and the way Wendy knew was this." The narrative goes on giving us some background information about Mrs. Darling and the ingenious way Mr. Darling won her; about the arrival of the three babies, and about the family's happy life. Then the presumptive hero makes his appearance: "There never was a simpler, happier family until the coming of Peter Pan" (13). I have elsewhere argued that Peter Pan is not the protagonist of the novel (Nikolajeva 2000, 87–93). Wendy's presentation before his supports this interpretation.

"The tramp was big and squarely built, and he walked with the rolling stride of the long road, his steps too big for the little streets of the little town" (*The Mouse and His Child*). The tramp is not the protagonist of the story, he is the *deus ex machina*, setting the plot in motion. He may also be interpreted as the metadiegetic narrator, the omniscient and omnipotent impersonation of the author. The story closes with the tramp contemplating the reestablished idyll of the doll house; therefore, we can view him as a metafictive figure, appearing outside the narrative of the two toy mice. The story's exposition thus presents different indications as to who the protagonist will be from the title and the contents.

Summing up the examples of beginnings, we can state that the criterion of the character first introduced as a protagonist is fairly safe, especially in combination with the character's name or appellation in the title. It cannot, however, always be used as an absolute guideline.

Frequent or Constant Presence

From the moment protagonists are introduced in the text, they are ordinarily present throughout the book. A further criterion might be that the protagonist is the character who appears in most episodes or on most pages in the book, although it cannot be a definite measure. There are novels that have several characters, with separate chapters devoted to each. A classic such as *The Prince and the Pauper* devotes alternative chapters to the two characters, as does the contemporary novel *The White Stone*. After the first chapter in which the two characters meet, the story alternates between the two; in each chapter, one is present, while the other is abandoned. In the concluding chapter, they are brought together again. In *Little Women*, most chapters are devoted to one of the four characters. Apparently, counting the exact number of pages devoted to each character would not prove very fruitful, and we will need other means of deciding on their interrelated importance.

In the *Pooh* books, Pooh is present in every chapter, although he may be occasionally absent from an episode within a chapter—for instance, when we meet Piglet "entirely surrounded by water" or when Tigger's and Roo's outing is described. This dominant presence clearly indicates that Pooh is the protagonist. However, in a more sophisticated reading with Christopher Robin as the true protagonist, we may make an interesting observation. Out of the twenty chapters in the two books, Christopher Robin is featured as a more or less central figure in merely one, describing the expedition to the North Pole (the chapter title stresses his central role). The main dramatic episode of the chapter, Roo falling in the river and Pooh's rescue of him, which leads to the discovery of the "pole," shifts the focus from Christopher Robin to Pooh. The last chapter of the first book, "in which Christopher Robin gives a Pooh Party," is a get-together of all characters, so it does not really single out the boy. Otherwise he is likely to appear at the end of a chapter to set things right. In chapter 6 of the first book, he only appears in the metafictive frame, and in chapter 8 of the sequel he is absent altogether. In chapter 5 of *The House at Pooh Corner*, "in which Rabbit has a busy day, and we learn what Christopher Robin does in the mornings," the boy is absent from the diegetic level and only mentioned by the other characters. For a protagonist, Christopher Robin is, in other words, too frequently absent from the story. We need other criteria to maintain his central position.

First-Person Perspective

First-person narratives often make us assume that the narrator is also the protagonist. The opening of the book may accentuate this: "I was born (as I have been informed and believe) on a Friday, at twelve o'clock at night"

(*David Copperfield*), or "My father had a small estate in Nottinghamshire; I was the third of five sons" (*Gulliver's Travels*). This is the most conventional way of starting a first-person novel. It is against this "David Copperfield kind of crap" that a modern first-person narrator, Holden Caulfield in *The Catcher in the Rye*, protests: "If you really want to hear about it, the first thing you'll probably want to know is where I was born." The difference may best be described in terms of Mikhail Bakhtin's theory as the difference between epic and polyphone narratives. By epic, Bakhtin means life stories, which indeed begin by "I was born . . ." and follow the protagonists through many trials toward a stable position or occasionally until their death. Contemporary polyphone novels seldom provide explicit background information about characters, and especially in the first-person perspective, the narrator seldom provides any information at all. Yet both David Copperfield and Holden Caulfield are protagonists in the stories they are telling.

We tend to assume that first-person narrators are homodiegetic, that is, identical with a character in a story. However, both the narrator's distance from the story and his degree of participation in it can be diverse. Consider the following opening:

> I have been asked to tell you about the back of the North Wind. An old Greek writer mentions a people who lived there. . . . My story is not the same as his. I do not think Herodotus had got the right account of the place. I am going to tell you how it fared with a boy who went there. (*At the Back of the North Wind*, 7)

The first-person pronoun seems to establish the narrator as the protagonist. The last sentence of the quoted paragraph indicates clearly that the narrator is metadiegetic; he is not telling us about himself or about anything he has experienced or has been witness to. The protagonist is a boy called Diamond, and exactly how the narrator knows about his experience (especially given the fact that Diamond is dead) is a metafictional question. Similarly, the intrusive "I" in *The Lion, the Witch and the Wardrobe* is naturally not identical with any of the characters. The narrator of Astrid Lindgren's *Emil* books is an adult, telling us about Emil's adventures long ago (extradiegetic). She is not a character in the story (heterodiegetic). Her knowledge of the events is, however, not firsthand; she has supposedly read the notes Emil's mother has put down in some blue notebooks. What she decides to tell us is selective: "No, don't ask me to tell you about that. I'm never going to tell anyone because I promised Emil's mother." We must therefore assume that Emil had many more adventures than the narrator has chosen to tell us. This first-person narrator is metadiegetic;

she exists in the metafictional frame, outside the actual story but inside the text (metadiegetic level). On this level, she can talk to Emil's mother and read her diary, and she also knows that Emil will eventually become the president of the local council and the finest man in the whole province.

Let us contemplate another example: "I, Penelope Taberner Cameron, tell this story of happenings when I was a young girl" (*A Traveller in Time*, 13). The narrator is telling about herself; she is autodiegetic. However, there is a substantial temporal gap between the narrator's time and the story time. The story is told in retrospect; the narrator is extradiegetic. Lisa, the first-person narrator of *The Children of the Noisy Village*, is homodiegetic, identical with Lisa the character. She is also intradiegetic, telling the story just as it unfolds, without any distance between the narrative and the narrating. However, she is obviously not the main character of the story. Lisa tells us about the daily life around her, the games, the chores, and the pastimes. Very seldom, if ever, are we allowed to enter her mind. Most often Lisa refers to the group as "we." Sometimes the "we" only includes the three girls, but just as often all the six children. She is simply a mouthpiece for the group; thus, the first-person narrator is not autodiegetic.

One of the most striking examples of the ambiguity of the first-person narrator is the pilot in *The Little Prince*. Applying the criterion of the title character, we will most probably suggest that the pilot is not the protagonist. He is an adult narrator, and he is not telling us about his childhood, but he is an adult character in his own story, who meets a child character. The simplest solution is to say that the Little prince is the protagonist, and that the pilot's presence in the text is merely an amplified version of the adult narrator's presence in the *Emil* books. However, *Emil's* narrator does not participate in the stories and is not affected by them, while the pilot's encounter with the Little Prince changes his whole worldview. In fact, a more sophisticated reading of the novel identifies the prince as the pilot's "inner child," the suppressed part of his self that he finally learns to acknowledge.[1] In an unsophisticated reading, the first-person perspective contradicts the criteria of the title character and dominant presence, which prompt us to choose the prince as protagonist. In a sophisticated reading, on the other hand, the first-person perspective supports the establishment of the pilot as the main character.

Mio, My Son starts with a description of a character, which is supposedly a radio announcement about a lost boy: "Karl Anders Nilsson has fair hair and blue eyes and at the time of his disappearance was wearing brown shorts, gray pullover, and a small red cap." Only a few sentences further into the novel, the narrator is revealed as being identical with the protagonist: "I am Karl Anders Nilsson." Comparing the titles *Mio, My Son* and *Johnny My Friend*, which may seem similar in structure, we can notice that the first indicates the protagonist or, rather, his transfiguration in the magical realm. The title quotes Mio's royal father's recurrent address to his son and thus reflects one of the central themes of the novel: the lonely orphaned boy's longing for his real father or at least for knowledge about his true origin as a means of discovering his own identity. The second title makes us assume that the story we are reading will be about a person called Johnny and that the narrator is not autodiegetic but a witness-narrator. However, reading the novel, we see clearly that Chris, in telling us about Johnny, is in fact telling his own story. The title contradicts the narrative perspective, which is part of the intricate narrative structure of the novel: the naive narrator *believes* that he is telling us about Johnny, while in fact he reveals far more about himself.[2]

The first-person narrator in *Mio, My Son* is, at first glance, autodiegetic. In fact, the narrative situation is more complicated. There is a narrator, whose name is Andy, who is sitting on a park bench, telling a story about another narrator, whose name is Mio, who is in Farawayland, telling a story, in retrospect, a year after the events, about a character, whose name is Mio, and occasionally about another character, whose name is Andy. The whole interpretation of the story depends on how we interpret the narrative situation. My suggestion is as follows:

ANDY (narrator) tells about →

           MIO (narrator) tells about → MIO (character)

ANDY (character) ← tells about

Mio the narrator can be considered autodiegetic, while Andy the narrator is extradiegetic or possibly metadiegetic, if we count "reality" as a different fictional level than Farawayland. When Mio the narrator at the end of the book starts talking about the character Andy in the third person, the different agents are definitely separated: "There's no Andy on any seat in the park. He is in Farawayland, you see[—]Karl Anders Nilsson is in Farawayland with his father the King" (179).

Thus, the difference in distance (extradiegetic or intradiegetic) is not decisive as a criterion for the protagonist; both may be protagonists but need not be. The narrator's participation in the story (heterodiegetic or homodiegetic) is, on the other hand, essential: only homodiegetic narrators can be protagonists; however, not all homodiegetic narrators are protagonists. The only really safe criterion is an autodiegetic narrator: a character telling his own story. The remaining problem is to decide whether the narrator is indeed autodiegetic. As we see from the examples of *Mio, My Son* or *Johnny My Friend*, this is not always straightforward.

Focalizer

One of the most radical and innovative statements to be found in Gérard Genette's *Narrative Discourse* is that there is no difference between the first-person and third-person narratives, which otherwise constitutes a strict division in most studies of children's literature (see Lukens 1990, 120–36). Instead, Genette speaks of narrators focalizing themselves in exactly the same manner as they can focalize other characters (Genette 1980, 198), either simultaneously or in retrospect, externally or internally. The pattern of focalization proves to be more important than the traditional difference between personal and impersonal narratives. We have already seen that the omniscient (meaning third-person) narrators often have very distinct voices and refer to themselves as "I"; in all other cases this omniscient "I" is simply hidden, covert. With this approach, there is no radical difference between the first-person adult extradiegetic narrator in *A Traveller in Time* and the third-person, presumably adult, extradiegetic narrators in *Tom Sawyer, Little Women*, or *The Lion, the Witch and the Wardrobe*. In each case, there is an adult narrative agency focalizing a young person. Applying the notion of focalization, rather than the criterion of the first-person (autodiegetic) narrator, we might come closer to a more precise definition of the protagonist.

Focalization as a narrative device denotes a limitation of the information that is allowed to reach the reader (another frequently used term is *central consciousness*). When a character is focalized, the text follows this person and cannot follow other characters. Focalization implies manipulation of the narrator's, character's and reader's point of view, resulting in our perceiving the narrative "as if" it were told by the focalizing character. This "as if" narrator deceives the reader and pushes the actual narrator into the background. In children's fiction, an adult narrator usually focalizes a child character, which creates an illusion that the events are rendered through the child's eyes. The notion of focalization is connected to both the narrator's presence in the text and the character's point of view.

A narrative can be nonfocalized (or zero focalized), externally focalized, or internally focalized. In a nonfocalized narrative (traditionally called the *omniscient perspective*), none of the characters is singled out. The narrator can follow all of them or one at a time, enter the minds of different characters, and switch between them. *The Lion, the Witch and the Wardrobe* is basically a nonfocalized narrative, whose perspective can switch between Edmund and the other three children when they have parted; the narrator can render all four children's thoughts and feelings, contrasting them; and he can even enter the mind of the evil White Witch, their enemy. The latter destroys some of the suspense of the story; it would have been a more powerful story if the readers were to discover the effect of the evil forces by themselves, together with Edmund or maybe before him.

A nonfocalized narrative gives us no help in deciding on the protagonist: all characters are presented as equally important. Although we quite often categorize narratives as nonfocalized (or having an omniscient perspective), in practice it is a very rare narrative device. If all the secondary characters were described as detailed and as often as the main characters, the narrative would be virtually impossible to handle. Normally we are dealing with limited omniscient perspective: the four children in *The Lion, the Witch and the Wardrobe* are focalized, but not Mr. Tumnus the faun or the beavers, or any of the other helping animals, and not even such a central character as Aslan.

External focalization means that the narrator follows the characters without entering their minds (traditionally classified as objective, or dramatic, perspective). We share their literal, perceptional point of view, but not their thoughts and feelings. As compared with the nonfocalized narrative, external focalization provides stronger support for our judgment of the protagonist. An external focalizer is more likely to be the protagonist than a nonfocalized character. However, if several characters are focalized, the problem remains. We can, of course, apply the quantitative principle and decide on the character who is focalized most. This criterion is likely to coincide with dominant presence.

Internal focalization means that the narrator enters the character's thoughts (traditionally called *introspective narrator*). If the narrator focalizes himself, we will probably call it a self-reflective narrative. Internal focalization almost eliminates the gap between the character and the reader. We are dissolved in the character; therefore, we almost unmistakably identify internal focalizers as protagonists. Unfortunately, it is not altogether impossible to have several internal focalizers in a narrative—the device is called *polyfocalization* (or *multifocalization*). The pattern is not the same as in a nonfocalized narrative, in which the narrator can be at several places *at once* or know what several characters think *at once*, as in *The Lion, the Witch and the Wardrobe*. In a polyfocalized narrative, when one character is focalized, the rest remain opaque. The shift of focalizers can present an exciting interplay, but our criterion for the protagonist fails and must be complemented by other means.

Yet the concept of focalization gives us more precise tools to decide on the protagonist. *Pippi Longstocking* is presented in critical works as an example of a text with an omniscient narrator, or a non-focalized narrative. In fact, Pippi is sometimes focalized externally, but the narrator never enters Pippi's mind and only accounts for her actions and utterances. Tommy and Annika are occasionally focalized, either externally or internally. When they meet Pippi and we as readers get the first description of Pippi's appearance, the focalization is external: "Just as they were standing there . . . the gate of Villa Villekulla opened and a little girl stepped out" (15). We share Tommy's and Annika's perceptional point of view, but we do not really know what they think. Moreover, at this point we already know who the little girl is, while Tommy and Annika do not. However, sometimes the narrator may enter their minds: "Tommy and Annika thought it sounded as if it would be fun and wanted very much to be Thing-Finders too" (27). Focalization in this sentence is rather vague, since the form is reported speech, involving a narrator. When Tommy and Annika pass Pippi's house on their way to school, the text says, "They would much rather have gone to play with Pippi" (49). Again, focalization is not very prominent. As already suggested, we are inclined to assume that focalizing characters also are the protagonists. When there are several focalizers, we must make a choice. We can choose the character who is focalized most, in this case Pippi. However, Pippi's subjectivity is too alien for us to share. Besides, internal focalization provides stronger subjectivity, in this case with Tommy and Annika, ordinary children. At the end of the book, Tommy and Annika go home. We share their point of view and look at Pippi standing at the window. This closure leads me to wonder whether Pippi is indeed the protagonist of the story. I prefer to see her as a catalyst who initiates a change, similar to Mary Poppins.

Evolution

Another criterion that would rule out Pippi as a protagonist is that of development and change. Whether we perceive literary characters as psychological entities or plot vehicles, we expect them to change in some way throughout the narrative. In plot-oriented stories, the change will be mostly, if not exclusively, in the character's power position, a development from underprivileged through trials toward material reward ("crowning"). This is mostly true in adventure stories. For instance, Tom Sawyer finds a treasure and thus remarkably improves his social status; Tom Canty in *The Prince and the Pauper* gains special privileges; and so on. Girls' books can also be primarily based on the change in social status: Heidi is rewarded for her virtue by material wealth.

In character-oriented narratives, we expect the character to obtain new—presumably higher—moral qualities, mature spiritually, gain knowledge and insights, and so on. The change may be quite explicit, typically in conventional didactic stories (e.g., *Pinocchio*). In a more sophisticated narrative, the change is implied, and the readers are supposed to draw their own conclusions. In *The Brothers Lionheart*, the first-person narrator Rusky says at the beginning that he is going to tell us about his brother. In fact, the story is much more about Rusky himself and about his spiritual growth, while his brother is a godlike model—handsome, clever, and admired by everybody from the start. There is nothing in this character that allows development. It is similarly obvious that Pippi does not change, because already from the start she has everything that the typical underdog must attempt to gain: physical strength, material wealth, superior power position, firm social status, remarkable self-assurance, superb mastery of language, and so on. Here we find further support for my argument that Tommy and Annika should be considered protagonists rather than Pippi.

Similarly, with this criterion, the title figure of *Peter Pan* is not the protagonist of the novel. Obviously, a boy who does not grow up does not change or develop. He exists wholly out of time. When he returns to Wendy after many years, when she has grown up, he is exactly as he was at the beginning of the novel. Furthermore, although omniscient and extremely intrusive, the narrator never enters Peter's mind. In fact, it is impossible to adopt Peter's subjectivity. Admire him in a way—yes, pity him—yes, but not share his subject position. On closer examination, he is the evil power of the story, the seducer, the revenger—betrayed by his mother, he wants to deprive other children of what he himself is missing most of all: "he was looking through the window at the one joy from which he must be for ever barred" (178). Moreover, Peter tries to prevent other characters from developing, by offering them eternal childhood in Neverland.

Thus, to define the protagonist we must also see who in the story undergoes a change; who gains a fortune, some knowledge, an insight; who matures physically or spiritually. Sometimes this change is almost negligible, which is what makes this issue so subtle. Even though this last criterion is perhaps the most certain and the most essential, it cannot be used as absolute truth. There are in fact protagonists who do not evolve or mature, do not gain any material wealth or moral improvement. The protagonists of formulaic fiction normally do not change, physically or spiritually: William, Biggles, Nancy Drew, Blyton's children, and so on. The absence of change is dictated by the nature of the genre. But also protagonists in some quality fiction show no evolution, perhaps because they are perfect from start, like Heidi.

Concluding Remarks

Summing up our experiences of determining the protagonist, we can state that none of the criteria in isolation is absolutely reliable. We must apply a combination of all the discussed criteria, and in many cases our decision will be a matter of interpretation. Much of the feminist criticism of adult liter-ature has involved a reevaluation of the protagonists of certain novels, in which the traditional interpretation identified the male characters as pro-tagonists, while the new reading suggests a possibility that it is rather the female character. Although the problem is mostly hypothetical with chil-dren's literature, it should not be totally dismissed. A reverse reevaluation can, however, be seen in some children's novels. For instance, in *The Secret Garden*, Mary, after having been the protagonist during the first half of the book, is suddenly reduced, giving way to Colin, who appears as the central and more important character. The focalization pattern of the novel com-pels us to shift to Colin as protagonist.

Sophisticated and unsophisticated readers may also have different per-ceptions of the main character. For an unsophisticated reader, *Winnie-the-Pooh* is undoubtedly about the toy bear, whereas a sophisticated reader will identify the gradual maturation of Christopher Robin and his inevitable farewell to childhood. In *The Little Prince*, an unsophisticated reader will most certainly point out the title character as protagonist. A sophisticated reader may choose to see the prince as the nostalgic fantasy of a lonely and unhappy man. While most readers will identify Ronia by a number of cri-teria as the protagonist of *Ronia the Robber's Daughter*, a sophisticated reader can also interpret the narrative as the story of Matt, the father. For a critic, it is possible to read *Heidi* as the story of an adult's moral improvement (Usrey 1985).

The decision about the protagonist is thus not as simple as it may seem, and in some cases we will need additional instruments to describe and ana-lyze character construction. These instruments will be discussed in the fol-lowing two chapters: the collective character and intersubjectivity.

Notes

1. A psychoanalytically oriented critic, such as Marie-Louise von Franz (1981), would say that the prince is the author's inner child (see further Nikolajeva 2000, 118–23).

2. It is not unusual that the novel's title contradicts the perspective. Comparing two very similar titles, *Carrie's War* and *Anna-Carolina's War*, we notice that the first of them corresponds to the third-person perspective of the narrative, while the second contradicts, totally unmotivated, the first-person perspective. While these particular titles do not affect our choice of the protagonist, in some other cases it can create confusion, especially in picturebooks addressed to very young children, in which a title such as *I Don't Want to Go to Bed* contradicts the omniscient perspective of the verbal text as well as the pictures.

CHAPTER FOUR

~

Collective Character

Many Actors—One Actant

In the previous chapter, I pointed out some difficulties in determining the protagonist. The dilemma becomes yet more complex when we are dealing with a group of characters who seem to be equally important in the narrative and who, by the proposed criteria, can equally lay claim to being sole protagonist. For instance, my students have throughout the years presented, based on criteria suggested in the previous chapter, very strong arguments for Lucy, Peter, or Edmund being the protagonists of *The Lion, the Witch and the Wardrobe*. Rather than discuss the possible solutions to this problem, I propose to treat these cases in terms of a collective, or multiple, protagonist—a concept that I have not met in any existing study of literary characters or in any study of children's fiction.

The concept of a collective protagonist follows naturally from the structuralist approach to character and the actantial model: all characters ("actors") who have the same role or function in a narrative constitute the same actant. Since collective protagonists are extremely unusual in mainstream fiction, general narratology has totally neglected this aspect of character theory. In fact, narratives representing different consciousnesses have been treated in criticism as exclusive examples of high artistic elaboration in modernistic fiction—for instance, *As I Lay Dying* or *The Waves* (Docherty 1983, 116*ff.*).

We must therefore regard collective characters as one of the specific narrative features of children's fiction, which has many assets. The collective protagonists of *Mary Poppins* or *The Lion, the Witch and the Wardrobe* supply a subject position for readers of both genders and of different ages. Collective characters may be used to represent more palpably different aspects of human nature—for instance, when one child in a group is presented as greedy and selfish, another as carefree and irresponsible, and so on. However, I would refrain from regarding a collective protagonist as an artistic device used restrictively for pedagogical purposes. As I will show, it is also an extremely complicated aesthetic issue.

Individual characters allow a deeper penetration into their psyche, a closer view of their thoughts and feelings, since an individual character naturally can be given more attention in the novel than several equally pivotal characters. Individual characters are usually more complex than any of the collective character's constitutive parts. Contemporary sophisticated novels for children tend to have individual characters. Early children's novels have individual characters (*The Nutcracker, Alice* books, George MacDonald's novels, *Pinocchio, Tom Sawyer, Heidi*, or *The Wizard of Oz*), presumably because they follow the conventions of the mainstream novel, before the specific children's fiction aesthetic emerged. These characters are rarely complex psychological existents; rather, they are actors in a plot. The tendency to use collective characters may historically be seen as writers' attempt at a more complex characterization.

The writer most often associated with "contemporary" children's fiction is Edith Nesbit (see the treatment of Nesbit's "twentieth-century narrative voice" in Wall 1991, 147–58; see further Crouch 1972). She was also the first to make the collective character her primary aesthetic principle, employing it in the Treasure Seekers series, the Five Children series, *The Enchanted Castle, The Railway Children*, and *The Wonderful Garden, or The Three Cs* (note that with just one exception, the collective protagonist is featured in the titles).

The characters of *Five Children and It* are first introduced as "the children" as they are walking from the station to their summer house, which will provide the setting for their adventures. They are then introduced individually as they express their admiration of the house:

> "How white the house is," said Robert.
> "And look at the roses," said Anthea.
> "And the plums," said Jane.
> "It's rather decent," Cyril admitted.
> The Baby said, "Wanty go walky." (19)

Although we do not learn much about the collective character apart from the names of its constituents, the individual children are indeed characterized quite colorfully by their lines: the first two are capable of perceiving beauty, Jane is thinking about food, Cyril is characterized as somewhat of a joy-killer; and we also realize that the fifth child of the title is merely a toddler. We never learn from the narrative how old the children are. We assume that Anthea and Cyril are the eldest, because they "knew that Australia was not quite as near as that" (24).

The children are further characterized in the first chapter when Robert "found the broken swing and tumbled out of it" and Cyril "nipped his finger in the door of a hutch" (21). Typically the boys are foregrounded when it comes to exploring the surroundings. This is, however, an exception rather than the rule, because all Nesbit's children are quite enterprising. Throughout the novel they are consistently described as a group, either as "the children" or, for instance, "Anthea and Cyril and the others" (22). Also, when referring to themselves, the children most often say "we" and "us," thus stressing that they perceive themselves as part of the group.

The dialogue between the children does not characterize them any further; it could be a stream of thoughts within one character. Moreover, Nesbit overtly makes a point of the siblings being very close: "these children were used to talking 'by fours,' as soldiers march, and each of them could say what it had to say quite comfortably, and listen to the agreeable sound of its own voice, and at the same time have three quarters of two sharp ears to spare for listening to what the others said" (66).

The individual features of the children are emphasized in different ways. Cyril comes up with ideas and suggestions of what they might do. He is also the bravest, or at least claims to be: "I am not afraid of snakes. I like them" (25). Robert is "not a brutal brother, though very ingenious in apple-pie beds, booby-traps, original methods of awakening sleeping relatives, and the other little accomplishments which make home happy" (40). The gender difference is conspicuous in, for instance, a statement like "Anthea, who meant to be a good housekeeper some day" (30). The girls behave in the predictable manner; for example, they burst into tears when distressed. However, our responses to such stereotyping should take the time when the novel was written into consideration. In fact, unlike most of her predecessors, Nesbit promptly avoids favoring a gendered addressee to her books, so she provides subjectivities for readers of both genders and various ages and temperaments. Her children are ordinary, "just like you," she often tells her readers ("Anthea and Jane and Cyril and Robert were very like you in many ways"; 105). Therefore, she obviously does not want them to be too individualized, but rather as universal as possible. However, typically for Nesbit, when events get totally out of hand, it is the girls who set them right.

Naturally, the best way to characterize the four children in the story is to examine their wishes. It is part of the plot that wishes are hastily and carelessly made and therefore turn out not quite the way the children have intended. Still the nature of wishes reveals more about the characters as individuals than anything else. The first wish is expressed by Anthea who, in haste, "did manage to remember a private wish of her own and Jane's, which they had never told the boys" (32). The wish is to be "as beautiful as the day," which is naturally gendered, and Anthea is aware of it: "She knew the boys would not care about it" (32).

An interesting detail is that no external description has been given of the children before their transformation, but after this wish they are described through each other's eyes: Jane "now had enormous blue eyes and a cloud of russet hair" (33); Cyril looked "like the picture of a young chorister, with your golden hair" and Robert like "an Italian organ-grinder. His hair's all black" (34). However, after they have turned back into their ordinary selves, we get a description, at least of Cyril: "your old freckles and your brown hair and your little eyes" (38). This is indeed a very clever way of describing characters without it feeling unnatural and authoritative, as it often feels in other novels (e.g., in *Little Women*; see also chap. 9 in the present work).

After the first disastrous experience, the children decide to make clever wishes and always agree among themselves as to what to wish for. However, their decisions clearly show how solipsistic and immature they are as a collective character, not one of them going beyond the very primitive, material wish for money. The fact that they repeatedly fail to benefit from their wishes is the didactic author's way of pointing out their immaturity. Indeed, she mentions the well-known fairy tale of the three wishes, intending this intertext to be recognized by her readers as the direct parallel to her characters' failures.

Although some of the unintended wishes are literally uttered by merely one of the children, none of them are allowed to have a wish of their own—the magic experience is pronouncedly collective. The episodes in which we are shown just one of the children are the chapter in which Anthea goes to see the Psammead at five in the morning to ask his advice about what to wish for and the chapter in which Cyril does the same. When the children are kept indoors as punishment for the day before, Robert is allowed to go out alone, to get the wish. Meeting the Psammead, he is tempted to wish for himself, "like toffee, a foreign stamp album, or a clasp-knife with three blades and a corkscrew . . . things the others would not have cared for—such as a football, or a pair of leg-guards, or to be able to lick Simpkins minor thoroughly when he went back to school" (120). The wishes certainly characterize Robert as a person, but it also does him credit that he refrains from these selfish wishes, at least long enough to make another careless wish for the whole group.

As it happens, this careless wish leads the children to be besieged in a castle, and almost all the rest of the chapter focalizes Robert as he is captured by a troop of soldiers taken out of a historical romance. We may think that he is individualized through this adventure, but this is merely a plot device. Any of the other three children would be completely interchangeable with Robert. A more individual experience (which, however, also could have happened to any of them, without much difference) is when Robert becomes "bigger than the baker's boy." Does this mean that Nesbit singles out Robert from the others? It is doubtful, especially as Robert is not focalized internally: we do not know how he felt being a giant, and the metamorphosis is merely a pretext for adventures.

The children do quarrel over what to wish for, and the boys even fight; the complex character has some inner struggle. They also blame their failures on each other. However, since none of them is individualized, and all have the same actantial role in the plot, with only slight shifts, I maintain that we are dealing with a collective protagonist. The text is plot oriented, and there is little room for thorough characterization, which we do not expect from a fantasy adventure story.

"The Nesbit Tradition" of Using Collective Characters

The title of Marcus Crouch's (1972) study of British children's literature, *The Nesbit Tradition*, refers to the overall impact of Edith Nesbit's works on several generations of British children's writers. Quite apart from her "contemporary voice" (Wall 1991) and the genre conventions that I have called her "magic code" (Nikolajeva 1988), the use of collective characters is part of her heritage. One of Nesbit's most straightforward followers, Edward Eager, has collective characters in all his novels for children, and their construction is much similar to that in *Five Children and It*, a group of siblings of both genders in identical actantial roles.

Another writer who has acknowledged her debt to Nesbit is Pamela Travers. Again, besides certain generic and thematic similarities, we notice the use of collective characters. In *Mary Poppins*, the children are presented as follows: "Jane, who was the eldest, and Michael, who came next, and John and Barbara, who were twins and came last of all" (9f.). The twins will get a chapter of their own, "John and Barbara's Story," but they only have subsidiary roles in the other chapters. Jane and Michael are, throughout the book, treated as one inseparable entity, referred to as "Jane and Michael," "the children," or "they," Let us consider some examples from chapter 1.

> Jane and Michael . . . *were glad* Katie Nanna had gone, for they *had never liked her.* She was old and fat and smelt of barley-water. Anything, they *thought,* would be better than Katie Nanna. (12; emphasis added)

The emphasized words convey simultaneous internal focalization of the two children, which by definition should be impossible, unless we treat them as one single subject position. The two children lack individuality; they think and feel identically.

The chapter continues to treat the two children as a single subject: "after supper Jane and Michael sat at the window watching for Mr. Banks" (12); "Jane and Michael saw a curious thing happen" (13); "The watching children heard . . ." (13); "they always had a good view"; "Jane and Michael could see . . ." (13); "Jane and Michael heard the stern voice" (14); "Jane and Michael, watching from the top landing" (14); "Such a thing, Jane and Michael knew, had never been done before" (16); "Jane and Michael edged toward Mary Poppins" (17); "Jane and Michael were more than surprised" (17); "Jane and Michael stared" (17); "Jane and Michael could tell" (19); "Jane's eyes and Michael's popped with astonishment" (19); "They noticed" (19); "they found themselves in bed and watching" (19); "Jane and Michael sat hugging themselves and watching (19); "they could find nothing to say. But they knew, both of them" (19). The literal point of view we are sharing in the chapter is the two children's common point of view, once again impossible by definition, but widely applied in fiction. As clearly seen from the examples, seeing, watching, and observing are the central activities in this chapter.

The dialogue between the children does not reveal any individuality either but could just as well be a monologue:

> "There he is!" said Michael . . . .
> "That's not Daddy," she said . . . .
> "How funny! I've never seen that happen before," said Michael.
> "Let's go and see who it is!" said Jane. (13)

The children are completely interchangeable here, as well as in their more individual questions to Mary Poppins:

"Will we do?" said Michael. (16)
"How did you come?" Jane asked. (17)
"What a funny bag!" he said. (17)
"Why," said Jane, "there's nothing in it!" (17)

Note that the children take turns in saying something. Choral speaking is not plausible in direct speech, but in fact, in each case the "Jane-and-Michael" entity is the source of the utterance. The same is apparently true about their first experiences of Mary Poppins's magical powers, when she gives Michael the medicine from her bottle: "Michael suddenly discovered that you could not look at Mary Poppins and disobey her" (18). This is presented as Michael's individual perception; however, the experience is immediately repeated by Jane, and thus the perception is shared. However, while we take part of the children's sensations ("A delicious taste ran round his mouth"; "Jane tasted it," 18), the twins' reaction is only presented through the older children: "by the few drops that were spilt on his bib, Jane and Michael could tell that the substance in the spoon this time was milk" (19). Finally, the children's articulated reaction to the evening full of wonders is presented through Michael: "Michael, charmed by this strange new arrival, unable to keep silent any longer, called to her" (20). We might interpret this as his individual perception if it were not immediately echoed by Jane's: "She was thinking about all that happened, and wondering" (20).

In the subsequent chapters, the two children are consistently treated as a single entity, in their literal point of view as well in the descriptions of their emotions. The occasional references to individual feelings, such as "Jane's heart was pitter-pattering with excitement" (36) or "his heart felt heavy" (179), can equally be ascribed to the other half of the collective protagonist. Chapter 6, however, is devoted solely to Michael, and he is focalized externally as well as internally. In the sequel, *Mary Poppins Comes Back*, there is a corresponding chapter devoted to Jane (the parallel narrative structure of the volumes has been observed in Bergsten 1978, 37).

Little Women or a Little Woman?

Nesbit's, Eager's, and Travers's novels are unmistakably plot oriented, and as earlier examples have shown, there is amazingly little characterization in them. The characters perform their actions or, at best, express the author's ideas. However, collective characters can also offer a deeper study of human nature. Several critics have discussed in all detail the various qualities of the March sisters in *Little Women*, without considering them as parts of a collective protagonist. Let us, however, view them as that. We can clearly see the difference between the four March sisters and the five Bennet sisters in *Pride and Prejudice*, in which Elizabeth is by almost every criterion the sole protagonist, while her sisters have supporting roles (see also Auerbach 1978, 35–73). By contrast, the protagonist in *Little Women* consists of four entities, each representing specific traits. In the opening scene we immediately become aware of the difference:

> "Christmas won't be Christmas without any presents," *grumbled* Jo, lying on the rug.
> "It's so dreadful to be poor!" *sighed* Meg, looking down at her old dress.
> "I don't think it's fair for some girls to have plenty of pretty things, and other girls nothing at all," added little Amy, *with an injured sniff.*
> "We've got Father and Mother and each other," said Beth *contentedly* from her corner. (3; emphasis added)

How does each line and the narrator's speech accompanying it characterize the four sisters? Jo grumbles, and she is lying on the floor in a most unwomanly manner. Meg sighs, and she is only thinking about her dress, showing vanity and selfishness. Amy, the youngest, is spoilt and immature and is personally offended by the world's injustices. Finally, Beth is humble and happy and tries to make everybody else happy as well. Throughout the novel, the initial impression we get from this opening is reinforced, presenting other traits, which all confirm this first description. Beth is pretty, nice, and shy; she is "the peace-maker" (4) of the family, always content with her fate. Meg is complaining, "elder-sisterly" (5), envious of other people's wealth. Amy is spoilt, vain, "particular and prim" (5), concerned about her looks; she suffers most from being poor, and she longs most for nice clothes. A bit further down on the opening page, the sisters are also characterized by the things they wish for Christmas presents: Jo, "who was a bookworm" (3), wants a new novel, Beth some new music, and Amy a box of drawing pencils. Each of the girls has a different talent, which is thus emphasized. Their self-imposed trials are also used to point out their specific faults.

Jo is singled out by the author (she is frequently identified as a self-portrait); in Part II, she more or less becomes the sole main character. Jo is the hot-tempered part of the collective protagonist, which must be suppressed. By allowing only a quarter of the collective protagonist to make a revolt, the writer can balance the societal demands on girls being well behaved and her own aspiration to portray a strong and independent girl. Seen from today's perspective, the revolt is rather innocent, mostly manifested in unladylike behavior. This behavior is presented immediately from the beginning: "Jo, examining the heels of her shoes in a gentlemanly manner" (3). Further we learn that Jo is using colloquial speech, does not care for clothes, and frequently spoils them, runs, whistles, throws snowballs, and so on. These actions are severely criticized by the other three sisters. Viewing the four characters as one single protagonist, we see how the "well-behaved," ladylike part of it chastises and tames the wild and independent part of her nature—a process that many a young woman in the nineteenth century had to go through. Jo is an androgynous figure—socially androgynous, meaning that she is trying to fight for her integrity through breaking the socially accepted gender norms. Like so many of her sisters, in literature as well as in real life, Jo wishes she were a boy, because she clearly sees that boys are valued more highly in her society and have more fun (even though part of the "fun" is the right to fight and die in a war). Not least, boys are allowed to go to college. But the author is careful enough to allow only one of her four characters to revolt and to counterbalance the rebellious Jo with the three genuinely feminine sisters.

Most studies of *Little Women* emphasize Jo's role as protagonist; indeed, some critics have stated that the book is only interesting because of Jo and her struggle for independence and integrity (Clark 1989; see further Alberghene 1998; Keyser 1999), while some maintain that Amy is the most interesting character of the four and a contrast to Jo in almost everything, including creative talent and sexuality (Hollander 1984). In any case, Jo's special traits only become prominent because they are presented against the background of the three other sisters. Treating the characters as parts of the same persona, we see the conflict and the competition in a new light, as a complex character's inner struggle. The life roads chosen by the author for the four sisters—Meg's marriage and a happy family, Beth's untimely death, Jo's aspiration as a writer, and Amy's indulgence in painting and her unscrupulous snatching of Laurie from Jo—reflect the various possibilities of the protagonist. The notion of the collective protagonist enables us to see clearly the complicated scope of emotions portrayed in this novel.

A brief comparison between *Little Women* and *Anne of Green Gables* can demonstrate the assets and drawbacks of collective and individual characters. Together the four sisters constitute a complex "character" with contradictory features, which also complement each other. On the other hand, each of the four girls is less individualized. The various traits are clear-cut and easy for young readers to recognize, as compared with Anne, who is complex and contradictory, and who also undergoes a change from the beginning to the end of the book. The revolt illustrated in *Little Women* by external means—that is, by portraying Jo as a rebel of the group—in Anne's case takes place within the individual protagonist, and the choices between marriage and career must also be made by one character rather than divided among several.

It is impossible and hardly fruitful to discuss which type of character construction is preferable, since both have educational as well as aesthetic purposes. For the sake of clarity and reader subjectivity, collective characters are certainly more suitable, while individual characters allow more complexity. As already noted, if we try to delineate the specific poetics of children's fiction, collective characters are definitely part of it.

Four Adults or One Child?

Another example of a novel in which the concept of collective character helps us circumvent the inevitable problems of determining the protagonist is *The Wind in the Willows*. Most studies discuss the four main characters separately (Hunt 1994; Kuznets 1987). Often they are examined in terms of class and social status; for instance, Mole is viewed as a lower-middle-class bachelor; Rat is a poetical, bohemian figure; Badger is a representative of the old aristocracy, while Toad is a conceited nouveau-riche. Many critics also discuss possible models from reality, thus reading the characters allegorically. The all-male community of the novel has been the focus of some feminist interpretations (e.g., Marshall 1994).

Using animals in a children's novel is a convenient way to circumvent the inevitable questions of age, race, and class. The question of the characters' age seems to be crucial for many critics: "although Mole may have childlike characteristics, he is clearly an adult" (Hunt 1994, 55). Similarly, Toad's infantile behavior seldom prevents critics from viewing him as an adult. However, if the characters of *The Wind in the Willows* are adults concerned with exclusively adult problems, why would this novel be considered one of the major children's classics? I rather share the opinion that the four figures are "ageless, timeless, genderless" (Gaarden 1994, 43), besides viewing them as parts of a collective child protagonist, representing different traits, often contradictory and thus enabling the author to describe an inner conflict. Rat is practical, intelligent, loyal, affectionate; he is also fully content with his life. Mole is the naive, curious, enthusiastic part of the child, eager to discover the world, but cautious and still very much homebound. Badger is the most grown-up part, on the verge of adolescence. He is sensible and reliable and provides a sense of security. Toad is the adventurous and anarchistic part of the child, a direct counterpart of Jo March. In the quadruple protagonist, the four parts are well counterbalanced: Badger's experience by Mole's innocence; Toad's lust for adventure by Rat's contentment; Badger's calmness by Toad's impulsiveness, and so on.

As in *Little Women*, the suppression of the wildest part of the collective protagonist is a matter of inner struggle. Toad is not intimidated by adults but by the three remaining parts of the collective protagonist who force the rebelling quarter into order. Is this not a direct parallel to Jo being chastised into becoming a well-behaved little lady? However, unlike the March sisters, Toad and his friends are freed from the necessity to grow up and adjust to societal demands. Instead, they can live happily ever after in their Arcadia—a convention of nonmimetic mode that allows characters to be completely static.

The Collective Romantic Hero

In *The Lion, the Witch and the Wardrobe*, we again see the protagonist divided between four figures, two boys and two girls of different ages. Naturally, this facilitates adopting a subject position. It is, however, more important that the four children represent different human traits. Peter is brave and dependable. He tries to defend Lucy when he thinks that she has lost her mind. He also feels responsible for Edmund, even though he feels little sympathy for his mean younger brother. Peter makes all the important decisions for the group: "Peter . . . began leading the way" (54). He is prepared to acknowledge his faults and apologize. Peter, after much hesitation, is the first to talk to Aslan when the children meet him, and he is to lead the final battle.

Susan is rational and comes with practical ideas (the narrator mentions "Susan's very sensible plan"; 54); she is also the peacemaker and tries to keep the group together. Yet, she is somewhat cowardly in her rationalism; she does not like Narnia and wants to go back home. However, she supports Lucy in her feeling of responsibility for Mr. Tumnus. Together with Lucy, Susan is allowed to witness Aslan's sacrificial death. At the end of the Narnia Chronicles, Susan is denied salvation alongside her siblings.

Lucy is emotional, spontaneous, mild, and, most significantly, truthful, which is stated explicitly: "Lucy was a very truthful girl" (29). Her foremost moral qualities are being loyal and trustworthy, as she explains to the others that they must rescue Tumnus because he has been punished for her sake. She is also inquisitive, curious, even stubborn, which is first shown by her actions:

[T]hey all trooped out again—all except Lucy. She stayed behind because she thought it would be worth while trying the door of the wardrobe, even though she felt almost sure that it would be locked. (12)

Almost at once the trait is mentioned explicitly: "Lucy felt a little frightened, but she felt very inquisitive and excited as well" (13). Furthermore, she is presented as clever and even rational, not unlike Susan: "She had, of course, left the door open, for she knew that it is a very silly thing to shut oneself into a wardrobe" (13). The sentence is repeated further on: "She did not shut [the door] properly because she knew that it was very silly to shut oneself into a wardrobe" (29f.). By contrast, Edmund "jumped in and shut the door, forgetting what a very foolish thing this is to do" (30); and Peter "held the door closed but did not shut it; for, of course, he remembered, as every sensible person does, that you should never shut yourself up in a wardrobe" (52).

At the beginning of the novel, Edmund is grumpy, cunning, greedy, and a liar. He is often bad-tempered and is portrayed as unpleasant right from the beginning: "Edmund could be spiteful, and on this occasion he was spiteful. He sneered and jeered at Lucy" (29); "he wanted to go on teasing her" (30). This presentation of Edmund prepares the reader for his becoming a traitor. The narrator is quite explicit in his judgment of Edmund, "who was becoming a nastier person every minute" (45), and "horrible ideas came into his head" (67). At the same time, the narrator defends Edmund, partly by ascribing his nastiness to the school he had attended but also otherwise:

You mustn't think that even now Edmund was quite so bad that he actually wanted his brother and sisters to be turned into stone. He did want Turkish Delight and to be a Prince. (81f.)

However, Edmund is the only character of the four who undergoes a change, which starts far before he is redeemed by Aslan: "Edmund for the first time in this story felt sorry for someone beside himself" (107). When the author allows a quarter of his collective protagonist to become a traitor, the consequence is that the other three feel responsibility and pain. They are prepared to fight for him, because they are fighting for themselves; or actually the battle is an inner one, within the protagonist. Edmund's transformation implies that the good three-quarters have won over the evil quarter, in a most tangible manner.

The focalization pattern of the novel supports our perception of the mutual importance of the four characters. Lucy is focalized most of the four children, which may prompt us to view her as the protagonist. She is focalized not only in the chapters where she is on her own but also when she is part of the group: "the first thing Lucy noticed" (68); "Lucy enjoyed it . . . she began to wonder" (95); "And at last Lucy was so tired" (96);, and so on. Edmund is naturally focalized, internally and externally, in the chapters where he is on his own but also in other situations: "That was what the others chiefly noticed, but Edmund noticed something else" (67). Peter is focalized very seldom, and only externally—for instance, during his battle with the wolves, and Susan hardly ever. One very prominent case of simultaneous focalization, which also strongly contributes to characterization, is when the children first hear Aslan's name mentioned:

> At the mention of Aslan each one of the children felt something jump in its inside. Edmund felt a sensation of mysterious horror. Peter felt suddenly brave and adventurous. Susan felt as if some delicious smell or some delightful strain of music has just floated by her. And Lucy got the feeling you have when you wake up in the morning and realize that it is the beginning of the holidays or the beginning of summer. (65)

Aslan, who is the central figure of the book but definitely not its protagonist, is never focalized. Instead, Lucy is allowed to guess about his feelings: "Up to that moment Lucy had been thinking how royal and strong and peaceful his face looked; now it suddenly came into her head that he looked sad as well" (118). Since Aslan is not even focalized externally, the dramatic episode of his sacrificial death must be told from some other's point of view, so Lucy and Susan are allowed to sneak after him—a very common narrative device, when the narrator or the focalizer "happens" to be present to witness an important event that they otherwise would never learn about. This, if anything, excludes Aslan as protagonist.

There is without doubt a grain of truth in the fact that Lucy is favored by the author and therefore perceived as the most important of the children and thus the protagonist. If we applied the criteria suggested in chapter 3, she would match many of them. For one thing, she is the first to enter Narnia. However, the character of *The Lion, the Witch and the Wardrobe* is unmistakably a romantic hero, summoned to fight the evil because of the inherent innocence. The heroic—male—features of the collective character are emphasized when the two girls are not allowed to participate in the battle, when Peter becomes High King, but most significantly when the only tangible evolution from traitor to hero takes place within the male character, Edmund. However, rather than maintaining that the evolution criterion qualifies Edmund for protagonist, I insist on viewing the four figures as one single protagonist with one single actantial role. On becoming kings and queens of Narnia, the children are awarded epithets: Peter the Magnificent, Susan the Gentle, Edmund the Just, and Lucy the Valiant. One specific trait is accentuated in each of them, as is common with romantic heroes. Throughout the novel, they are repeatedly referred to collectively as "the children."

A brief comparison between the collective romantic hero in *The Lion, the Witch and the Wardrobe* and the individual hero in *Mio, My Son* shows clearly how a romantic narrative is deconstructed by means of a complex character. Mio is at times ready to give up; he almost becomes a traitor, like Edmund. The most important battle takes place within himself. Moreover, the characters appearing in the secondary world are clear projections of the real people in his real life, and the whole adventure is a psychodrama, an inner quest. As the case of Jo March, in *The Lion, the Witch and the Wardrobe* the collective character's internal struggle is externalized for didactic purposes. The individual character in *Mio, My Son* is much more complex, and we as readers perceive him more as a real human being (low mimetic or ironic) than as a fairy-tale hero (romantic). The four children in *The Lion, the Witch and the Wardrobe* are rather pale; they merely perform the actions that the plot demands of them.

The Pseudo-collective Character

The mere fact that there is a group of characters in the center of a plot does not automatically mean that we are dealing with a collective protagonist. Although the character construction of *Peter Pan* may seem similar to that of *Mary Poppins*, the similarity is superficial. Not only is Wendy featured in the title of at least some of the many editions, introduced first, and focalized most of the three siblings; more important is that her role in the narrative is distinctively different from those of John and Michael. These two boys join the gang of the Lost Boys whose purpose is to have adventures and assist Peter. Wendy's role is to be mother to Peter and the Lost Boys, and her female dilemma is to accept that Peter's feelings toward her are "those of a devoted son" (117). If anyone undergoes a change in the Neverland, it is undoubtedly Wendy, and she indeed comes back to her real world with a better insight about herself and the process of growing up.

In *Elidor*, we meet four siblings, superficially much like the characters in the Narnia Chronicles. In the first pages they are certainly presented this way as they talk to each other deciding what to do. All four have strong characterizing traits: Nicholas is rational, David is acquiescent and sticks with his older brother, Roland is imaginative, and Helen is the peacemaker (gender stereotyped). These initial traits are reinforced later in the novel: Nicholas promptly refuses to discuss the siblings' experience in Elidor and even denies that the adventure has taken place; David first supports Nicholas but is honest enough to admit his fault after the children have seen the unicorn. Roland is stubbornly faithful toward Elidor, and he is also the most sensitive and vulnerable, while Helen is all the time trying to reconcile the brothers. In Elidor, the children are given magical objects, just as the Pevensie children receive magical gifts in Narnia. But while the Narnian gifts have practical purposes and are used in the story (Peter's sword, Susan's horn, and Lucy's medicine bottle), the objects from Elidor are simply to be kept safe. However, they certainly add to their individual characterization: Nicholas gets a stone, a symbol of wisdom; David, a sword; Roland, a spear; and Helen, a cauldron, a feminine symbol.

The very first question that arises in discussing this multiple character is about the gender imbalance: three boys and a girl. If the collective character had been exclusively chosen for the purpose of offering readers a number of suitable subjectivities (as the case might be with the previously discussed text), we would expect an equal gender proportion with a group of four. In fact, by applying a functional or actantial model, we immediately see that the roles of the four children in Elidor are radically different from those of the Pevensie children. The three brothers are similar to the characters of a traditional fairy tale: two elder brothers who, for different reasons, fail the task (see Propp's notion of false hero) and the youngest— despised and oppressed—brother who turns out to be successful. In fact, Roland is given many traits of the fairy-tale fool. The brothers are constantly teasing him for letting his imagination run away with him ("'Come off it, Roland. You are always imagining things.' It was a family joke"; 71). Later they try to make his strong involvement with Elidor appear a childish play. But he is the one chosen to save Elidor. The sister's role is that of a "princess," similar to Jill in The Silver Chair or Polly in The Magician's Nephew. In fact, Helen is enchanted, and her brothers' assignment is to save her. Her further function in the story includes taming a unicorn, a traditional female role in myth. The hypotext of the Child Roland story amplifies this role distribution.

In Elidor, the didactic omniscient narrator of the Narnia novels is replaced by strong focalization of just one of the four characters, Roland. Although in the beginning the children seem to have equal roles in the plot, as soon as Roland enters Elidor, he becomes the sole hero. Moreover, we can see Elidor as his inner landscape—mindscape—reflecting his fears and anxieties projected onto his real life, in which his brothers and sister have supporting roles. In Jungian terms, Roland is the one who is going through an individuation process. If we believe the author's own interpretation of the ending, Roland is also the one who pays the high price for involvement with Elidor by going mad. Thus, in *Elidor* we have indeed an individual rather than a collective character.

I find it necessary to distinguish between collective and pseudo-collective characters since, having accepted the concept of the collective character, overlooking the cases in which only one in a group is the real protagonist is easy. Although not an absolute rule, one character in a group is more likely to be individualized in contemporary novels. While the characters of the Famous Five series or *Swallows and Amazons* are unmistakably collective, having exactly the same function in the plot, in the modern Robinsonnade *Homecoming*, Dicey is the sole protagonist: we follow her dilemmas, her responsibilities, and her inner maturation.

The Collective Character as a Projection of the Individual Character's Inner World

In the previous chapter I have mentioned that the choice of protagonist in *Winnie-the-Pooh* lies between Pooh and Christopher Robin, depending on the level of sophistication we apply in our interpretation. Taking this argument further, we may suggest that all the characters in the Hundred Acre Wood are parts of a collective protagonist, representing the various traits of the individual character outside the Wood—Christopher Robin. As with the characters of *The Wind in the Willows*, rather than discussing what each character might represent by himself, as most critics do (Lurie 1990, 144–55; Hunt 1992), I find it more gratifying to see how each of them contributes to the construction of a complex protagonist.

Christopher Robin is, in the outer frame, the cocreator of the plot and the characters, bestowing upon them the faults and defects he possesses himself. Even viewing him as a passive narratee, we have reasons to suspect that the adult narrator, the father, invents the characters to suit the narratee's psychological needs. Thus, Pooh, the nucleus of the collective character, is the imaginative dreamer—a character type who attracts most of the reader's sympathy but who is constantly mocked by the narrator for being silly and naïve. In Piglet, the most primitive fears of the child are reflected, and by letting Piglet overcome some of them, the narrator empowers the child. Eeyore is the skeptical and suspicious part of the child. Tigger is the wild, untamed, and the most childish part, and Roo the part that is frantically trying to liberate himself from the overprotective mother. Owl and

Rabbit are the most controversial parts of the collective protagonist. Peter Hunt claims that they are adults (cf. his interpretation of *The Wind in the Willows*, noted earlier), while their particular features appear much more clearly if we treat them as projections of the child. Rabbit is the rational and stubborn part of Christopher Robin, who has made up his mind never to accept change. His mistrust first of Kanga and Roo and later of Tigger reflects the child's intuitive fear of a new sibling and rival. Typically, Rabbit immediately falls for the tiny Roo since he feels superior to him, but he has problems accepting the big and strong Tigger. In fact, it is Rabbit who attempts to "unbounce" Tigger, much like the three animals in *The Wind in the Willows* try to intimidate Toad or the three March sisters try to intimidate Jo. Rabbit, the sensible part of the child, is trying to counterbalance the wild and as yet unsocialized part. Besides, Rabbit is the only character who seems to be able to read and write properly and therefore feels contempt toward everybody who cannot, most obviously Pooh. Owl is especially interesting in this respect. He pretends that he can read and write, while in fact he cannot, which is clearly demonstrated in two chapters: first when he writes "Hipy papy" on Pooh's honey jar, and later when Rabbit shows him Christopher Robin's written message. Since Christopher Robin's path to literacy is one of the strongest underlying themes of the two *Pooh* novels, Owl's attempts to conceal his inadequacy are an excellent reflection of the child's hidden shame.

The superficial events of the novels are in fact playful representations of the child's thorny road to self-knowledge, with many questions on the way. It is also noteworthy that the characters are introduced successively, one or two at a time in every chapter, as in a cumulative narrative. This may be viewed as the child's successive discovery of her own traits.

One final argument for the treatment of *Pooh* figures as a collective protagonist is to be found in the introduction to the first volume, in which the narrator first talks about Pooh and then lets Piglet interfere with, "What about *Me?*" (x; author's emphasis), the capital letter emphasizing the very young child's egocentrism; and finally invites the chorus of voices saying, "What about *Us?* suggesting that all the characters are equally important.

The Moomin books can also be viewed as having a collective character, which consists of Moomintroll as a nucleus, complemented by other characters, in the first place Sniff. Sniff is the worst side of Moomintroll's personality: grumpy, cowardly, greedy, and selfish. Snufkin represents the most independent and mature part of Moomintroll, the part that is already prepared to leave home. *Moominvalley in November* is a particularly clear example how the writer makes it easier for the reader to accept the traumatic process of growing up (or maybe for herself to depict) by substituting a collective character for Moomintroll. The different parts of this collective character each go through a separate maturation process and acceptance of their own identities (see Nikolajeva 2000, chap. 10).

The difference between the collective character of the *Pooh* stories and the Moomin stories is that in the latter, there is no individual character like Christopher Robin whose projections all the other characters can be. The only possible interpretation is to go beyond the text and see the characters as representations of the author's various traits and traumas, which is quite legitimate in the author-centered Jungian analysis (see Mueller Nienstadt 1994); however, I find such approaches less fruitful.

Siblings: Duplication or Interplay?

When siblings of the same gender are used in central roles, they are likely to have identical actantial positions. We are dealing with a mere duplication of a character, perhaps primarily for didactic purposes. *The Wind in the Moon* is a good example, in which the entity "Dina and Dorinda" always appears as a single actant; the two sisters have no individual traits, and their alliterated names further accentuate their duplicate roles. By contrast, in *The Brothers Lionheart* the two brothers have radically different roles: Rusky is the romantic hero, while his older brother Jonathan is the model, the guide, the helper, who is never focalized and whose psychological qualities are nonexistent. It is thus essential to distinguish between the use of siblings as collective characters and the use of a sibling as a supporting character.

I have already discussed several texts presenting a brother and a sister as a collective character—for instance, *Mary Poppins*, in which the siblings are interchangeable, and the specific masculine or feminine roles are minimal. This is true of many novels in which reaching out to readers of both genders seems to be the only reason for using characters of different genders, from *Puck of Pook's Hill* to *From the Mixed-up Files of Mrs. Basil E. Frankweiler*. Most often there is a slight difference in gender stereotyping. Tommy and Annika in *Pippi Longstocking* are practically interchangeable and are usually treated as an entity. However, they are also portrayed individually as a typical boy and a typical girl. For instance, Annika is always more cautious, even cowardly.

On the other hand, the use of a brother and a sister as a collective protagonist may have a subversive purpose, to present a female character who would otherwise not be quite acceptable. In *The House of Arden*, the author first introduces Edred as the main character. We are given a brief history of the glorious Arden family and informed that there are two male Ardens left, and one of them is a child called Edred, who lives with his aunt. First at the bottom of the second page the text says, "Edred and his sister were at school. (Did I tell you that he had a sister? Well, he had, and her name was Elfrida)" (8). From this presentation, we are almost forced to believe that Elfrida will be a secondary and insignificant character. However, already in the next page, the siblings are referred to as "Edred and Elfrida" (never "Elfrida and Edred") or "the children"; that is, they are treated as a collective protagonist. Nevertheless, the character construction is different from Nesbit's previous novels. The children have adventures in which they are not interchangeable, and in most cases, when they are separated, we follow Elfrida. While Edred sits on the magical clock to stop time, Elfrida has some breathtaking adventures in Queen Anne's time. She is in the center of the Gunpowder Plot episode (except in the passages describing Edred's friendship with Sir Walter Raleigh). She is also focalized in the chapter on Henry the Eighth and Anne Boleyn. Judging by the criterion of dominant presence, Elfrida has more right to be called the protagonist.

It is repeatedly stressed that Edred is Lord Arden, the strong and clever; he is to be made "brave and wise" and to find the treasure. But Elfrida is the creative one, writing poems to summon the Mouldiwarp when needed. She is depicted as being more intelligent, as well as understanding more of the events around them. Thus, she realizes at once that their wish of travelling back into the past has been granted, and that they have "got turned into somebody else" (53), and the old lady they have met is their grandmother. The narrator's comment is: "I don't know how it was that Elfrida saw this and Edred didn't. Perhaps because she was a girl" (53f.). Although Nesbit does not use the actual word, she lets the reader understand that Elfrida is intuitive—a feature traditionally believed to be feminine—while Edred is rational and therefore slow to accept the magical adventures. Edred often despises his sister, saying, "You're only a girl" (17) or "you're not clever enough" (110); and his plans for the future are to "go to Eton and Oxford . . . and Elfrida can have a pony" (212). But the narrator lets the reader understand that Elfrida is more generous, agreeable, and willing to compromise. She is "always less daring, but more persevering than her brother" (26), which helps them in their endeavors. While Edred is skeptical and easily gives up, she is prepared to go on searching and is always rewarded. She is not afraid or reluctant to meet the witch, Betty Lovell. In fact, Elfrida feels sympathy for Betty, and is rewarded for it too, as Betty recognizes her kind heart. Elfrida is also bold and can talk reasonably to adults, where Edred gives up and is prepared to take his punishment. While Edred is most interested in his title and in finding the treasure, Elfrida is interested in adventure for its own sake; she is imaginative and inquisitive. The Mouldiwarp definitely has a higher opinion of Elfrida than of Edred. Of course, Nesbit could not, publishing her novel in 1908, make Elfrida a fully emancipated girl, but there are all these small details pointing toward the idea of women being equal or even superior to men.

If Elfrida's distinction can be accounted for by the author's gender, the special position of Susan in *The Weirdstone of Brisingamen* cannot be explained similarly. Nesbit, writing in the beginning of the twentieth century and being a radical Socialist, apparently wished to foreground women by showing that girls were not inferior to boys, that they could be smarter and braver. She had to do it very carefully, so as not to irritate the masculine literary establishment (publishers, critics), and her female heroine has a subversive impact, especially, I would guess, on contemporary female readers. Alan Garner writes from different premises, most likely out of his own fears of feminine mysticism, and of a subconscious acknowledgment of female otherness. Susan is depicted as having stronger intuition and a considerably stronger direct connection with the magical forces, good as well as evil. Her sensitivity and hence vulnerability toward dark powers are externalized by her wearing a bracelet with a magic stone connecting her to the triple, ambivalent goddess, one of the many literary reincarnations of the mythic chthonic figure. Thus, even though the "Colin-and-Susan" entity in *The Weirdstone* and its sequel, *The Moon of Gomrath*, mostly appear as a collective protagonist, Susan is singled out as somewhat more important.

It is quite unusual in children's fiction to place two siblings with a big age difference in the center of the narrative. The simplest explanation is the construction of the implied reader: a reader who will identify with a significantly older sibling will find the younger one childish, and the other way round, which impedes choosing a subject position. The combination may present an interesting narrative challenge; however, I have not encountered a text in which this challenge would be met in a satisfactory manner. *The Hounds of the Morrigan*, a fantasy novel, portrays two siblings, a boy of fourteen and a girl of seven, in identical actantial roles. For a young reader, the difference between seven and fourteen is profound. In his mental development, the brother is infinitely ahead of the sister; therefore, psychologically they are not interchangeable while structurally they are. This contradiction interferes with the psychological impact of the novel, if any has been intended by the author.

Pedagogical Implications of Collective Characters

As stated earlier, collective protagonists seem to be a very prominent part of children's literature poetics. The two main purposes of using collective protagonists are both didactic. First, such usage offers suitable subject positions to readers of various ages and genders. It is also conceivable that the extensive use of collective protagonists in the past has to do with the practice of reading aloud: a group of listening children was encouraged to empathize with the group of characters in the story. Second, this device presents character traits more palpably, clearly divided between separate figures in the plot. This may also be part of children's literature's heritage from myths and folktales, in which characters are endowed with only one particular feature. In any case, the use of collective protagonists is a conscious and deliberate narrative device on the part of children's writers, who thus adapt their writing to the assumed needs of the implied audience. Since collective characters seldom appear in adult fiction, we must indeed agree that this is the case. Adult fiction has, however, another method of constructing complex subjectivity by using multiple characters, and children's fiction has subsequently adopted this form, which will be discussed in the next chapter.

~

CHAPTER FIVE

From Collective Character to Intersubjectivity

In addition to collective and individual, a third way of constructing a protagonist is intersubjective.

The postmodern notion of intersubjectivity presupposes the absence of a single, fixed subject in a literary text, instead suggesting that the complex "subject" of a narrative has to be assembled by the reader from several individual consciousnesses. This phenomenon may be best described through Mikhail Bakhtin's (1984) concept of polyphony or heteroglossia: an interplay of different voices and perspectives within a narrative. In an interesting manner, this concept is also connected, as are many postmodern ideas, to quantum physics and its complementarity principle. The decisive difference between the collective and the intersubjective character lies in the absence, in the latter case, of an omniscient perspective in which the narrator has simultaneous access to several characters' minds. While a collective character is a simple sum of its constituents, an intersubjective character is constructed through an intricate interplay of subject positions in the text.

Although intersubjectivity as a term has not been in circulation for more than ten to fifteen years (it is not included in Gerald Prince's *Dictionary of Narratology* from 1987), the phenomenon itself has naturally existed long before. In the mainstream, it is often associated with modernistic fiction, in which, as mentioned in the previous chapter, it has been treated as an example of high artistic elaboration—for instance, in *As I Lay Dying* or *The Sound and the Fury*.

Naturally, the boundary between the collective and the intersubjective constructions of character is sometimes extremely subtle. It is quite possible to treat the character in *Little Women, The Lion, the Witch and the Wardrobe*, or the Moomin novels as intersubjective rather than collective. In fact, I find that *Moominpappa at Sea* features an intersubjective character, while all other Moomin novels have collective characters. The primary criterion for a collective character is the identical actantial roles of its constituents in the plot, which also presupposes identical, or almost identical, subject positions. In *Moominpappa at Sea*, the subject positions of Mamma, Pappa, and Moomintroll are not identical, while, for instance, in *Comet in Moominland*, Moomintroll and his travel companions can be viewed as a collective protagonist, because they appear as a single actant.

The concept of intersubjectivity enables us to reconcile many of the incompatible interpretations of children's novels where the point of departure is the decision on the protagonist. Some examples of such incompatibilities are Malcolm Usrey's (1985) reading of *Heidi* with Grandfather as protagonist, which contradicts the more common and more logical treatment of the title character as protagonist, or Lissa Paul's (1990) criticism of *The Secret Garden* on the basis of Colin's coming into the foreground and ousting Mary as protagonist. Just as I have demonstrated how different opinions on protagonists in *The Wind in the Willows* or *Winnie-the-Pooh* can be reconciled by treating them as collective characters, many problems, not least involving child–adult balance, can be solved by applying the idea of intersubjectivity.

Cross-gender Intersubjectivity

Let us start with a very simple case, *The White Stone*. The book begins:

> This is going to be a story about all kinds of things. I'm not sure yet who is who and what is what. But I can tell you right now that the story will not be about two children named Hampus and Fia.
> Fia was a thin little girl with flying dark hair. She was the daughter of a piano teacher. (1)

The two main characters are introduced by stating that the book will not be about them. This is in a way true, since the adventures that the two children experience happen to them in the capacity of their imaginary personae, Fideli and Prince Perilous. The opening sentences stress that both children are dissatisfied with their identities and therefore invent new ones; the book will not be about two ordinary children but about two exciting fairy-tale figures. However, after this declaration, Fia is introduced first of the two, and the whole first chapter is dedicated to her. Since Fia is introduced first and because she is focalized in the opening chapter, we may tend to perceive her as the protagonist. This decision is enhanced by the fact that the author is female and that the book has strong autobiographical features, which makes us connect the author with the character. However, this initial decision is subverted already during the first encounter between Fia and the strange boy in the end of the first chapter. As he is described, we share Fia's point of view:

> He looked at her in that funny way again, and suddenly Fia *felt* that there was something special about her today. She *felt* as though she could turn into a wild animal or a crybaby or an enchanted princess all at one and the same time. (14; emphasis added)

Fia tells the strange boy that her name is Fideli, and she asks him his name. At this point, something happens with the subject position:

> He turned around toward the shoemaker's house, as if he did not mean to answer, but he was only looking to see what all the sudden commotion on the road was about. Four circuswagons were passing on the way to the fairground near the marketplace. On one of the wagons was a gaudy poster showing a man dressed in nothing but a leopard skin. "Prince Perilous" stood in huge letters on the poster. "That's my name," Hampus said. (15)

The first part of the first sentence in this quotation is told from Fia's point of view; the statement "as if he did not mean to answer" is her comprehension of the situation. The point of view is limited, since Fia does not know more about the boy than the reader. The continuation, "but he was only looking," shifts to the boy's point of view. We share his thoughts. The indirect inner speech, "what all the sudden commotion . . . ," can be transformed into direct: "What is all this sudden commotion, he thought." The rest of the quote is a description of what the boy sees, employing his literal point of view. He is referred to by his name, Hampus. By this time, we have lost Fia's point of view, and although we cannot ignore our previous knowledge of Fia, we now see her through Hampus's eyes, in an estranged manner. This technique is naturally different from the omniscient perspective, where the narrator knows what is going on in several minds at once and watches the scene from a detached position.

For the rest of *The White Stone*, the point of view alternates from chapter to chapter between the two children. In the beginning of each chapter, we are informed whose point of view this chapter expresses: "When Prince Perilous went home . . ." or "When Fia woke up next morning . . . ." The established point of view is then consistent throughout the chapter. Unlike the omniscient perspective, which would enable the narrator to say something like: "While he was doing this, she . . . ," one character is abandoned while the other is focalized. At any given moment, we only have one character's view of the events, and the final picture has to be assembled by the reader by uniting the two parallel sets of evidence. Developing Bakhtin's concept of polyphony, I propose to call this technique *antiphonic*, two minds described in interplay.

The alternating focalization in this novel makes it radically different from most children's novels depicting cross-gender friendship, such as Maria Gripe's *Hugo and Josephine* trilogy or Katherine Paterson's *Bridge to Terabithia*, in which only one of the two children is consistently focalized. The protagonist in Maria Gripe's books is without doubt Josephine, and the protagonist of *Bridge to Terabithia* is Jess, while the roles of Hugo and Leslie are, respectively, those of a helper (Propp) or Wise Old Man/Woman (Jung). Both Hugo and Leslie are opaque characters in the sense that we do not know anything about their internal life and only see them through the eyes and minds of the protagonists. In *The White Stone*, the roles and consequently subjectivities are constantly reversed.

The question of gender in this novel is not without significance. Like so many contemporary psychological children's novels, it features a boy and a girl in the main roles, apparently to provide models for readers of both genders. The tasks that the children give each other in their competition over the white stone reflect their genders: Hampus has to perform dangerous deeds, involving courage and physical strength, while Fia's trials demand ingenuity and imagination. However, in their narrative functions, the children are equal. In Jungian terms, they represent each other's Anima/Animus—creative, imaginative powers; in Proppian terms, they are each other's senders (assigning the task), as well as givers (providing the "magical" agent, the stone), helpers, and "princesses" (quest objects). Their maturation is parallel, and in the end they both achieve a higher status. Since they are very young children and no romantic relationship is explicitly mentioned, the female character does not have to be subjected to the patriarchal form of existence, marrying her prince and submitting to his superior social position. On the contrary, since both children are underprivileged at the start, at the end they are both equally empowered, and neither is presented as having gained more.

Seemingly the same technique appears in Susan Cooper's *Seaward*, in which we follow one of the two characters while the mind of the other remains closed, or opaque. The profound difference between this novel and *The White Stone* follows from the level of complexity involved. *The White Stone* is a series of exciting adventures, describing an external reality. Even though we might see these external events as metaphors for the characters' inner growth, this translation of mimetic reading into symbolic feels a little far-fetched. *Seaward* takes place in the complicated mindscape of the two adolescents who have both endured losses and psychological traumas. The dreamlike narrative prompts a reading of the text as a description of internal, rather than external, reality. However, this stance usually demands that we determine who is dreaming. Writing about *Seaward* in 1990, I without the slightest doubt interpreted it as Cally's story, viewing Westerly as her companion, Animus, or helper. I believe that my choice was affected by the author's as well as my own gender. Several years later, one of my female students wrote a paper about *Seaward*, interpreting it just as unproblematically as Westerly's story. This gave me serious reasons to reconsider subjectivity in the novel.

Westerly is introduced first of the two characters, in the first sentence of the first chapter: "Westerly came down the path at a long lope, sliding over the short moorland grass" (7). In this chapter, nothing suggests that the story is other than mimetic or that the setting is other than perceptible reality. We do not know where the boy is going or why, but there is nothing to lead our genre expectations toward the extraordinary. In the next chapter, Westerly is abandoned, and we meet Cally in a similar *in medias res* manner: "Cally sat in the apple tree" (10). Unlike the Westerly chapter, this chapter immediately initiates us into Cally's dilemma: her father is dying. The woman who has come to take him, ostensibly, to a hospital, may be seen as the symbolic figure of death. She says to Cally: "'We've met before . . . but only at a distance. We shall meet again soon'" (11). Apparently, Cally has seen death before, "at a distance," perhaps when a distant relative died; the mysterious woman will soon come to collect Cally's mother, and Cally will presently meet Death itself, Lady Taranis, in the dark landscape of her mind. At the same time, Taranis can be also viewed as the darker side of Cally's mother, which Cally has to recognize and accept:

> Cally had a sudden nightmare image of her mother hostile to her, of a malevolence aimed at her which somehow was retribution for everything she had ever failed to do, or done wrong. In place of the loving forgiveness she had always known, in her mind she saw her mother's face twisted with ill-wishing. (17)

After Cally has escaped from her dismal reality through a mirror—a straightforward Jungian symbol representing the darker side of the ego, the Shadow—the narrative switches back to Westerly, and several more chapters are written in this antiphonic manner (chaps. 3 and 4 for Westerly; chaps. 5 and 6 for Cally), until the two characters finally meet. From this point onward, they must cooperate, trust, and help each other to succeed. They are focalized alternately, yet the two points of view almost coincide. The characters merge in their actantial roles, but continue to complement each other psychologically: Cally has intuition; Westerly is rational and resolute. Their actions have immediate impact on each other; they must learn to be sensitive and considerate. In Jungian terms, Cally is Westerly's Anima and he is her Animus. These positive, creative sides of their respective psyches must counterbalance their dark sides, the Shadows, Lugan and Taranis. Although Lugan seems to be benevolent, while Taranis is evil, both are ambiguous in their messages and in the end both are equally treacherous and supportive.

For Westerly, too, Lady Taranis is the symbolic maternal figure. His real mother has somehow managed to send him over to the Otherworld just before she was brutally murdered in a unnamed totalitarian country, far away from Cally's peaceful British countryside. Westerly feels guilty for her death. He is searching for his father, and Lugan, the male parental substitute, plays the natural role of guide:

> "I am your . . . watchman. As a hawk hangs watching in the sky. I see those things that happen to you—but only when they are happening, not before. Sometimes I may intervene. Not always. There are perils in this country, but there are also laws." (30)

Interpreting the Otherworld as Westerly's mindscape, full of fear and anxiety, the novel presents his inner journey toward acceptance of his parents' death, thus paralleling Cally's quest. The description of the journey is illogical, almost incoherent; it evokes the unmistakable sense of a nightmare. The world where Cally and Westerly wander is unstable, unpredictable, undeterminable. During the journey, both come to the understanding that their parents are neither perfect nor totally reliable. They recognize the time has come to liberate themselves from parental protection and continue on their own.

The goal of Cally's and Westerly's quest is the sea. The sea in Jungian psychology represents the unconscious, and it is a very transparent symbol in this novel. It is introduced in the second chapter: "Cally had never heard the sea, or seen it" (10). Characteristically, as it turns out, Cally is a descendant of selkies, the mythical seal-people. However, the sea is also a symbol of death. Cally's mother tells her, in the beginning of the novel: "'Your father's going away for a little while' . . . 'He's going to a special hospital by the sea'" (10). The mother soon follows him, supposedly to visit. Eventually, Cally has to accept that her parents are not coming back. Similarly, Westerly has been told by his mother to travel seaward in search of his father. Taranis, death incarnated, tries to tempt Westerly into following her:

> "Come with me, Westerly. I will take you to the sea, and there shall be no more pursuing and no more peril. Come with me, and I will send you over the ocean, to the land of Tir n'An Og, the ever young, where there is neither loss nor age nor pain. You will find your father there." (32)

Taranis promises Westerly eternal youth, but she entices him to follow her into the realm of death—on the mimetic level, to commit suicide. She then says the same to Cally: "'Come with me, Cally. I will take you to the sea, to your mother and your father, and you will be safe again. All together'" (49). The duplication of the temptation emphasizes the identical roles of the two characters in the story.

The intersubjective reading of the characters enables us to reconcile the two separate narratives, the two separate inner journeys, viewing them as two sides of the same quest for self, in which the two concrete figures are interchangeable, not least because their gender complementarity makes their story more universal. They learn to understand and trust each other just as an individual would explore his or her own psyche in an extreme situation. They share their fears, nightmares, and visions; they virtually become one. Just as their parental figures are the two sides of one inseparable whole: day and night, Life and Death, impossible without one another, so Cally and Westerly are ultimately two sides of the same mind and soul.

The works of Susan Cooper offer good material for contemplating the different forms of character construction. *Over Sea, under Stone*, a completely plot-oriented story, presents a collective character, consisting of the three siblings—Simon, Barney, and Jane—in identical actantial roles. The individual romantic hero in *The Dark Is Rising* allows some psychological depth. In *Greenwitch*, Jane, the female part of the collective protagonist, is emphasized. *The Grey King* and *Silver on the Tree* show a more complex interplay of collective and individual roles: the three Drew children have similar functions, while Will and Bran have separate roles. Finally, we meet complex intersubjectivity in *Seaward*. However, in *The Boggart* and sequel *The Boggart and the Monster*, Cooper goes back to a plot-oriented narrative and thus the collective character.

Child–Adult Intersubjectivity

Intersubjectivity in children's fiction presents a special challenge when the protagonist is constructed in an interaction between child and adult. In *The Mouse and His Child*, we are faced with the dilemma of determining the protagonist, unless, of course, we choose to neglect it all together—a strategy adopted by many critics who have dealt with this equivocal novel. Lois Kuznets (1994, 171) views the mouse child as the protagonist since it is a children's story, which for me is a circular argument. Other critics would perhaps maintain that the father is more central. After all the title is *The Mouse and His Child*, not "The Mouse and His Father," prompting an adult perspective that manipulates a sophisticated reader to interpret the story as the father's quest. The sociohistorical readings of the novel, whether they focus on the depiction of the American immigration, the Jewish Diaspora, or a more general history of the Jewish people, will also emphasize the father's role as the leader, the preserver of traditions, bearer of values, and protector of the coming generations (see some interpretations in Allison 2000). A young reader, missing the deeper levels of the narrative, will most likely identify the mouse child as the protagonist. Moreover, since both the father and the child are toys, which usually represent the child, it is very easy to treat them as an entity, as the-mouse-and-his-child that they are almost until the end of the story.

What is the implication of father and child literally stuck together? Are we dealing with a collective hero, in an unusual combination of child and adult? The focalizing pattern of the narrative rather suggests intersubjectivity. The father and child constantly replace each other as focalizing characters, without any omniscient narrative agency haunting them. The choice of one or the other as focalizer may seem arbitrary; however, on closer examination a pattern emerges. The much-quoted first dialogue between the child and the father already reveals their radically diverse view of the world:

> "Where are we?" the mouse child asked his father. . . .
> "I don't know," the father answered.
> "*What* are we, Papa?"
> "I don't know. We must wait and see." (4; author's emphasis)

The child is inquisitive; the adult, resigned. The child is rewarded as his curiosity is immediately satisfied; however, the elephant's straightforward explanation is merely the first step in the search for identity. Also, further on, the child will receive answers to his existential questions from the Frog

("What are shrews? . . . Do they eat frogs?"; 39); from the shrew drummer boy ("What's a territory?"; 45); or from Serpentina the turtle ("What do you contemplate? . . . What is infinity?"; 103). He will pursue self-knowledge while forced to watch his own reflection in the can of dog food. The father does not ask questions and is obviously not preoccupied with his identity; not because his identity is strong—he lacks it totally—but because the identity-seeking role is given to the child, as a more natural part of the double persona. Serpentina's summary goes, "The child is father to the mouse" (103).

The complementary nature of father and child is maintained throughout the book. When the child says that he does not want to go out into the world, the father simply tries to pacify him. Ashamed in front of the other toys, he does not interrogate his and his son's predestination, and he offers no words of consolation. He has an invariably submissive attitude to life; when the child asks where they should go after the tramp has repaired them, the father says: "Who knows? . . . There seems to be a good deal more to the world than the Christmas tree and the attic and the trash can. Anything at all might happen, I suppose" (14). In fact, although the father is assumed to be an adult, he is just as inexperienced as the child, lacking any knowledge of the world and its ways.

During the journey, the father looks forward, while the son looks backward, although logically it should be the other way around. Like so many characters in children's fiction, the mouse child does not wish to grow up and become independent but rather seeks to go back to the security of his early childhood, symbolized by the dollhouse. The father, forced to look forward, is much more skeptical about the future: "Our motor is in me. He fills the empty space inside himself with foolish dreams that cannot possibly come true" (35). The father is repeatedly prepared to give up, while the child never loses hope: "Maybe we'll succeed . . . . Maybe we'll have a lucky day" (60). However, it is not hope for the future, but hope for a return to the mythic past in which the father, an adult, does not believe: "the whole idea of such a quest is *impossible* . . . . It would be *hopeless* to attempt to find any of them . . . . Finding the elephant would be as *pointless* as looking for her" (34f.; emphasis added). The emphasized words reflect the father's philosophy, which, incidentally, does not support the idea of him being a great leader who totally trusts in the Almighty. Rather, he is a pessimist, lamenting every new turn in their fate: "How can we find anything? How can we ever hope to have our own territory?" (71); "We are helpless, as always" (104). To which the child replies, "Maybe we shan't always be helpless, Papa . . . . Maybe we'll be self-winding one day" (72). While the father despairs, the child acts. The child keeps asking every creature they meet about the seal and the elephant; he uses his wits to escape from Manny Rat during the Crow theater performance, to get them out of the pond or to make the hawk drop them. To the father's defeatist "Why not give up the struggle?" as they are carried away by a hawk, he replies bravely: "Don't say that, Papa! . . . I've got you! You won't fall!" (118). Applying Bakhtin's notion of polyphony, we see a battle of voices and wills going on within the single persona of "the-mouse-and-his-child," a battle in which the two halves of the persona carry equally heavy loads.

Besides the physical perseverance and his determination to reach his goal, the mouse child keeps seeking the truth beyond the last visible dog, the father's skepticism notwithstanding:

> "I fear that Serpentina is right," said the father. "Nothing is the ultimate truth, and this mud is just like all other mud."
> "I don't care if it is," said the child. "I want to get out of here." (111)

The remarkable resilience of childhood is emphasized by the fact that the toys do not have to eat, do not age, and cannot die—except for the very specific form of death and resurrection that the author invents for them. Being inedible is part of their identity; not aging allows great spans of time to pass without affecting them. Unlike human characters, the toy mice literally can wait forever for fate to smile on them again.

When the father sees the seal, the elephant, and the house, after his second rebirth, he is prepared to fight for his territory. In a way, the father takes over the child's role as protagonist, because now he also wants to retreat into the mythical world of childhood. Paradoxically, this wish is combined with a clear erotic desire:

> The elephant was shabby and pathetic; her looks were gone, departed with the ear, the eye, the purple headcloth and her plush. The father saw all that, and yet saw nothing of it; some brightness in her, some temper finer than the newest tin, some steadfast beauty smote and dazzled him. He wished that he might shelter and protect her . . . . He fell in love. (95f.)

The erotic subtext of the novel is obvious, especially in the rivalry between the mouse father and Manny Rat. As the father is developing plans for recapturing the dollhouse, showing determination for the first time during the story, the image of home merges for him with the image of his beloved: "His eyes were fixed on the elephant as he spoke, and there was new energy in his voice" (133). However, the intersubjective construction of the protagonist allows the author to subdue the sexual undertones by shifting the focus back to the child and his need for a mother, rather than the father's need for a partner.

As a result of one of their many subsequent transformations, the mice become separated. Normally, this would signify the child's inevitable and healthy separation from the parent as part of the maturation process. However, since the end of their quest brings the toys back to the restored paradise of childhood, symbolized by the dollhouse, their function in the narrative remains identical. They merely duplicate each other, and this time without the contradictory dialogue of inner voices. Moreover, drawing on Jungian notions, their persona has become split rather than achieving the wholeness of the Self. When Manny Rat makes the mice self-winding, it results in a life without change: "self-windingly and interminably walking" (167). Even though the winding stops, the mice are entrapped in a never-ending happiness: "'Your fortune has been made,' said Frog, 'and needs no more telling'" (181). The toys have no future; they are immortal and therefore dead. The mouse child will forever be a child, and his father has regressed into the eternal childhood. The implication is the child restoring childhood to an adult—a motif observed by many critics of Arcadian fiction, dating back to Heidi, Anne of Green Gables, and The Secret Garden. In this process, the child merges with the adult, they become interchangeable, and the complete picture of the persona must be put together from the intricate score of the two voices.

The intersubjective construction of the protagonist is still more complicated in Tom's Midnight Garden. The natural way of reading this novel is by treating Tom as the protagonist and by exploring the tension between his desire to stay forever in the childhood paradise of the garden and his acknowledgment of the necessity to grow up and return to the linearity of real life. Tom's dominant presence in the narrative, his function as the sole focalizer, his psychological development, and not least the title support this interpretation. A feminist re-vision of such a reading would perhaps suggest that Hatty's role in the story is grossly overlooked. In old Mrs. Bartholomew's account of the events in the last chapter of the novel, we suddenly see the whole story from another perspective. It appears not only (and maybe not primarily) to be the story of a young boy who is tempted to "exchange time for eternity," but the tragic story of an old woman who knows from experience that time is irreversible. From this point of view, we are not dealing with Tom's midnight garden, but with Hatty's midnight garden. The garden, which Tom is able to enter during the magical thirteenth hour of the night, exists in Hatty's memory time (cf. Krips 2000, 60–64). It is evoked by Hatty's nostalgic memories of her happy, albeit lonely, childhood. It is a paradise where there is always summer and fine weather, since memory is selective. There is only one winter scene, which is also the last encounter between Hatty and Tom, thus suggesting departure and the inevitable movement toward growth, aging, and death. The garden symbolizes irretrievably lost childhood and, like the Neverland in *Peter Pan*, it offers the child merely a temporal retreat. The question is, which child, Tom or Hatty?

Some of my students have been disturbed by the novel, claiming that old Mrs. Bartholomew emotionally abuses Tom, drawing on his youth, imagination, and vigor like a vampire, to procure energy as she senses her own approaching death. In fact, Tom looks "thinner," more transparent and ghostlike as the story goes on. A simple explanation is that Hatty is less and less interested in him, her imaginary playmate, as she grows up and becomes more involved in substantial relationships. But this is only true if we accept the interpretation that Tom really travels in time and exists, although ghostlike, in Hatty's childhood. However, if the garden only exists in Mrs. Bartholomew's memory, then her experience of Tom in the garden is merely a phantasm, in the Lacanian sense, a product of sick imagination. She is anguished about her old age and imminent death, she goes back to her lonely and unhappy childhood, and in a last frantic attempt to recapture it, she inhabits her memories with an imaginary playmate, ascribing him the traits of the boy she has seen in passing in her tenants' flat. The intensity of her desires affects Tom and evokes his dreams—or perhaps, from this perspective, nightmares. As quite a few readings of children's fiction suggest, writing for children turns out to be a therapeutic vehicle for frustrated adults, both the adult characters in the texts and the adult writers.

However, such a radical rereading of *Tom's Midnight Garden* seems to me just as insufficient as the more straightforward reading with a focus on Tom alone. Unless Mrs. Bartholomew is lying, Tom has indeed existed in her childhood, because on the night before her wedding, Hatty thinks "of all I would be leaving behind me: my childhood and all the times I had spent in the garden—in the garden with you, Tom" (211). Mrs. Bartholomew's memories are, in their turn, evoked by Tom's longing for a playmate. A plausible explanation is that Hatty and Tom are cocreators, while the creative source itself is their innocent, prelapsarian, presexual love. The question of who of the two characters is real and who is the ghost, which has occupied many a scholar, including myself (Nikolajeva 1988, 101ff.), can be viewed in a new light here. An intersubjective reading of the novel avoids reducing it to merely one dimension, either the child or the adult perspective, and instead enables us to see the complexity and ambiguity that account for its vitality and appeal.

My last two examples predate by several decades the declared phase of postmodern children's fiction of the 1990s, which is also claimed to eliminate clear-cut borderlines between children's and adult literature. The two novels I have discussed present in their character construction a complexity that has long been denied children's fiction, and many critics still deny it today.

A More Complex Case of Intersubjectivity: *The Secret Garden*

A number of recent interpretations of *The Secret Garden* have illuminated the fact that Mary, clearly perceived as the protagonist for the first two-thirds of the text, is forced aside by Colin (Murray 1985, 39ff.; Paul 1990, 159; Foster and Simons 1995, 189). These re-visions, utilizing the tools of feminist criticism, make us aware of the recurrent pattern in stories of the Beauty-and-the-Beast type, to which *The Secret Garden* unmistakably belongs: the sacrificial female is in the end supplanted in her hero role by the male whom she has successfully restored to power. The formal reason for this perception of Mary and Colin is that we are usually trained to identify focalizers with main characters, and from chapter 19 Colin becomes the focalizer, while Mary is, according to these readings, abandoned.

To begin with, I do not agree that she is indeed abandoned. Colin's point of view is instead added to Mary's, to enhance the internal development portrayed. It is not until Mary is strong enough emotionally that Colin's voice can be fully introduced into the score, but rather than silencing Mary, as the feminist rereadings suggest, his voice joins in to emphasize the intersubjective character's growth and change. Mary is the sole focalizer in eighteen out of the novel's twenty-seven chapters. Although we may see Dickon as a part of her persona, reflecting the positive, creative sides of her otherwise somber psyche, I am more inclined to see him as the guide and helper, supporting and speeding up her emotional awakening. In fact, Dickon fits perfectly into the archetype of the "green-world lover" (Pratt 1981, 140). Dickon's function in Mary's narrative may be more prominent than that of his sister Martha, his mother, or the sulky gardener, Ben Weatherstaff; however, all these characters affect Mary's evolution without being projections of her inner features.

Colin is indirectly introduced in chapter 5, "The Cry in the Corridor":

> It was a curious sound—it seemed almost as if a child were crying somewhere. Sometimes the wind sounded rather like a child crying, but presently Mistress

Mary felt quite sure this sound was inside the house, not outside it. It was far away, but it was inside. (49f.)

Mary, presented as an emotionally cold and indifferent child, has apparently never cried in her life, not even over her parents' death. In this episode, she is confronted—as she constantly is in her new life at Misselthwaite Manor—with an emotional response she does not recognize. By this time, Mary has already learned the sensations of joy, empathy, and compassion. As a new subject position is introduced through Colin, we witness Mary's slow transformation from a self-centered monster to a sensitive and nurturing young girl. However, the way she is presented in the beginning of the novel, she cannot show any understanding of another human being unless she learns to understand herself. By watching Colin, she is forced to take a more objective view of herself. Colin is her mirror reflection, the archetypal double, whose role is to show to the protagonist her own faults amplified tenfold. The author's successive enlargement of Colin corresponds to Mary's growing understanding of herself. It is not an instant illumination but a slow and painful process.

Mary's exploration of the hundred closed rooms of the manor is a rather transparent metaphor for her exploration of her own sealed-off self. As she first hears the distant crying, we may interpret it as her psyche's calls to draw her attention and stimulate her curiosity. When she discovers Colin, she has reached the center of her self. What she sees, disturbs and repels her, until she realizes that she is confronted with her own mirror image:

"I hate fresh air and I don't want to go out."
"I didn't when I first came here," said Mary. (121)

The physically sick, hypochondriac Colin represents Mary's former dormant, sickly mind. She is immediately determined to get him out of bed and into the healing freshness of the garden; thus, Colin's physical improvement parallels Mary's mental and emotional growth, her self-fulfillment. Yet, this growth cannot proceed too fast. The reason Mary can handle Colin lies in the remnants of her former, unsympathetic person. Unlike the servants, who pity the poor cripple, Mary recognizes her own self-centered attitude in Colin and has no inclination to humor him: "She was no more used to considering other people than Colin was and she saw no reason why an ill-tempered boy should interfere with the things she liked best" (157). This is, of course, a selfish action on Mary's part, but this selfishness and resolution provide the best remedy for Colin's disposition. After a quarrel, she leaves Colin saying that she is never coming again. However, she is not merely curious and in need of a playmate: she sees Colin's improvement as an essential step in her own progress. Mary's infamous "contrariness" is her best weapon in her struggle against—or rather for—Colin. In her handling of Colin's tantrums she is far from being silenced; in fact, she "shouted" (165), "contradicted . . . fiercely," and "commanded" (166). Even after Colin has taken over as the main focalizer, she is still the most active character, taking initiative in bringing Dickon to see Colin, and then arranging for Colin to be taken out in his wheelchair. She talks a lot, she shouts "in her fierce indignation" (208) at Ben Weatherstaff, she tells Colin how rude and ill mannered he is, and she is anything but an oppressed, submissive female.

However, we cannot dismiss Colin merely as Mary's immaterial projection, since he has in fact his own, tangible presence in the novel (unlike Tom's ghostly existence in *Tom's Midnight Garden*). In his turn, Colin cannot be understood without Mary. His miraculous transformation is far too abrupt to seem plausible, but viewing Mary as a catalyst we can accept it. In Mary, Colin sees that change is possible. In fact, he changes his mind already during their very first conversation, as he says, "I should not mind fresh air in a secret garden" (126), and he allows Mary to pat, sing, and soothe him to sleep. Mary's transformation is not quite complete at this point, but the more she changes, the more Colin is inspired to change. He becomes curious about the garden, he starts eating and gaining weight, he stops caring only about himself, and very soon he discovers that he can walk and run like any other child. Just as Mary looks at him to see her own reflection, he realizes, with amazement, that Mary once experienced some of his own feelings:

"Did you feel as if you hated people?"
"Yes," answered Mary without affectation. "I would have detested you if I had seen you before I saw the robin and Dickon." (176)

"It's always having your own way that has made you so queer," Mary went on, thinking aloud.
Colin turned his head, frowning.
"Am I queer?" he demanded.
"Yes," answered Mary, "very. But you needn't be cross, " she added impartially, "because so am I queer . . . . But I am not as queer as I was before I began to like people and before I found the garden."
"I don't want to be queer," said Colin. "I am not going to be." (218f.)

This point is, of course, of overall importance. Mary could not have had the positive influence on Colin before she had gone through a substantial change herself. Colin, on the other hand, would not have trusted Mary unless he recognized the change undergone by her. The process in the two characters is interactive and interdependent. Mary's maturation is speeded up as she sees her remaining faults in Colin. Colin has many problems similar to Mary's and many different. His recovery is quicker and more tangible, but the two children not only support each other within the plot but complement each other in characterization. In this double description, the restoration of the garden serves as an additional metaphor of the resurrection of body and spirit, an observation too trivial to be elaborated on.

It is also not without significance that the two characters very clearly break the traditional gender stereotypes. Mary is stubborn, naughty, strong-tempered, and unemotional, and, despite her intuition leading her to the discovery of the garden, she is rational and determined in a specifically masculine way. Her sphere of actions is predominantly outdoors. Colin is weak, melancholy, and suspicious, and his tantrums are described as "hysterics," a typical feminine psychotic state. He is isolated indoors, in a traditionally feminine sphere. The process of self-knowledge is for both very much connected with discovering contrasting gender-specific traits in each other.

Yet the novel does not end with Colin's recuperation, but the point of view is changed once again, and in the same direction as observed by the feminist critics—that is, toward a stronger power position. If Colin, a male character, supplants and suppresses the female, as feminist readings maintain, the emergence of Mr. Craven as focalizer is an obvious case of an adult supplanting and suppressing the child. Following Malcolm Usrey's *Heidi* interpretation, we can easily see Mr. Craven as a "Byronic hero," voluntarily isolated from the world after his adored wife's death, a lonely wanderer without peace of mind:

> [H]e was the man who for ten years had kept his mind filled with dark and heart-broken thinking. He had not been courageous; he had never tried to put any other thoughts in the place of the dark ones . . . . A terrible sorrow had fallen upon him when he had been happy and he had let his soul fill itself with blackness and had refused obstinately to allow any rift of light to pierce through . . . . Most strangers thought he must be either half mad or a man with some hidden crime on his soul. (263)

The garden also represents *his* withered soul. We witness how his son's physical improvement—in its turn initiated by Mary's physical and spiritual awakening—suddenly brings about a change in the father's attitude to life. Formally, he is summoned home by a letter from Mrs. Sowerby, Dickon's and Martha's mother, and the fairy godmother of this fairy tale. But already prior to this letter, Mr. Craven feels that something is calling to him, a voice that he perceives as his dead wife's, but which may be a mystical transmission of his son's and niece's evocations: "In the garden! In the garden!" (266). The garden thus becomes the meeting place of all subjectivities, the focus where the points of view intersect.

Seeing Mr. Craven "restored" and "reformed" by two innocent children (as an Usrey-inspired reading would prompt) would oblige us to interrogate the novel as a piece for young readers, since child characters then would be merely vehicles for an adult's resurrection. At the least, we should regretfully state that the objective of the narrative is to bring the adult back to the eternal paradise of childhood. However, just as I am reluctant to admit that Mary is silenced by Colin, I cannot see that the (multiple) child is silenced by the adult, since Mr. Craven's subject position is melted into the amalgam of the intersubjective character. The bridging of male and female, child and adult in this character construction presents us with a remarkably powerful portrait.

Intersubjectivity of Narrator and Protagonist: *The Little Prince*

The Little Prince is one of the most enigmatic works of children's fiction and also one of the most often interrogated as a children's book. One of the main reasons is the double and highly ambivalent perspective. On the one hand, we have the story of the little prince and his painful quest for self-knowledge. On the other hand, we have the story of an odd and lonely adult, recollecting his encounter with the little prince six years ago, as he was stranded in a desert after a plane crash. Since the pilot is telling the story, his memories of the little prince may just as well be visions or hallucinations. Another interpretation suggests that the little prince is the pilot's inner child. A biographically oriented psychoanalytical interpretation views the little prince as a projection of the author's anxieties (Franz 1981).

I have offered a reading of *The Little Prince* elsewhere (Nikolajeva 2000, 118–23), so here I will just concentrate on the character construction. It is quite difficult to reconcile the two ways of approaching the story: one with the prince as the protagonist and the pilot as an outsider narrator; the other with the pilot as the protagonist and the prince as the product of his imagination. Obviously, the first is an unsophisticated reading, and the second is a sophisticated reading. By applying the concept of intersubjectivity, we can see how the two characters complement and illuminate each other.

The prince appears out of the blue as the pilot realizes that he only has drinking water for six days. He is desperate, and the little prince is his frantic attempt to hold on to life, to recollect everything that he has ever valued. The figure also gives him confidence: "my little man seemed neither to be straying uncertainly among the sands, nor to be fainting from fatigue or hunger or thirst or fear. Nothing about him gave any suggestion of a child lost in the middle of the desert" (8). The pilot has now created another subjectivity, apart from his helpless and desperate self.

The pilot puts the prince through the test he has tried on his adult friends: he draws an elephant inside the boa. He wants to make sure that he has not lost the ability to use his imagination. But he discovers that he has: "[The prince] thought, perhaps, that I was like himself. But I, alas, do not know how to see sheep through the walls of boxes. Perhaps I am a little like the grown-ups. I have had to grow old" (17). Through the prince, the pilot fights his reluctance to grow old and ultimately his fear of death.

Having invented his inner child, the pilot supplies him with a background that would be relevant for a child. In fact, the pilot keeps drawing parallels between what adults find essential ("The planet he came from is Asteroid B-612") and what children would want to know ("The proof that the little prince existed is that he was charming, that he laughed, and that he was looking for a sheep"; 16). Unless we see the prince as the pilot's creation, his ontological status presents several problems. His coming from an asteroid gives the story a slight touch of science fiction, while its clear fairy-tale nature is maintained throughout the narrative: it is not explained how the little prince can breathe, where his food or clothes come from, or how he can travel to other planets. Still less clear are his origins. Did he ever have parents? Who were they? Where and when did they disappear?

None of these questions are touched upon in the book, and they may seem totally irrelevant on the story level; however, they are essential if we want to assess the symbolic meaning of the character as the narrator's inner child. If the pilot creates the little prince from his imagination, naturally he need not supply him with a "boring," "grown-up" biography. He ponders the loneliness of his little friend, which is a reflection of his own loneliness. But he does describe the planet, the fight with the baobabs, and the appearance of the flower. Since we do not know much about the pilot's life, we can only speculate that the story of the arrogant flower grows out of his own romantic experience. The story comes while the pilot is desperately trying to repair his aircraft and retorts to the little prince's questions by saying: "I am busy with matters of consequence!" (24). The phrase, echoed by the responses the prince receives from strange adults on the planets he visits, stands in sharp contrast with everything that the prince believes to be important: beauty, joy, and love. Having uttered the phrase, the pilot suddenly realizes that he has been busy with trifles, forgetting the essential aspects of life: "I had let my tools drop from my hands. Of what moment now was my hammer, my bolt, or thirst, or death? On one star, one planet, my planet, the Earth, there was a little prince to be comforted" (26). This is the point when the pilot makes true contact with his inner child and acknowledges the importance of everything he has been trying to reject or repress as an adult.

The subsequent account of the prince's travels is a disguised story of the pilot's self-examination. He discovers and renounces the qualities represented by the grown-ups whom the prince meets on the different planets; he comes to the realization, articulated by the fox, that "[i]t is only with the heart you can see rightly; what is essential is invisible to the eye" (68). He listens to the story of the merchant who sells the thirst-quenching pills "as I was drinking the last drop of my water supply" (72). His little friend "has never been either hungry or thirsty" (72). Being merely an imaginary child, he is free from the burdens of living men, including the threat of death. The pilot says to himself: "What I see here is nothing but a shell. What is most important is invisible" (74). This most important thing may again be the pilot's inner child; anyway, it is clear that the figure of the little prince is less important than what he represents.

The parting of the pilot and the prince, repeating the parting of the prince and the fox, implies that the pilot has realized that he must let his inner child go. At the same time, he knows that the memory of his remarkable friend will stay with him forever, and that it is more important than the desire to remain young. The pilot's insights thus repeat step by step the prince's self-discovery, and the final cognizance presented to the reader has to be assembled from the two stories. Although we superficially have the same type of child–adult intersubjectivity as in some texts discussed earlier, the pattern is more complicated, since the adult character is also the homodiegetic narrator.

Metafictive Intersubjectivity:
The Neverending Story

The Neverending Story shows how the reader's subjectivity is created. The protagonist, Bastian, is reading a book. He is so fascinated by what he is reading that he gets more and more involved, until he is literally drawn into the narrative and becomes a character in it. This is a metafictive device aimed at erasing boundaries between reality and fiction, and interrogating our perception of reality as "real" (see Hutcheon 1988; Nikolajeva 1996, chap. 7).

The two parts of the novel repeat each other, showing the hero's quest, with a vast repertoire of recognizable events and figures. However, while Atreyu in Part I behaves like a real hero, showing bravery and ingenuity, Bastian in Part II acts not even as an antihero but as a false hero of the fairy tale, making wrong decisions and undoing everything that Atreyu has accomplished. Reading the two narratives as mirror images of each other and interpreting the two characters intersubjectively, we see that in the first part Bastian adopts the subject position of the protagonist in the story he is reading (just as real readers would adopt Bastian's subject position) and shows such a great empathy that he finally gets into direct contact with Atreyu. First, as Bastian is reading about Atreyu's encounter with the monster Ygramul, he cannot refrain from crying out:

> *A cry of fear escaped Bastian.*
> A cry of terror passed through the ravine and echoed from side to side. Ygramul turned her eye to left and right, to see if someone else had arrived, for that sound could nor have been made by the boy who stood there as though paralyzed with horror.
> *Could she have heard my cry? Bastian wondered in alarm. But that's not possible.* (76f.; author's emphasis).

Later, looking into the magic mirror, Atreyu sees Bastian instead of his own reflection:

> He saw a fat little boy with a pale face—a boy his own age—and this little boy was sitting on a pile of mats reading a book. The little boy had large, sad-looking eyes, and he was wrapped in frayed gray blankets. . . .
> *Bastian gave a start when he realized what he had just read. Why, that was him! The description was right in every detail.* (106; author's emphasis)

In terms of metafiction, we can note that on these occasions the boundary between the diegetic level (Bastian's reality) and the hypodiegetic level (Atreyu's reality) is tentatively breached, only to be completely eradicated later on. In terms of intersubjectivity, it is essential to remember that Bastian is a fat, unlovable, unhappy boy, bullied in school and neglected by his father; his mother has recently died. By adopting Atreyu's subjectivity, he becomes everything he wishes to be: handsome, brave, endowed with magical powers, and dispatched on an exciting and dangerous mission. Atreyu is an archetypal fairy-tale hero: of unknown origin and chosen for a heroic deed. However, while Atreyu possesses all the qualities of which Bastian dreams, Atreyu's task is to find someone who is more powerful, someone who can save Fantastica and its ruler the Childlike Empress. This someone is, of course, Bastian, and his powers are language (he can give people and things names) and imagination. Thus, although Atreyu does not know as much about Bastian as Bastian knows about him, he is very much aware of the existence of this double. As confirmed by the second part, the novel is really about Bastian and his identity quest. Atreyu's story is used to show the way, to create a pattern. Part II is the deconstruction of the pattern. Atreyu is constantly beside Bastian, as his squire and also as a voice of conscience, which Bastian tries to silence. The final portrait of the protagonist is created by the interplay of the two subjectivities.

An attempt at metafictive intersubjectivity is also to be found in *Sophie's World*, where the protagonist is created through the interplay of characters on different diegetic levels.

Aesthetic Implications of Individual, Collective, and Intersubjective Protagonists

By contemplating the implications of collective, individual, and intersubjective characters in children's fiction, I find the most profound differences in the way authors communicate with the readers on the issue of the "reality" of the depicted events. The use of a collective protagonist creates an illusion of an objective, "realistic" narrative. Basically, the assumption is that if several people share an experience, then this experience must be a product of a tangible, existing world.

The use of individual characters creates ambiguity since a single focalizer, especially one reflecting internal existence, questions the objectivity of the character's experience. In children's novels with an individual character, devices such as estrangement and filter may be used to emphasize the immaturity of the mind through which the narrative is presented. Even in narratives where primarily external focalization is employed, such as *Tom Sawyer*, the naive perspective leads to doubt in our perception of the described events as wholly objective.

Intersubjective character construction definitely interrogates the possibility of objectivity in portrayal of human consciousness. Especially child characters cannot be plausibly described as possessing an ability to understand and interpret the world around them. Instead, a number of different subjects are brought together to present a more complex consciousness than an individual child character allows. By using cross-gender intersubjectivity, authors can avoid gender stereotypes, instead making the most of the archetypal masculine and feminine features within their characters. By using child–adult intersubjectivity, authors can circumvent many of the problems arising from the child characters' inability to perceive and evaluate their external as well as internal reality. I find it significant that Philip Pullman develops the character of his trilogy from individual in *Northern Lights* to intersubjective in the following two volumes, adding adults to the two child characters in *The Amber Spyglass*.

~

CHAPTER SIX

Secondary Characters and Character Constellations

In the previous chapters I have discussed protagonists—that is, main characters. In the vast majority of children's novels, we have at least several other
characters besides the protagonist. In children's literature, characterization
through human relationships is, if possible, still more essential than in the
mainstream, because the protagonist in a children's novel is extremely seldom portrayed in complete isolation. Fairy tales, which, as I have repeatedly
demonstrated, provide the model for most of children's novels, are based on
a complex web of human relationships. It is basically impossible to construct
a fairy-tale plot with one single character. Literary characters are normally
depicted in their interaction with other characters, since our interest in fiction is primarily based on its treatment of human relationships.

A completely solitary protagonist is possible, although not common in
adult fiction. In children's fiction, a solitary protagonist is impossible for several reasons. First, a child living completely on his own is not plausible,
unless there are some special circumstances. One example of such special
conditions might be a Robinsonnade, in which the character is indeed isolated and is depicted in interaction with nature, rather than with other
characters. However, even Robinson Crusoe on his desert island finds a
companion, characteristically in children's editions much sooner than in
the original. This does not mean, of course, that the protagonist cannot be
abandoned for a while, which often is the very mechanism of the plot, but
sooner or later the other actants must enter the story. A modern Robinsonnade, either in nature, such as *Hatchet,* or in urban hostile surroundings,
such as *Slake's Limbo,* illustrates this well.

Second, there are pedagogical reasons: young readers must be socialized, trained to handle human relations. There is usually at least one adult figure in the child character's vicinity, acting as a guide and teacher.

Finally, an isolated character does not allow much variety in terms of actions and interactions. Since traditional children's literature is action oriented rather than character oriented, a wholly self-reflective, actionless narrative would contradict the aesthetics of children's literature. Interestingly enough, the only type of children's fiction that allows a solitary protagonist is the picturebook, in which a character is often depicted in interaction with inanimate objects rather than other people. This may reflect the very young child's solipsistic worldview.

Certain types of relationships are, for obvious reasons, more important in children's novels than in mainstream: with parents or guardians, teachers, and siblings. These characters correspond roughly to the fairy-tale personae of dispatchers, helpers, donors, and false heroes. On the other hand, we may expect the central relationship in the mainstream, that toward a lover or spouse, to be irrelevant in children's fiction. However, in the actantial model, a lover or spouse has the function of the object of the hero's quest ("desire" in psychological terms). In a children's novel, this function can be taken by a friend, including a friend of the opposite gender, or otherwise a lost parent or a lost toy. Certain genres presuppose a symbiosis between characters, in which one is impossible without another (hero-villain in an adventure story, two lovers in a romance, etc.). In Jungian theory, supporting characters are viewed as projections of the protagonist's various personality traits. Thus, supporting characters are necessary from many different points of view.

A common attitude to children's books is that they must not contain too many secondary characters, since young readers cannot remember them and distinguish between them. As compared with many mainstream novels, such as *Mansfield Park*, *Bleak House*, or *War and Peace*, children's books tend to contain relatively few characters. I would argue that the limited number of characters in children's fiction is a deliberate aesthetic device, reflecting a young person's limited experience. The younger the main characters, the less likely they are to know many people outside their closest environment. Normally only parents, siblings, grandparents, and possibly neighbors are included in novels for and about very young children. At school age, the characters would know classmates and teachers, in positive as well as negative roles. Adventure stories and fantasy presuppose encounters with a large number of characters, helpers as well as opponents. In the teenage novel, the horizons open still wider.

Typology of Secondary Characters

In his *Character and the Novel*, W. J. Harvey (1965) distinguishes between four kinds of characters: protagonists, background characters, cards, and ficelles.[1] Cards are, according to this approach, what is normally called a *type*, or even *stereotype*, in which one trait is amplified, becoming "larger than life" (58). According to Harvey, these are often comic characters and very seldom protagonists, although he mentions some exceptions, such as Oblomov and Don Quixote (in my opinion, he grossly oversimplifies both these characters). Ficelle, a term introduced by Henry James, is a character who only exists for a certain purpose or function in the plot (Harvey 1965, 62f.). Harvey is a mimetic critic who judges characters not by their function in the plot but by the degree of mimetic completeness or entirety in their presentation. We may, however, agree that secondary characters show a wide range of functions as well as complexity. The most common and simple division of characters into main and secondary does not seem quite sufficient.

My own classification according to the characters' position in the plot and partially even completeness would be as depicted in the figure.

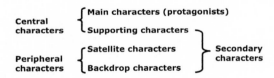

The various criteria for determining main characters have been discussed in the previous chapters, where it has also been stated that protagonists can be individual, collective, or intersubjective. All characters other than protagonists are secondary. Supporting characters are all secondary characters essential for the plot. Together, main and supporting characters constitute central, or integral, characters. The plot cannot develop if we remove any of them. Basically, they correspond to Propp's dramatis personae or Greimas's actants: the hero, the helper/donor/sender, the princess/object, and the antagonist. Among the supporting characters I would like to single out one very important role, which I have already mentioned in connection with my discussion of the protagonist: a character who sets the plot in motion. I have chosen to call this character a *catalyst*. Good examples of catalysts are Mary Poppins and Pippi Longstocking, who both bring a radical change into protagonists' lives. In some interpretations, Peter Pan would also be a catalyst. Johnny in *Johnny My Friend* is without doubt a catalyst.

Yet a catalyst is not the same as a *macguffin*, a notion used by Alfred Hitchcock to denote an insignificant detail that initiates the plot but does not participate in it. A catalyst character may be central to the plot as well as a quite complex personality.

I would not extend the notion of catalyst to antagonists, since the antagonist's role is by definition to set the plot in motion. It is rather in some plots without visible antagonists (character-against-nature or character-against-self plots) that we can find the notion of catalyst useful. Likewise, antagonists cannot, by definition, be main characters. It is therefore important to distinguish between main characters and central characters, who can be either main or supporting. The White Witch in *The Lion, the Witch and the Wardrobe* is undoubtedly a central character, but she is not the main character (as many of my confused students have suggested).

Both main and supporting characters can be flat or round, static or dynamic. It is, however, likely that integral characters are more complex than peripheral ones. The difference between central and peripheral characters is that the latter can be removed from the plot without the plot being radically changed. There is a difference in the degree of importance between satellite and backdrop characters. Satellite characters are not essential for the plot, but they may serve to illuminate some aspects of the plot, or for contrastive characterization or simply for variation. In books where the depiction of society plays an important role, satellite characters represent a variety of human types. For instance, in a school story we are likely to encounter a large gallery of satellite characters, children as well as adults. The Harry Potter novels are a good example. Of Harry's many classmates, Ron, Hermione, and Draco Malfoy are supporting characters, while all other Hogwarts students are satellite characters. Of the teacher wizards, Dumbledore and possibly Minerva McGonagall are supporting characters (parental substitutes) throughout the series, while each individual novel also has an additional supporting adult figure. There are a large number of satellite teacher characters, each with an individuality, but not necessarily pertinent for the plot.

Besides carrying the plot, a satellite character may contribute to the portrayal of the protagonist. A younger or older sibling may not be essential for the plot, but through the protagonist's attitude to them, he will be characterized. For example, Holden Caulfield is thoroughly described through his relationship with his older brother, younger sister, and younger dead brother.

Backdrop characters may flip in and out of the narrative, without leaving any substantial traces; they are mostly used to add color to the narrative;

often they have comic roles. They may also be used for the purpose of authenticity—for instance, figures like milkmen, mail carriers, police officers, school janitors, errand boys, and so forth. They have no essential role in the plot but make the setting more familiar and believable.

Let us illustrate the character typology with *Anne of Green Gables*, a text with an unusually large number of characters for a children's novel. Anne is without doubt its sole protagonist. Matthew, Marilla, Diana, Gilbert, the schoolteacher Miss Stacy, and Aunt Josephine are supporting characters. Without them, the plot would not be possible. They all play an essential part in Anne's evolution as a character; in Propp's terms, they perform functions in the plot. By contrast, Mrs. Lynde the neighbor, Diana's mother Mrs. Barry, Mr. Philips the old schoolteacher, and Mrs. Allan the minister's wife are satellite characters. They are not indispensable for the plot, but they certainly add to the character gallery. For instance, Mrs. Lynde is a stereotype of a old busybody, opinionated and hypocritical. There are also a large number of backdrop characters: the awful Mrs. Blewett, who is willing to take charge of Anne until Marilla changes her mind; Anne's schoolmates at Avonlea and at Queen's; teachers; the artist at the concert who praises Anne's pretty hair, and so on. They do not add anything essential to the plot or the depiction of society; however, they make this society more varied and therefore more plausible. They also provide additional comments on Anne and her life.

A character's status in a narrative may change as the story progresses. A seemingly peripheral character may suddenly come to the foreground—for instance, Luke in *Lyddie*. In sequels, a peripheral character may be given a more central role or even become the protagonist. Cousin Richard, whom the Arden children meet on some of their time travels in *The House of Arden*, becomes the protagonist of *Harding's Luck*. In this book, the Ardens are mentioned in passing. On closer examination, the protagonists' mother and aunt in *Knight's Castle* appear to be the main characters of Eager's earlier novel, *Half Magic*. A little boy hiding behind the fence in *Night Daddy* becomes the main character in *Elvis and His Secret* and the four sequels. The opposite is also possible; for instance, Lyddie is a satellite character in *Jip: His Story*. In an episodic narrative, a character may be integral in one chapter and never reappear again. For instance, in the individual chapters of *Pippi Longstocking* we meet a variety of characters who are indispensable in this particular chapter (the two burglars, the circus director, or Miss Rosenblom are some of Pippi's antagonists) but are never mentioned again.

Both central and peripheral characters can be presented as stereotypes (although peripheral characters are more likely to have stereotypical traits).

A *stereotype* is a character possessing only one feature amplified almost to caricature (cf. Harvey's definition of *card*). Some examples of child stereotypes are the naughty boy and the model boy, the bully and the wimp, and the tomboy girl and the model girl. Some examples of adult stereotypes are a restrictive parent, an overprotective parent, an evil teacher, a model teacher, a hypocrite neighbor, and a helpful neighbor. Examples of racial and national stereotypes include big and strong sporty blacks, blond Swedes, passionate Italians, dark-haired and dark-skinned immigrants, and so on. A stereotype of a villain is a dark-haired figure, often with some visible disfigurement and excessive facial hair (see further interesting discussion of stereotypes in formulaic fiction in Cawelti 1976, 11*f*.).

Gender stereotyping implies that girls and boys, men and women in books behave exactly in accordance with the prevailing conventions. Girls are nice and well behaved, like "little women," while boys are full of pranks, like Tom Sawyer or Emil. Annika in *Pippi Longstocking* may be seen as a stereotype, with her nice frocks and frightened attitude. But she can also be viewed as a parody on a stereotype. Since male and female stereotype traits are opposed to each other, it is easy to present a schematic abstract pattern of "masculinity" and "femininity," as does John Stephens, describing masculinity in terms of strong, violent, tough, aggressive, competitive, and femininity in terms of beautiful, nonviolent, soft, submissive, sharing, and so on (Stephens 1996). It does not mean that all male and all female literary characters follow this schema, but the schema can help us evaluate gender stereotypes. In our culture, masculine features are implicitly superior. Of course, our ideas about typical masculine and feminine traits change with time. Female characters have changed especially radically since *Little Women*, and boys in contemporary novels are allowed to be soft and caring.

In assessing gender stereotyping in secondary characters, we must be aware of the narrative perspective of the text. In *Karlson on the Roof*, the mother can be very easily perceived as a stereotype, since she is only portrayed in stereotypical situations: baking cinnamon rolls and making hot chocolate drinks for her son, bandaging his wound after a fight, comforting and caring. However, the narrative is focalized through the young protagonist, and the portrait of the mother is *his* image of a perfect parent: "I want you to be in the kitchen every day when I come home from school, and you must wear your apron and bake rolls." This is not the narrator's point of view, but the child's: mothers exist in order to provide children with cinnamon rolls! Indeed, we do not know what else Midge's mother does beside baking rolls, since it is irrelevant for the focalizing character.

Constellations of Characters

The main character and secondary characters have different relations to each other. As shown before, within structural theory, characters are treated merely as agents who perform certain actions. Structural models, whether functional or actantial, describe the characters in relation to the plot and only superficially in relation to each other. Yet this is a good starting point for discussing the various roles that secondary characters may play in a story.

Not all plots have a clearly delineated antagonist, but most plots do. Likewise, not all plots demand helpers, dispatchers, and donors, but most frequently we will indeed find helping and providing figures around the protagonist. The main reason seems to be the need for interaction of characters in plot development. The Disney version of *The Little Mermaid* is an excellent illustration of its creators' drive to supply the protagonist with a set of supporting characters in order to clarify (and oversimplify) the plot. In the original version, the little mermaid's chief enemy is herself, and as she leaves the sea, there is no one to assist or comfort her on land. In the Disney version, the witch—originally the agent of magical transformation, a helper—is turned into an antagonist, and three helpers, the crab, the fish, and the seagull, accompany the mermaid during her adventures. The conflict becomes more tangible and concrete, while the philosophical implications of Andersen's tale are gone. The victory over the antagonist reestablishes the protagonist's power position. The Disney plot is thus substantially closer to the traditional folktale plot with its agents and actants.

Let us now contemplate some common types of secondary characters in children's novels. Naturally, this cannot be anything but a brief catalogue, since each of these types certainly deserves a special study.

Parents and Parental Figures:
Dispatchers and Donors

The difference between typical combinations of characters in children's fiction and in the mainstream literature is that in children's books secondary characters are indispensable, notably adults, since it is hardly plausible that children can cope entirely on their own (Pippi Longstocking and Momo are clear exceptions, only credible within the fantasy genre). For obvious reasons, parents play a more prominent part in children's fiction than in the mainstream. Children are dependent on their parents, physically and emotionally, and part of growing up involves liberation from parental protection. In adult fiction, this process is usually fulfilled, and other processes have taken over. While quite a number of mainstream novels do indeed focus on generation conflicts, not least various versions of Oedipal situations, in children's novels parents or parental figures are absolutely essential.

In traditional narratives, such as folktales, the role of parents is mostly that of dispatchers and occasionally donors. The dispatcher role means that the parents either directly send the child away from home into the dangerous world (*Little Red Riding Hood; Hansel and Gretel*) or by their absence, often death, expose the child to dangers (*Cinderella*). The parents thus presented cannot be evaluated psychologically, as "bad" or "evil," since they necessarily must have this particular function in the narrative. Sometimes the absent parent may act as a guardian and donor. In the Grimm Brothers' *Cinderella* (or *Aschenputtel*), the dead mother, transformed into a tree, provides her daughter with fancy clothes; in the Perrault version, the mother takes a more tangible form in the fairy godmother. Again, we cannot judge this figure as "good" but merely state that her role in the story is providing the protagonist with magical agents (donor). In children's novels, parents have generally retained the traditional folktale roles, even though the relationships are substantially more psychologically complex. However, the scope and function of parental characters vary between kinds and genres of children's fiction, and it has also changed over time.

In her insightful study of the adolescent novel, *Disturbing the Universe*, Roberta Seelinger Trites (2000, 54–69) proposes three patterns of parental presence in literature: *in parentis, in loco parentis*, and *in logos parentis*. *In parentis*, literally "in possession of parents," is, paradoxically enough, a rare case in children's fiction. To initiate a physical, emotional, and spiritual growth in the character, children's authors have to remove the parents, either permanently, by death, or temporarily, in the form of physical or emotional absence. While in reality parents or guardians are the most important figures in a child's life, in fiction, parents seldom play any significant role in the child character's development. If they do, they have a negative role, denying the child physical and spiritual freedom and thus preventing independence and growth. Most often, parents are merely a nuisance that need to be got rid of: "Father had to go away suddenly on business, and mother had gone away to stay with Granny, who was not very well" (*Five Children and It*, 22). This may seem a strange arrangement in this novel, since the parents have just taken their children to the countryside for vacation; but it has several implications. The children still get all the necessities of life, notably regular meals, because they have servants. However, since they do not feel the same loyalty toward the servants as they would toward their parents, they can make a magical wish so that the servants do not notice any-thing strange going on; they can lie or pretend without feeling guilty about it. On the other hand, "[i]t was very difficult indeed not to tell her [the mother] all about the Psammead at once, because they had got into the habit of telling her everything" (206).

In loco parentis, "instead of parents," describes the most common situation in children's fiction, when a substitute parent is provided for the young character, either because the real parent is permanently removed, or because he or she is insufficient in offering the support and guidance necessary for the child's growth. The substitute figure may be a grandparent or other relative, a foster parent, a teacher or in fact any adult (for instance, the school janitor in *The Planet of Junior Brown*). In fantasy novels, this role is commonly given to a wizard or witch (Wise Old Man/Woman in Jungian terminology): Galdalf in *The Hobbit*, Merriman in *The Dark Is Rising* series, and so on.

Parent substitutes, often a relative or a foster parent, can be kind and well wishing, like Tom Sawyer's Aunt Polly, or wicked, like Aunt Hulda in *Mio, My Son*. They can also be more round and dynamic, like Matthew and Marilla in *Anne of Green Gables* or Maime Trotter in *The Great Gilly Hopkins*. Despite this mimetic-psychological difference, they have the same function in the narrative. In classic books, there is often an elderly female relative who has the role of a fairy godmother and helps the protagonist in difficult situations. Even though a character may have a real mother, another female can be portrayed in the book as a mother substitute, providing food as well as care and love (Mae in *Tuck Everlasting*). Conversely, the use of a parent substitute may make the liberation process less offensive (in the same manner that a wicked stepmother is less offensive than a wicked mother). In *Tom's Midnight Garden*, the protagonist is first removed from his biological parents and provided with substitutes, whereupon he exercises his identity quest. Using psychoanalytical terminology, a substitute parent works as a transitional object to make separation less painful.

The linguistic hybrid *in logos parentis*, which may be roughly translated as "parents made out of words," refers to the cases of young characters inventing a substitute parent in their imagination, not seldom as an imaginary correspondent or confidant. *Daddy-Long-Legs* is the most obvious case, but a number of contemporary novels clearly utilize this pattern—for instance, *Dear Mr. Henshaw* or *Dear Bruce Springsteen* (observe the similarity of titles). In both novels, young protagonists create an image of an ideal parent when their own fathers fail them. Also, Gilly Hopkins creates an ideal mother on the basis of two postcards she has received from Courtney.

If we interpret the magical journey in *Mio, My Son* as the protagonist's wishful fancies, both the benevolent "my father the king" and the evil Sir Kato are his *in logos parentis*.

In *Disturbing the Universe*, Trites makes an interesting observation that protagonists of young adult novels are in greater need of parents than their counterparts in novels for younger children, in which parents are indeed comfortably removed to allow the characters full freedom to explore the world on their own. The adolescent protagonist needs a parent authority at hand to revolt against it. Therefore, *in loco parentis* and *in logos parentis* are a stronger issue in adolescent novels. If anything, this is a good indication of the profound difference between children's and adolescent fiction.

Furthermore, there is a difference in the presentation of parents between various genres. In classic boys' and adventure stories, parents often hinder adventure. They restrict the protagonist's freedom, demand that he come home for meals, have decent clothes, and wash his hands. Aunt Polly in *Tom Sawyer* is a good example. Other adults are seldom models for the male protagonist; rather they are presented as hypocrites who create rules, set limits, and make demands. In this respect, rebellious teenage fiction has inherited the secondary character gallery from boys' books. In classic girls' novels, adults are commonly models and idols. The March girls adore their mother and the absent father. Laura in the Little House series has full trust in her parents and loves them without reservations. The teacher Miss Stacy is the paragon for Anne Shirley. Contemporary psychological novels often depict a harmonious relationship with at least one adult, although not necessarily a parent. In many contemporary children's novels, parents are "an issue": they fail to understand the child's needs, and they are emotionally absent. Examples are too many to enumerate; for instance, most parents in Katherine Paterson's and Patricia MacLachlan's novels are emotionally inadequate. The mother in *Homecoming* literally abandons her children. For a mimetically oriented critic, this may reflect the societal changes and attitudes, the general alienation and despair of our times. I have heard critics outside Sweden expressing concern over the negative portraits of parents in contemporary Swedish children's novels, wondering whether Swedish parents are indeed that bad. From the structural and narrative points of view, emotionally absent parents are just as fundamental as physically absent parents in fairy tales and classic children's stories.

Since the 1960s, a large number of children's books from all over the world portray single parents, both mothers and, more rarely, fathers. An absent, divorced, or missing parent is obviously a suitable "issue" for a children's book, in which it can be treated mechanically or in a more subtle way.

Many contemporary novels also have positive and ambivalent portraits of parents. Ronia's father in *Ronia the Robber's Daughter* loves her more than anything in the world, but his love is selfish and smothering, and becomes the source of the central conflict in the novel. Rusty's mother in *Back Home* is generally kind, yet she fails to assist her daughter in readjusting to her life in England. Leslie's parents in *Bridge to Terabithia* may appear caring and loving; they have provided their daughter with excessive intellectual stimulus and change their lifestyle for her sake, so that she can grow up in a natural and healthy environment. On closer examination, however, they have left Leslie just as much starving for human warmth as Jess's more obviously negligent parents. Ultimately, their decision to move to the countryside leads to Leslie's tragic death. Chris's parents in *Johnny My Friend* are seemingly supportive: they invite Johnny to share meals with the family and buy him new shoes, but they do not interfere when they clearly see that Johnny is being abused, physically and possibly sexually. The fact that Johnny has no parents presents Chris in a favorable light: he has two loving and caring parents; however, they are emotionally absent, just as so many other parents in children's books. One of the recent examples of utter ambiguity in portrayal of parents is to be found in the *His Dark Materials* trilogy. Not only does Lyra discover to her dismay that the beautiful but obviously evil woman is her mother. The father's moral qualities are dubious, and the young protagonist is torn between loyalties, unable to make an adequate judgement or to detach herself from either parent. The child's inherent trust in and dependence on her parents is brought to the extreme. Significantly, Will, the coprotagonist of the trilogy, is obliged to take care of his sick mother.

Naturally, the role of a parental figure depends heavily on the protagonist's gender. The relationships between mother and son (*Elvis and His Secret*), mother and daughter (*Back Home*), father and son (*Dear Mr. Henshaw*), and father and daughter (*Ronia the Robber's Daughter*) are profoundly different (on mother–daughter relationships, see Trites 1997, chap. 7; Crew 2000).

To evaluate the depiction of parents in children's novels, we must take into consideration their function in the narrative. The infantile and demanding mother in *Elvis and His Secret* has often been referred to as an extremely negative parental image. However, this is only true in a strictly mimetic reading. Since the novel consistently uses Elvis as the focalizing character, the mother is not presented objectively, but through the eyes and mind of a very young child, who feels neglected and oppressed. What his mother really might be like is beyond the reader's comprehension, and more or less irrelevant, since she is only interesting for us in her relationship with the protagonist. From the structural and psychoanalytical viewpoint, Elvis's mother has the function of the wicked stepmother of the folktale—in itself a late euphemism of a biological mother. Her neglect and emotional coldness is a prerequisite for the young boy's maturation (on the function of fairy-tale mothers, see Birkhäuser-Oeri 1988; Lundell 1990). In *Mio, My Son*, a similar role is given to the foster mother, which is naturally less offensive and disturbing than the biological mother in *Elvis*. However, the wicked (step)mothers of children's fiction still have the traditional function of dispatcher and not of the antagonist, since their "wickedness" becomes the driving force behind the child's maturation. The folktale stereotype of a wicked stepmother is counterbalanced in contemporary children's novels by portraits of nice stepmothers, such as Sarah in *Sarah, Plain and Tall*. This is one of many recent children's books all over the world in which children try to provide a wife for their divorced or widowed fathers. Nice stepparents in contemporary fiction frequently have the function of positive substitute parents.

Grandparents often have an important role in children's fiction, especially when the parents fail to play their parts, either because they are dead (*Heidi*), have abandoned the children (*Homecoming*), or are emotionally detached (*Elvis and His Secret*). In the *Elvis* books, the two pairs of grandparents illustrate two radically different worldviews, which is perhaps harder for the child to accept in parents. In addition, grandparents are used to introduce death. It is more natural and less frightening when an old person dies, and a child may accept this easier than a parent's death. Grandparents are obviously more central in children's fiction than in the mainstream. Proust creates a vivid portrait of a grandmother, but only in the part of his novel devoted to the protagonist/narrator's childhood.

Teachers are habitually ridiculous in boys' books, just like all other adults, while in girls' books there is commonly one special female teacher who becomes the heroine's model. Contemporary children's novels have inherited both patterns. For instance, in *Bridge to Terabithia*, Jess has a very special relationship with his music teacher. Chris's teacher in *Johnny My Friend* turns out to be a real monster, presumably a criminal. The rest of the teachers are presented in a not too flattering manner, either: "ancient, mouldy gents with walking sticks and ear trumpets and gravely coughs and other aches and pains, each with one and a half feet in the grave" (Pohl 1985, 9f.). Many children's books portray the first day of school (alternatively, the first time in a new school), and usually there is at least one stupid teacher, often the principal, and at least one nice. The title character of the Ramona series meets a new teacher in every sequel, and most of them are kind and supportive on closer examination.

I have already mentioned the servant figure in classic children's novels. In Edith Nesbit's books, servants merely provide the basic necessities for the children, while their parents are comfortably removed. However, in *The Secret Garden*, servants, especially the young maid Martha and her mother, play an important role in the protagonist's development. Many classic American children's novels have the figure of a black Mammy, which today's critics find controversial. She stands closest to the child during early childhood, often much closer than the biological mother, while later on the child learns to despise her because of her race.

Peers: Helpers and Quest Objects

Although many classic and contemporary children's authors choose to portray a single child, accentuating the protagonist's loneliness and isolation, just as many supply the protagonist with siblings in a variety of roles. An older sibling may serve as a model, even a parent substitute, as in *The Brothers Lionheart*. A younger sibling may be the object of the protagonist's love and care, occasionally even the quest object. However, just as often siblings are "an issue," especially well-behaved siblings to a naughty boy, like Tom Sawyer. Ramona feels inferior because her sister can do all the things she cannot yet do herself. Jess in *Bridge to Terabithia* has four sisters, yet he feels lonely and misunderstood by his family. However, toward the end of the novel he develops a truly warm relationship with his little sister Maybelle. Stepsiblings and foster siblings are a type of relationship that has become more usual in real life, and many writers describe the advantages and the problems. Part of Gilly Hopkins's maturation involves acceptance of her retarded foster brother.

However, as noted before, it is common in contemporary books that the protagonist is the only child, which creates an additional sense of loneliness and abandonment. Then friends acquire a significant position. Friends may be helpers, and they may also be quest objects, when friendship is sought and gained. Friendship is depicted differently in boys' and girls' fiction. A boy has many friends, who build a gang. Tom Sawyer's very best friend is Huck Finn, but he also has Joe Harper. Friendship with Huck is prohibited and therefore especially attractive. Male friends in adventure novels have the traditional helper function from fairy tales. Girls, on the other hand, are often described as having a relationship in pairs, a "bosom friend"—for instance, Anne and Diana in *Anne of Green Gables*. Such a friendship can have a romantic undertone. Since the female protagonist's plot seldom involves external quest, the helper role of her best friend may feel less prominent. Male friendship rarely has romantic or erotic connotations, except in young adult fiction—for example, in *Dance on My Grave*, in which Barry is unquestionably the "quest object" for Hal.

Some contemporary books portray cross-gender friendship; according to some investigations, this happens more frequently in books than in reality at the age protagonists are described. Cross-gender friendship in children's fiction has its origin in the hero–princess relationship in folktale: the hero must save and protect the princess; they have nonequal, subject–object positions. However, in contemporary novels, a friend of the opposite gender can also fill the gap left by the "absent" parent. Such a friend—for instance, Leslie in *Bridge to Terabithia*—has the function of a dispatcher rather than a helper (even in fairy tales, the donor/helper/dispatcher functions are not seldom combined in one actor).

The Antagonist

As pointed out before, antagonists are not absolutely indispensable in children's novels; yet most classic writers definitely choose plots involving an antagonist and thus a person-against-person conflict, the simplest and most clear-cut type of conflict in a narrative. Antagonists are easiest to define in certain genres, such as fantasy, adventure, and the crime novel. Yet, most time-shift fantasies lack antagonists, and adventure can be constructed without an antagonist—for instance, a search for treasure. In heroic fantasy, we will most certainly find an antagonist (Sauron in *Lord of the Rings*; Arawn in the Prydain Chronicles; the White Witch in *The Lion, the Witch and the Wardrobe*), and a villain adds to the thrill of adventure, such as that in *Treasure Island* or *Tom Sawyer*.

Typically, most antagonists in fantasy and adventure novels for children are adults. On the symbolic level, the protagonist meets the adult world and proves to be stronger, smarter, and more virtuous than his adversary (and than other adults). There can also be an additional villain, who is a child. For instance, Voldemort is Harry Potter's primary antagonist in his global struggle against evil, but on a more everyday scale, his enemy is Draco Malfoy, a peer. The gender pattern in the relationship between protagonist and his enemy is interesting from the psychological point of view. Do protagonists meet evil in the form of their own or the opposite gender, and what is the implication? Both Freudian and Jungian critics have interesting arguments around these questions (see Veglahn 1987; Nikolajeva 1996, 76–79). The Harry Potter novels deviate from the common pattern identified by scholars, as Harry's antagonist is of the same gender.

In many contemporary fantasy novels, good and evil become ambivalent. For instance, is Malebron in *Elidor* a helper or an antagonist? He seems to be on the good side, but he does not assist the children in their quest; on the contrary, he tricks them into Elidor's dangerous games of power. I have already pointed out the ambivalent roles of Mrs. Coulter and Lord Asriel in *His Dark Materials*. Furthermore, we can sometimes see a reversal of roles: in *Darkangel*, the villain turns out to be a victim.

Contemporary psychological novels seldom contain any pronounced antagonists; the characters are involved in person-against-self conflicts. These are naturally more complex than face-to-face combats in fantasy. I have already mentioned *The Little Mermaid*, which in the Disney version acquires an antagonist to clarify the plot. Similarly, a Russian retelling of *Pinocchio* develops the peripheral figure of the puppeteer in Collodi's novel, giving him the role of the protagonist's pursuer and enemy. An inner quest is transformed into an external one. Such changes point at the adult storytellers' mistrust in young readers, as a plot without a recognizable antagonist apparently is believed to be insufficiently appealing.

Deus ex machina

The last type, which does not appear in fairy tales and is therefore not featured among Propp's character gallery, is the character, most likely an adult, who sets things right. It can be a missing parent who suddenly turns up with a huge amount of money, a forgotten distant relative who bequeaths the protagonist his title and estate, or merely an authoritative adult who neatly disentangles the problems into which the characters have got themselves. The *deus ex machina* figure was quite common in traditional children's literature; today's demands for credibility have almost eliminated this type, at least in quality fiction. However, this figure is not uncommon in fantasy novels, in which a powerful magician appears in the end to take over the rule of the world, which young protagonists cannot manage on their own. We see such an authority figure step forward in, for instance, *The Tale of Time City*. The appearance of a *deus ex machina* usually disempowers the child protagonists, since whatever problems they might encounter, the adult figure will take care of them. Contemporary psychological novels prefer to allow characters to solve their problems unaided or otherwise leave them unsolved.

We can partially ascribe the *deus ex machina* role to Christopher Robin, to whom the other characters turn for help and advice in all their predicaments. Since in a more sophisticated interpretation the toys represent the inner qualities of Christopher Robin in the frame, the Christopher Robin of the embedded narrative has the power position normally reserved to adults; the child projects himself into a godlike figure with unlimited power and wisdom.

Nonhuman Characters

In his chapter on characters in fiction, E. M. Forster (1927) claims that "actors in a story are usually human" and continues, "Other animals have been introduced, but with limited success, for we know too little so far about their psychology" (43). Forster seems to have overlooked the possibility of using animals, supernatural creatures, and inanimate objects as masks for human beings—a strategy widely employed by children's fiction. In fact, children's novels and especially picturebooks abound in clothed and humanized animals, living toys, supernatural creatures (witches, ghosts), as well as personified objects and machines, such as cars or trains. Some scholars of children's literature prefer to view such books as separate genres. However, let us not be deceived by the superficial form. Animals, toys, baby witches, and animated objects are always disguises for a child. They behave like children and have similar problems, even when they are depicted in seemingly natural surroundings—for instance, *Bambi*, a coming-of-age story that includes the indispensable elements of death and sexuality. We see the disguise especially vividly as fairy-tale conventions enable authors to describe unnatural communities of animals—for instance, making a pig and a spider best friends, or bringing together Rat, Mole, Toad and Badger, Toad and Frog, Bear and Tiger. To represent characters as animals or toys is a way to create distance, to adjust the plot to what the author believes is familiar for child readers. This reflects a stereotypical and obsolete attitude to children as not fully human, at least not fully developed as human beings (see Schwarcz 1991, 9). Fables, which represent human faults in animal figures, were considered suitable for children during certain periods. Animals are seldom portrayed as protagonists in books for teenagers or in mainstream literature, outside allegory, such as *Watership Down*, or satire, such as *Animal Farm*.

The depiction of a character as an animal (or toy or inanimate object) allows the writer to eliminate or circumvent several important issues that are otherwise essential in our assessment of character: that of age, gender, and social status. For instance, the protagonists of *The Mouse and His Child* can spend years at the bottom of a pond, without having to eat or growing any older. Pinocchio can endure more than a human child would. As shown earlier, the characters of *The Wind in the Willows* are referred to as male, but their age and social status are unclear. They behave like small children but live on their own; the source of their living (e.g., food) is never mentioned. We may say that these characters represent very young children, at the stage where such issues are more or less irrelevant (see my discussion of animal and toy stories as pastoral, Nikolajeva 2000, 47–55). Generally, in an ani-

mal character, one specific trait can be amplified—for instance, Curious
George's "monkeyhood." Animal characters are more easily accepted as flat
and static.

Since I am more interested in the character's function than in its external form, I make no difference among texts involving animals, toys, minia-
ture people, supernatural creatures, or animated objects, since all these figures can have one of the two roles in a narrative. They can be either the
subject of the story—that is, the protagonist—or the object—that is, the
protagonist's friend, helper, or, occasionally, antagonist. This chapter is,
however, devoted to supporting characters, and I will now take a brief look
at some functions that nonhuman characters can have in children's fiction
(see also Blount 1974; Kuznets 1994; Nikolajeva and Scott 2001, 88–96).

Wonderful pets or animated toys who can communicate with the child
protagonist are transformations of a magical animal-helper in folktales. In
using nonhuman beings as supporting characters in children's novels, three
strategies can be employed. First, the animal or toy can perform the role of
a substitute parent. For instance, *Indian in the Cupboard* provides the child
character with a father figure. Anthony Browne's picturebook *Gorilla* is
another straightforward example. The psychological implication is naturally slightly different depending on whether the protagonist is a boy or a
girl. In Edith Nesbit's fantasy novels, we find a number of magical creatures
who have the function of a guide and adviser, bringing excitement and
adventure into the lives of the protagonists: the Psammead, the Phoenix,
and the Mouldiwarp. On the other hand, an intelligent animal or an animated toy can allow the protagonist to perform the role of a parent, being
cleverer, stronger, showing care and concern. Paddington the bear has primarily this function. The most common role is playmate on more or less
equal terms.

The only difference in using a nonhuman being for depicting a peer relationship is circumventing some mimetic conventions. A toy or a pet can
stay in the same house as the protagonist, including sharing a bed in a cross-
gender relationship, which would certainly be unacceptable if a human
friend were portrayed. A nonhuman companion has no social obligations
(in the first place, has no parents) and can be loyal toward the protagonist
without reservations. The function of animals in horse and pony novels is
that of a best friend and often of a "transitional object" for a young girl heading toward a real sexual relationship. Dorothy's three companions in *The
Wizard of Oz* illustrate, in a slightly transformed manner, the three transformations of a nonhuman supporting character: a rag doll, a machine, and
an animal. In a science fiction fairy tale, *Star Wars*, we find similar combi-

nations of companions: on the one hand, mechanical friends R2D2 and C-3PO; on the other hand, friendly monsters Chewbacca and Jar-Jar Binks.

Very often, however, the role of the nonhuman beings is more ambivalent than the three outlined possibilities. Indeed, Dorothy's three companions are superficially adults—that is, acting as parent substitutes. On closer examination, they are all inferior to Dorothy, since she possesses the personality traits they are seeking: she is smart, brave, and kind-hearted. Furthermore, reading the novel as a psychological quest, the three creatures are projections of Dorothy's inner qualities, which she discovers during her sojourn in the land of Oz. Similarly, Karlson-on-the-roof, an ingenious human–machine hybrid, has the external form of an adult, and he is superior to Midge because he can fly. On the other hand, Karlson is definitely less mature than Midge, and in the relationship between the two, Midge is the strongest. On a deeper psychological level, the protagonist transfers his own faults and shortcomings onto his imaginary companion: greed, hot temper, sibling jealousy, and so on.

Note

1. The French word *ficelle* refers to the string used by a puppeteer to steer the puppets.

CHAPTER SEVEN

$\sim$

Complexity and Development

Among the foremost conditions that classic poetics (e.g., Aristotle or Lessing) put on literary characters, we find consistency and unity. Consistency implies that a literary character cannot have contradictory traits. Neither can characters behave in a manner incompatible with what has already been revealed about them, in description, actions, or the narrator's comments. Normally we place a higher demand for consistency on literary characters than on real people. Since children's literature is generally didactic, we place still higher demands for consistency on children's literature characters. Characters must be understood from the text alone; therefore, any radical deviation in the way a character is presented will be perceived by readers as an artistic flaw.

Unity presupposes the character to be an artistic whole that is appearing to the readers as a single, complete, and structured individual, which is naturally entirely different from real people. It also implies that none of the character's traits revealed to us are accidental, that they are all indispensable for our understanding of the character.

Contemporary poetics has deviated significantly from these demands, following the evolution of narrative prose in the twentieth century. However, they are a good starting point for discussing characters in terms of their complexity and ability to change. Yet another connected question is whether characters are to be treated as typical or individual (see Scholes and Kellogg 1966, 204–6). Depending on the approach, we will perceive the complexity and dynamism of characters in different lights. If we apply Perry Nodelman's (1985a) concepts of "sameness" or variation on the same theme to character rather than plot, as he does himself, children's fiction should operate with a more or less fixed gallery of types, similar to the gallery of the fairy-tale figures. We do, indeed, find a number of recurrent types in children's novels, such as the jealous sibling, the bright, but cruel classmate, the grim teacher, the nice teacher, and so on. These are normally called stock characters. However, the characters we remember and love are indeed unique and nonrepeatable: Alice, Jo March, Huck Finn, Anne Shirley, Peter Pan, Pooh, Pippi Longstocking, Taran the Assistant Pigkeeper, or the Cat in the Hat. They may have some typical traits, familiar from other characters, but it is the unique combination of traits that makes them immortal and the books "classic." In fact, attempts at imitations of classic characters usually fail, such as *More Alice* or *The Willows in Winter*.

Static and Dynamic, Flat and Round

In assessing character complexity and development, we can start by applying two binarities used in narrative theory. The concept of flat versus round character goes back to E. M. Forster and his *Aspects of the Novel*. The pair static/dynamic was added later and has been widely applied in character analysis. Both pairs have been introduced in children's literature criticism—for instance, in Joanne Golden's (1990) *The Narrative Symbol in Childhood Literature*. Like all binarities, these should be perceived as two extremes of a broad continuum (Rimmon-Kenan 1983, 40–42; Golden 1990, 36). Golden speaks quite correctly about flat orientation or dynamic orientation rather than about characters who are flat or dynamic (41–52). The concepts flat/round and static/dynamic are abstractions, while every actual literary character is more complex than merely flat or merely round. Furthermore, the concepts demonstrate the nonmimetic approach to characters. The fact that the author chooses to emphasize one single trait in a character does not mean that the character reflects a real person with only one trait, which by experience we know is impossible. There are no two-dimensional people in the real world; all people have a body, a head and face, limbs, and so on, even though the narrative does not mention any of these. Real people have multiple personal traits. Real people are generally more complex than any of the round, dynamic literary characters. The author decides to present the characters as flat or round. Consequently, literary characters are, as a rule, easier for us to understand and relate to; we can interpret their motivations more easily. The creation of a character approximating a real person in complexity and unpredictability is a matter of the writers' skills, and in many cases it is not the writers' intention. In fact, in most children's novels, characters are intentionally less complex than real people.

The terms static/dynamic and flat/round are quite self-explanatory. Dynamic characters change throughout the story, while static characters do not. Both main and secondary characters can be dynamic or static. Tom Sawyer does not change, since there is not much room for him to do so. First, the duration of the story is too short for a radical change. Second, it is not part of the writer's intention. The book ends by stating that since this is a story of a young boy it must stop; otherwise, it becomes a story of a man. Changes imply, among other things, growth and maturation. The story about Anne of Green Gables takes several years, and Anne does not only grow up but changes inside. This is typical of girls' fiction. As some critics point out (Scholes and Kellogg 1966, 168), character development can be of two kinds, chronological (changes due to the flow of time) and ethical (changes in the character's moral and ethical qualities). In Anne, we note both aspects. Golden (1990, 44) claims that characters in realistic fiction, unlike fantasy, are dynamic in chronological rather than ethical terms. Since I do not make any generic distinction between fantasy and realism, I find this observation irrelevant. Moreover, there are many examples of ethical changes of characters in realistic modes, such as Mary Lennox in *The Secret Garden*.

Old didactic children's fiction tends to have static characters. Since the foremost goal of the contemporary psychological children's novel is to depict inner growth, such novels presuppose at least one dynamic character, whom we usually perceive as the protagonist. Formulaic fiction commonly contains static characters. But even quality fiction may have static characters, and they are in no way a sign of lower artistic merit. Such lovable and popular figures of children's fiction as Dorothy in *The Wizard of Oz* or Winnie-the-Pooh are unquestionably static.

Flat characters are by definition two-dimensional and colorless. They are not fully developed, which once again does not imply an artistic flaw. Flat characters are usually depicted as having one typical trait, or none at all. They can, for instance, be ascribed features such as "good" or "evil." Their actions are easily predicted. Characters in formulaic fiction are often flat. Yet characters representing parts of a collective protagonist can also be flat. Piglet is scared and cautious, Tigger is bouncy, Eeyore is a thinker, Rabbit is bossy, and Kanga is a good mother and housewife. Most secondary characters in Moomin books are flat: Hemulen is a bore; Muskrat, a hypochondriac; Snork, rational; Snork Maiden, vain; and Fillyjonk, mean and pedantic. Meeting characters in a Moomin sequel, we already know what to expect of them. Flat characters can rarely surprise us.

By contrast, round ("multidimensional") characters possess a number of traits, both positive and negative; they are fully developed; we really get to know them well as the story progresses, but we cannot predict their behavior. The various traits are revealed to us in different ways—for instance, through repetition, similarity, contrast, and so on.

Protagonists are not necessarily round characters, and secondary characters need not be flat (although that is frequently so). Some secondary characters of *Tom Sawyer* or *Treasure Island* are more round than the rather flat protagonists. Neither are protagonists always dynamic. Round characters can be both dynamic and static. Alice, an extremely multidimensional character with many exciting traits, is not allowed to go through a change within the frame of her adventures (other than superficial, of course, when she constantly grows and shrinks). Flat characters who possess but few traits have little chance to be dynamic. If a flat character suddenly changes from evil to good, it is not very plausible (we might call it a "miraculous" conversion or metamorphosis). A radical change is more convincing in a round character, who from the beginning possesses both good and bad traits. Of the four children in *The Lion, the Witch and the Wardrobe*, only Edmund is both round and dynamic. His feelings are contradictory. He knows that he is behaving wrongly, but continues anyway. He is, of course, under a spell, but all the time he knows that he is doing wrong. On seeing the White Witch turn animals into stone, he feels the first signs of remorse. Edmund's trial and transformation are thus the most essential events of the book.

There are, however, certain genres and kinds of children's fiction that presuppose a total change of a flat character to the other extreme, most often from "evil" to "good," from "lazy" to "diligent," and so on. Many nineteenth-century didactic children's books describe such a change. Formulaic fiction also sometimes provides this pattern. The difference between character development in children's fiction and in the mainstream depends on the dynamics of childhood itself. A child character is still moldable, so that the depicted evolution is never fully accomplished. A further development may be hinted at—for instance, by means of an open ending. There are also certain pedagogical criteria governing character evolution in children's fiction. Normally, a child character cannot develop into a villain or a morally depraved person (which is not unusual in general fiction), since it is believed that young readers will have problems detaching themselves from such a character.

There is no quality value in the notions of flat or round, dynamic or static character (cf. Rimmon-Kenan's [1983] critique of Forster's terms, 40f.). A flat character is not necessarily artistically "worse" than a round one; it is merely a matter of constructing characters and giving them a function in the plot. As Scholes and Kellogg (1966) demonstrate, Achilles in *The Illiad* is characterized through one single trait, wrath, which does not make him a failed character (161f.), and "Bloom is not a 'better' characterization than his Homeric prototype. Only a different kind" (165). Such a vivid and charming character as the Little Prince is both flat and static.

In the following subsections, I shall illustrate the flat/round and static/dynamic orientation in characterization with four well-known female characters.

Katy: Flat and Static

Twelve-year-old Katy Carr, the protagonist of *What Katy Did,* is a charming but hardly complex character. Her primary feature is being naughty, by accident or on purpose. "Katy tore her dresses every day, hated sewing, and didn't care a button about being 'good'" (9). The main devices used to reveal the character are the narrator's comments and judgments, such as:

> She was a dear, loving child, for all her careless habits, and made bushels of good resolutions every week of her life, only unluckily she never kept any of them. She had fits of responsibility about the other children, and longed to set them a good example, but when the chance came, she usually forgot to do so. (14)

This exhaustive presentation of the character at the beginning of the novel is then illustrated by all kinds of pranks and other examples of "what Katy did." In fact, Katy cherishes grand plans and very seldom does anything at all. The everyday events do not add much to characterization, and Katy does not change either. If we expect her to change, we will be disappointed. She is constantly late, loses her things, gets into mischief, and has recurrent fits of bad temper, but she is also kind-hearted and ready to admit her faults. After meeting her disabled cousin Helen, she decides to become a model of virtue, but fortunately for the reader, her attempts fail, so Katy continues being herself. She does learn to be patient and humble during her prolonged illness, but these qualities do not in any way contradict her initial traits. She takes on some household responsibilities when her Aunt dies; yet she is in a way her old mischievous self as she makes the servants cook exotic meals or forces the whole family go on a healthy diet. Even though the narrator states, "Month by month she learned how to manage a little better, and a little better still" (159), characterization never goes beyond these statements—we do not actually see Katy perform, nor do we learn how she feels about her performance. When we suddenly meet Katy after a gap of two years, the only change we notice is that she is now running the house firmly, from her wheelchair upstairs, with the rest of the family coming up to consult her about every trifle. Katy's transformation from a little good-for-nothing into a respectable young lady is thus declared but not shown; therefore, we can hardly speak of character development in the true sense of the word. In fact, we are merely informed about a transition from one static condition into another. As mentioned earlier, static and flat character orientation does not imply inferior literary quality. *What Katy Did* has been popular ever since its publication, but certainly not due to its deep characterization.

Heidi: Flat yet Dynamic

Heidi is one of the favorite characters of classic children's fiction, whose charm lies in her innocence, her inherent goodness and capacity to bring joy and salvation to everyone around her. The character is flat, since the only prominent feature she possesses is her unlimited virtue. Even though the plot presupposes some trials, Heidi never shows any unpleasant traits, staying nice, patient, and cheerful throughout the novel. As pointed out previously, flat characters have little room for evolution. Indeed, Heidi is so perfect that you would not expect any change in her (a change from good to depraved would be highly unlikely in a children's book, especially one written in 1880). Yet, on closer examination, Heidi does go through a profound change that brings her as far away from her initial state as possible.

The book starts with the archetypal pattern of myth, fairy tale, and children's literature, the protagonist's physical and emotional dislocation, as the five-year-old orphan Heidi is sent to stay with her grandfather. This is, however, not a Cinderella-like exile, connected with humiliation, in which a formerly uplifted protagonist is deprived of her privileges. In fact, we do not know much about Heidi's life prior to her arrival at Alm-Uncle's mountain hut, other than what we learn from her aunt's account to a curious neighbor: that Heidi's mother died when she was one year old and that she has since then been in the care first of her grandmother and later of another old woman, "shut up within four walls" (29). From this background we cannot decide whether Heidi's transition is a degradation or an ascent; however, the mountain symbolism rather suggests the latter. More importantly, however, one of the initial scenes in which Heidi takes off her clothes and shoes and enjoys the feeling of mountain air and sun on her bare legs and arms symbolizes liberation from civilization ("able now to move at her ease"; 17) and unity with nature, the discarding of a tangible, protective, but confining border between Self and the world (cf. Scott 1992). "Heidi and the goats went skipping and jumping joyfully" (19)—she becomes literally part of nature, merging into it as layer by layer she strips off her restrictive clothes.

This liberation process is conscious on Heidi's part, as she says that she will not need her clothes anymore because she wants "to go about like the goats with their thin light legs" (22).

Furthermore, Heidi not only immediately adapts to the new situation but enjoys it immensely and manages at once to win her hermitic grandfather's heart. She also makes friends with Peter the goatherd, his mother, and his blind grandmother. She disseminates joy, love, kindness, and generosity around her. In Frankfurt, she makes the manservant Sebastian her ally, the tutor is prepared to put up with her mischief, and Herr Sesemann takes her part against the discontented housekeeper. Finally, she contributes to the miraculous healing of the wheelchair-bound Clara, brings consolation to the grief-stricken doctor, and not least brings her grandfather back to Christian faith and society.

In quite a number of children's books, conquering territory (including captivating the foster parents, gaining the approval of the neighbors, and acquiring friends) proves sufficient to constitute the plot—for instance, in *Anne of Green Gables*. Spyri builds her plot around a conflict that is very easy to reduce to a simple juxtaposition between the nature of the mountains and the civilization of the city. Indeed, this is the most obvious way to read the novel. Heidi is a "natural" child, simple—although far from simple-minded—naive, innocent, with a keen eye and healthy spirit. Sent away to a big city, she withers like a bird in a cage but has enough of her will not only to come back to the mountains but to redeem her little rich foster sister, demonstrating that the natural way of life, healthy peasant food (goat's milk, bread, and cheese), fresh air, and positive attitudes are superior to the dubious comforts of urban life. However, the evolution imposed on Heidi during her sojourn in Frankfurt is far too profound for her to be able to regress to her natural state as painlessly as the novel seems to suggest. In doing so, Heidi loses the "natural" ways and, among other things, must learn to read.

The question of formal education is first brought about in connection with Peter the goatherd, who in winter must "turn to his pen and pencil" (43), which he obviously dislikes. Neither does the grandfather see any value in education. While Heidi learns "all kinds of useful things from her grandfather" (53), he promptly rejects the schoolmaster's appeal to send Heidi to school. To the pastor he says, "I am going to let her grow up and be happy among the goats and birds; with them she is safe, and will learn nothing evil" (55). At this point of the novel, the reader will certainly have formed an image of the grandfather as a kind and good person, contrary to his bad reputation among the villagers. He has been exceedingly kind to Heidi, he has been nice to Peter, and he has without hesitation made the necessary repairs on grandmother's hut at Heidi's request. Grandfather's statement that Heidi will learn "nothing evil" in the mountains exposes the reader to an ethical dilemma. We are prepared to support grandfather's opinion, and we definitely sympathize with Heidi's love of nature. Consequently, any attempt to take her away from her Arcadia is perceived by the reader as a crude violation. On the other hand, as a feminist critic might point out, grandfather employs his patriarchal power to keep Heidi in ignorance and under his oppression. The pastor represents civilization, culture, learning, which the grandfather denies Heidi, apparently on the basis of his experience of human vice in the big world— let us remember his earlier statement: "people who live down below in the villages . . . go huddling and gossiping together, and encourage one another in evil talking and deeds" (39).

The further development toward civilization follows during Heidi's forced stay in Frankfurt. The housekeeper finds Heidi's natural ways abhorrent and immediately sets about to tame her. She is also terrified at the very idea of Heidi not being able to read. However, this is far from a feminist view of education as a road to independence; on the contrary, literacy is for Fräulein Rottenmeier an instrument for learning obedience and good Christian morals. The tutor fails to teach Heidi to read, but a miraculous transition is brought about by Grandmamma Sesemann, who thus introduces Heidi to scholarly knowledge. It may also be of interest to note Clara's attitude to education: she seems to have never questioned what the adults around her have indoctrinated her to believe: "of course you must learn to read, everybody must" (67). Later, Heidi will use exactly the same argument in her entreaty to Peter: "You must learn how to read . . . you must learn at once" (179f.). Having herself been coerced into learning, Heidi is now prepared to impose it on others.

The consequences of Heidi's conversion are far-reaching. Grandfather's return to human community, under Heidi's pressure and guidance, results in the opposite of what has been Heidi's desire and what has brought her back from Frankfurt. Instead of living the simple and natural life in the mountain hut, grandfather moves down into the village and becomes a respectable member of the community he has despised for so long, while Heidi goes to school and is integrated into the community as well. Interpreting the literal movement downhill metaphorically, we cannot but view it as a moral and spiritual degeneration.

Several details mark the transition from nature to culture, which can easily be overlooked. The first and perhaps most obvious is Grandfather's visit to church the day after Heidi has read the story of the prodigal son to him. For this occasion, Grandfather dresses up in Sunday clothes and forces Heidi to put on her pretty Frankfurt frock—which she promptly took off as inappropriate when approaching the hut, saying, "I would rather go home to grandfather as I am" (132). The phrase "as I am" conveys Heidi's last desperate—and perhaps subconscious—attempt to recover the natural self she has irreparably lost in Frankfurt. This scene, echoing and reversing the undressing episode in the beginning of the novel, is deeply symbolic. Once again clothes function as a clearly delineated boundary between nature and culture.

Furthermore, Heidi happily trades the sweet-smelling hay mattress she enjoyed so much during her first years in the mountains for a proper bed "with bedding of all kinds and . . . beautiful new white coverlid[s]" (205). Insignificant as these details may seem, they are tokens of the irreversible change in Heidi, which are reinforced by the fact that she is now materially well-off and provided for. Money, an unmistakable sign of civilization, has ruthlessly destroyed Heidi's initial innocence. While her previous affinity with Peter's blind grandmother was based on her oral stories, involving free imagination and spontaneity, after her return from Frankfurt Heidi reads the hymns from the prayer book—that is, fixed texts, conveying the morals of the existing order, among other things humility, patience, obedience, and other Christian, patriarchal virtues.

The novel cannot be brought to a satisfactory closure under its initial premises; that is, although Heidi's natural state is throughout the novel presented as preferable to the villagers' and the townspeople's corrupt ways, she cannot be allowed to be brought back to nature. A compromise is inevitable. The title of chapter 11, "Heidi Gains in One Way and Loses in Another," although referring to something else, is an excellent description of this compromise. While a less sophisticated reader may find the compromise quite satisfactory ("a happy ending"), it reveals the eternal dilemma of children's fiction, since the child cannot be allowed to retain her natural, innocent state, unless she dies young, before socialization becomes unavoidable. The incompatible desires of the author—to allow the child to keep her natural innocence and at the same time be forced into civilization—must succumb to societal expectations.

In a way, Heidi may seem a static character. In fact, although the flow of time is evident in the novel, Heidi does not seem to age, physically or mentally, although by end of the novel she must be at least nine or ten. However, the dynamism of this character lies on a deeper level, in her "corruption" and irreversible change from nature to culture. The dynamism is thus ethical rather than chronological.

Pippi: Round but Static

Pippi Longstocking is a more complex character than Katy or Heidi, and the author uses a variety of narrative devices to reveal her character. We first learn that Pippi is nine years old and that she does not have a mother or a father. Already the following passage is ambivalent: "that was of course very nice because there was no one to tell her to go to bed just when she was having the most fun" (11). Is this Pippi's opinion or an extradiegetic narrator's? If we are never allowed to enter Pippi's mind and only external characterization devices are used, the character can never become truly round.

The fact that Pippi lives in an "old house" in an "old overgrown garden" characterizes her indirectly, through the setting. The opening itself, "Way out at the end of a tiny little town," alludes to fairy tales and also the famous Swedish picturebook *The Tale of the Little, Little Old Woman*, by Elsa Beskow, which encourages us to view Pippi as a fairy-tale figure. We then learn that Pippi once had a mother and a father. Neither fact is very reliable. In the mother, who is up in Heaven, we recognize the convention from early sentimental children's books, while the story of the father who disappears in a storm is reminiscent of a sailor's yarn. When we get to know Pippi better, we can suspect that the story of the father is just one of her many tall tales (even though he does make a physical appearance in the end). In *Pippi Goes on Board*, we read, "She really believed it when she said her father was a cannibal king" (10). Pippi's ontological status is therefore different from that of Katy or Heidi, who must be provided with a background to be plausible.

The plausibility of Pippi's background—that is, her life before she came to live in Villa Villekulla—depends on the reader's judgment of the narrator's reliability. We do not believe Pippi's own tall tales about her experiences in Egypt, Argentina, and Congo, but can we believe the narrator? The first evaluation of Pippi comes from one of the sailors on her father's ship: "A remarkable child" (13). The narrator hurries to confirm this: "he was right. Pippi was indeed a remarkable child" (13), adding that she was extremely strong. We learn that Pippi "had always longed for a horse" (14), which many young readers will empathize with, recognizing their own longing for a pet. The first pages of the novel are thus devoted to a detailed presentation of Pippi, her background, and her most important inner traits.

However, the author waits for quite a while before giving us a description of Pippi's looks, which we receive through Tommy and Annika. The description is, once again, preceded by the statement that she was "the most remarkable girl" they had ever seen (15). The repetition of the word *remarkable* is a powerful device for establishing Pippi's constant epithet. The external description is long and detailed:

> Her hair the color of a carrot, was braided in two tight braids that stuck right
> out. Her nose was the shape of a very small potato and was dotted all over
> with freckles. It must be admitted that the mouth under this nose was a very
> wide one, with strong white teeth. . . . On her long thin legs she wore a pair
> of long stockings, one brown and the other black, and she had on a pair of
> black shoes that were exactly twice as long as her feet. (16)

This description accentuates all Pippi's specific features: hair color, freckles,
potato nose, big mouth, and her unusual clothes, the features we remember
best. Her hair and freckles will later be often referred to—for instance,
through other people's reactions to them or through the episode when Pippi
sees an advertisement in a beauty parlor, asking, "Do you suffer from freckles?" and responds to it by entering the parlor with a resolute "No!" (*Pippi
Goes on Board*, 18). However, this initial description of Pippi is so vivid that
it does not need frequent reinforcement. In the beginning of the third
sequel, we encounter another description of Pippi, as seen through the eyes
of a fine gentleman: "The girl in the middle had lots of freckles on her face
and two red pigtails which stuck straight out" (*Pippi in the South Seas*, 12).
Since the reader is supposed to be familiar with Pippi already, there is really
no reason to describe her looks again, but in the beginning of the sequel this
description has a didactic function, as a reminder. A similar "estrangement"
is used in the chapter about burglars, when Pippi is seen through their eyes.
This occasional reinforcement of Pippi's looks is unobtrusive and creates a
comic effect.

The description does not mention Pippi having two arms and two legs,
two eyes and two ears—these are the details we fill in ourselves. If the text
did not specify that Pippi's hair was red, we would also fill in this detail,
assuming, for instance, that Pippi, a Scandinavian, is blond. Incidentally, it
is never specified what color Tommy's and Annika's hair might be. The
color of Pippi's eyes is not mentioned, either, and we assume that they are
green, since red hair is—at least in literary characters—frequently combined with green eyes.

Everything else we learn about Pippi from the three books is primarily
revealed through her speech and actions. The narrator never says that Pippi
is kind or generous, but we make this inference because she treats Tommy
and Annika to nice meals, gives them presents, and so on. Later, she buys
sweets for all the children in the town and comforts children who have
failed Miss Rosenblom's examination—the repetition of her actions amplifies our perception of Pippi as a generous person. However, when we view
Pippi all alone in her house in the evenings, her daytime magnanimity
acquires a different flavor. She is not merely generous because she is strong

and rich but also because she is lonely—a well-known phenomenon of a lonely, unhappy child who "buys friendship." Perhaps the difference between the two phenomena is not so rigid.

Watching Pippi's behavior, we come to the conclusion that she is brave, independent, and smart (e.g., when she figures out how to save the two children from the fire). From an adult perspective, she is ill mannered. She lies a lot—or, rather, tells a lot of imaginative stories. Her ways of cooking or scrubbing the floor are highly original. It is essential to note that Pippi never abuses her strength. In fact, she only uses it against those who are themselves nasty toward the weak: the big boy Bengt, the police officers, the burglars, and so on. Otherwise, she prefers to talk her opponents down. There are practically no negative traits in Pippi. Some of my students have objected to Pippi teasing the little girl who is looking for her father. Her lack of manners may of course irritate prudish adults, but most young readers find delight in them.

The narrator's comments on Pippi are scarce: "she caught [the eggs] *skillfully* in a bowl" (20; emphasis added) or "Pippi could work fast, she could" (26). These comments cease completely as the novel unfolds. The other characters' comments on Pippi are also rare. The morning after they have met Pippi, Annika wakes her brother saying: "let's go and see that funny girl with the big shoes" (24). The adults in the little town promptly dislike Pippi. The schoolteacher thinks Pippi is "an unruly and troublesome child" (55), and Miss Rosenblom believes Pippi to be "the most stupid and disagreeable child" she has ever seen (*Pippi in the South Seas,* 48). However, most of the adults change their minds on getting to know Pippi better, especially after she has rescued two children from the fire, tamed the escaped tiger, and intimidated the ruffian Laban. The most radical attitude change is noted in Mrs. Settergren, Tommy's and Annika's mother, in the last book. The ladies of the little town wonder whether she indeed is considering sending her children to the South Seas with Pippi, and she says, "As long as I've known Pippi she has never done anything that has harmed Tommy and Annika in any way. No one can be kinder to them than she. . . . [H]er heart is in the right place" (*Pippi in the South Seas,* 66f.). The mother has realized that Pippi's inner qualities are more important than her lack of table manners.

Another consistent aspect of Pippi's characterization is her total absence of feelings. The closest we come to an expression of sentiment is when Pippi is "wild with delight" (148) on getting a music box for her birthday. Indirectly, we take part in her feelings when she weeps over a dead bird in *Pippi Goes on Board.* Typically enough, Pippi herself denies that she is crying, and she also seems to forget about the bird quite soon. She is full of compassion for Countess Aurora during a sentimental theater performance. Sometimes the text will tell us that Pippi is angry—for instance, when she sees a man beat his horse. She also cries after the adventure with the shark, but not because Tommy has almost been eaten up, but because "the poor little hungry shark no get breakfast today" (sic; *Pippi in the South Seas*, 85). Pippi's statements about herself are not worth much; mostly she just brags: "Grace and charm I have at least" (76), "I do think freckles are so attractive" (80), or "I should imagine I'll be the most stylish person of all at this party" (118). The most decisive of all Pippi's actions that characterize her is that she refuses to go away with her father when she sees how upset Tommy and Annika are. Until now, Pippi's generosity did not cost her too much—she has access to an endless supply of golden coins. But to abstain from her own pleasure in order not to make her friends upset demands more.

So far, the traits we have discovered in Pippi certainly make her a round and complex character. But what about dynamism? I have already, in discussing Pippi as a possible protagonist, mentioned her static nature. The main reason Pippi cannot evolve as a character is that she already possesses every property desirable for a young reader: she is the strongest girl in the world, she is rich beyond imagination, and she is independent of the adult hierarchy, including all rules and laws. In this way, Pippi is from the beginning placed in the power position that otherwise is the strongest motivation for character development. Consequently, Pippi lacks the desire to grow up—she simply does not have to. The only conceivable change would be to strip Pippi of all her power, which certainly contradicts the author's intention, as well as conventions of children's literature. Thus, if the common dream of many child characters is "to grow up and become strong, rich and admired," Pippi's motto is to be strong, rich, and admired and never have to grow up (see my comparison of Pippi and Jacob Two-Two in Nikolajeva 1997d).

Anne: Round and Dynamic

In terms of complexity and dynamism, Anne Shirley, the protagonist of *Anne of Green Gables*, is one of the most fascinating characters in children's fiction. Anne is eleven years old when the book starts and sixteen and a half when it ends. But it is not exclusively the fact that she grows older (chronological dynamism) that governs our sense of character evolution. The author constructs an extremely complex character, using different ways of both revealing Anne's traits and of making the reader aware of the moral changes in Anne and the reasons for them.

We get the very first evaluation of the protagonist from the stationmaster, who tells Matthew that the girl waiting for him is "a case" (10) and that she has "got a tongue of her own" (11). It is also the stationmaster who first quotes the phrase that will soon become Anne's signature tune: "There was more scope for imagination" (10). In the stationmaster's view, the statement and the quote present the yet nameless girl in a rather unfavorable light; however, they certainly evoke the reader's curiosity. At this stage, we know that Matthew has come to collect a boy, not a girl; but the title of the novel makes us anticipate, quite correctly, the protagonist. We get the first external description of the girl as seen literally through Matthew's eyes, but in a way that Matthew is incapable of expressing:

> Matthew was not looking at her and would not have seen what she was really like if he had been, but an ordinary observer would have seen this:
> A child of about eleven, garbed in a very short, very tight, very ugly dress of yellowish gray wincey. She wore a faded brown sailor hat and beneath the hat, extending down her back, were two braids of very thick, decidedly red hair. Her face was small, white and thin, also much freckled; her mouth was large and so were her eyes, that looked green in some lights and moods and gray in others. (11)

Already this first description gives us a very clear picture not only of Anne's looks, but her background as well: the ugly clothes that are too small for her and the pale, thin face witness an impoverished existence. Her braids hang down her back, unlike Pippi's. The large mouth perhaps suggests that she is far from pretty. But we immediately get another portrait of Anne as the text continues:

> So far, the ordinary observer; an extraordinary observer might have seen that the chin was very pointed and prominent; that the big eyes were full of spirit and vivacity; that the mouth was sweet-lipped and expressive; that the forehead was broad and full; in short, our discerning extraordinary observer might have concluded that no commonplace soul inhabited the body of this stray woman-child. (12)

While the first description pretends to be impartial, the second one immediately enforces the reader's empathy. The narrator draws our attention to the fact that inner qualities are not necessarily manifested on the outside. At the same time, the description is based on the assumption—today quite outdated—that external features, such as a prominent chin or broad forehead, directly reflect inner qualities (physiognomy was widely spread at the time the novel was written). We also learn that

Anne has a "peculiarly clear, sweet voice" (12), and when she without hesitation starts a conversation with Matthew, this characterizes her as brave and self-confident.

Like Pippi, Anne is most frequently described through what she says as well as how she says it. Already her first monologue reveals her exceptional verbal capacity and her temperament. Her ceaseless talking on the way to Green Gables enhances this first impression. Everything that Anne says in the first chapter discloses her views on life and other people. She prefers to think that the merchant who donated three hundred yards of fabric to the orphanage did this because of his kind heart and not because he could not sell his goods. She wants the world to be good and kind. We soon learn that Anne always tries to find excuses for all her former foster parents and see their positive sides, even though in our eyes they have clearly maltreated her. It is, however, not until many pages later that we learn anything about Anne's background, and she tells her story herself. Consequently, we do not get any impartial facts but rather Anne's substantially beautified version of them, colored by her romantic view of life.

The change that Anne goes through in the novel is a perfect illustration of the various devices that authors have to describe literary characters. Anne's attitude to life changes, as well as her appreciation of herself. Other characters' attitudes toward her changes. The narrator's manner of depicting her changes. There are other, perhaps less conspicuous, but extremely important changes. One such essential detail in Anne's development and her maturation is her attitude toward her looks. In the beginning, she is extremely dissatisfied with her red hair: "Now you see why I can't be perfectly happy. Nobody could who had red hair" (17). At the time the book was written, red hair was still associated with witchcraft, something that Astrid Lindgren parodies in *Pippi Longstocking*. Anne dreams of having "a beautiful rose leaf complexion and lovely starry violet eyes" (17). But she is very critical of herself and considers herself ugly, which in her view as well as the surrounding's is the main hindrance to happiness: "I don't ever expect to be bride myself. I'm so homely nobody will ever want to marry me" (14). But in her imagination, she sees herself differently: "My hair is of midnight darkness and my skin is a clear ivory pallor" (61). Anne is irritated beyond measure when anyone comments on her looks. In the chapter suitably titled "Vanity and Vexation of Spirit," Anne tries to dye her hair with such dreadful results that she has to cut it off. It is interesting to draw a parallel with Jo March, who also cuts off her hair, but for a noble cause. In the end, Anne grows to like her hair, especially after she has heard a famous painter refer to it as "Titian" (275).

Already in the first chapter where we meet Anne we learn about her dream of a "beautiful pale blue silk dress" (14), which sometimes transforms into a "a gown of trailing white lace" (61). Marilla sews three dresses for Anne: "She had made them up herself, and they were all made alike—plain skirts fulled tightly to plain waists, with sleeves as plain as waist and skirt and tight as sleeves could be" (78). This description illustrates the enormous discrepancy between Anne's dreams and the harsh reality she lives in. To Marilla's annoyance, Anne cannot conceal her disappointment with the dresses. She can just "imagine that one of them is of snow-white muslin with lovely lace frills and three-puffed sleeves" (79). When Anne gets a dress for Christmas from Matthew, it is the happiest moment of her life, and it is certainly not accidental that the dress is described in detail:

> Oh, how pretty is was—a lovely soft brown gloria with all the gloss of silk; a skirt with dainty frills and stirrings; a waist elaborately pin-tucked in the most fashionable way, with a little ruffle of filmy lace at the neck. But the sleeves—they were the crowning glory! Long elbow cuffs, and above them two beautiful puffs divided by rows of stirrings and bows of brown silk ribbon. (201*f.*)

The dress symbolizes a new phase in Anne's life. When she eventually gets her long-desired white organdy dress and a blue-flowered muslin dress, they seem like a natural part of her personality. She also gets a pearl necklace she has been dreaming of, but at this point she values it most because Matthew has given it to her.

Anne's name is another essential aspect of her identity quest. When she first comes to Green Gables, she detests her name. She finds Diana to be a "perfectly lovely" name; what she means is that the name has an unusual and romantic connotation, while her own name is too plain and lacks originality. Matthew on the other hand thinks that there is "something dreadful heathenish about it. . . . I'd ruther Jane or Mary or some sensible name" (21). When Marilla inquires about her name, Anne wonders if she can be called Cordelia: "It's such a perfectly elegant name. . . . And Anne is such an unromantic name" (25). However, as Anne grows more self-confident she also comes to terms with her name.

Also Anne's way of viewing her immediate surroundings changes. Her first night in the gable chamber at Green Gables is described with dislike:

> The whitewashed walls we so painfully bare and staring that she thought they must ache over their own bareness. The floor was bare too. . . . The whole apartment was of a rigidity not to be described by words, but which sent a shiver to the very marrow of Anne's bones. (28)

But already the next day Anne discovers the cherry tree in bloom outside her window, and we realize that she is capable of appreciating beauty. The author mentions her "beauty-loving eyes" (32). When allowed to stay at Green Gables, she tries to "imagine things into this room so that they'll always stay imagined" (61). Her imagination fills the empty room with velvet carpets, pink silk curtains, gold and silver brocade tapestry, and mahogany furniture—she has never seen such things, but read about them in books. Four years later in the plot, the room is described again, and now it bears the traces of Anne's personality; the description carries words such as "pretty matting," curtains "of pale green art muslin," "dainty apple blossom paper" (266f.), and instead of mahogany furniture, we see a white-painted bookcase. The text says explicitly that Anne likes her room and enjoys living in it.

The changes in Anne's behavior are described by very subtle means. When Anne has had a temper tantrum and refuses to apologize, she changes her mind after a conversation with Matthew, saying that she can do anything for his sake. This is perhaps the first time in her life that Anne learns to take other people into consideration, for which she needed to have the experience of being loved. On receiving chocolate from Matthew, she immediately wants to share it with Diana. These episodes are left without comment, but the reader will draw the necessary conclusions. Neither is there any comment to the chapter in which Anne comes up with a false confession to be allowed to go on a picnic.

It is illuminating to hear Anne herself summarize her development as she grows older:

> Ever since I came to Green Gables I've been making mistakes, and each mistake has helped to cure me of some great shortcoming. The affair of the amethyst brooch cured me of meddling with things that didn't belong to me. The Haunted Wood mistake cured me of letting my imagination run away with me. The liniment cake mistake cured me of carelessness in cooking. Dyeing my hair cured me of vanity. I never think about my hair and nose now—at least very seldom. And today's mistake is going to cure me of being too romantic. I have come to the conclusion that it is no use trying to be romantic in Avonlea. (229)

The changes Anne has observed in herself are external, "useful" changes; she does not comment on her more important inner evolution. However, in this case she is talking to Marilla, fully aware that her foster mother is mostly interested in hearing how Anne has become cleverer and more reasonable. At another point she says: "I'm not a bit changed—not really. I'm only just pruned down and branched out. The real *me*—back here—is just the same" (277; author's emphasis). This statement in itself is a token of maturity.

Also in other people's attitudes toward Anne, the changes are obvious. Matthew is the first to appreciate Anne: "she's an interesting little thing" (30). The practical Marilla, who wants a boy to help in the household, is very negative toward Anne. Anne's talkative nature does not make it easier, as Marilla says, "I don't like children who have so much to say" (30). As Marilla watches Anne during the first morning at Green Gables, her attitude slowly changes, and her brother's wish to keep the girl influences Marilla strongly. On learning Anne's story, Marilla is sympathetic and starts considering keeping her, especially after she hears Mrs. Blewett, the lady who wants Anne for a servant, talk coldly and rationally to Anne: "I'll expect you to earn your keep, and no mistake about that" (46). Marilla "looked at Anne and softened at sight of the child's pale face with its look of mute misery" (46)—the same Marilla who a few pages earlier is characterized as "merciless." On hearing Anne pray to God to let her stay at Green Gables, Marilla gives in.

In the chapter with the eloquent title "Matthew Insists on Puffed Sleeves," we receive still another description of Anne after she has been at Green Gables for a year and a half: "Anne had a brighter face, and bigger, starrier eyes, and more delicate features than the others" (195). Matthew observes that Anne does not have the same clothes as the other girls, and it is interesting that a man should detect this. Matthew starts viewing Anne as a young woman rather than a little girl, and he understands her need and longing for pretty clothes. Watching her at a concert, he feels proud of her: "our Anne did as well as any of them" (205). Marilla is as always more reserved: "I was proud for Anne tonight, although I am not going to tell her so" (205). After several more years, Marilla loves her foster child dearly: "she had learned to love this slim, gray-eyed girl with an affection all the deeper and stronger from its very undemonstrativeness" (239). Therefore, Marilla feels certain sorrow noticing that Anne has become a young woman:

> The child she had learned to love had vanished somehow and here was this tall, serious-eyed girl of fifteen, with the thoughtful brow and the proudly poised little head in her place. Marilla loved the girl as much as she had loved the child, but she was conscious of a queer sorrowful sense of loss. (255)

Other adults' attitudes also reflect Anne's evolution. Mrs. Rachel Lynde is initially negative toward Anne and does not hide it. Marilla's defense of Anne does not help. However, Mrs. Lynde changes her mind and takes

Anne's side after the first trouble in school. When Matthew asks Mrs. Lynde to get a new dress for Anne, she expresses strong sympathy: "The way Marilla dresses her is positively ridiculous, that's what, and I've ached for her so plainly a dozen times" (200).

Diana's mother, Mrs. Barry, is nice from the start, but after Anne has accidentally given Diana wine, Mrs. Barry forbids the two girls to meet. The whole society's attitude toward Anne changes radically after she saves a little sick girl's life—in the same way the townspeople change their attitude toward Pippi after the fire. The dramatic episode with the sick girl serves the purpose of a turning point in the people's opinion of Anne. The chapter title is "Anne to the Rescue." Mrs. Barry also changes her mind at this point. Thus Anne influences her surroundings while she changes herself. The most important barometer in the adults' opinion of Anne is Aunt Josephine, who appreciates Anne so much that they "became firm friends" (161). Aunt Josephine's judgment is straightforward: "If I'd a child like Anne in the house all the time I'd be a better and a happier woman" (237).

Anne's peers' attitudes are relatively uncomplicated. Diana accepts her immediately, her "queerness" notwithstanding, and this friendship means a lot for Anne's development. Gilbert, the most successful and popular boy in school, seems to be interested in Anne from the start. Most of the classmates, both boys and girls, like Anne and show it openly. It may seem a bit unmotivated, even implausible, but it is the author's deliberate choice to emphasize Anne's qualities that are appreciated by other children.

However, the most essential—and the least explicit—change in Anne concerns her language. In the beginning of the book, she says: "people laugh at me because I use big words. But if you have big ideas you have to use big words to express them, haven't you?" (16). In the early parts of the book, Anne uses phrases such as "the White Way of Delight" (19), "the Lake of Shining Waters" (20), "alabaster brow" (17), "my hair is a glorious black, black as a raven's wing" (17), "I am in the depth of despair" (27), and "My life is a perfect graveyard of buried hopes" (38). Anne's own comment is that "it sounds so nice and romantic" (38). Anne's exalted mood is often emphasized by exclamation marks in her speech: "Oh, Mr. Cuthbert! Oh, Mr. Cuthbert!! Oh, Mr. Cuthbert!!!" (18). She often uses hyperbole, such as "children should be seen and not heard. I've had that said to me *a million times*" (16; emphasis added). She also keeps using amplifying adjectives and adverbs such as "divinely," "scrumptious," and "excruciatingly."

When Anne is allowed to stay at Green Gables, she is told that she will have to restrain her talking, which also means restraining her imagination and keeping back her hot temperament. Marilla repeatedly warns her not to talk too much in front of other people. After two years, Anne still uses high-flown language in her school essays, and together with Diana she starts the Story Club, where they write beautiful and romantic stories. But at fifteen Anne suddenly becomes silent—or rather is silenced. In the chapter "Where the Brook and the River Meet," we gain access to her thoughts:

> I don't want to talk as much. . . . It's nicer to think dear, pretty thoughts and keep them in one's heart, like treasures. I don't like to have them laughed at or wondered over. And somehow I don't want to use big words any more. It's almost a pity, isn't it, now that I'm really growing big enough to say them if I did want to. . . . There's so much to learn and do and think that there isn't time for big words. Besides, Miss Stacy says the short ones are much stronger and better. (256)

The schoolteacher, Miss Stacy, is an important model for Anne, but paradoxical as it may seem, she becomes the one who makes Anne lower her voice and adapt to the rules of society. "Children should be seen and not heard," especially girls.

We must necessarily view Anne's development in the light of gender stereotyping. Together with Jo March, Anne has been described by critics as the most typical tomboy girl. The way Anne is presented does not match the normal traits associated with femininity. If we turn to the very schematic presentation of masculinity and femininity—for instance, as suggested by John Stephens (1996)—we will see that Anne is, of course, emotional, caring, and vulnerable (feminine traits), but she is strong rather than beautiful, and she is independent both in her thoughts and deeds and far from passive. On the contrary, she is extremely determined; for instance, she refuses to go to school after she has been, as she sees it, offended by the teacher. Her decision to decline the desirable scholarship and stay at Green Gables witnesses both her independence and her maturity. She can also be aggressive if not violent (e.g., when she shouts her hate toward Mrs. Lynde or when she hits Gilbert with her slate), and she is definitely not submissive, least of all verbally. She is not obedient by nature, and she interrogates many things around her, including evening prayer, since she thinks she has no reason to feel grateful toward God who has been unfair to her. She hates the traditional female chores, such as sewing and cooking, but she is quite good at outdoor activities. Anne's constant competition with Gilbert—a male—goes against the principles of femininity.

The changes that Anne goes through in the novel bring her closer to the feminine stereotype: she must learn to be obedient and humble, restrain her temper, and also give up her poetic feminine language. One of the key episodes in the novel is revealing: when Anne is saved by Gilbert. The author does describe this scene with irony (the chapter title is "An Unfortunate Lily Maid"), but she allows Anne and Gilbert to act according to gender stereotypes: she is a helpless victim, he the brave rescuer. Since the readers at this point have guessed about Anne's true feelings for Gilbert, although she herself does not admit them, the traditional gender roles are further accentuated.

We can see this development as negative, since we today appreciate strong, independent female characters. We must, however, put the novel into its historical and social context. In 1908, Montgomery could hardly depict a young woman taking a decisive step toward independence; it would not have been plausible. The way Anne is described, in the first place as an independently thinking individual, she is subversive enough. Even forty years later, when Astrid Lindgren describes her independent heroine Pippi, she must invent special conditions for Pippi to be acceptable (see a comparison of Anne and Pippi in Åhmansson 1994).

Transgressional Characters

A particular group of characters that does not fit into clear categories may be called transgressional. Mostly, transgressional characters appear in nonmimetic modes. One such type is a character undergoing a metamorphosis, either reversible or irreversible. Pinocchio the puppet is transformed into a living boy—we cannot account for it in terms of the normal character development as seen in mimetic narratives. Eustace in *The Voyage of the Dawn Treader* is transformed into a dragon and for a short period seems to acquire a dragonlike mentality. The popular Animorphs series shows a number of human–animal or human–monster transformations (see Lassén-Seger 2000).

Fantasy novels occasionally feature characters with supernatural powers. Fantasy heroes often have supernatural helpers. However, depicting a protagonist with magical powers demands special characterization devices, since as readers we cannot immediately relate to such experiences. The character's discovery of his extraordinary powers and the consequences of those is one of the central driving forces for Will Stanton in *The Dark Is Rising*, Christopher in *The Lives of Christopher Chant*, and, most recently, Harry Potter. In assessing these characters, we cannot directly apply our usual criteria of consistency and unity, since they are deliberately created as different from ordinary human beings.

A very special and interesting case involves characters who change identity as a result of time displacement. Edred and Elfrida take the place of their distant relatives in the past in *The House of Arden*; however, mentally they remain themselves and retain full memory of their own time. Penelope in *A Traveller in Time* and Abigail in *Playing Beatie Bow* get so much involved with the past that their identities seem to dissolve, and their behavior and many personality traits change. The protagonist of *Charlotte Sometimes* literally becomes someone else. Discussing these characters, we must bear in mind the peculiarity of their situations, in which normal psychological criteria may not be applicable. In fact, time travelers present a kind of narrative schizophrenia, since their identity is split into two separate persons in the different time frames. It may be of less importance in plot-oriented stories, such as *The House of Arden*, but all the more essential in time-shift novels with psychological and ethical dimensions (see Scott 1996).

Finally, a type of transgression that has become prominent in children's fiction in the 1980s and 1990s is androgyny, mostly in its social form, involving cross-dressing (see Flanagan 1999; Westin 1999; Österlund 2000). A girl disguised as a boy, such as Johnny in *Johnny My Friend*, defies common logic and cannot, for one thing, be discussed in standard terms of masculinity or femininity. While this character type has been examined in general literature (Gilbert 1980; Lehnert 1994) and has recently come into focus in children's literature research, the nonmimetic transgressional characters of fantasy have been for obvious reasons totally ignored by general criticism. They are, however, an essential part of children's fiction, and their very peculiar complexity and dynamism are indispensable features of the aesthetics of children's literature.

A Further Taxonomy of Characters

While we may be satisfied with the two simple binarities—flat/round and static/dynamic—for a rough differentiation between types of characters, we surely need more subtlety. Baruch Hochman suggests in his *Character in Literature* some categories that enable us to classify characters in greater detail. All the categories represent the extremes of a continuum, so any given character can possess various amounts of each quality:

Stylization	Naturalism (or minimal stylization)
Coherence	Incoherence
Wholeness	Fragmentariness
Literalness	Symbolism
Complexity	Simplicity
Transparency	Opacity
Dynamism	Staticism
Closure	Openness (Hochman 1985, 89)

Two of the binaries, complexity/simplicity and dynamism/staticism, naturally correspond to our earlier categories round/flat and dynamic/static. The other categories do not perhaps offer a radically new approach to characters as compared with what has already been discussed; however, Hochman's taxonomy provides some structure for the previous argument.

The distinction between stylized and natural characters is extremely important in children's fiction, in which stylization is a commonly used didactic device. I have partly touched upon this aspect in the discussion of stereotypes, and I have also earlier mentioned the question of typical versus individual. Katy, Heidi, Pippi, and Anne are all stylized, in different manners and to various degrees. Contemporary psychological novels tend to have more natural characters than traditional children's fiction, which becomes immediately apparent through a comparison of a modern character such as Gilly Hopkins with any of our four classic heroines.

Coherence and consistency, partly discussed already, are, according to Hochman, culturally determined. As he points out, most postmodern characters are deliberately incoherent (some critics also use the term of instability when referring to such characters; see Phelan 1989). It would be strange to demand coherence, for instance, from the characters of *One Hundred Years of Solitude*. In labeling a character incoherent, we should therefore take into consideration whether the incoherence is an artistic flaw or a conscious device. Pippi may be seen as incoherent, but this is the author's intention. However, as compared with contemporary mainstream literature, characters in children's fiction tend to be more coherent, for didactic purposes.

Wholeness does not mean wholeness or completeness of a real person, only of what is relevant for our understanding of the character. Fragmentariness can be a deliberate characterization technique—for instance, when a person is associated with an attribute. Hochman's example is Anna Karenina's handbag; we can recall Moominmamma's handbag as a parallel example. Synecdoche (using a part to signify the whole) and metonymy (using a word to denote another, closely associated notion) can be very strong characterization devices. Anne Shirley is definitely a whole character, and while I would not call Pippi a totally fragmentary character, her red hair, extremely big shoes, and nonmatching stockings are good examples of characterization by attributes. In fact, her last name, Longstocking, is a synecdoche.

Literalness and symbolism are connected to the previously discussed mimetic and nonmimetic approaches to characters. Literal characters are constructed in a way that prompts us to interpret them mimetically, while symbolic characters suggest the opposite. Katy, Heidi, and Anne are more literal characters than Pippi. Symbolism prompts us to interpret characters as a representation of something else. Indeed, Pippi has been treated as a witch and even as Satan.

Hochman's concept of closed and open characters differs slightly from the way these terms have been discussed in chapter 1. By closure he means resolution, finality; a closed character is to be wholly and totally understood from the text. An open character leaves the reader puzzled, as there are still qualities that can develop beyond the text. Of my four examples, all four characters are rather closed than open; there is little to wonder about them once we have finished the novels. Modern characters, such as Gilly Hopkins (*The Great Gilly Hopkins*), Jess Aaron (*Bridge to Terabithia*), or Chris Nordberg (*Johnny My Friend*) are open, since the ending of the novels leaves unlimited possibilities for their development and growth.

Finally, transparency and opacity are ways to describe our access to information about characters. Are we allowed to penetrate their minds or do we see only their external appearance? So far we can state that Katy, Heidi, and Pippi are opaque characters, while Anne is transparent. Pippi is the most opaque of the four characters. But how exactly does it work? This question will be the essence of part 2 of this book.

PART TWO

EPISTEMOLOGY OF CHARACTER

From Opaque to Transparent

Most critics who have been interested at all in theoretical approaches to characters dwell on a number of epistemological questions surrounding characters—that is, the ways we can get to know and understand them. Several critics, following E. M. Forster, argue that literature allows us to gain an intrinsic knowledge of other people, while in real life we only have intrinsic knowledge of ourselves and extrinsic knowledge of other people. Although real people are always opaque to us, literary characters may be presented in a vast continuum from opacity to full transparency. For Forster and many other scholars, this is the main attraction of fiction.

Baruch Hochman (1985) emphasizes the importance of historical and social context in our understanding of character (55). This is extremely important for children's literature, since young readers may not be aware of the changing values presented through characters. For instance, child abandonment and abuse were acceptable before, but not today. We cannot judge a parent beating his children in a Victorian novel by the same measure we would judge a parent nowadays. The societal norms encoded in such adjectives as "nice," "virtuous," "well-mannered," or even "pretty" differ considerably over time and from culture to culture. However, we do not always have the knowledge of exactly what these qualities denoted to their bearers. Again, this is especially important for children's literature, since young readers may lack not only knowledge but also interest in this aspect. Therefore, they can easily fall victim to racist, sexist, and other prejudices.

What is the minimal amount of information we need about a literary character? As compared with real people, literary characters are always incomplete. What is sufficient for a reader to "construct" a personality from a number of words? We would assume that a name alone would be enough. Indeed, we meet many peripheral characters in literature who are little more than a name. In a central character, we certainly expect more than a name. On the other hand, a name is not in itself necessary to understand and relate to a character. A first-person narrator may omit his or her name and thus remain anonymous throughout the novel and yet be revealed to us as a complex character. This is rather unusual in children's fiction, since names have a strong connection with identity, and it is therefore believed that young readers need a name to associate with the character whose subject position they adopt.

Going further though "censuslike" questions, we might suggest age, gender, and race as minimal requirements. We assume that characters have an age, even though age is not necessarily revealed explicitly. In the mainstream, we can determine the characters' age from their social position (a university professor or a company president are presumably older than a freshman student or a junior clerk); from their childhood memories (if a character remembers John F. Kennedy's assassination or the Vietnam War, it gives us clear clue about his age); from their reading or music tastes, and so on. Furthermore, if a character's parents and grandparents are still living, we assume that he is young; if he has children and grandchildren, we assume that he is old. In children's literature, the scope of a character's age is limited by the concept of childhood as such.

Most frequently, characters have a gender, if only revealed by the pronouns *he* or *she*. Theoretically, it is possible to manipulate a text so that the character's gender will not be disclosed. Some languages do not have grammatical gender (e.g., Finnish), which makes it possible to write about characters without referring to their gender by personal pronouns. In combination with gender-neutral names, this device will allow the character's gender to remain ambivalent. Naturally, in a novel such as *Johnny My Friend*, in which the character's gender is one of the mysteries of the plot, the personal pronoun *he* is just as much a disguise as Johnny's masculine appearance and name.

As to race, it need not be mentioned in a text but will be understood from the plot, setting, and other textual elements. In such novels as *Roll of Thunder, Hear My Cry*, or *The Planet of Junior Brown*, the characters' race is essential to understanding both the events and the characters' situation; however, the characters are not specifically presented to the reader as people of color. However, if a character's race is not mentioned, we will judge it by "default value," which in our Western culture is Caucasian. We have no reason to assume that Anne Shirley is Chinese, even though we are not explicitly told that she is not. We have no reason to believe that Huck Finn is black, because if he were, the author would have told us, just as he tells us that Jim is "the small colored boy" (*The Adventures of Tom Sawyer*, 9).

In all these cases, except for names, illustrations in children's books contribute to our perception of character, giving an instant and immediate external portrait. Even when a novel is not illustrated, a cover picture may be revealing enough. Even a very brief examination of a number of covers to classics such as *Anne of Green Gables* shows how a visual portrait of a character can influence our expectations. In existing covers, Anne is portrayed sometimes older, sometimes younger, sometimes happy, sometimes sad, sometimes very pretty, which contradicts the text, and sometimes plain, in consistency with the text. In any case, the cover signals that the protagonist is a young white female. This may make adult, male, and non-Caucasian readers reject the novel. The covers of *Roll of Thunder* and *The Planet of Junior Brown* show black characters, filling the gap left by the text and signaling the characters' social status. Book covers are paratexts that contribute to our understanding of the character. Unlike adult novels, it is almost inconceivable that a children's novel would not have a cover illustration. A character's portrait on the cover or in illustrations enhances the verbal description of the character or replaces it.

As we remember, Aristotle claimed that characters should only possess one of two traits: noble or base. In many cases this is also true of characters in children's fiction: they can be easily divided into "good guys" and "bad guys." The traits of noble or base, good or bad, are revealed to us primarily through the characters' actions. Adopting the protagonist's subject position, we perceive all actions geared toward his ascent as noble, and all actions bringing about his descent or destruction as base. We do not speculate about the villain's motivation for being mean, since being mean is the only trait a villain can have. We also have a repertoire of actions that we inherently evaluate as noble or base. Helping other people is noble; stealing, cheating, lying, and killing are base. These values are not absolute; in fact, in ancient tragedies, heroes are constantly engaged in stealing, cheating, and killing.

In psychological novels, we normally expect characters to have other traits than merely good and bad, and we expect the traits to add up to a consistent whole. However, these traits are not necessarily revealed to us all at once; they are not necessarily all revealed by the same means—for instance, through actions; they are not necessarily revealed explicitly. As readers, we get to know literary characters successively, from a number of incidents. "In principle, any element in the text may serve as indicator of character" (Rimmon-Kenan 1983, 59). One may assume that this is similar to our getting to know real people; there is, however, a profound difference. Since literary characters are created by writers, these may employ different strategies in revealing characters. Writers can give us contradictory information through different characterization devices. For instance, a character's self-evaluation may contradict the other characters' opinion or the narrator's overt comments. Writers may even omit essential information or withhold it until later.

Martin Price (1968) remarks in his study of character that in many cases essential features are missing from characters' portraits; he further points out that omissions may be part of a genre's specifics or even part of the individual author's poetics: "the things revealed about Emma Bovary are the very things ignored in Henry James's heroines. Rarely does a critic speculate about Robinson Crusoe's sexual frustration during his long years on the island" (284). Price goes on to argue that the amount of information we demand is highly dependent on the kind of text we are dealing with: "We can make surmises about the attributes that are missing, but we are hardly inclined to do so unless the novel invited us" (284). In fact, we are rarely interested in all properties of a character. Instead, we should ask what is sufficient in order to understand a character in a particular text type. In children's literature, the question is especially relevant, since young readers may misjudge characters or fail to assemble a number of traits into a whole. In an empirical reader survey, the mother in a short story by Astrid Lindgren was perceived by six-year-old readers as "kind" because she gives her daughter a puppy. The readers failed to connect this action with the mother having neglected the protagonist, causing loneliness, depression, and escape into the realm of fancies.

The question of the characters' completeness as compared with real people is crucial for any epistemological discussion. Peter Lamarque (1996, 23–39) discusses character as having a set of properties. For every property, a real person either possesses it or lacks the same property. A fictional character can both possess and lack it. A much-discussed example is whether Sherlock Holmes has a mole on his back (Lamarque 1996, 37). We can equally ask whether Pippi or Anne Shirley have moles on their backs. They may have them or may not have them, which for a real person is not an alternative. We know that Johnny has a chipped front tooth, because the narrator has told us about it. If we had not been told about this detail, we could equally assume that Johnny had or did not have a chipped tooth. These examples may seem fruitless speculations, but they demonstrate the danger of discussing characters as if they were living people.

How is information about characters revealed to us? Seymor Chatman (1978, 126ff.) suggests that while reading, we register every trait we encounter in a character and add them up into what he calls a trait paradigm. Every new trait we meet may slightly or substantially change our perception of this particular character. For instance, in the combination "brave" + "clever" the trait of "brave" is different from the combination "brave" + "stupid," where it probably equals "reckless." The value of "generous" is different in the combinations "rich" + "generous" and "poor" + "generous." The combination "brave" + "clever" + "generous" almost adds up to "perfect." These are, of course, primitive examples, since characterization is usually significantly more complex even in very simple stories. However, they show the principle of Chatman's trait paradigm.

By contrast, Shlomith Rimmon-Kenan (1983, 59) speaks about a network of traits. I like this concept better, since it indicates that a character is made not out of a sum of traits but out of a complex system of interactions. If Chatman's paradigm is a list, Rimmon-Kenan's network could probably be represented only by an intricate three-dimensional geometrical figure. Rimmon-Kenan also distinguishes between direct definition (by which she basically means narrative statements of the type: "She was stupid") and indirect presentation, including actions, speech, external appearance, environment, and analogy (59–70). I find this distinction too narrow to describe the broad spectrum of characterization devices. Each chapter of this part will be dedicated to a particular type of characterization, moving from direct (or authorial) to indirect (or figural) representation.

Description and narration are two characterization devices in which characters are the most opaque. We become acquainted with them more or less in the same manner that we become acquainted with real people, seeing their external appearance and hearing somebody's direct judgment of them. In characterization by actions and reactions, the characters are still relatively opaque; however, we are sometimes allowed to follow them through events and situations that would be impossible with real people. This may range from accompanying a character on a lonely and dangerous journey to witnessing their visit to the bathroom. Characterization by speech brings us closer to the characters' inner world, especially if we assume that they are sincere in their utterances. Internal representation makes characters completely transparent in a way no real person can ever be, not even somebody we have known intimately for our whole life. Finally, implicit characterization may seem to take us back to opacity, which would be the case with real people, since we would be making inferences from external details. However, literary characters are deliberately constructed by the author, which means that elements that are inconsequential in real life are arranged in fiction to support (or occasionally subvert) our understanding of character. Like everything else in a narrative, character is part of the overall design.

~

CHAPTER EIGHT

Character and Plot

Although I have repeatedly referred to plot in the previous chapters, I feel it necessary to return to this central concept in connection with the epistemology of character, since characters are essentially revealed to us through their involvement in the plot. A passage from Henry James's *The Art of the Novel*, "What is character but the determination of incident? What is incident but the illustration of character?" already quoted in chapter 1, maintains the close interdependence of plot and character, which is often interrogated within other approaches to literary texts. As mentioned several times before, in classic Aristotelian poetics, characters are subordinate to the plot, while, for instance, E. M. Forster gives the character priority. Scholes and Kellogg note that the connection between plot and character changes throughout history. While ancient literature indeed shows characters as instrumental to plot, in classic novels, character and plot are closely intertwined, and in contemporary fiction, there is a clear separation of plot-oriented (entertaining) and character-oriented (serious) narratives (Scholes and Kellogg 1966, 233–39). One of the few recent studies discussing the character's function in the plot is James Phelan's (1989) *Reading People, Reading Plots: Character, Progression, and the Interpretations of Narrative*. With my specific focus on character, the function of the plot is to reveal the character, even though I admit that in many types of narrative, characters are indeed subordinate to the plot. In this chapter, I will discuss how various elements of plot contribute to our understanding of characters (see also Docherty 1983, 127–55).

Is There a Specific "Children's Plot"?

The most traditional narrative plots are to be found in oral stories, and these have been adopted by children's fiction. The typical plot in children's literature, which we may call a *basic* plot or a *master* plot, follows the pattern: home—departure from home—adventure—homecoming. Home provides safety, but the character must depart from home, since nothing exciting ever happens there. Being away is exciting but also dangerous, so the characters must return home, often after they have found a treasure or gained knowledge and maturity.

The type of plot with the normal development from complications through the climax toward a closure, the *progressive* or *epic* plot, allows considerable character evolution and a vast scope of characterization devices. In children's books, usually for young children, other types of plots occur. In an *episodic* plot, single events or short episodes are linked together by common characters, settings, or themes. Within each episode, however, we can often distinguish the master plot. *Pippi Longstocking* and *Mary Poppins* have episodic plots. Episodic plots allow little room for thorough characterization since each episode is too short for character evolution. Episodic plots are usually action oriented rather than character oriented. However, by repeating and accentuating a particular character trait in each episode, a character will be made more vivid. For instance, Pippi is recurrently portrayed as generous and hospitable. First, she treats her new friends to pancakes, then invites them to have coffee up in the tree, takes them out on a picnic, buys sweets for all the children in town, and so on. She is also presented as witty (although some adults would perhaps rather say "cheeky"), clever, and brave in each adventure. Our image of Pippi is thus constantly reconfirmed. However, the episodes can be read in an arbitrary order, without our understanding of character being affected.

Episodic and progressive plots may be combined within one and the same narrative—for instance, *The Adventures of Tom Sawyer*. Tom's pranks, running away from home, romance with Becky, and so on, are single episodes. In each one Tom leaves home, has adventures, and returns home. Each episode reiterates his naughtiness as his dominant trait. There are, however, at least two progressive plots that hold the book together. The first one involves conflict with Injun Joe and the murder accusation of Muff Potter. The second one, connected with the first, involves the treasure hunt. The two plots are interwoven, but they develop at a different pace, reach climaxes at different points, and have different closures. Both make use of suspense and cliff-hangers—for instance, when Tom and Becky get lost in a cave. In these plots, a certain degree of character development is possible. Tom's witnessing against Injun Joe in court shows considerable maturity and presents the protagonist in a new light. Finding the treasure changes his power position.

Another example of combined episodic and progressive plot is the Ramona series. Ramona obviously does grow up physically as she moves from kindergarten to third grade. However, each chapter is more or less a self-contained adventure or prank. Within each book, the episodes can change place, and even episodes from different books in the series can be read out of order, because the connection between them is thematic rather than temporal or causal. Most episodes underscore our initial understanding of Ramona as a mischievous but imaginative and strong-minded girl, without adding any substantial new information.

Cumulative plot is a pattern in which a new character or event is added in every subsequent episode. For small children this is an excellent device to help them remember the characters. I have already mentioned the cumulative protagonist as a specific feature of children's literature poetics; it is also a good illustration of the interdependence of plot and character, since the cumulative character naturally presupposes a cumulative plot. In *Winnie-the-Pooh* a new character with its special features is introduced in every chapter: first Pooh and Christopher Robin; in the second chapter we meet Rabbit, then Piglet, next Eeyore and Owl, and so on. All of them partake in a feast in the final chapter. It is possible that the order of appearance was suggested by the order in which the boy—both the fictive character and the real Christopher Robin—received his toys. It also represents a little child's successive discovery of the surrounding world.

Episodic and cumulative plots are uncommon in adult novels. (We can perhaps view a collection of short stories with the same protagonist as a narrative with episodic plot, such as V. S. Naipaul's *Miguel Street*.) We must therefore consider episodic and cumulative plots as specific devices in the aesthetics of children's literature. Characterization in these plot types is different from that in progressive plots.

Embedded plot, on the contrary, is a common pattern in the mainstream—for instance, such classics as *The Canterbury Tales* and *Decameron*. In children's literature, *Winnie-the-Pooh* has an embedded plot: in the outer frame, a little boy is listening to his father's bedtime stories, in the inner frame, a number of episodes, held together by setting and characters, take place. The outer plot is, however, barely discernible and not really essential. We learn very little about the characters in the outer frame, the father and the son. Some overtly postmodern children's novels have intricate embedded plots—for instance, *The Solitaire Mystery*. This Chinese box puzzle of narratives leaves almost no room for characterization; the characters are metafictive and "canceled."

It is otherwise usual for children's books to have one, clearly delineated plot. It is sometimes believed that children cannot remember or follow more than one plot line. This, of course, depends on the readers' age. Books for younger children often have one plot. Books for older children can have one primary plot and one or several auxiliary plots. I have already shown how single episodes are combined with a progressive plot in *Tom Sawyer*. The most famous Swedish children's book, *The Wonderful Adventures of Nils*, has several auxiliary plots in which the main character participates more or less or sometimes not at all. In *Moominsummer Madness*, the Moomin family is separated during a flood, and the reader follows sometimes Moomintroll and Snork Maiden, sometimes Snufkin, and sometimes the rest of the family who are left on the floating theater. One reason why Tolkien's *Lord of the Rings* trilogy is often treated as an adult book, unlike *The Hobbit*, may be the many parallel plots when the Fellowship of the Ring splits up.

Auxiliary and parallel plots allow the reader to follow several characters one at a time. It may be necessary and desirable for the actions involved; however, it limits the scope of characterization. While an adult novel of 800 pages can have a number of parallel plots and yet leave ample room for the portrayal of several characters, a children's novel of 120 pages does not have the same prerequisites. Children's literature's preference for a single plot, especially when the novel is character oriented, is therefore not merely an adaptation to the presumed readers but an intrinsic quality.

There is essentially a limited number of plots in literature. Some typical plots in children's fiction include the dragon-slayer story; the underdog story (or Cinderella story); the journey into distant countries, real or imaginary; the solution of a mystery, or the fulfillment of a difficult task. All these plots may be found both in fantastic and in realistic texts, or, to use Frye's terminology, on all levels of displacement. Associating a certain plot with a certain genre, as is commonly done, is therefore fruitless. It is instead a challenge to recognize a plot originating from a heroic tale in an everyday story. For characterization, seeing the characters' position in a plot is more important than their dependence on certain genres.

Several types of conflict make up the basis for a plot. *Person-against-person* conflict is probably the most common in children's novels, since it originates from traditional literature, myths, and folktales. The protagonist meets his adversary in some sort of combat (Alice meets the Queen of Hearts, Dorothy meets the Wicked Witch of the West, Tom Sawyer meets Injun Joe, etc.). This conflict is presumably easiest for a young reader to understand, since this is the type of confrontation children encounter in their everyday surroundings, with adults and peers. A person-against-person conflict usually involves external characterization: the characters are revealed through their actions and reactions.

In a *person-against-society* conflict, the character meets social conventions that prevent him from reaching a goal or compel him to make a moral choice (Pinocchio has to adapt himself to society before he can become human; Holden Caulfield has to accept the prescribed norms of behavior; and Pippi's ways are a revolt against the existing rules). This conflict, too, demands external characterization, based on the character's behavior. The narrator's or other character's comments add to it. Naturally, the characters may reflect over the origin and consequences of the conflict, as Holden Caulfield undoubtedly does.

In a *person-against-nature* conflict, the character is confronted with natural elements in a struggle for his life or survival, as is Robinson Crusoe. All Robinsonnades have this type of conflict. Since the character in a person-against-nature conflict is isolated from other people, this type encourages self-reflection and internal focalization, even though the larger portion of the plot may be focused on external events.

Finally, in a *person-against-self* conflict, probably the most sophisticated, an inner struggle is depicted. The dominant characterization devices are the various kinds of internal representation. In most books, several conflicts are combined. Furthermore, the conflicts may look different at the different levels of the text. In *Mio, My Son* we find a conflict of the "person-against-person" type on the surface: Prince Mio is struggling against the evil Sir Kato. On a more symbolic level, we meet a lonely boy struggling with his own problems: a conflict of "person-against-self." In *Ronia the Robber's Daughter*, there is a person-against-person conflict in the rivalry between the two groups of robbers; there is Ronia's conflict with the society she is growing up in; there is Ronia and Birk's struggle for survival in the wilderness; but most important are the inner conflicts within Ronia. At each level, Ronia is revealed to the reader through different means.

Some specific plot elements, or motifs, that we find in children's novels are not as prominent in the mainstream fiction. The first is coming to a new home. Naturally, this element—connected to the basic motif of dislocation, inherent in all fiction—is present in quite a number of mainstream novels, such as *Jane Eyre* or *Mansfield Park*. However, I would state that the new home is more dominant in children's fiction and also more significant, since the change of setting is a more dramatic event in a child's life than in an adult's. The character's reaction to the change is very revealing. Mary Lennox's initial hatred of her new Yorkshire home adds to our general negative impression of her. The Pevensie children's eagerness to explore their new surroundings characterizes them as keen, inquisitive, and not so dependent on their parents (by inference, we know that they have spent most of their lives in boarding schools, and have no close relationship with their parents). In *Tom's Midnight Garden*, Tom's reluctance to go away and his disappointment in the house without a garden, on the contrary, shows his immaturity and dependence on his family.

Some other key moments in a children's plot include birthdays and Christmas (or other culturally dependent seasonal celebrations, such as Halloween in the United States or Midsummer in Sweden), the first and last days of school, and, alternatively, school examinations. These moments are often used to start or finish a narrative. For instance, *Little Women* starts just before Christmas, while *Pippi Longstocking* ends with Pippi's birthday. *Ramona the Pest* starts on Ramona's first day in kindergarten, and the sequel, *Ramona the Brave*, on her first day in first grade. Apparently, at least in the writer's view, these events are more important in a child's life than in an adult's. For one thing, these events mark the regularity and stability of existence, essential for the child's (character's as well as reader's) sense of security. In terms of characterization, a character's attitude toward such events is revealing. For instance, Chris in *Johnny My Friend* is happy about his birthday and about getting older; while Johnny denies age and does not celebrate birthdays, which Chris has problems understanding. The March sisters complain that Christmas will not be the way it should be without presents, which characterizes them as indulged and selfish.

Quest is by far the most common motif in children's literature, especially if we treat it broadly, not limiting it to the search for objects or persons but also including the quest for identity. Quests are common in folktales in which the hero leaves home in order to search for treasure, a kidnapped princess, or simply fortune. We see the motif most clearly in genres closely related to folktale, primarily heroic fantasy—for instance, the Prydain Chronicles, *The Dark Is Rising* series, *Mio, My Son*, and *The Brothers Lionheart*. Quest may be manifest on different levels of the text: on the symbolic level, the protagonists of all these novels are searching for their own identities. Furthermore, in contemporary psychological novels quests are predominantly of the symbolic nature, which may be emphasized by the title, such as *Park's Quest*. A classic quest narrative, the Holy Grail legend, is used as an intertext in this novel, obviously very differently than in the concrete search for the grail in *Over Sea, Under Stone*, the first volume in *The Dark Is Rising* series. Depending on the nature of the quest, external or internal characterization will be used.

In adventure stories, there are many examples of searching for treasure,

Treasure Island being the best known, but also *The Story of the Treasure Seekers* or *Five on a Treasure Island*. There are more humorous variants of treasure hunt in some chapters of *Pippi Longstocking*—for instance, when Pippi is a "Thing-Finder" or when she is looking for "spink." In everyday stories, too, we can find quests for things or people as a recurrent pattern. Often there is also another, symbolically charged, meaning. For instance, Elvis is looking for a missing bit of the jigsaw puzzle or for a lock to open with the key he has found. Both objects have a concrete as well as a symbolic significance. A more sophisticated version is looking for a missing relative, especially a father—a very common motif in children's books (see Nikolajeva 1994). Quest is one of the best ways of revealing a character's inner qualities, as well as the change occurring during the process of searching.

Journey is another fundamental pattern in children's fiction, even found in picturebooks for very young children. The classic Swedish children's book *The Wonderful Adventures of Nils* is based on the journey motif. We find a variety of journeys in fantasy novels, such as *The Wizard of Oz*, *The Phantom Tollbooth*, or *Seaward*. In mimetically oriented narratives, the most famous example is perhaps Huckleberry Finn's journey on the raft down the Mississippi. Running away, pursuit, and escape are auxiliary motifs associated with journey as well as quest. Robinson Crusoe runs away from home, Nils Holgersson is forced to leave home, Moomintroll leaves with his mother's blessing to have some adventures, and Ronia the robber's daughter moves from home after a conflict with her father. Throughout his whole journey, Nils is pursued by an antagonist, which adds to the suspense and reveals Nils as a character in his reactions to the antagonist's tricks.

Survival in some threatening surrounding is the central motif of Robinsonnade, having its origin in *Robinson Crusoe*. It is also found in an episode in *Tom Sawyer* and is parodied in *Pippi Goes on Board* when Pippi stages a shipwreck herself. If we consider the motif of survival as such and not the setting (a desert island) as the most essential feature of Robinsonnade, then we can classify such diverse books as *The Catcher in the Rye* and *Ronia the Robber's Daughter* as modern Robinsonnades.

The motif of struggle between good and evil is typical of fantasy, but it can also be found in detective and adventure stories. A mystery is associated with crime novels, but it can once again be the mystery of somebody's identity, such as Johnny's in *Johnny My Friend*. In children's fiction, we seldom find murder; more often the mystery concerns a less serious crime, such as theft or smuggling.

Apparently, all these plot elements put characters in extraordinary situations, in which character traits can be more vividly revealed. Two more everyday events, however, also radically change the protagonist's situation. The arrival of a new sibling is a crucial point in a children's plot, while it is for obvious reasons almost nonexistent in the mainstream novels. A new family member shatters the child's universe, not seldom disrupting the child's self-centered position; in most children's novels, it is described as a traumatic experience. The protagonist's attitude toward the new sibling is a significant characterization device. Finally, the death of a parent, a grandparent, a friend, or a pet brings insight about the character's own mortality (see Butler 1984; Nikolajeva 2000).

The reason certain motifs are more widespread in children's fiction than in mainstream is most probably the characters' (and the readers') age. Journeys, both real and imaginary, discoveries, the search for identity, and survival on one's own without adults' assistance are all important components in a young person's psychological development. The insight about death is necessary for a young person to be able to go further and become adult. On the other hand, some motifs that are more essential in adult life, such as marriage and adultery, professional career, parenthood, fighting a terminal illness, and old age, are unusual in children's fiction, although they can, of course, be present as secondary motifs.

Beginnings and Ends

In discussing some key moments in a "children's plot," I have already suggested that certain elements are widely used in children's novels to mark the beginning or ending of the plot. These elements are, however, different from those typical in the mainstream. In their discussion of classic plots, Scholes and Kellogg (1966) suggest that human life provides the most impeccable plot: "What more perfect beginning than birth or more perfect ending than death?" (211). For obvious reasons, such a plot would not work in children's fiction, in which a character cannot even enter adulthood without the novel ceasing to be children's fiction (see the much-quoted ending of *Tom Sawyer*). Not even the whole life span of a seven- or ten-year-old protagonist is easily grasped by a young reader and therefore of little interest. Yet most plots in children's fiction are indeed constructed in the traditional manner, with a beginning, a middle, and an end, following other plot patterns suggested by Scholes and Kellogg, apart from the biographical: the romantic, "desire to consummation" (212), or occasionally the moral, "redemption and atonement" (216).

A standard plot begins with an exposition in which characters and setting are introduced. The exposition in a children's novel may be of two kinds. As already mentioned, a vast number of novels open with the characters' physical dislocation, so that the characters are presented to us not in their usual surroundings but in alien ones, sometimes idyllic (*Heidi*), sometimes threatening (*The Mouse and His Child*), sometimes undetermined, allowing the reader to guess whether the new situation is benevolent or not (*Tom's Midnight Garden*). By contrast, the protagonists may be introduced in their normal environment, into which an unusual element is brought, once again, exciting (*Five Children and It, Mary Poppins,* or *Karlson on the Roof*) or dangerous (*Comet in Moominland*). The characters' reaction to their changed situation is an excellent way of exposing their most prominent traits.

In any case, some change in the character's situation is essential to set the plot in motion. However, unlike adult protagonists, child characters seldom, if ever, can decide their fate themselves. They do not choose to leave home, but are forced to do so by the adults. For instance, Heidi is first taken to live with her grandfather in the mountains, then ruthlessly and without warning snatched away from him and placed in a family of complete strangers in Frankfurt. Tom in *Tom's Midnight Garden* is sent away to stay with his relatives, despite his violent protests. True, some young characters run away from home; however, this reaction is nearly always provoked by some action on the part of adults—for instance, in *The Adventures of Huckleberry Finn.*

After the character has been taken through complications in a rising action reaching the climax point, a resolution, a falling action, follows. Resolution, at least in classic Aristotelian poetics, does not imply the solution of the conflict; it is merely the part of the plot following the climax (the culminating and turning point of the plot). The character's participation in the resolution allows a good deal of characterization. The final pages of *The Lion, the Witch and the Wardrobe,* describing the children's happy rule as the kings and queens of Narnia after the climax of the victory over the Witch, is a good example, as the various deeds of the characters are presented. Resolution should therefore not be confused with denouement, in which the fate of the character is known, the initial order restored, and the narrative brought to a closure. For a child character, the closure can imply either a further empowerment or a disempowerment. When Tom Sawyer finds the treasure and, albeit indirectly, wins over Injun Joe, he not only enhances his position as a hero, he also gains higher status in adult society. The Pevensie children, on the other hand, return from their adventures in Narnia and are stripped of their regalia, their wisdom, and glory.

It is further necessary to distinguish between structural closure (a satis-

factory round-up of the plot) and psychological closure, bringing the protagonist's personal conflicts into balance. Normally, in a children's story
these coincide. When Pinocchio is turned into a human boy, the plot,
involving his achieving this transformation, is concluded, and the protagonist's conflicts with the external enemies as well as with his own self are
solved. Peter Pan's victory over Hook is synchronized with Wendy's accomplished quest for Self and her readiness to go home. However, the structural
and psychological closures may stand in discrepancy to each other. For
instance, the arrival at their grandmother's house is a natural way to finish
the Tillerman children's journey in *Homecoming*; however, it does not solve
the main conflict of the story, does not bring back the children's mother,
and does not necessarily promise an easy and happy future for the characters. The superficial plot is concluded; the "human" plot is left open-ended.
The ironic title adds to the ambiguity of the ending. For characterization,
psychological closure is naturally more interesting than structural.

The happy ending—which in most cases presupposes a combination of
structural and psychological closure—is something that many adults immediately associate with children's literature and that many scholars and
teachers put forward as an essential requirement in a good children's book.
Folktales always have a happy ending, expressed by the coda "lived happily
ever after." Since children's fiction borrows many of its structures from folktales, most traditional children's books have a happy ending, at least superficially: Dorothy returns home, the White Witch is eliminated, the treasure
is found, and so on. In contemporary novels for children, we notice a deviation from the obligatory happy ending, on a structural as well as psychological level. Instead of a closure, implying a rounding off of the plot, a
happy reunion of the protagonist and his object of quest (often a kidnapped
friend, pet, sibling, or parent), victory over the antagonist, and so on, we
see a new opening, *aperture*, for the character.

Unlike a structural open ending, aperture does not in the first place imply
the possibility of further character development (providing an opportunity
for a sequel) but an indeterminacy concerning both what has actually happened and what might still happen to a character. Aperture is thus an ending that allows an infinite bifurcation of interpretations. Aperture in fact
precludes a sequel, since depending on the bifurcation we choose, the
course of further events would be radically different. I would therefore suggest reserving the terms *closed ending* and *open ending* for denoting structural
settlement of the plot, while *closure* and *aperture* would describe the psychological completion of the character at the end of the narrative. Closure

presents the character as fully depicted, leaving no questions about his qualities. Aperture allows us to contemplate further.

Let me illustrate the concept of aperture with *The Giver*. In the end of the novel, Jonas has escaped from his community with his baby brother Gabriel, and we see him struggling through the hostile snowy landscape toward an unknown destination. There are several indications in the final chapter that Jonas is dying of exposure and that the vision of a sledge on the slope and the sounds of Christmas carols are his death-agony hallucinations. Since the word *Elsewhere* has been used in the novel as a euphemism for death, Jonas's heading for and reaching Elsewhere can be interpreted as his dying. Yet, we may also decide that Jonas survives and reaches Elsewhere, which actually exists outside his community. However, this Elsewhere may either prove just as cruel as his own community or be different. If it is another totalitarian society, Jonas may either be killed or extradited to his own community (back to square one). If it is a free world, he and Gabriel may be accepted, adopted into a nice and loving family, and live happily ever after. But he may equally be rejected as an alien and a spy from an antagonistic world. If he is rejected, he either dies or returns to his own community, and so on. This bifurcational argument may seem a fruitless speculation, but I have deliberately stretched the text to illustrate my point.

We could interpret the ending of *The Giver* in yet another way. Upon his escape, Jonas releases part of his memories into the community (the science fiction genre saves us the unnecessary question of the technicalities of this action). We also know that upon a Receiver's death, all the memories accumulated in his or her mind are released—this happened once before with Rosemary, the previous Receiver. The recovery of memory may have two effects on the community. The authorities may capture the memories and prevent them from entering the inhabitants' minds (which happened with Rosemary). On the other hand, we know that Jonas has received considerably more memories than Rosemary ever did, and that he is a more powerful Receiver than Rosemary was. The scope and force of Jonas's memories may be so great that the community will be affected radically and eventually restored to what we perceive as normal human existence. If so, Jonas's sacrificial death makes him exactly the Savior figure the novel hints at, and his escape is meaningful (even though dubious as a satisfactory closure for a children's book, since a child is given a role that no adults can shoulder). In terms of characterization, it certainly makes a difference whether we see Jonas as a successful or a failed hero or whether his failure is indeed his victory. The ending of *The Giver* creates the indeterminacy without setting the reader into frustration. The readers who are reluctant to see Jonas as dying are equally allowed to decide that he lives happily ever after.

Thus, aperture leaves it for the reader to decide what happens next to the character, sometimes even what has actually happened and what conclusions the character must draw. We find examples of aperture in novels as different as *The Catcher in the Rye* and *The Brothers Lionheart*. Has Holden been cured now? Will he manage to attend a new school, and will he live up to the expectations that his parents and society have for him? Would a sequel depicting Holden adjusted to societal norms satisfy the reader's appreciation of this complex character? Is Rusky dying in the end of the novel, or has he actually been dead all along? Would a sequel depicting Rusky's further adventures in the next world add anything to the moral dilemma of the protagonist? Aperture stimulates the readers' imagination in a way traditional closure can never do.

On the other hand, it may leave a less sophisticated reader frustrated. Astrid Lindgren has received many letters from young readers demanding a sequel to *The Brothers Lionheart*. Fortunately, she resisted the temptation; however, for the sake of dissatisfied readers, she published a ten-line epilogue describing Rusky's and Jonathan's happy life in Nangilima. In any case, aperture seems a more natural ending for a children's novel, because child characters are always left halfway in their maturation; they are by definition not fully developed as individuals, or we would not be dealing with children's fiction. By contrast, happy endings in fairy tales, which children's stories have inherited, involve young people of marriageable age (with some rare exceptions, such as Little Red Riding Hood or Hansel and Gretel).

The happy ending is one of the foremost criteria in the conventional definitions of children's literature, as well as one of the most common prejudices about it. However, the notion of the happy ending is culturally and historically dependent. In the Western sentimental and moral nineteenth-century stories for children, the death of the main character was a happy ending: the child was united with God and thus was rewarded for his earthly sufferings—for instance, in *The Little Match Girl* or *At the Back of the North Wind*. Today we would not view death as a happy ending. Endings are also genre-dependent. In a love story, the reunion of the hero and heroine is a happy ending. In a western, the hero rides away from the heroine toward the setting sun—an opening rather than closure. If a character in a contemporary existential novel suddenly marries a film star, inherits a million dollars from an unknown aunt, and finds himself heir to a newly diseased count, we will certainly view this as a serious style deviation, or more likely a parody; however, such things happen daily in soap operas. In Disney's version of *The Little Mermaid,* the tragic ending of the original was changed into a happy ending, apparently to adapt the story for the unsophisticated young American audience, used to action and suspense and obviously untrained to appreciate introspection.

Consider an episode in *The Little Prince:* the prince has tamed the fox, and it is time to say farewell. Is this a happy or unhappy ending, to have gained a friend but to have to part? What is more important—for a child and for an adult? And how does the Little Prince's decision characterize him: as unfaithful or as strong in spirit? We agree that *Mio, My Son* is a children's book, but from an adult perspective it has a deeply unhappy ending: the boy is still sitting on a park bench, and nothing has changed. Or do we see a change in the protagonist's attitude toward himself? A happy ending is a relative notion. It is not even definite as a literary convention. Aperture has become so common in contemporary children's fiction that some scholars have begun to interrogate its effect: it has become banal. Some recent novels return to the happy ending, but often with an ironic undertone.

Such a dominant ending of the mainstream novel as marriage (with all its variations, implying the protagonists' reunion with the objects of their desires) is seldom employed in children's fiction. We may see as its variant the child's reunion with the missing parent (*The House of Arden, The Secret Garden, The Neverending Story,* or *Gathering Blue*); however, the power position in this event is not the same as in marriage. Reunion with a parent brings the child back into parental protection, limiting the freedom the protagonist has enjoyed during the parent's absence. In *Gathering Blue,* the happy reunion of daughter and father hovers on the edge of sentimentality, but the author avoids it by letting her character take a mature decision. Furthermore, in contemporary children's fiction, we are more likely to find a pseudo-reunion, in which the recovery of the absent parent brings disappointment rather than joy. In *The Great Gilly Hopkins,* Gilly's recovery of her biological mother implies the loss of her foster family, which she has learned to value—an important insight, marking the character's substantial growth. Likewise, in *Come Sing, Jimmy Jo,* the character meets his real father at the point when he is mature enough to accept his foster father, who has brought him up with love and care: "'I guess in a matter of speaking I am your son. But'—he took a deep breath—'you ain't my daddy'" (194). These examples show very well the relativity of a happy ending and the way the open endings reveal characters' emotional maturity.

Upward and Downward Plot Movement

To understand the character's role in the plot, we can consider two main types of characters according to their power position: the underdog and the trickster, both originating in myth and folklore. The most common hero in a folktale is an underprivileged child or young person, the youngest son or youngest daughter, often a child of unknown origin. At the end, the hero finds his fortune, "the princess and half the kingdom," and he triumphs over those who seemed cleverer and stronger in the beginning. The abandoned orphan is also the most typical character in children's fiction. The degree of abandonment can vary from the parents being away for work to their being away traveling or dead; as shown before, they may also be absent emotionally. Tom Sawyer's and Anne Shirley's parents are dead. The March sisters' father is away at war. Pippi's mother is dead and her father absent (maybe also dead, if we interpret Pippi's stories about him as tall tales, including his "actual" return). The parents of the four children in *The Lion, the Witch and the Wardrobe* remain in London, and we know almost nothing about them; they could be dead. The children are free to have their adventures, since the old professor they are staying with does not mind what they get up to. We can call such children, whose parents are alive but do not care about them, "functional orphans." Elvis Karlsson and Holden Caulfield are two more examples.

Another typical character in children's fiction, originating in folklore, is the trickster. Tom Sawyer is a trickster. Jacob Two-Two is a trickster. Emil in *Emil's Pranks* is a trickster, and as such he has his permanent attributes, his cap and his toy rifle; by the end of the first book he has also acquired a horse, like a real hero. Many "naughty boy" books, such as *Just William*, have the same origin. However unlike the static William, Emil is a dynamic character and becomes a real hero at the end of the third volume, much like his folktale model Tom Thumb. A "tomboy girl," like Jo March or Anne Shirley, alludes to a trickster figure as well, while in *Pippi Longstocking* a girl is put into a typical male trickster role. While the trickster is more common in entertainment literature, the first character type, the underprivileged child, is the most widespread in contemporary psychological children's novels.

Both the underdog and the trickster are characters who, as the plot progresses, change their power position from low to high or at least higher. This is what we often refer to as the intrinsic hope and optimism of children's literature. This upward plot movement is typical in fairy tales and in classic novels. In traditional poetics, this type of plot is called comic (for analyses of comic heroes in literature, see Torrance 1978). In ancient literature, Renaissance drama, and contemporary mainstream novels, we encounter protagonists who start by having power and lose it as the plot progresses—the tragic plot. In Greek tragedy, characters are subjected to

Fate; in Shakespeare they often bring about their own defeat. Contemporary characters lose their life partners or friends, fail in their careers, face a major illness or death, and so on. While a conventional plot will inevitably find solutions for these problems and restore the power balance (new partner, new friend, new career opportunity, miraculous cure), most contemporary existential novels leave the plot unresolved, thus describing a consistent and definitive downward movement for the protagonist. Young adult novels quite often show the protagonist's defeat—in extreme cases, death or suicide.

In a children's novel, a downward movement is unlikely. The major decisions that form human lives are seldom made during childhood, such as the choice of a profession or partner. The temporary defeats that a child protagonist may experience are usually followed by success. If they are not, the protagonists' young age leaves many possibilities open for them. They can repair their social relationships and reestablish broken bonds with their parents; they can improve their academic results and athletic achievements; they can recuperate after traumatic losses. Thus, a protagonist of a children's novel is seldom if ever depicted as an ultimate failure. Naturally, there are exceptions. *Gummi-Tarzan*, a novel by the Danish writer Ole Lund Kirkegaard, portrays a little wimp of a boy, bullied in school, intimidated by teachers, and despised by his father. He meets a witch and gets all his wishes granted—for one day. He wishes to be strong and fights his bullies, displays incredible athletic achievements, reads the most difficult texts in front of his teacher, and so on. One would assume that this day of magical total empowerment would radically change the character's life; for instance, his father would see him a new light, his classmates would fear and respect him, and the teachers would change their minds about his learning abilities. However, the next day, the character is once again exposed to all the bullying, molesting, and humiliation we have seen in the beginning. His power position has not changed, and his self-esteem has apparently sunk lower still, since he is now aware that his situation could be changed but never will. This is an unusual resolution in a children's book, so unusual that it meets considerable resistance in young readers. While this book in the early 1980s topped the library loans in Sweden—an unmistakable sign of its popularity—a unique empirical examination shows that most young readers suppressed the ending. When asked about the resolution, they would answer that the protagonist gets complete power from the witch and can thus obtain revenge on all his enemies. The reversal of power was not acknowledged, and on being prompted, the young readers in the experiment denied it. Trained in conventional narratives with an upward movement, they chose to ignore the deviant ending and interpret the story in a conventional manner (see Asplund Carlson 1996). I do not know of any similar empirical studies, but I would not be surprised if other unresolved narratives were equally misinterpreted by young readers and even by university students.

In my experience, most college students of children's literature perceive the ending of *The Giver* as positive: Jonas and Gabriel have reached a society where they will be accepted and happy. When I point out the strong indication in the text that the character instead is dying of exposure, the imagery amplifying his hallucinations, the students are reluctant to accept this interpretation. I do not necessarily claim that young readers need happy endings. Rather, they are conditioned to see conventional endings, which in our Western tradition happens to be a happy ending, reestablishing the characters in their power position.

On the other hand, it certainly takes some sophistication to see the positive aspects of endings that superficially seem tragic. When the little mermaid sacrifices herself rather than kill the prince and be saved, readers often fail to realize that she has in fact attained the promise of what has been the object of her quest, an immortal soul. In *Bridge to Terabithia*, we may be thoroughly upset by Leslie's death, but for Jess it provides a substantial thrust toward spiritual maturity. In fact, the ending shows him at least partially recuperated and definitely strong enough to go further.

To conclude this argument, while the character's role in the beginnings is relatively uniform, the ends, especially in contemporary children's fiction, offer a variety of means to reveal characters to us, more often posing questions than providing answers.

"Middle Narrative"

Plot design and especially the significance of endings have been thoroughly investigated by Frank Kermode (1968). In standard narratives, which employ a beginning and an end, we meet characters at the moments of crisis and epiphany, that is, in extreme situations, dislocated, exposed to dangers or emotional disturbances, forced to act heroically, and so on. The crisis brings about loss of innocence, resulting in knowledge, insight, and maturity. Character traits are revealed more prominently under such conditions; therefore, it is natural for authors to portray their characters in out-of-the-ordinary settings and situations.

Contemporary narratives tend to deviate from this pattern. Scholes and Kellogg (1966) distinguish between historical and mimetic narratives, pointing out that mimetic narrative is "the antithesis of mythic in that it tends toward plotlessness. Its ultimate form is the 'slice of life'" (13). In a "middle narrative," we meet characters in their everyday life, without any critical or turning points. This is the type of narrative Mikhail Bakhtin (1984) calls polyphonic, to distinguish from epic, or the beginning-middle-end narrative (see further Nikolajeva 1996, chap. 4). There is little chance for characters in middle narratives to gain insights or learn lessons. They cannot show their reactions to extreme situations. The process of maturation is slow and gradual, without sudden and explicit twists. Therefore, the characterization devices in middle narratives must necessarily be more subtle, internal rather than external.

There are very few examples of middle narratives in children's literature; I am thus confined to the books that I have discussed in another context, Maria Gripe's Elvis series (Nikolajeva 1996, 100–1). This five-volume series, of which only two books are available in English, starts when Elvis is six and follows him until he is eight. There are no beginnings or endings in any of the five volumes. The story frames are completely arbitrary, as if suggesting that real life does not conform with the prescribed patterns of a literary plot. The main conflict between Elvis and his mother remains unresolved, possibly accelerating and becoming more hopeless than ever. Friends appear and disappear, and even the most dramatic episode of the series, a car accident in which Elvis is badly hurt, does not bring any climax or reconciliation.

Middle narrative implies that the plot movement goes neither upward nor downward, that the protagonist ends up where he started without even having gone through any considerable changes. *Slake's Limbo* is a good example, with its open ending stressing the character's unresolved situation.

Causality and Motivation

The discussion of the "middle narrative" leads us to the question of causality. In real life, we do not necessarily see events around us in a cause-and-effect relation. In literature, we expect that if an event or an action is depicted it must be important for the plot. From this I conclude that we place higher demand on causality and intentionality in fiction than in real life. Apparently children place still higher demands on causality as compared with adults (children often ask the question "Why did he do so?"). Therefore, the way events and actions are combined in children's fiction is of overall importance. Causality is also a powerful means of revealing characters. Lets us consider the following options:

1. An event/action follows another event/action (very weak causality). Example: Pippi moves into Villa Villekulla. Tommy and Annika make her acquaintance. We do not learn anything essential about the characters from these events.
2. An event/action makes another event/reaction possible (stronger causality). Example: Pippi moves to Villa Villekulla because her father has disappeared in a storm. Although Pippi could have reacted to her father's absence differently—for instance, by taking over the ship and becoming the sea captain herself—her character is revealed to us through her decision to start a new life.
3. An event/action directly causes another event/reaction (very strong causality). Example: Nils Holgersson is rude to the elf and is therefore transformed into a midget. The punishment immediately indicates that Nils's action was wrong; his character is revealed through cause and effect.
4. An event/action is arranged so that it will cause another event/action (intention). Example: The White Witch enchants Edmund with Turkish Delight to prevent Aslan from taking power in Narnia. The witch's behavior reveals her as evil since we know that Aslan represents goodness. Without this intention, we would judge the witch as generous and benevolent.

Naturally, when reading novels, we do not consciously make all these causal connections; however, in the long run they certainly help us to assemble the image of the character from the details provided by the author.

In fiction, we also expect characters to have motivations for their actions. In his discussion of the structure of romance, Northrop Frye (1976, 47f.) points out the difference in design between realism and romance, labeling them as the "hence" narrative and the "and then" narrative. In the former, we expect a good deal of logic in the events and motivation behind the character's behavior; in the latter, the demand for logic, consistency, and continuity is considerably weaker. The characters behave in a certain way simply because the plot requires it of them.

Many critics have pointed out that the literature of romance is, to a high degree, based on coincidences, and children's literature, with its strong inherent links to romance, has the same tendency (see Pinsent 1989). As Frye (1976) remarks, "one of the functions of rhetoric is to present an *illusion* of logic and causality" (48; Frye's emphasis), but certainly in many cases the logic is not too convincing. One of my favorite examples from the mainstream is King Lear's totally unmotivated, plainly foolish decision to divide the kingdom between his three daughters, based on the amount of love they feel for him. This episode has indeed puzzled many mimetically oriented Shakespeare scholars because it lacks logic and motivation. In the obvious hypotext to *King Lear*, a fairy tale known as "Salt and Bread," we do not seek motivation since we have different genre expectations. However, since Lear's irrational decision sets the whole plot in motion, it is as indispensable in the tragedy as it is in the fairy tale. The character's actions are not prompted by his intentions, but by the demands of the plot. In this case, I see Lear as less "human" than Harold Bloom (1998, 476–515) would make him.

Similarly, we may expect characters in realistic children's novels to behave reasonably within the scope of their cognitive potentials, while we more readily accept fantasy characters' behavior according to the plot design. For instance, a fantasy hero fights the dragons because this is his role in the story, and not because he has high moral standards and a strong sense of right and wrong. Frye (1976) points out that the less displaced the characters are, the more rigidly they follow the prescribed patterns of behavior: "Characters occupy the *designed* time and space of their creators; they may as logically end their fictional life at marriage as at death; their paths may cross in sheer 'coincidence.' The more undisplaced the story, the more sharply the design stands out" (38; Frye's emphasis). However, we do ascribe to all characters certain motives, whether ethical or material, altruistic or selfish. Such a motive may be, for instance, fighting evil (the Pevensie children fight the White Witch because it is the right thing to do); revealing external secrets (Tom Sawyer exposes the murderer because it is morally correct); eliminating dislocation (Dorothy goes through the trials in the land of Oz because she wants to go home); finding one's identity (Gilly is reluctant to accept Maime as a substitute parent because she feels strong bonds with her biological mother); or fulfilling desire (the Arden children keep going into the past because they hope to find a treasure and become rich). Frequently the various motivations appear on the different interpretative levels of the text. For instance, eliminating dislocation causes Dorothy to fight evil, and at the same time it can be interpreted as her identity quest. Typically, the conventions of children's literature preclude one of the strongest motivations that drive the characters of adult fiction: sexual desire (unless we interpret oral gratification—e.g., Pooh's love for honey—as a circumscription of sexuality; see further Nikolajeva 2000, 11–16).

What clearly follows from this argument is the fact that we cannot always draw conclusions about characters on the basis of their behavior and motivations, because these may be wholly dictated by the plot. Furthermore, our demand for motivation leans on our general approach to literary characters. As Scholes and Kellogg (1966) point out, "[i]llustrative characters are concepts in anthropoid form or fragments of the human psyche masquerading as whole human beings. Thus we are not called upon to understand their motivation as if they were whole human beings but to understand the principles they illustrate through their actions in a narrative framework" (88). In other words, if we liberate ourselves from the view of literary characters as living human beings, we will not seek any motivation behind their actions, instead trying to examine the writers' design behind them.

Character and Temporality

The various aspects of temporality (duration, order, and frequency) are not directly connected with characterization. Thomas Docherty (1983, 156–213), however, devotes two chapters to the characters' existence in the fictional time of the novel and their experience of time. On closer examination, we can, first, state that temporality in children's fiction is in several respects different from the mainstream and, second, that different types of character demand their special temporality; that is, temporality can to a certain extent function as a characterization device.

Let us first consider the difference in temporality between children's fiction and the mainstream. The duration of children's novels is generally limited. An adult novel can continue for many years in the fictional time. For a child reader, a year is a substantial time span, in proportion to the child's life experience; as psychologists show, a child's perception of time basically cannot stretch beyond the child's age. A brief comparison will illustrate the point.

Fanny Price's arrival in her rich relatives' home in *Mansfield Park* is not unlike a similar opening of many children's novels—for instance, *Heidi* or *Anne of Green Gables*: a physical dislocation as a way to set the plot in motion. Fanny is ten years old; however, the novel is not concerned with her childhood or growing up, and after a very short description of her first confrontation with the new surroundings, there is a gap of five years that the readers are to fill to their best ability. By contrast, the first days after Anne's arrival at Green Gables take several chapters, and her first year out of the five described in the first volume takes over half of the book, before time accelerates and separate events in Anne's life are described with considerable temporal ellipses between them. In *Heidi*, the protagonist's first evening and morning at her grandfather's take three chapters, and even though there are some ellipses between the episodes, the flow of time is somewhat continuous. A gap of five years, as in *Mansfield Park*, is almost inconceivable in a children's novel, since young readers would not be able to fill them from their experiences. A children's novel may end in a kind of epilogue, telling the reader about what happened when the protagonist grew up (the last chapter of *Peter Pan*, titled "When Wendy Grew Up"), but this is a vision rather than an actual part of the plot.

Temporality in *Heidi* and *Anne of Green Gables* is typical of classic girls' novels, based on cyclical time, repetition of seasons, and recurrent events in the protagonists' lives. The difference between the two novels is that despite the flow of linear, chronological time, Heidi does not seem to be growing up, changing, or maturing; she seems to be stuck in an atemporal state of perfect happiness, a primeval, mythic time, *kairos* (see Nikolajeva 2000). Anne, as shown in chapter 7, is developing and changing. The temporality of the novel is thus interconnected with the character construction.

The temporal structure of adventure stories, especially with episodic or combined progressive/episodic plots, is based on the disjunctive pattern: each episode is described in detail, but substantial temporal ellipses exist between episodes. Since the duration of each episode is limited, it does not allow any character evolution, while ellipses do not encourage the reader to fill in the missing information about the characters, because this information is not essential to the plot.

On the other hand, many contemporary mainstream novels have a very short duration, the extreme being perhaps *Ulysses*, where discourse time by far exceeds story time, the temporal pattern called stretch. By concentrating the plot on one single day or several days, authors can show characters literally at the moment of crisis, rather than unveiling their evolution during the course of many years. Clearly, the characterization devices used in combination with such temporality will be different. The lesser the time span, the more dramatic the change in character. Most of contemporary, character-oriented children's novels involve a short duration, often just a few days. The plot is focused on some turning point in the protagonist's life, rather than describing a long process. This has several consequences for characterization. First, a short duration means that scenes dominate over summaries as the principal temporal pattern. Summary (in which discourse time is shorter than story time) is narrator's discourse, which implies that the information we get about the character is mediated through the narrator. In the summary, "Two years passed, and Katy had now changed," we only hear the narrator's statement; we have not witnessed the process, and we cannot even be sure that the change has indeed occurred. A scene (in which discourse time equals or approximates story time), which may be a dialogue, a description involving external focalization, or a mental representation of a character's inner life, is closer to figural discourse. It allows us to know and understand the characters better, share their literal views and internal changes. Even though we cannot use the ratio of scenes to summaries as the absolute measure of literary quality, scenes definitely allow more profound characterization than summaries. For extremely intense experiences, stretch can be used—for instance, the fight episode in *Dance on My Grave* or Johnny's reckless biking down the stairs in *Johnny My Friend.*

On the other hand, short duration naturally excludes gradual change. Here some other temporal patterns may come in handy. *Analepsis*, or flashback, is a form of anachrony in which the narrative precedes the main story. Analepsis is a powerful characterization device since it can provide additional information about the characters' background. Most of *Johnny My Friend* is narrated in an analepsis, in which the protagonist recollects a year he has experienced together with Johnny. The primary story takes a couple of hours while Chris is interrogated by the police. *Prolepsis*, or flashforward, is an anachrony in which the narrative antecedes the main story. It may take the form of: "as he learned later." A prolepsis may thus illuminate the character's naïveté or lack of understanding at the time of the events by providing the insights gained later.

A *paralepsis* is a side narrative that can be connected with a given moment within the main narrative but does not take any of the story time. Magical journeys in space and time can be regarded as paralepses. In terms of characterization, a paraleptic narrative enables a significant maturation which would perhaps take many years otherwise. This is especially vividly shown in *The Lion, the Witch and the Wardrobe*, in which the children grow up in Narnia, while they can still return to their own world and become young again. Similarly, the whole story of Mio's struggle against Sir Kato presumably takes place during a couple of hours while he is sitting alone on a park bench in Stockholm, and the whole story of *The Brothers Lionheart* takes place during Rusky's death agony. A paralepsis thus allows a short story time and a significant moment of crisis while simultaneously providing a longer time span in the secondary narrative, which enables gradual change and growth.

Such temporal plot elements as foreshadowing, backshadowing, and sideshadowing allow some interesting additional means of characterization. *Foreshadowing*, or anticipation, mainly gives us a hint of events to come, but it can also contribute to characterization. For instance, Dorothy's silver shoes foreshadow her safe return home. Throughout the story, we are given hints about the power of the silver shoes, and Dorothy is shown as naive since she never even reflects upon this matter. Backshadowing and sideshadowing are concepts coined by analogy with foreshadowing (Morson 1994). *Backshadowing* implies an explication of an event or an action in retrospect. It is a very powerful characterization device. Most of Chris's understanding of his enigmatic friend Johnny, conveyed to the reader, is revealed through backshadowing. *Sideshadowing* implies a revelation of an event by means of a parallel event, real or imaginary, showing what could have happened under different circumstances. For instance, when Chris contemplates what a happy life Johnny might have had if he and his family had interfered in time to prevent Johnny's brutal death, this shows that Chris has now abandoned his childish solipsism and is more prepared to take responsibility for other people.

Narrative frequency may supply us with essential details about characters. Iterative, marked by such words as *always, often, every day*, and *each spring*, provides important information about the characters' habits, their repeated actions and reactions, which confirm and amplify facts that we already know (see more on iterative in Nikolajeva 2000).

Thus, although temporality is strictly speaking not an element of the plot, characters undoubtedly exist within the temporal structures of the text, and the various temporal patterns can enhance or impede our understanding of them.

CHAPTER NINE

～

Authorial Discourse
Description and Narration

External representation is the least complex way of revealing a character, and it is also the way that most clearly resembles our getting to know real people: by their appearance and by their actions and reactions. In external representation, characters are opaque, and we do not know any more about them than other characters would.

Scholes and Kellogg (1966) suggest characterization in Icelandic sagas as "an almost pure and perfect example of the external approach to character" (172). It is seldom that external representation is the only means of characterization in a novel; normally it is combined with other devices. However, we can speak about external orientation in characterization, meaning that most of the facts that we learn about a particular character are conveyed through external means: description, narrator's comments, actions, and events.

External orientation is closely connected with several literary factors. First, it occurs in older rather than in contemporary texts. Second, for obvious reasons, it is more common in plot-oriented narratives focused on what characters do rather than on how they feel about their doings. Third, it is more frequent in formulaic fiction than in psychological narratives. Fourth, it is more likely to be used in texts addressed to younger children. Finally, external orientation more or less presupposes an omniscient perspective. None of these are absolute rules, and the examples that follow will show how external representation can be used in combination with other characterization devices.

External orientation does not imply deficient characterization. While we today attribute higher aesthetic quality to psychological portrayal, penetrating the innermost parts of the human mind, it is wrong to assume that external characterization is artistically inferior; it is merely a different device. Moreover, external characterization is part of the overall didactic adaptation of children's fiction to the cognitive level of its implied readers. Young readers can more easily understand and judge characters' actions, external descriptions, or the narrator's direct statements about them than subtle psychological changes and motivations. Since literature is dependent on language to describe emotional life, it demands a rich and multifaceted vocabulary to convey the nuances of meaning, which young readers may not master yet. There is a clear tendency in fiction for younger children toward external characterization, while young adult fiction frequently employs internal means.

Description

Description is the most elementary way of presenting a character. Historically, however, it is a late invention. We do not find it, for obvious reasons, in ancient drama; it is sparsely (although quite efficiently) used in epics—for instance, Icelandic sagas. It is totally absent from fairy tales, in which characters instead are given epithets: Vasilisa the Beautiful, the Brave Tailor, Faithful Johannes, or Clever Elsa. As a consistent means of characterization, description emerges in Western literature with the rise of the classic novel. Its abundance in classic literature, including classic children's novels, also has to do with the late eighteenth-century theory of physiognomy, directly connecting people's physical appearance with their psychological traits. As Shlomith Rimmon-Kenan (1983, 65) notes, although this theory has been completely discredited in the twentieth century, its influence is still manifest in fiction.

We assume that descriptions have a purpose in a novel, that they have deeper significance, although they may be included in the novel merely because the author wants to create a fuller portrait of the character (see Docherty 1983, 9–42). We should also distinguish between mimetic and nonmimetic description. In a formulaic novel, blond hair will indicate innocence, while dark hair will indicate evil. In a realistic novel, the color of hair does not necessarily imply moral qualities (cf. Price 1983, 24). Yet, certain external traits, such as crooked teeth, moles, extreme facial hair, and so on, are often ascribed to evil characters even in realistic modes.

Generally, in formulaic fiction, description is limited to a few stereotypical traits: "Nancy [Drew], a slender attractive girl of eighteen with reddish-blond hair . . . George Fayne, a trim-looking brunette with short hair and a boyish name" (*The Haunted Bridge*, 1).

In picturebooks and illustrated books, illustrations are naturally better suited to serve the purpose of description. Even if the edition itself is not illustrated, the cover may provide a portrait of one or several characters. The text usually does not have to supply any additional information about the characters' looks, or, if it does, we regard this as unnecessary duplication. Also in theater and film, we get an immediate and more or less complete picture of the characters' appearance. Verbal description lacks this immediacy and completeness. To begin with, a story may omit character description altogether, leaving the characters' appearance up to the reader to invent. Exactly how we fill in such gaps depends partly on our experience, partly on our imagination. From experience, we know the difference between men and women, boys and girls, children and adults, people of different races, and so on. Even a brief mention of a fact ("The old lady put her spectacles down"; *Tom Sawyer*, 7) may help us to create a portrait of a character. However, it depends on our imagination how detailed this portrait will be.

Character descriptions are seldom complete in the sense that they provide all details about the character's looks. When meeting a person in real life, we usually pay attention to certain features: face, eyes, hair, perhaps the general shape of the figure, height, and so on. Unless the person has any specific traits, such as a beard, spectacles, or a very prominent birthmark, we do not register the absence of those; likewise, we do not register the fact that the person has two eyes, two ears, two legs, two arms, and five fingers on each hand. However, if a person only has three fingers, as does a character in *The Devil's Arithmetic*, we will immediately observe this.

Authors construct character descriptions on the same principle. Unless the character is supposed to have a deviating feature—one leg (John Silver), missing hand (Hook in *Peter Pan*), a scar (Harry Potter), one eye, extremely big ear lobes—the description will concentrate on the general traits. Figure, posture, face, eyes, and hair are the most common features used in descriptions, since these are the traits we normally notice first. The characters' clothes are often included in descriptions, which may serve various purposes—for instance, to convey information about the characters' social status.

Unlike an illustration or a film, where our perception of the characters' looks is instantaneous, a novel needs a descriptive pause to provide the reader with a character description. A pause (a temporal narrative pattern

in which story time is zero) stops the natural flow of events. It was once customary in novels to stop the plot and provide a description, such as by saying, "As young readers like to know 'how people look,' we will take this
moment to give them a little sketch of the four sisters who sat knitting away
in the twilight" (*Little Women*, 5). The description is not motivated otherwise than by convention: the presumed expectations of the implied readers.
The description itself is quite detailed:

> Margaret, the eldest of four, was sixteen, and very pretty, being plump and fair,
> with large eyes, plenty of soft, brown hair, a sweet mouth, and white hands,
> of which she was rather vain. Fifteen-year old Jo was very tall, thin, and
> brown, and reminded one of a colt, for she never seemed to know what to do
> with her long limbs, which were very much in her way. She had a decided
> mouth, a comical nose, and sharp, gray eyes. . . . Her long, thick hair was her
> only beauty, but it was usually bundled into a net, to be out of her way. Round
> shoulders had Jo, big hands and feet. . . . Elizabeth—or Beth, as everybody
> called her—was a rosy, smooth-haired, bright-eyed girl of thirteen, with a shy
> manner, a timid voice, and a peaceful expression. . . . Amy . . . a regular snow
> maiden, with blue eyes, and yellow hair curling on her shoulders, pale and
> slender. (*Little Women*, 5–6)

I have allowed myself to quote this long description almost in its entirety
to demonstrate how well it matches my outline above of what details are
included in a description (hair, eyes, complexion, posture). It can be added
that the description clearly intends to contrast the four sister to each other
(plump—thin, fair—brown, smooth-haired—curly, gray eyes—blue eyes,
rosy—pale). It is almost incredible that four sisters born to the same parents
can have such different looks, but this is a literary convention used to help
the reader distinguish among them.

As already suggested, the description is a narrative pause, not motivated
by the plot. Obviously, the four sisters have seen each other hundreds of
times. Even if it is plausible that they are watching each other as they knit,
they would hardly take notice of each other's eye or hair color, their permanent features. If anything, they might state that Jo's hands and feet have
grown lately or that Amy is paler than usual. However, the description does
not even pretend to be coming from the characters' point of view, rather it
is the omniscient narrator's voice, emphasized by the didactic comments
dispersed throughout the passage: "of which she was rather vain,"
"reminded one of a colt," or "was her only beauty." The author also hurries
to assure her readers that external description is by no means enough to
know the four protagonists: "What the characters of the four sisters were we

will leave to be found out" (6). However, already the description carries substantial information about the sisters' inner qualities: Meg's vanity, Jo's insecurity, and Beth's timidity.

This description is by no way unique in early children's fiction; in *What Katy Did*, a similar narrative device is used: "I want to show you the little Carrs, and I don't know that I could ever get a better chance than one day when five out of six were perched on the top of the ice house" (11).

As in *Little Women*, the author invites us to get acquainted with the characters posing in front of us, as if in a photo.

> Clover . . . was a fair sweet dumpling of a girl, with thick pig-tails of light brown hair, and short-sighted blue eyes. . . . Pretty little Phil . . . Elsie, a thin, brown child of eight, with beautiful dark eyes, and crisp short curls covering the whole of her small head. . . . Dorry was six years old, a pale, pudgy boy, with rather a solemn face. . . . Joanna . . . was a square, splendid child, a year younger than Dorry; she had big grave eyes, and a wide rosy mouth, which always looked ready to laugh. (11*ff.*)

In this description, we recognize clichés from *Little Women*: eyes, hair, and complexion are emphasized, and opposites are used to help the reader distinguish between the characters. Since Katy's siblings are not as prominent in the novel as the four March sisters, the description is very much a purpose in itself, as if the author knows that her readers will expect it, following her fellow author's statement that "young readers like to know how people look."

Katy herself is described last, after and in contrast with her best friend Cecy,

> a neat, dapper, pink-and-white girl, modest and prim in manner, with light shiny hair which always kept smooth, and slim hands which never looked dirty. How different from my poor Katy! Katy's hair was forever in a tangle. . . . Katy was the *longest* girl that was ever seen. (14; author's emphasis)

Moreover, Katy's appearance is also presented as a contrast to her dreams, much like Anne Shirley's:

> Her eyes, which were black, were to turn blue; her nose was to lengthen and straighten, and her mouth, quite too large at present to suit the part of a heroine, was to be made over into a sort of rosy button. (15)

Unlike the previous descriptions, this one is very clearly Katy's evaluation of herself, even though it is presented in free indirect discourse rather than in direct speech, like Anne's, which I discussed in chapter 7.

A detailed description of characters immediately in the beginning of the novel, by way of introduction (called *block description*), is the most common way of using this device. A slightly more sophisticated way is to let the character be observed by someone else, which can occur in the beginning of the novel or later on, as I have shown in chapter 7, when I discussed Pippi Longstocking and Anne of Green Gables. Yet another, widely used device is to let a character go past a mirror and look at her own reflection; we may call this autodescription. It occurs, for instance, in *Emily of the New Moon*. In the Ramona series, the author repeatedly lets the protagonist take a mental look at herself from the outside:

> She felt as if she were standing aside looking at herself. She saw a stranger, a funny little six-year-old girl with straight brown hair, wearing grubby shorts and an old T-shirt. (*Ramona the Brave*, 19)

A description can also be a natural part of the protagonist's comparison of herself to another girl:

> Susan's hair looked like the hair on the girls in the pictures of the old-fashioned stories. . . . Ramona put her hand to her own short straight hair, which was ordinary brown. (*Ramona the Pest*, 18)

At one point, Ramona also sees her reflection in a mirror:

> For the first time Ramona looked into her own mirror in her very own room. She saw a stranger, a girl with red eyes and puffy, tearstained face, who did not look at all the way Ramona pictured herself. Ramona thought of herself as the kind of girl everyone should like, but this girl. (*Ramona the Brave*, 95)

Clearly these descriptions have a radically different purpose than those in *Little Women* or *What Katy Did*. When Ramona watches herself from aside or looks at the stranger in a mirror, this is a part of her self-evaluation and as such of character development. A similar, although infinitely more poignant, episode occurs in *Bleak House* when Esther looks at herself in a mirror after having been sick with small pox.

Yet another natural way of giving an external detail is letting a stranger comment on it: "Everybody kept touching my hair. 'Don't you ever cut it?' they said. 'Can you sit on it? It is naturally black, like that? Do you use conditioner?'" (*Walk Two Moons*, 11). From this passage, we learn that the narrator/protagonist's hair is extremely thick, long, and black, without her looking at herself in a mirror.

In contemporary novels, authors seldom give us a complete description of the physical appearance of the characters; instead, they tend to focus on a detail, which may then be reiterated and amplified throughout the text. This is a more effective means of description since it conveys a sense of the character as individual, rather than a standard set a features. In *Johnny My Friend*, for instance, the phrases "half a tooth missing. At the top on the right. From where I am" are recurrently used to describe Johnny's most conspicuous feature; this is his "special trait," also appearing in the police report. Johnny's red hair, on the other hand, is marked in the beginning and not referred to often, since after the first acquaintance Chris, the narrator, does not pay much attention to Johnny's appearance. The portrait of Johnny in the beginning of the book comes naturally since Chris is asked to describe his friend to a police officer:

> The cop noted down this freckles business as well. Can you describe them in more detail: dense, patchy, just dotted about? Even, uneven? Forehead, nose, chin, neck?
> Johnny's girlish face hovered there in front of us: freckles dotted evenly all over it, apart from the chin.
> Not his chin? Neck? Forehead?
> The cop wanted to know exactly.
> It wasn't easy to comment on his forehead. His red quiff blocked the view.
> OK, freckly. And red-haired. No doubt he had green eyes as well, then?
> The cop could be damn sure of that: Johnny's lights flashed green! . . .
> There's plenty to say about Johnny's peepers all right. But let's cut! You can't describe him like that: hair, eyes, skin, and colours. Smile, voice, deportment, gestures. That's just wishy-washy, and Johnny was anything but wishy-washy. (24)

This description is very different from the descriptions of the March sisters or Katy Carr. It does not come from an objective, outsider narrator but is an attempt to recollect the looks of a best friend in an extreme situation, a police interrogation. It is emotionally charged; the protagonist/narrator uses a good deal of colloquial idiom, and the description itself has a purpose in the plot. At the same time, the narrator makes it clear that the external description does not in any way present his friend the way he really was.

Already from the examples given it is clear that descriptions can be authorial (presented through an extradiegetic narrator) or figural (presented through a focalizing character). A good example of the latter is to be found in *Bridge to Terabithia*, as Jess sees a newcomer to his little village for the first time:

[S]itting on the fence nearest to the old Perkins place, dangling bare brown legs. The person had jaggedy brown hair cut close to its face and wore one of those blue undershirtlike tops with faded jeans cut off above the knees. [Jess] couldn't honestly tell whether it was a boy or a girl. (18)

Although this description also focuses on hair and clothes, it is radically different from the description of the March sisters. Leslie is seen through another character's eyes, and we cannot be sure whether it is indeed an objective portrait. However, the casual dress immediately pinpoints one of the most prominent traits of Leslie as a character. We also learn something about Jess and his way of viewing other people. The word *jaggedy* is apparently Jess's judgment. The phrase "one of those tops" is also part of the character's discourse. Figural description is always subjective and commonly emotionally colored.

As demonstrated in these examples, description is predominantly used to introduce female characters. This is one of the consequences of gender stereotyping in characterization. Feminist criticism employs the notion of "male gaze" when dealing with stereotypical portrayal of women. Here is, for instance, an example of a female character's looks conveyed through a male focalizer: "a lovely little blue-eyed creature with yellow hair plaited into two long tails, white summer frock, and embroidered pantalettes" (*Tom Sawyer*, 22). We immediately recognize the clichés of eyes and hair as the prominent traits. However, as the examples above show, stereotyping in external description is frequently practiced by female writers. Moreover, in the all-female world of *Little Women*, the initial description of the four sisters does not denote a male gaze. By contrast, as Jess views Leslie, she is ascribed androgynous traits, in a deliberate attempt to break the stereotype.

Classic male characters, appearing in texts by male authors, are seldom characterized by description. For instance, Tom Sawyer is never described externally, apart from the brief mention of the clothes he is wearing or his dirty face and hands. We know nothing about the color of his eyes and hair, the shape of his ears, or the proportions of his body. This common negligence may be accounted for by the authors' inherent "masculine" style of writing, the authors' preconceived opinions about their implied readers' lack of interest in description (which, as we remember, slows down the plot), or the authors' preconceived opinions about their male characters' lack of interest in their looks. Whatever explanation we come up with, description as means of characterization seems to be one of the strongly gendered narrative patterns in children's fiction. One of the rare descriptions of a male character involves cross-dressing; as in some prior examples, the character is watching himself in a mirror:

> He was gazing at a girl with fluffed, slightly frizzed blonde hair that haloed a tanned face touched with a blush of colour on high cheeks. She had a wide, generous mouth, perhaps a too prominent chin. She wore a loose white sum- mer dress. (*Dance on My Grave,* 213)

Hal has for a short time adopted a female identity, but he studies himself as if from outside, as he would have gazed at a girl. He even wonders "whether this girl would attract him" (214). Since Hal is homosexual, the use of fem- inine characterization device is appropriate and efficient.

Description as Part of Character Evolution
The examples so far examined show that authorial description is most fre- quently an objective in itself as a fill-in, while figural description provides deeper characterization of the focalizer as well as of the focalized person. Description can further be used for more profound reasons—for instance, to show change in a character. In *The Secret Garden*, external description, combined with the narrator's comments, is one of the most prominent characterization devices. Our first impression of Mary Lennox is far from favorable:

> [E]verybody said she was the most disagreeable child ever seen. It was true, too. She had a little thin face and a little thin body, thin light hair and a sour expression. Her hair was yellow, and her face was yellow because she had been born in India and had always been ill in one way or other. (7)

This description can cause two types of response from the readers. Sharing the narrator's position, we will immediately develop a disliking for the character, which will hamper our empathy and which will have to be overcome as Mary improves in the eyes of the narrator, as well as in the eyes of other characters. It is also possible that we will feel sympathy for Mary, especially since the text goes on describing how unwanted and neglected she is by her parents. Fur- thermore, the conventions of reading will prompt us to recognize that Mary is the protagonist and that we therefore must adopt a subject position as close to her as possible. This position is, however, once again hampered by the fact that the description above is not Mary's picture of herself—she is happily unaware of herself being "sickly, fretful, ugly" (7)—but an outsider's view. The description creates an ambiguity in the reader's subjectivity: apparently, the less sophisticated the reader, the stronger the empathy.

The purpose of the description is to provide a starting point for Mary's evolution. Like many other narratives in which protagonists are introduced at the lowest mark of their power position, Mary lacks love and care, a home, parents, siblings, pets, and friends. However, unlike the Cinderella archetype, she is neither pretty nor virtuous, and the coming change is all the more profound. This first external description of the main character is very soon contrasted to that of her mother:

[S]he stared most at her mother. She always did this when she had a chance, because the Mem Sahib . . . was such a tall, slim, pretty person and wore such lovely clothes. Her hair was like curly silk and she had a delicate little nose which seemed to be disdaining things, and she had large laughing eyes. (9)

The first thing we can state about this description is naturally that it presents the mother and daughter as direct opposites: "pretty—ugly"; "hair like curly silk—thin light hair"; "delicate nose—thin face"; "laughing eyes—sour expression." But unlike Mary in the first description, her mother is not seen through an objective narrator's eyes, but through a neglected daughter's. Mary may not be aware of being neglected, but the passage definitely indicates that she is aware of her mother's pretty appearance. She enjoys watching her mother, and subconsciously she must be comparing the pretty Mem Sahib to herself. This suggests that Mary is perhaps not as unaware of her own plain looks as it may seem. Moreover, that the first description is after all not an objective narration, but a representation of Mary's judgment of herself: "Everybody says I am the most disagreeable-looking child ever seen. It is true, too. I have a little thin face . . . because I was born in India and have always been ill." With this interpretation, the description acquires a different value than if it came solely from an objective narrator.

The next comments on Mary's appearance come from other characters, first from Mrs. Crawford, the clergyman's wife who takes care of Mary before she is sent to England:

"She is such a plain child," Mrs. Crawford said pityingly, afterwards. "And her mother was such a pretty creature. She had a very pretty manner, too, and Mary has the most unattractive ways I ever saw in a child." (15)

The statements reinforce the contrast between Mary and her mother, but they also show that the previous description of Mary was after all objective: Mary is plain and disagreeable in other people's eyes. The next evaluation, from the housekeeper Mrs. Medlock, is not much better: "'My word! She's a plain little piece of goods!' she said. 'And we'd heard that her mother was a beauty. She hasn't handed much of it down, has she, ma'am?'" (16). Mrs. Medlock herself is introduced as "a stout woman, with very red cheeks and sharp black eyes" (16).

If the contrast between Mary and her mother is based on the opposites "pretty—plain," Mrs. Medlock provides the contrast between Mary's "sallow" face and the housekeeper's healthy complexion, a contrast that will in the course of the novel become more important than the first one. Mary will never be directly described as pretty, but she will soon be described as more healthy. But so far we see Mary in a railway carriage, through Mrs. Medlock's eyes:

> Mary . . . looked plain and fretful. . . . Her black dress made her look yellower than ever, and her limp light hair straggled from under her black crêpe hat.
> "A more marred-looking young one I never saw in my life," Mrs. Medlock thought. (Marred is a Yorkshire word that means spoiled and pettish.) (18)

Mary's next confrontation is with Martha the young housemaid, who is described as "round, rosy, good-natured-looking creature" (28), and with Martha's brother Dickon: "a funny looking boy about twelve. He looked very clean and his nose turned up and his cheeks were as red a poppies and never had Mistress Mary seen such round and such blue eyes in any boy's face" (92). Both descriptions are once again used to provide a contrast with Mary. But the first person who really makes Mary aware of her appearance is the old gardener: "She had never thought much about her looks, but she wondered if she were as unattractive as Ben Weatherstaff and she also wondered if she looked as sour as she had looked before the robin came" (42).

The gardener becomes the first mirror reflection of Mary which she discovers and which makes her wonder about her own appearance. The author makes Mary's development very palpable with these concrete observations: "the bright-breasted little bird brought a look into her sour little face which was almost a smile" (38); "the big breaths of rough fresh air blown over the heather filled her lungs with something which was good for her whole thin body and whipped some red color into her cheeks and brightened her dull eyes" (44f.); "Poor little thin, sallow, ugly Mary—she actually looked almost pretty for a moment" (46); "She had such red cheeks and such bright eyes and ate such a dinner" (79).

Mary's indifference to food is presented as one of the sources of her poor physical condition: "She has always had a very small appetite" (33). As she begins to spend more and more time outdoors, run, and skip the rope, she "wakened one morning knowing what it was to be hungry" (45). Let us remember that the ideal of female beauty at the time the novel was written differed radically from the late twentieth-century models. Women and girls were expected to be plump and rosy (cf. the description of Meg in *Little Women:* "very pretty, being plump"; or Anne Shirley's laments over her looks: "I am dreadful thin, ain't I? . . . I do love to imagine I am nice and plump"; 13). Thinness and paleness were considered signs of poor health, not least due to the widely spread fear of consumption. Martha is the first to point out for Mary that good, plain food will make her feel better, and Mary very soon discovers the truth of this. Gaining weight is the most tangible result of her physical improvement, but it is also reflected in her hair getting thicker and shinier. The gardener is the first to comment on the change in Mary's appearance:

> "Tha's a but fatter than tha' was an' tha's not quite so yeller. Tha' looked like a young plucked crow when tha' first came into this garden. Thinks I to myself I never set eyes on an uglier, sourer faced young 'un." (88)

Martha's judgment echoes Ben's:

> "Th' air from th' moor has done thee good already. . .Tha'rt not nigh so yeller and tha'rt not nigh so scrawny. Even tha' hair doesn't slamp on tha' head so flat. It's got some life in it so as it sticks out a bit. . . . Tha'rt not half as ugly when it's that way an' there's a bit o' red in tha' cheeks." (143)

Dickon joins in the appraising chorus: "Tha's beginning to look different, for sure" (156), and Mary herself is aware of this, as she replies: "I'm getting fatter and fatter every day . . . . Martha says my hair is growing thicker. It isn't so flat and stringy" (156). The narrator condescends to utter a few words of approval: "the plain child who at that moment could scarcely be called plain at all because her face was so glowing with enjoyment" (180). Finally, the change in Mary's appearance is confirmed by Mrs. Medlock: "She's begun to be downright pretty since she's filled out and lost her ugly little sour look. Her hair's grown thick and healthy looking and she's got a bright color" (242).

The external description is paralleled throughout the novel by the narrator's comments, associating Mary's mental state with her physical condition. If, at the beginning, she is described as ugly in appearance, the narrator's opinion about her inner qualities is not much better: "by the time she was six years old she was as tyrannical and selfish a little pig as ever lived" (8), "she was a self-absorbed child" (13), and so on. The narrator is quite hard on Mary, but at the same time repeatedly tries to

explain and excuse her bad temper by the living conditions in which she
has grown up:

> In India she had always been too hot and too languid to care much about any-
> thing. The fact was that the fresh wind from the moor had begun to blow the
> cobwebs out of her young mind and to waken her up a little. (47)

> In India she had always been too hot and languid and weak to care much
> about anything, but in this place she was beginning to care and want to do
> new things. (67)

The changes in Mary's attitude toward life is very subtly accentuated by
the repeated contrastive use of the verbs *hate* and *like* to describe her feelings. In the beginning, most of Mary's feelings are, without distinction,
negative: "Mary hated their untidy bungalow" (13), "Basil was a little boy
with impudent blue eyes and a turned up nose, and Mary hated him" (14),
"I hate it [the moor]" (28), and "she hated the wind" (45). As she gets to
know her surroundings, the words used to describe her emotions change:

> [S]he began to feel a slight interest in Dickon, and as she had never before
> been interested in any one but herself, it was the dawning of a healthy senti-
> ment. (33)

> She had begun to like the garden just as she had begun to like the robin and
> Dickon and Martha's mother. She was beginning to like Martha, too. That
> seemed a good many people to like—when you were not used to liking. (63f.)

> She was beginning to like to be out of doors; she no longer hated the wind,
> but enjoyed it. She could run faster, and longer, and she could skip up a hun-
> dred. (86)

Mary becomes curious, explores the house and the garden, and finds ways
to bring the garden into bloom again and to bring Colin back to a normal
life. But this internal change is constantly accompanied by repeated external descriptions, as shown above. The mental change is stimulated by physical exercise: running (first to keep warm, later for pleasure), skipping rope,
and finally working in the garden.

Descriptions of the garden parallel the description of Mary and the
changes in her. The first description, at the beginning of chapter 9, echoes
the description of the ugly, passive girl in the beginning of the book. Just as
the gardener serves as Mary's reflection, the garden—on a much more symbolical level—reflects her looks and her state of mind. The changes in the
garden, brought about by Mary's caring hands, evoke her physical and emotional transformation and anticipate the similar process she is about to initiate in Colin. The fact that Mary's mind and spirit are described symboli-

cally through the garden contributes to the overall sense of predominantly external characterization in the novel.

Descriptions of Colin are used once again as a contrast to Mary, but since Colin is introduced after Mary has considerably improved in her looks, Colin's appearance serves as a reminder of what Mary used to be:

> The boy had a sharp, delicate face the color of ivory and he seemed to have eyes too big for it. He had also a lot of hair which tumbled over his forehead in heavy locks and made his thin face seem smaller. He looked like a boy who had been ill. (118)

Interestingly enough, the author amplifies the similarities in the two children's dispositions by echoing the word "hate" in Colin's speech: "My father hates to think I may be like him"; "he almost hates me"; "I hate fresh air" (120*f.*); "Sometimes I hate [my mother for dying]" (127). The rapid changes in Colin's looks repeat—and therefore reinforce—the changes in Mary. He too is immediately affected by the healing power of the garden: as she steps into it, "he looked so strange and different because a pink glow of color had actually crept all over him—ivory face and neck and hands and all" (199). Mary's healthy appetite is also echoed in Colin, who discovers the luxury of fresh milk, eggs, and baked potatoes, and his doctor is not late to note the change: "You are getting flesh rapidly and your color is better" (235). Unlike Mary, Colin is initially presented as handsome, but the author definitely prefers health to pallid beauty:

> The waxen tinge had left Colin's skin and a warm rose showed through it; his beautiful eyes were clear and the hollows under them and in his cheeks and temples had filled out. His once dark, heavy locks had begun to look as if they sprang healthily from his forehead and were soft and warm with life. His lips were fuller and of a normal color. (241)

While this description seems to come from the narrator, the next one is Ben Weatherstaff's view: "the once sharp chin and hollow cheeks which had filled and rounded out and the eyes which had begun to hold the light" (251). The images of health, mainly connected with complexion and roundness, are repeated just as in descriptions of Mary.

Obviously, the author does not trust her readers to recognize and account for the profound physical and mental evolution in her characters. Not only does she promptly spell out all the changes, but she also sums them up in a most didactic manner (261–62). This summary is the best illustration of the function of external description in depicting a dynamic character.

Narration

From the discussion of Mary Lennox, we see clearly that description is used in combination with the narrator's explicit comments. Scholes and Kellogg (1966) call narrative statement the "simplest way of presenting the inward life" (171). Indeed, we move one step further from purely external description toward a portrayal of the character's inner qualities. However, these qualities are not revealed to us by means of representation (showing, mimesis) but by means of narration (telling, diegesis). Since they are part of the narrator's discourse, narrative statements are by definition authoritative. They force us to accept the narrator's judgments of characters rather than allowing us to make our own inferences. Some of the narrative statements about Mary contradict what we as readers can infer from her behavior. While the narrator continues to call Mary lazy, passive, and spoiled, we see that she is improving rapidly.

Narrative statements are widely used in classic novels—for instance, Jane Austen's: "[Mrs. Bennet] was a woman of mean understanding, little information, and uncertain temper" (*Pride and Prejudice*, 53); "[Elizabeth] had a lively, playful disposition, which delighted in any thing ridiculous" (59); "[Lydia] had high animal spirits, and a sort of natural self-consequence" (91). In most cases, they are redundant since the characters' behavior and speech reveal their traits vividly enough. Similarly, the initial description of the March sisters in *Little Women* is soon followed by narrative statements: "Margaret had a sweet and pious nature" (13); "Beth was too bashful to go to school" (37); "[Amy was] good-tempered . . . . her small vanities and selfishness were growing nicely" (38); "at fifteen [Jo] was as innocent and frank as any child" (47); and so on.

Narrative statements can be used to comment on a variety of characteristics, such as the character's external appearance (pretty, ugly, tall, fat), social position (rich, poor), intelligence (clever, stupid), actions (brave), attitudes (greedy), manners (well behaved, kind), and finally on the character's temporary feelings (cold, hungry, tired) or state of mind (agitated, frightened, glad). They can refer to a permanent, inherent quality (brave or clever by nature) or to a concrete action or reaction (brave or clever in this particular situation).

Narrative statements are often associated with traditional, didactic children's fiction: "Flopsy, Mopsy, and Cottontail, *who were good little bunnies,* went down the lane to gather blackberries/But Peter, *who was very naughty*" (*The Tale of Peter Rabbit;* emphasis added). At the time the story was written, it was usual to have such comments in children's books, as if the author did not trust her readers to recognize the three bunny girls as well behaved and Peter as naughty. Similarly, the protagonist of *Curious George* is immediately introduced as "very curious." Interestingly enough, in the first edition of this picturebook from 1941, the narrator condemns George for his trait: "But he had one fault. He was very curious," while in the purified edition from 1969 the text is changed into: "He was a good little monkey and always very curious." The value of being "curious" was apparently negative in the original edition, but somewhat ambiguous in the later one.

Narrative statements are widely used in *Tom Sawyer*, where we find such judgments as "simple-minded soul" (9) about Aunt Polly or the presentation of Sid as "a quiet boy, [who] had no adventurous, troublesome ways" (9). They are also abundant in *Anne of Green Gables*, alongside external descriptions. For instance, Matthew "was the shyest man alive" (2); Marilla "looked like a woman of narrow experience and rigid conscience, which she was" (5); Aunt Josephine "was a rather selfish old lady" (237); and so on. And even in *The Lion, the Witch and the Wardrobe*, written much later, we constantly come across explicit comments both on the characters' permanent traits and their states of mind: "Lucy was a very truthful girl" (29); "Edmund could be spiteful" (29); "Edmund . . . was becoming a nastier person every minute (45); "For the next few days [Lucy] was very miserable" (28); "Lucy . . . was happy and excited" (41); "Edmund had been feeling sick, and sulky, and annoyed with Lucy" (44); "They felt very glad, but also solemn" (99); "They were pretty tired by now" (114); "Peter did not feel very brave; indeed, he felt he was going to be sick" (120). We will hardly find any such narrative statements in contemporary children's fiction, in which characterization is more internally oriented.

Narrative statements are examples of the author filling textual gaps for the readers. Rather than allowing the reader to assemble the characters' portraits from their behavior, the author serves up a complete portrait, with clear and unambiguous labels. Like many other didactic narrative devices, narrative statements can be viewed as inherent to children's fiction; however, contemporary authors employ a number of more sophisticated characterization means, as will be shown in the following chapters.

CHAPTER TEN

~

Authorial Discourse

Actions and Events

Actions and events are elements of discourse that indicate a change of state. "He is hungry" is a state. "He became hungry" is an event. "He became hungry and got some food from the fridge" is an action. It is not always possible to draw a clear-cut border between actions and events. We can say that actions by definition imply the character's active role, while events are something that happens to or around the characters. Some narratologists define an action as a particular form of event that is brought about by an agent, unlike a happening, which occurs without an agent's interference. While actions reflect the character's intentions, motivations, opinions, and beliefs, events as means of characterization are interesting because of the character's response to them.

Characterization by actions is external and hence authorial; however, readers are free to interpret actions and reactions according to their own understanding. Is Tom Sawyer clever or naughty when he cheats other boys into whitewashing the fence for him? How does attending his own funeral characterize him: is he clever, cynical, silly, thoughtless, witty? Is Anne Shirley stupid and wicked when she gives Diana wine to drink, or does she simply not know better? Do characters act according to their intentions, on impulse, or do things merely "happen" to them?

Two devices frequently used for characterization by actions are repetition and juxtaposition. Repeated actions show the characters' determination, perseverance, or occasionally stubbornness. Tom Sawyer's repeated actions characterize him as naughty but not evil. Anne's repeated actions in the beginning of the novel—for instance, her "confessions" of crimes she has not committed—reveal her immaturity. Pooh's actions very consistently characterize him as naive. He pretends to be a cloud trying to get honey from the bees, not realizing how stupid it is; he follows his own steps in the snow convinced that he is chasing a dangerous animal, and so on. Juxtaposition allows a contrast either between a character's actions in different situations or between two characters' actions. Tom's witnessing against Injun Joe in court is worlds apart from his and Huck's childish oath of silence; it shows Tom's moral growth. Anne's hot temper is juxtaposed to Diana's well-mannered nature. While repetition and juxtaposition are naturally very effective techniques, even singular actions can strongly contribute to characterization.

It is impossible and hardly fruitful to analyze the whole scope of actions and events possible and frequent in children's fiction. Moreover, I am not interested in actions and events as such—that is, as elements of the plot, but exclusively in the way actions and events contribute to our understanding of characters. In this chapter, I will concentrate on several areas of human activity in which characters are revealed to us.

The Human Condition

In *Aspects of the Novel*, E. M. Forster (1985, 47ff.) elaborates on the five main facts of human life: birth, food, sleep, love, and death. In his discussion, Forster observes that two of these, birth and death, are secondhand experiences in real life, while in novels they often occupy a central place and can be presented as if they were actual experiences. Forster provides no examples, but we can easily supply them—for instance, the two remarkable childbirth scenes in *Anna Karenina* (i.e., the birth described from the perspective of the woman in labor and from that of the new father) or *Tristram Shandy*, describing the protagonist's supposed memory of his own birth. Death as experienced by a character or by someone close to a dying character is a motif that appears so often in novels that further examples may seem superfluous. It is indeed one of the most prevalent motifs in world literature. Forster (1985, 52) observes that death is also a convenient closing element in a novel.

Quite a few children's novels have death, the fear of death, and "coping with death" as a central or peripheral motif, and writers can deal with death as an "issue" ("How to help children cope with the death of a relative"; see Rudman 1995) or an existential problem (see Butler 1984), in a realistic (*Bridge to Terabithia*) or fantastic (*The Brothers Lionheart*) mode. Most often, the person who dies in a children's book is the protagonist's older relative, quite often a pet ("transitional object"), more rarely a parent, occasionally a sibling or a friend. The event very seldom concludes the novel, as Forster suggests; on the contrary, it is introduced in the beginning to set the plot in motion. By the end of the book, the trauma has been successfully healed. In many novels, the parents' death (utter form of "absence"), as in fairy tales, is the necessary prerequisite for the character's quest (*The Secret Garden*).

The treatment of death in children's literature has changed radically during the past two hundred years, as has the general attitude with regard to death in our society (see Ariès 1962). While the nineteenth-century practice of letting the young protagonist die (see Plotz 1995) may seem improper to us today, it reflects the contemporary views on childhood as the period of blissful innocence, the Christian perspective on death as well as the actual child mortality of that time. Today we may view the ending of Andersen's *The Little Match Girl* as tragic; Andersen's contemporaries were supposed to see the happy reunion of the child and her grandmother in heaven. The taboo on death in children's literature during the first half of the twentieth century gave way to a more serious treatment of the theme in contemporary psychological children's novels. As I show in my study of mythic and linear time in children's fiction, death is one of the three essential components of human growth, together with the sacred and sexuality, and therefore always present in children's fiction in some form (Nikolajeva 2000).

However, it is still uncommon to describe the protagonist's actual death experience. The delicacy of the subject has meant that death is most often described on a symbolical level. By making the protagonist nonhuman, the writer can alienate the death experience. For instance, the Steadfast Tin Soldier is melted down, and the little mermaid dissolves into sea foam. The Mouse and his child are smashed and repaired—death is presented as reversible. Diamond's death in *At the Back of the North Wind* is depicted as a fantastic journey, and so are the seven characters' deaths in *The Last Battle* or Rusky's death in *The Brothers Lionheart*. In all these cases, the reader is given the opportunity to interpret the story literally, as an actual magical transportation rather than death. If we choose to view Rusky's adventures in Nangiyala as his dreams or hallucinations prior to his actual death, the final words of the novel, "*I can see the light!*" (183; author's emphasis) convey the recorded clinical near-death experiences, whether we believe them or not.

In young adult novels we meet a number of depictions of young protagonists anticipating their own imminent death—for instance, *Admission to the Feast*. However, the depiction seldom goes as far as the actual death agony. There are two main reasons for this. First, the depiction itself puts tremendously high demands on the writer, since it is seldom, if ever, a first-hand experience (unless writers have been through a near-death condition and are capable of detaching themselves from the memory well enough to describe it). Second, some unwritten taboos still exist in children's and juvenile literature, and a naturalistic portrayal of death agony is apparently as yet considered unsuitable for young readers, while many other kinds of emotionally disturbing events have been accepted. The ending of *The Giver* may be interpreted as the main character's death, although it is never stated explicitly. If we read it so, the last pages of the novel are indeed a poetic and poignant description of death agony.

Like death, birth is described as a mediated experience in children's fiction; the most common and widely exploited motif is the birth of a sibling. It is often treated by critics as an "issue" ("How to cope with sibling rivalry"; see Rudman 1995). However, like death, the birth experience can be described in a children's book on a symbolical level, the best example being the birth of Annabel in *Mary Poppins Opens the Door*.

Food is the next field of human activity that Forster (1985) pays attention to, noting that in fiction it mainly has a social function; food "draws characters together, but they seldom require it physiologically, seldom enjoy it, and never digest it unless specially asked to do so" (53). Since I have coauthored a whole book devoted to the function of food in children's fiction (Bergstrand and Nikolajeva 1999; see also Nikolajeva 2000, 11–16 and *passim*), I will not dwell on this fascinating subject here. For all that Forster denies the characters of mainstream fiction the joys of food, they are all the more explicit in children's fiction. Furthermore, as several critics have maintained, food in children's fiction is the equivalent of sex in the mainstream. Still more important is that for child protagonists, food is the essential link between themselves and the surrounding adults who have the power to provide food or to deny it. Food symbolizes love and care or lack thereof. A number of well-known children's texts, from *Hansel and Gretel* to *Where the Wild Things Are*, rotate around this theme. Last but not least, food in children's fiction is, much more often than in the mainstream, used for characterization. James Bond may be characterized through his passion for "shaken, not stirred," but we are more likely to remember Winnie-the-Pooh through his passion for "hunny."

Sleep in fiction is dismissed by Forster (1985) as "perfunctory" (53). Although, as he notes, we spend a third of our lives sleeping, literary characters may be described as going to bed or getting up but very seldom asleep. Forster deeply regrets that no novelists have made attempts "to indicate oblivion or the actual dream world . . . neither copied sleep nor created it" (53f.). Here, children's literature shows a radical difference from and, I would venture, superiority over the mainstream. Some of the best children's novels and picturebooks are dream narratives, in which dreams are not merely a parable used to illuminate the main plot, but constitute the plot itself. Sometimes the narrative is explicitly stated to be a dream, as in *Alice in Wonderland*; more often it is implied, as in *Tom's Midnight Garden*. While Alice, on waking up, is comfortably relieved of the necessity of taking responsibility for her actions in the dream, the character of *Marianne Dreams* finds that there is a significant connection between her dreams and her real life. Picturebooks allow vast possibilities in the interaction of word and image to create ambiguity of meaning in dream narratives (see Nikolajeva and Scott 2001, 173–209). It can be said in Forster's defense that, writing his lectures in 1927, he could not have foreseen the emergence of the prominent trend of modern and postmodern fiction exploiting the dream as the central narrative device. However, children's fiction used it as early as in *The Nutcracker,* and in many cases it is also more inventive and imaginative than most of the mainstream dream narratives.

In addition to dream narratives, a variety of bedtime situations constitute a substantial part of children's books plots and not seldom become the plot itself, especially in picturebooks. It can be anything from pure mischief to the anxiety of sleeping in an unfamiliar place, from the security of loving parents to the fear of darkness or serious separation trauma (see Galbraith 1994). Obviously, going to bed, falling asleep, and thereby losing control over oneself is a much more significant event in a child's daily life, which is therefore treated so ardently in children's fiction. Most children's novels contain at least one scene with the child in bed and an adult, often a parent or grandparent, by the bedside comforting, reading or telling a story, saying a prayer or listening to the child's confessions. In *Heidi,* for instance, there are two scenes in which the grandfather watches the sleeping Heidi and which convey a strong sense of affinity between the child and the adult. In *Ramona the Brave,* the six-year-old protagonist discovers that the pleasure of having a room of her own is eclipsed by the horror of sleeping all alone. In an adult novel, when two characters go to bed together, it is most likely to have sex. A child creeping into the parents' bed, a friend staying overnight, a night spent camping have different, and, as often as not, more profound implications. Sleep is thus, in children's novels, as much a social activity as food.

Finally, there is love, which Forster defines very broadly, as all kinds of human relationships. Forster notes that, as compared with daily life, novels are significantly more preoccupied with this activity, that it is in fact the central element in a novel. He observes, furthermore, that the novel characters' obsession with human relationships "is remarkable and has no parallel in life, except among people who have plenty of leisure" (Forster 1985, 54). There is no radical difference between children's and mainstream fiction in this respect. The child protagonist's relationships to parents, other adults, siblings, and friends are as central as any relationship in a mainstream novel. Moreover, a writer is free to focus the temporal span of the novel on the most condensed periods or even moments in a relationship, while omitting, in a temporal ellipsis, quite substantial amounts of "uneventful" time. Thus, an illusion is created that literary characters live infinitely more intense lives than we ordinary people. In children's novels, the temporal span, as mentioned before, is often shorter than in the mainstream, to adjust to the life experience of young readers. A large number of events may seem to be voluntarily squeezed into a very short period of time, sometimes one day. This contributes to suspense, as well as conveying a young child's immensely intense perception of the world.

As Forster (1985) remarks, love "is congenial to a novelist because it ends a book conveniently" (55). Two lovers united in the end indeed present one of the major commonplaces in Western fiction. Since marriage is seldom if ever an objective in children's fiction, the relationships involved do not necessarily demand a resolution. However, as shown in a previous chapter, it is a common device to end a children's book with an established or reestablished relationship: a long-lost father returns home; the protagonist gains a friend or receives a puppy for his birthday. A conflict with a parent or friend is most likely to end in reconciliation. Naturally, just as a contemporary mainstream novel can leave a relationship unresolved, a children's novel today can end in separation and despair.

Forster (1985) concludes his comparison of *Homo sapiens* and *Homo fictus* by describing the latter as follows: "He is generally born off, he is capable of dying on, he wants little food or sleep, he is tirelessly occupied with human relationships" (56). Judging exclusively from this consciously oversimplified description, characters in children's fiction are both more complex and more true to life than characters in mainstream novels—a paradox I would not pursue.

Labor

Sleeping and eating belong to the category of actions that I would call ordinary, actions that every writer and reader has experience of and therefore can easily relate to. There is another important activity, which Forster does not mention, perhaps because this activity is seldom relevant in the classic bourgeois novel he is discussing but all the more prevalent in human life today, and that is work. The nature and amount of work differ substantially in novels and in real life. As with sleep, one-third of our daily adult life is spent at work; however, amazingly little portrayal of work appears in novels. Various kinds of human relationships connected with our work places may take a large space in novels: relationships between bosses and subordinates, professional competition, romance, and so on. However, there is very little depiction of the actual working process, especially in proportion with the amount of time we spend at work in reality. From novels, one can get the impression that people seldom work at all. Manual labor was indeed irrelevant for most of the characters in classic novels, and a large amount of modern popular fiction portrays characters unencumbered by the need to earn their daily bread. From classic literature, we may recollect Levin in *Anna Karenina* involved in agriculture, which is a symbolic act rather than a necessity. We often see ladies in classic novels busy with needlework. However, we are unlikely to encounter any lengthy depictions of conveyor belts, mining, plowing and harvesting, or even office work. We may find a vast number of professions mentioned, but no depictions of actual labor. Not even Charles Dickens, who is perhaps the closest of the English-language novelists to probe into the living conditions of the working classes, has any extensive pictures of labor. As George Orwell (1954) observes in his essay on Dickens, "If you look for the working classes in fiction, and especially English fiction, all you find is a hole" (57); and "one cannot point to a single one of the central characters [in Dickens] who is primarily interested in his job" (93).

Let us first contemplate why work occupies such a negligible place in literature in general. Apart from the upper- and middle-class writers' lack of interest or knowledge, the main reason seems to be that work is an ordinary action, and ordinary actions, such as sleep, meals, or going to the bathroom, are omitted in literature, until they for some reason become extraordinary (Marcel's insomnia or Leopold Bloom's bowel movements). Like sleep and meals, work constitutes a narrative gap which we as readers normally fill with our experience from real life. We assume that all adult characters have an occupation, unless we are told that they live off their dividends. If their occupation is mentioned, we can usually imagine what their work day is like; if not, we still ascribe to them some way of making a living.

Traditional children's literature was written for and about upper- and middle-class children, since these classes were the strongest, if not the sole, consumers of children's books. Fathers in classic children's novels have respectable upper- and middle-class occupations—they are bankers, lawyers, medical doctors, church pastors, or military officers. Mothers are almost without exception homemakers. Child characters in upper- and middle-class children's novels are exposed daily to a huge amount of manual labor, namely the servants'; however, this is taken for granted and never described in detail. Basically, in children's fiction, the adults' work is insignificant. The only professional occupation that characters of children's fiction regularly come into contact with is that of the teacher, and most teachers in children's fiction are objects of hatred and mockery. Child characters seem to be surprisingly ill informed about their parents' professions, as illustrated by the following ironical passage:

> Now, the City was a place where Mr. Banks went every day—except Sundays, of course, and Bank Holidays—and while he was there he sat on a large chair in front of a large desk and made money. All day long he worked, cutting out pennies and shillings and half-crowns and threepenny-bits. And he brought them home with him in his little black bag. Sometimes he would give some to Jane and Michael for their money-boxes. (*Mary Poppins*, 3–4)

The parents' occupation is seldom relevant for the plot. In fact, often the profession is chosen to get rid of the parent to comply with the plot's demands; for instance, if the parent is an explorer, a navy captain, or a missionary in Africa, the necessary "absence" is easily provided. More important, however, is that in traditional children's literature, work is not an issue by definition. In fact, one of the strongest conventions of children's fiction is the absence of all the prominent aspects of human (i.e., adult) civilization, including law, money, and labor (see Nikolajeva 2000, 21*ff*.). Children, real as well as fictional, are supposed to grow up unaware of and unrestricted by these tokens of adulthood. Hence, the conspicuous absence of labor in children's literature has its aesthetic reasons as well as social and historical reasons. Notably, in children's editions of *Robinson Crusoe*, most of the depictions of the protagonist's hard labor on the island are omitted, presumably as being uninteresting—for one thing, uneventful—for young readers. In some of the prevalent genres of children's fiction, such as fantasy, adventure, or the detective story, labor is never mentioned since the characters are preoccupied with killing dragons, searching for treasure, or hunting bandits—once again extraordinary actions chosen in favor of ordinary. In animal and toy stories, labor is naturally not an issue, either.

Work as a life necessity, a means of earning money, is normally beyond a young child's sphere of interest or concern. In classic domestic children's novels, such as *Little Lord Fauntleroy* or *The Railway Children*, "being poor" means that the family has to do with merely one maid and a cook instead of a whole staff as before. We may also recollect how the characters regard the inability to give each other expensive Christmas gifts as the worst result of their poverty. The four March sister also complain of having to work hard; however, their toil does not go beyond reading aloud to old ladies, teaching young children, or doing simple domestic chores. The alleged poverty never forces the young protagonists to earn their living by working in a factory or a mine. A well-known exception is the French classic *The Foundling*, which among other things describes the protagonist working in a coal mine and nearly being killed in an accident. A novel by the German writer Lisa Tetzner, *The Black Brothers*, deals with child labor in Italy in the 1840s. In both stories, the characters are eventually liberated from the hell of manual labor: Remi, when he turns out to be the child of a rich aristocratic family; the poor chimney sweep Giorgio, by being adopted into a rich family and getting proper education. A vast number of Victorian stories deal with poor working-class children who are always comfortably killed off by the authors to provide examples of good morals for their middle-class readers.

One of the most vivid depictions of work in classic children's fiction, Tom Sawyer whitewashing the fence, mocks the whole idea of labor by turning it into a game. As if uncertain that the reader will understand the point, the author puts the following didactic summary into his narrative:

> If [Tom] had been a great and wise philosopher, like the writer of this book, he would now have comprehended that work consists of whatever a body is obliged to do, and that play consists of whatever a body is not obliged to do. And this would help him to understand why constructing artificial flowers, or performing on a tread-mill, is work, while rolling nine-pins or climbing Mont Blanc is only amusement. There are wealthy gentlemen in England who drive four-horse passenger-coaches twenty or thirty miles on a daily line, in the summer, because the privilege costs them considerable money; but if they were offered wages for the service that would turn it into work, then they would resign. (*The Adventures of Tom Sawyer*, 19–20)

Children's fiction is basically about play. It can be serious and dangerous play, involving killing dragons in faraway mythical worlds, but the young characters are inevitably brought back to the security of home and the protection of adults. Creative play is an essential way of training for adult life, and it may contain elements of work. But since young characters, as well as young readers, have vague ideas about what labor in fact is, the depiction seldom goes beyond building a tree house, hunting, or cooking. For instance, Wendy in *Peter Pan* seems to be working hard in Neverland, and the author tries to convince the readers that his heroine indeed enjoys this dull and monotonous work, simply because women are made this way:

> Wendy's favourite time for sewing and darning was after they have all gone to bed. Then, as she expressed it, she had a breathing time for herself; and she occupied it in making new things for them, and putting double pieces on the knees. (84)

However, since everything in Neverland is pretense and make-believe, Wendy's domestic endeavors are merely part of the game.

In *The Secret Garden*, Mary discovers the joys of simple manual work, digging in the garden to make it come alive after ten years' dormancy. This work is used for symbolic purposes, alongside fresh air, exercise, and plain food, that bring about crucial mental and emotional changes in the character. Unlike the hard-working Martha and Dickon, two youngsters from the lower classes who function as catalysts for her improvement, Mary, orphan as she may be, is exceedingly wealthy and will never have to worry about her daily bread. Her gardening is therefore a healthy and useful hobby, not a life necessity:

> She went from place to place, and dug and weeded, and enjoyed herself so immensely. . . . Mistress Mary had worked in her garden until it was time for her to go to her midday dinner. . . . she could not believe that she had been working for two or three hours. She had been actually happy all the time. (78–79)

Observe that the task of preparing "midday dinner" is taken care of without the protagonist contemplating it, as are all the other duties of the enormous Craven household. By contrast, Mary's attitude to her occupation is explicit:

> She worked and dug and pulled up weeds steadily, only becoming more pleased with her work every hour instead of tiring of it. It seemed to her like a fascinating sort of play. (87)

The last sentence is revealing: if Mary were forced to dig the garden to earn her keep at her uncle's, she would not be enjoying it. As it is, she is creating a sanctuary for herself, her cousin, and ultimately her uncle, where they can be forever free from everyday worries and anxieties. Moreover, Mary only has to give the garden a start, the rest takes care of itself, by "magic" that her cousin Colin so strongly believes in.

In the Swedish Noisy Village series, work is also part of play, a nice way for the children to be together and have fun while they are thinning turnips or picking strawberries. The description of these events are joyful and adventurous. Although not particularly rich, the Noisy Village children are not forced to work in order to make their living, and they are too young and carefree to notice the hard work of their parents. Similarly, the endless depictions of the adults' toil in *Little House in the Big Woods* are refracted through the young character's mind. Laura finds them exciting, since she is as yet not concerned about earning her bread. Actually, most of the parents' work is closely connected with providing food, which is the focus of the young protagonist's attention: hunting, fishing, salting and smoking meat, churning, baking, cooking maple syrup, or making cheese. The sight of the adults at work signifies for Laura that there will be plenty of good things for her to eat; her contemplation of work does not stretch further than that (although in the later volume of the Little House series, Laura, getting older, does learn a good deal about manual labor).

In contemporary fiction, children, especially urban children, are if possible still more detached from labor, just as real children in our society are usually detached and protected from "real life" (there are naturally exceptions, rarely reflected in fiction). A matter-of-fact mention of domestic chores is to be found, for instance, in *Bridge to Terabithia*; it does not occupy any prominent place in the novel. Moreover, Jess's farm work is primarily used to emphasize the difference between himself and Leslie, the daughter of rich parents, who is never worried about pecuniary matters. In *Jacob Have I Loved*, the main character contributes to her family's meager budget by crabbing; she feels resentful toward her pretty and talented twin sister who is never expected to do any manual work:

> I would come in from a day of progging for crab, sweating and filthy. Caroline would remark mildly that my fingernails were dirty. How could they be anything than dirty? But instead of simply acknowledging the fact, I would fly into a wounded rage. How dare she call me dirty? How dare she try to make me feel inferior to her own pure, clear beauty? . . . Wasn't it I who brought in the extra money that paid for her [music lessons]? (93–94)

Work is once again used symbolically, for contrasting characterization. Partially, it is self-imposed, a "curse" that Louise believes she is carrying, as the unloved, unwanted twin.

In all these examples, work is marginal, and the descriptions of work are peripheral to the plot; even if work adds to characterization, the depiction of work can be removed from the plot without substantial changes. Under what conditions and circumstances then can labor become central in a children's novel, especially contemporary novels? The most common type of story that allows a depiction of labor is a historical novel; here a profound difference can be observed between the nineteenth-century novels describing their own time and contemporary novels set in the past. Contemporary authors are not restricted by their class, race, or gender, which allows them to break the taboos that the nineteenth-century authors had to respect. A nineteenth-century heroine, such as Jo March, could dream of a professional career but was finally forced, by the conventions of her creator, to find herself in the bondage of matrimony, albeit "equal." The heroine of *Lyddie* is a product of her creator's time and can therefore be portrayed through an unmasked feminist lens. Hired out by her mother as a maid at a tavern, the thirteen-year-old Lyddie dreams of freedom and financial independence:

> Once I walk in that gate, I ain't free anymore, she thought. No matter how handsome the house, once I enter I'm a servant girl—no more than a black slave. She had been queen of the cabin and the straggly fields and sugar bush up there on the hill. But now someone else would call the tune. (18)

As soon as she gets a chance, Lyddie starts working as a weaver at a factory in Lowell. Her ambition is to earn enough to pay off the debts on her childhood home and return to a place where she feels she belongs. But the cabin is eventually sold, her mother dies, the younger brother and sister are adopted by another family, and for a while it seems that Lyddie's drudgery has been all in vain:

> She worked hard because work was all she knew, all she had. Everything else that had made her know herself as Lyddie Worthen was gone. Nothing but hard work—so hard that her mind became as calloused as her hands—work alone remained. (148)

Labor has a double significance here, both a road to freedom and a road into enslavement. Slavery is an essential issue in this novel, set in Vermont and Massachusetts in the 1840s. Lyddie believes herself to be free in comparison with the black slaves in the South, but she soon realizes that she is also a slave in the tavern owner's power. She believes that she will be free through working at the factory, failing to see that she is heading for worse slavery. She does not fully recognize how humiliating factory work is; she gladly allows herself to be increasingly exploited and oppressed, accepting the male bosses' conditions and showing no solidarity with her sister workers if it jeopardizes her wages:

> So it was that when Concord Corporation once again speeded up the ma-
> chinery, she, almost alone, did not complain. . . . She needed the money. She
> had to have the money. . . . Lyddie was given another loom and then another,
> and even at the increased speed of each loom, she could tend all four and felt
> a satisfying disdain for those who could not do the work. (89)

The novel is unique in its detailed depiction of the factory workers' everyday life, the inhuman working conditions, and the first attempts at protest.
Together with Lyddie, we get the first horrifying glimpse of the weaving room:

> Creation! What a noise! Clatter and clack, great shuddering moans, groans,
> creaks, and rattles. The shrieks and whistles of huge leather belts on wheels.
> And when her brain cleared enough, Lyddie saw through the murky air row
> upon row of machines, eerily like the old hand loom in Quaker Stevens's
> house, but as unlike as a nightmare, for these creatures had come to life.
> They seemed to be moved by eyes alone—the eyes of neat, vigilant young
> women—needing only the occasional, swift intervention of a human hand
> to keep them clattering. (62)

The depiction continues for another paragraph and is reinforced a few pages
later, when Lyddie watches another girl work:

> Everything happened too fast—a bobbin of weft thread lasted hardly five
> minutes before it had to be replaced—and it was painfully deafening. . . .
> There were moments when all three looms were running as they ought—all
> the shuttles bearing full quills, all three temples hung high on the cloth, no
> warp threads snapping. (65)

The author uses a lot of professional terms, which are almost certainly
unfamiliar to contemporary young readers but which add a strong sense of
authenticity to the description. There are the terms and the skills Lyddie
has to master, as she begins working herself:

> Within five minutes, her head felt like a log being split to splinters. She kept
> shaking it, as though she could get rid of the noise, or at least the pain, but
> both only seemed to grow more intense. If that weren't trial enough, a few
> hours of standing in her proud new boots and her feet has swollen so that the
> laces cut into her flesh. She bent down quickly to loosen them, and when she
> found the right lace was knotted, she nearly burst into tears. Or perhaps the
> tears were caused by the swirling dust and lint. (75)

By repeating the naturalistic descriptions of Lyddie's working conditions,
her pain and exhaustion, sick lungs, and recurrent accidents, the author

makes us understand that work does not take care of itself, that it is a long and strenuous process, going on for thirteen hours every day, day after day, for the two years of the novel's duration. Remember, Lyddie is merely fourteen when she starts at the factory.

Work is undoubtedly a way to liberation for Lyddie; it is used symbolically to show that women could only become emancipated through economic independence. It is also significant that Lyddie eventually realizes that education will give her a still better societal status; in fact, in *Jip: His Story*, we meet Lyddie as a certified teacher—that is, freed from the burden of hard manual labor. Although I fully understand the author's intention, the underlying message is that manual labor is less worthy of respect and definitely less desirable than intellectual occupations. In a way, the ultimate solution for the character is not unlike that of Remi in *The Foundling*, who after years of misery and toil turns out to be a rich heir. This is one of the constant dilemmas of children's fiction: as adults, we strive to protect children from the hard facts of life, which sometimes results in ambiguous messages about them. Incidentally, in *Jip: His Story*, work is peripheral, even though the protagonist is a poor farm boy. The text merely states, "He worked hard, as he and Sheldon were the only able-bodied residents" (5). The social and human issues of the novel are too important in themselves; once again labor is left in the gap for the reader to fill.

Another example of a narrative set in the past, although not as distant as *Lyddie* and *Jip*, is *Roll of Thunder, Hear My Cry*. This novel is not as focused on labor as *Lyddie*, since its central theme is racism; however, both texts share the view of the present-day authors on the social injustices of the past. Children's authors writing in the 1930s, the time when the events of *Roll of Thunder* take place, could obviously not address the issues raised in this novel; by choice or by force, they wrote about middle-class white children for whom work was not an issue. Giving a voice to her black female protagonist, the author cannot possibly circumvent manual labor which is an essential part of Cassie Logan's existence.

The family's cotton land cannot feed them anymore, and the father is away working on railroad construction. The children are thus very much aware both of the economic situation and of the working conditions of their parents. While the father is away earning money to pay taxes and mortgages, the mother runs the farm, in addition to being a school-teacher, and "Big Ma, in her sixties, would work like a woman of twenty in the fields" (7). Unlike the middle-class heroines of classic children's novels, Cassie knows all too well where food, clothes, and other necessities come from.

Writing for young Americans in the last quarter of the twentieth century, the author must let her first-person narrator explain some things, which presumably are so self-evident to her that she would never reflect on them:

> Because the students were needed in the fields from early spring when the cotton was planted until after most of the cotton had been picked in the fall, the school adjusted its terms accordingly, beginning in October and dismissing in March. But even so, after today a number of the older students would not be seen again for a month or two, not until the last puff of cotton had been gleaned from the fields. (16)

This didactic passage, however, puts the readers in the right frame of mind, reminding them that child labor among the black population was a fact in the not so remote past. This short passage is occasionally reinforced by the depiction of the family working in the fields or about the house, which almost becomes a backdrop for all the other, much more dramatic events. The author does not present field work as hard or unpleasant; on the contrary, Cassie seems to prefer it to school (which perhaps says more about school than work):

> I was eager to be in the fields again. . . . In the last week of March when Papa and Mr. Morrison began to plow the east field, I volunteered to sacrifice school and help them. (196)

Even with this attitude, the difference between these depictions and the idyllic thinning of turnips in *Noisy Village* is profound. For Cassie and her family, child labor is a matter of life and death. If we as readers perceive the Noisy Village children's agricultural endeavors as a natural part of their games and adventures, we certainly feel indignation when confronted with the depictions in *Roll of Thunder*, viewing them as an essential element of the overall social injustice imposed on the character. It is clearly understood that the children of the white community are never forced to work.

Another event of recent history, which contemporary children's authors have cautiously started to explore, is the Holocaust. The subject is so difficult in itself and so profoundly incompatible with the basic premises of children's fiction (innocent, optimistic, with happy endings) that few writers even attempt any descriptions of the actual living and working conditions in concentration camps (see Bosmajian 2001). *The Devil's Arithmetic* is a rare exception. Upon arrival in the camp, the Jews see the infamous slogan over the gates: "Work makes you free." The young protagonist Hannah very soon realizes the true meaning of these words, even though most of the book focuses on humiliation, hunger, and physical suffering rather than labor. However, the story would not be credible without at least some reference to work: "the three-fingered woman came forward to tell them about the work that lay ahead and what they were to expect each day" (110). The depiction of actual work is sparse, its essence conveyed by some vivid details:

> The work was the mindless sort. Some of it was meant to keep the camp itself running: cleaning the barracks, the guards' houses, the hospital, the kitchen. Building more barracks, more privies. But most of the workers were used in the sorting sheds, stacking the clothing and suitcases and possessions stolen from the prisoners, dividing them into piles to be sent back to Germany. . . .
>
> [Hannah was] set to work with Rivka in the kitchen hauling water in large buckets from the pump, spooning out the meager meals, washing the giant cauldrons in which the soup cooked, scrubbing the walls and floors. It was hard work, harder than Hannah could ever remember doing. Her hands and knees held no memory of such work. It was endless. And repetitive. (124–25)

I allow myself to quote these two lengthy passages since they comprise the only actual depiction of labor in a labor camp. True, they are narrated in iterative frequency, expressing recurrent events taking place day after day, which produces a strong effect. Yet the author evidently does not wish to draw too much attention to the physical suffering caused by labor. She cannot omit mentioning that anybody not fit for work is sent to the ovens, but the book is more concerned with the relationship between the prisoners and their struggle for survival against all odds; in fact, it amplifies the positive camp experiences, such as hope and mutual support.

The narrative device employed, time displacement, brings the character safely back from the horrors of the Holocaust. Her experience thus becomes an important part of her identity quest, as she understands her place in the family as well as in the Jewish tradition. But this final escape diminishes the overall impact of the story, making it nothing but an exciting, albeit horrifying, adventure or perhaps a bad dream. Back to her own place and time, a wealthy Jewish home in New York in the 1980s, Hannah may remember the drudgery of the camp, but the risk is that readers will feel that it was not that bad after all, since she returned safely.

Contrary to the historical genre, *The Giver* takes place in an indefinitely remote future, where all children, even very young, participate in the so-called volunteer work, in practice forced labor, and are assigned their permanent adult occupations at the age of twelve. The author carefully avoids the depiction of actual manual labor, although presumably somebody in the depicted society is still doing such work. Instead, we get a glimpse of working conditions in an old people's home, which is actually a pretext to start the young protagonist contemplating the hierarchy of the dystopian society he lives in. Jonas's parents are, typically enough, a lawyer and a nurse (in inverted gender roles). The contempt for manual workers is something the depicted society shares with many adult dystopias, such as *Brave New World* and *1984*: "he didn't envy Laborers at all" (17); "Fish Hatchery Attendant. Jonas was certainly glad that *that* Assignment was taken, he wouldn't have wanted it" (53; author's emphasis). The protagonist is assigned an intellectual rather than menial job. None of the painful, traumatic memories he receives from the Giver involve labor, perhaps because, if anything, labor is well known in Jonas's society. However, it is obviously more gratifying for children's authors to create smart and intellectual characters than ones who would be confined to a job as a fish hatchery attendant.

Historical novels and science fiction are thus two genres that allow some depiction of work, because they present society in a detached and thus distorted perspective, in a kind of estrangement effect, since the ordinary is described as extraordinary. In a children's novel set in contemporary Western society, there must always be some element of estrangement to present labor, because only taken out of its everyday context does it become interesting enough as a plot or characterization element. This estrangement can, for instance, take the form of depicting seasonal workers, immigrants, homeless people, or any other expression of the Other.

Finally, yet another extraordinary situation enables a contemporary author to show a young person at manual work: the depiction of forced labor in a contemporary environment. One would certainly not associate this motif with children's literature, but modern children's fiction has gone a long way from the idyllic world of *The Secret Garden*. In *Holes*, the young protagonist is sent to a labor camp for a crime he has not committed. Stanley comes from an underprivileged family, but even in this book there is no substantial mention of the parents' work. Stanley's father is an unsuccessful inventor, a further development of the stereotype of a mad scientist. Moreover, Stanley's original problems do not result from poverty; rather, he gives the impression of a spoiled brat, even though he is bullied in school for being overweight. Manual labor is alien to Stanley, but he immediately becomes aware of its meaning when faced with the task of digging "one hole each day, including Saturdays and Sundays. Each hole must be five feet deep, and five feet across in every direction. Your shovel is your measuring stick" (13).

Since digging holes totally fills the life of the young protagonist for the eighteen months of his sentence, the author cannot simply dismiss it by stating that Stanley indeed dug a hole every day. Labor is a shock for Stanley, and the naturalism of the descriptions adds to the poignancy of the protagonist's emotional life:

> The shovel felt heavy in Stanley's soft, fleshy hands. He tried to jam it into the earth, but the blade banged against the ground and bounced off without a dent. The vibrations ran up the shaft of the shovel and into Stanley's wrists, making his bones rattle. (26)

The description of Stanley's first working day at camp takes many pages: a detailed description of hard, meaningless, and painful toil. "[B]y the time Stanley broke past the crust, a blister had formed in the middle of his right thumb, and it hurt to hold the shovel" (28). The author effectively uses repetition as a narrative device to convey the prolonged time of action. The word *blisters* keeps appearing to remind the reader that while the narrative goes on, shifting into other temporal dimensions, Stanley is still digging his holes in the unbearably hot sun: "He had blisters on every one of his fingers, and one in the center of each palm" (32); and further on again:

> Stanley's blisters had ripped open, and new blisters formed. He kept changing his grip on the shovel to try to avoid the pain. Finally, he removed his cap and held it between the shaft of his shovel and his raw hands. This helped, but digging was harder because the cap would slip and slide. The sun beat down on his unprotected head and neck. (33)

This ruthlessly graphic passage sets up the whole atmosphere of the novel and is reinforced a few pages later: "His cap was stained with blood from his hands. He felt like he was digging his own grave" (38). Comparing these descriptions with those of Mary Lennox digging for pleasure in the secret garden, we see clearly how far children's fiction has moved in its relationship to reality. In addition, the author is not satisfied with letting the readers imagine the rest of Stanley's suffering. His second day and second hole are described just as meticulously:

> He stepped on the shovel blade, and pushed on the very back of the shaft with the base of his thumb. This hurt less than trying to hold the shaft with his blistered fingers. . .
> He took one shovelful at a time, and tried not to think of the awesome task that lay ahead of him. After an hour or so, his sore muscles seemed to loosen up a little bit.
> He grunted as he tried to stick his shovel into the dirt. His cap slipped out from under his fingers, and the shovel fell free.
> He let it lie there. (48–49)

Even though the actual depictions of digging eventually become less prominent, we are constantly reminded of what the character is doing while his thoughts are occupied elsewhere. The phrase "He dug his shovel into the dirt" is used as a refrain throughout the text to emphasize that the first graphic descriptions of Stanley's misery were only several in a series of endless, identical days of hard labor.

The author of *Holes* is quite ironical toward the practice of forced labor. Indeed, he starts the novel by stating:

> If you take a bad boy and make him dig a hole every day in the hot sun, it will turn him into a good boy.
> That was what some people thought. (5)

The idea is not far away from the Nazi camps' slogan, but in Stanley's case he really benefits from being exposed to hard labor. He becomes physically more fit, and he makes some friends, which he lacked in his previous life. To use a cliché, Stanley finds his identity through manual work. Eventually he also finds the treasure that ensures him and his family a prosperous life ever after. Here the author has fallen into the common pit of children's literature conventions: a sentimental and implausible happy ending, which completely eradicates the physical and spiritual torture that the protagonist has endured.

The examples I have discussed show some significant similarities, both among themselves and with most of the previously mentioned classic children's books. Labor is used symbolically, as a temporary trial through which the young protagonists have to go before they can find their true place in society. The depiction of labor is highly ambiguous: it is a punishment, and even when chosen voluntarily, as in Lyddie's case, it is a burden that brings neither joy nor satisfaction. The message young readers will get from these novels is thus somewhat dubious. Labor seems to be a curse, and is in any case a transitional state, lasting merely until the characters have miraculously been freed from it. Like the case with so many other dominant themes in children's fiction, the authors seem to be trying to keep their readers in comfortable innocence about the hardships and anxieties of adult life.

Other Ordinary Actions

While the adults' working lives occupy only a minimal space in children's novels, the child protagonists' equivalent, school, is naturally more prominent, but once again not in proportion with the amount of time a child spends in school in real life. School as setting is not uncommon, especially in the school stories from *Tom Brown's Schooldays* to *Harry Potter*. Various relationships within school, closely corresponding to the relationships at a work place in adult novels, are also inevitable: conflicts and friendships with teachers and peers, academic and athletic competition, and so on. The *Ramona* books are a very good illustration of this.

Very seldom do we encounter any elaborate description of actual school-work. A lesson may be used to introduce an issue, such as democracy, gender, ecology, or birth control. It may also be used for humorous purposes, like the chapter "Pippi Goes to School" in *Pippi Longstocking*. School stories seldom depict lessons but rather mischief, recreation, and sports. In fact, the tradition of portraying school in children's fiction is remarkable, from the point of view of the messages conveyed to readers. School is an inevitable evil in *The Adventures of Tom Sawyer*, an arena of "slow suffering" (42) that children are meant to escape as much as possible. Pinocchio is seduced into a carefree existence in the Land of Toys by the following promise: "Where would you look for a healthier place for us children to live? There are no schools there; there are no teachers there; there are no books there. In that blessed country no one ever studies" (*The Adventures of Pinocchio*, 119). When confronted with the prospect of being adopted by Wendy's mother, Peter Pan's first question is "Would you send me to school?" Upon getting an affirmative reply, he retorts, "I don't want to go to school and learn solemn things" (*Peter Pan*, 181). His less determined friends, the Lost Boys, very soon realize that having loving parents has its dismal sides: "Before they had attended school a week they saw what goats they had been not to remain on the island; but it was too late now" (183). Edith Nesbit's opinion on education is as skeptical and ironic as most of her other views: "Edred and Elfrida went to school every day and learned reading, writing, arithmetic, geography, history, spelling, and useful knowledge, all of which they hated quite impartially, which means that they hated the whole lot—one thing as much as another" (*The House of Arden*, 10). In all these examples, school is presented as the opposite of freedom, integrity, and imagination. The aforementioned *Ramona* books may seem to contradict this statement; on closer examination, they focus on pranks and mischief rather than learning.

Another reason the ordinary actions in connection with school are of less importance is, of course, that they are familiar for the reader, and the gaps left by this omission can be easily supplied with information from the readers' experience. *Harry Potter* may seem an exception to the rule with its detailed descriptions of lessons in Hogwarts School, but then lessons in Potions, Herbology, Arithmancy, and Intermediate Transfiguration can hardly be called ordinary. It is not so easy for readers to fill in the gaps about the content of lessons in the school of wizards. Yet, Harry's and his friends' extracurricular activities take considerably more space in the books.

Since child characters cannot, without a very good reason, have a professional occupation, a whole number of typical mainstream characters and, consequently, plots and conflicts tied to these characters, are excluded in children's fiction. In fact, most of the several hundred occupations suggested for characters in writers' manuals (see Lauther 1998) are not relevant for children's fiction. Child protagonists can neither be brokers nor ambassadors, medical doctors nor jet pilots, college professors nor tax collectors.

Naturally, certain genres allow a substitute for an occupation. For instance, a child detective is a widely used figure. A journalist in a mainstream novel may become an editor of a school newspaper; a company president will correspond a class president. Furthermore, child characters may be field workers, horse trainers, circus artists, baby-sitters, and so on. Hobbies and school achievements can provide some insight into professions. Still, certain limitations will always be present. For instance, the artist figure, so dominant in the twentieth-century Western novel, is by definition impossible in a children's book, since the anxiety of failure and the joys of recognition will be totally irrelevant even for a child with artistic talents. A children's Künstlerroman portraying a young writer (*Harriet the Spy; Cassie Binnegar*), a musician (*The Facts and Fictions of Minna Pratt*), or a dancer (*Ballet Shoes*) may focus on hardships and temporary failures, but the character's age alone allows a good deal of optimism.

Recreation and leisure are still other human activities that take a relatively large part of our time in reality, and both novels for adults and for children devote substantial space to these. Naturally, certain types of entertainment common in mainstream fiction appear in children's books less frequently—for instance, hunting, gambling, drinking, or sex. However, children's novels have their own specific forms of recreation and pastimes: bicycling is popular, as well as fishing, hiking, swimming, looking for treasure, or more recently, playing computer games. There are several genres in children's fiction built wholly around recreation, such as sports novels, horse and pony novels, or stories about ballet schools. While these novels most often are formulaic, in some quality novels, sports and hobbies are used for characterization. For instance, Leslie in *Bridge to Terabithia* is unbeatable at running and has an unusual hobby for a girl: scuba diving.

An important pastime that often has a prominent position in a character's life is reading. Reading habits contribute considerably to characterization. Reading is often opposed to active sports, and a reading child is bullied by classmates and not seldom misunderstood by parents. The amount and content of the character's reading may indicate development and change. Indirectly, by depicting reading, writers promote their own profession.

As to other, perhaps less exposed, but nevertheless essential aspects of everyday human life, very little attention has been paid to the most basic needs such as going to the bathroom. This action is completely absent from classic mainstream novels, while it appears in many texts from the Middle Ages and Renaissance, always with frivolous undertones (e.g., in Rabelais). Urination is also depicted in the famous scene in *Gulliver's Travels*, when Gulliver extinguishes a fire in the royal palace. In children's editions of Rabelais and Swift, this transgressional behavior is purged. In modern adult novels, the character's bowel movements are described in detail in *Ulysses*, but once again not as an everyday detail but as a transgressional, deliberately offensive element. In children's fiction, Roald Dahl is considered the master of transgressional humor and the grotesque, including defecation, belching, farting, and other bodily functions.

Recently there has been a strong wave of potty-training picturebooks for the youngest readers, perhaps produced in the first place for utilitarian purposes. However, this trend reflects the need to acknowledge an activity of paramount importance in a very young child's life. Bathrooms are frequent settings in the depiction of school bullying, but very seldom otherwise. While adventure and fantasy books often focus on the character's encounter with hunger, it is almost impossible to imagine that the four children wandering in the winter landscape in Narnia should consult each other about the necessity of relieving themselves. As Forster (1985) remarks, literary characters "need not have glands" (51), and in most cases they need not have bladders. We are usually not disturbed by this fact; however in certain situations, ignoring the problem subverts the credibility of the narrative. In a book about Vietnamese boat refugees who spend several weeks in a boat on the open sea, the problem is evident, and since every other practical problem is dealt with—cooking, fresh water, sleeping—the natural needs cannot be easily circumvented. Similarly, in a book about Jews being transported to camps, this detail might add to the credibility of the story. One excellent example comes from *The Devil's Arithmetic*: "Somewhere a child cried out that she had to go to the bathroom. A little while later, a smell announced that she had" (78). This minute detail conveys the horror of being locked in a cattle car, without going into a too disturbing naturalism.

Cleaning teeth, combing, dressing, and undressing are not as offensive to the general reading public as going to the bathroom, but also these everyday actions are often omitted unless they for some reason acquire a special significance. In *Homecoming*, the everyday survival of the children wandering on foot down the American East Coast is the focal point of the story, and such details are an essential part of it.

Just as literary characters seldom have bladders or intestines, they almost never have kidneys, livers, middle ears, breathing tracts, or other organs that can cause trouble. Adventure and fantasy characters normally do not have colds, stomachaches, blisters, or sunburns. They persevere where most ordinary mortals would die of exposure. Occasional or prolonged illness may be part of the plot (*What Katy Did; Marianne Dreams*). Most often the illness is cured by the end of the book. In *The Brothers Lionheart*, the protagonist's illness is terminal. In all these books, illness is the character's antagonist rather than a human condition; it is stated but not described. Characters with disabilities have also become common after a long period of absence. In classic children's literature, a little invalid in a wheelchair or permanently in bed was almost a commonplace, such as Clara in *Heidi* or Colin in *The Secret Garden*. However, Clara is not the protagonist, and we do not learn much about her except that she has been ill for a long time; we do not share her experience of having a disability. Colin is first seen through Mary's eyes, but in the latter half of the novel he becomes the focalizer. In contemporary novels, a disabled protagonist may allow us an insight into his or her situation (see further Coats 2001).

Finally, a most important aspect of the life cycle for half of humanity, menstruation, belongs with the many other unmentionables. According to some critics, the first explicit mention of menstruation in an American children's book occurred in *The Long Secret*. In Sweden, a number of children's novels in the 1960s and 1970s broke this taboo. However, this fact is as conspicuously absent from most children's novels as other bodily functions. Although it is common knowledge that young women stop menstruating under extreme conditions, very few adventure or war narratives focus on this detail.

Procreation is seldom relevant in children's novels, but it can appear in young adult fiction, both as unwanted pregnancy and teenage parenthood. Once again, it is stated but not represented, and many of these "issue" or "utility" novels read like educational brochures. Like illness, procreation, when it appears in juvenile fiction, is a problem to be dealt with rather than a human experience to be artistically investigated. There are of course exceptions, such as *Dear Nobody*.

When ordinary actions are depicted at some length, we start perceiving them as extraordinary and feel compelled to interpret them symbolically.

Normally we do not think of cutting one's hair as a significant action. When Jo March in *Little Women* sacrifices her pretty hair to earn money, this action becomes a powerful means of characterization. Dressing and undressing are everyday actions to which we normally pay scant attention. When Heidi sheds one garment after another in her excitement over arriving at the mountain, we interpret this action as a liberation from the restricting tokens of civilization.

Extraordinary Actions

For obvious reasons we are more interested in the characters' extraordinary actions, since these frequently go beyond our everyday experience and allow us to adopt a subjectivity that we lack in real life. Defamiliarization, or estrangement, is a powerful characterization device, which allows authors to expose characters to conditions that are unfamiliar and therefore exciting for readers (cf. Martin 1986, 48).

Fantasy novels empower the characters by putting them in situations that are impossible otherwise. The first prerequisite is physical dislocation (transportation into a magical realm), which gives young characters freedom to have adventures without adult supervision. When the means of empowerment appears in the ordinary world (a magical helper, a magical object), the characters tend to keep it a secret from the adults, thus also creating a world separate from the ordinary. In the magical realm, children can perform heroic deeds that are not available for them in reality: fight battles, kill dragons, fly, have their wishes come true, and so on. As adult coreaders, we tend to interpret fantasy novels nonmimetically, as a symbolic depiction of an inner journey and a maturation process. Most unsophisticated readers interpret the same texts mimetically, finding pleasure in sharing the experiences of their peers in being strong, brave, rich, and powerful. It is, however, seldom that child protagonists are endowed with magical powers; far more often they are assisted by magical agents. Christopher Chant and Harry Potter are among the few exceptions.

In realistic novels, heroic deeds are restricted. We may find examples of wartime heroism in historical novels. An interesting recent trend is Holocaust novels, in which child characters are allowed to survive far more often than any historical records demonstrate. Peacetime heroism may include saving somebody from a fire or from drowning; on a more modest level, we find many examples of bravery or honesty that young characters display. Running away from home is a popular motif in adventure stories, starting with Robinson Crusoe as a model. In children's novels, escapes are seldom permanent; instead, protagonists either return voluntarily (*Tom Sawyer*) or find a new home (*Homecoming*). Finding treasure is another widely exploited motif. All these narrative elements have been thoroughly investigated in children's literature research, not surprisingly, since they are much more prominent and exciting for the writer as well as the reader than ordinary actions such as washing or dressing (see Fisher 1986).

The last essential aspect in which children's fiction has so far been different from adult literature is violence. Children's writers have always avoided overtly violent depictions, to the degree that this seemed unnatural—for instance, in war novels. This restriction has been recently broken. In Scandinavian children's and juvenile fiction, a vast number of novels describe violent death and suicide of young characters, and the very last taboo, a young person killing another young person, seems to have been broken as well.

In assessing extraordinary actions in children's fiction, we should bear in mind the credibility of the action within the given genre frames. Extreme heroism in an everyday psychological novel will probably feel unreal, while it is accepted in adventure stories. Nancy Drew's miraculous skills in driving, sailing, shooting, and flying airplanes do not surprise us any more than James Bond's. The young characters' easy proficiency in driving heavy trailers or handling automatic weapons in *Tomorrow When the War Began* is rather dubious. Notably, in contemporary psychological novels for children, we are more likely to find an absence of heroism and extraordinary actions. Writers seem to prefer to offer their readers credible subjectivities rather than escapist adventures. This has to do with the overall transition "from hero to character," discussed in an earlier chapter.

The characters' actions and the events in which they participate are the least investigated means of characterization, as compared with external and internal descriptions, speech acts, or point of view. The aspects of texts I have examined may seem less essential, but they affect the reader on the subconscious level, as they convey values and beliefs as to what childhood is or should be. Even the very brief comparison with adult novels offered here reveals some profound differences in how these artistic devices work, which considerably enriches our understanding of the specific nature of children's fiction.

~

CHAPTER ELEVEN

Figural Discourse

Speech Acts

Some Preliminary Discussion on Speech Acts

Speech acts have several functions in narrative. They can be the essential part of plot progression; they can supply additional, background information about the events; and they can naturally contribute to characterization, by what the characters say, how they say it, and why. We can thus distinguish between *locutionary* acts (acts of saying), *illocutionary* acts (the reason something is said), and *perlocutionary* acts (the impact the speaker intends to make). My goal here is not to go deep into a deeply theoretical discussion of speech acts, least of all into terminology (see Austin 1962; Searle 1969; Pratt 1977). I am interested in the way speech acts in narrative are used as characterization devices. For this purpose, seeing what types of speech acts characterize the speakers directly and what types reflect the narrator's rather than the character's views is of overall importance.

Let us first distinguish between two basic types of speech acts: direct speech and indirect (or reported) speech.[1] In the following discussion, I will use an arrow ($\rightarrow$) to indicate the grammatical transformations that I perform on authentic quotations to illustrate my point.

Let us begin by considering some very simple examples of direct speech.

Direct statement: "It's an owl," Peter said (*The Lion, the Witch and the Wardrobe*, 10).

$\rightarrow$ Indirect statement: Peter said that it was an owl.

Direct question: "What is a moor?" she said suddenly to Mrs. Medlock. (*The Secret Garden*, 23)

→ Indirect question: Suddenly she asked Mrs. Medlock what a moor was.

Direct order: "Go away!" cried Mary. (*The Secret Garden*, 14)

→ Indirect order: Mary ordered the boy to go away.

Direct threat: [H]e said: "Siddy, I'll lick you for that." (*Tom Sawyer*, 10)

→ Indirect threat: He promised (or threatened) to lick Sid for that.

Direct greeting: "Good morning, Christopher Robin," he said. (*Winnie-the-Pooh*, 8)

→ Indirect greeting: He wished Christopher Robin a good morning (or even "He greeted Christopher Robin").

From these very simple examples, we see that the main difference between direct and indirect speech lies in the use of tenses and deictics (see Banfield 1982; Ehrlich 1990, 21f.; Galbraith 1995). Furthermore, indirect speech allows ambiguity in perspective (the source of speech) and ambiguity between uttered and unuttered speech—that is, thoughts. The tense of direct speech is independent of the tense of the tag (speech verb, *verbum dicendi*). The difference between "'It's an owl,' Peter said" and → "'It's an owl,' Peter says" indicates the narrative (situational) time. The difference between "'It's an owl,' Peter said" and → "'It was an owl,' Peter said" (and the less likely, but not impossible → "'It will be an owl tomorrow,' Peter said") reflects the relationship between the time of the speech act and the time of the action described in direct speech (hearing an owl hoot).

The tense of indirect speech is dependent (at least in English) on the tense of the tag: → "He says that it is an owl" and → "He said that it was an owl" implies the simultaneity of the speech act and the described action. → "He says that it was an owl" and → "He said that it had been an owl" indicates that the action preceded the speech act. → "He said that it would be an owl the next day" indicates that the speech act precedes the action. Some hypothetical variants may also include → "He will say that it is an owl," → "He will say that it has been an owl," and so on. In other languages—for instance, Russian, which has no forms like perfect and pluperfect—the temporal relationship between the speech act and the described action is instead expressed by deictics, such as "the day before" or "the next day." Together with tenses, deictics help us discern the temporal relationship between actions and speech acts. The deixis "tomorrow" is related to the speaker, and it is only relevant in connection with the speaker. In indirect speech, it has to be changed into "next day."

Occasionally, grammatical rules can be broken in indirect speech, for instance:

> So it was arranged that they should start *next morning*, and that Rabbit . . . should now go home and ask Tigger what he was doing *to-morrow* (*The House at Pooh Corner*, 111; emphasis added).
>
> Transformed into direct speech: → Rabbit said: "We shall start tomorrow morning, and I shall now go home and ask Tigger what he is doing tomorrow."

In indirect speech, deictics are indispensable to distinguish between objective and subjective statements. The statement "He said that I had seen an owl" is different from "He said that he had seen an owl," since it presupposes the presence of an "I" who is the character in the text, most probably the first-person (homodiegetic) narrator. However, in the first case the speaker is making a statement on behalf of someone else, while in the second case he is speaking for himself. It may be easy in this particular simple statement, but it can create problems even in just slightly more complicated cases—for instance, "He said that I claimed to have seen an owl" (possible accusation of lying). Here we must pay attention to the illocution and perlocution of the utterance.

Together, the combination of tense and deictics creates a large number of possibilities for conveying speech. Yet how do these speech acts contribute to characterization? We assume that we can learn something about characters from what they say and from what other characters say about them. However, only direct speech acts are more or less "nonnarrated" (Chatman 1978, 166–81). By "nonnarrated," scholars such as Chatman mean statements that supposedly come directly from the characters. For instance, → " 'It's an owl,' Peter said, 'There are lots of them around at this time of year' " can characterize the speaker as observant and familiar with the habits of birds. Already the tag ("he said") presupposes a narrator. A specific speech verb, an adverb, or any additional comment will immediately manipulate our understanding of the character. For instance:

> "Who is going to dress me?" *demanded* Mary. (*The Secret Garden*, 29; emphasis added)
>
> "I'm sorry I was late," he said *shyly*. (*Anne of Green Gables*, 12; emphasis added)
>
> "I suppose you are Mr. Matthew Cuthbert of Green Gables?" she said *in a peculiarly clear and sweet voice*. (*Anne of Green Gables*, 12; emphasis added)

Compare the following statements:

→ "It's an owl," Peter lied.
→ "It's an owl," Peter said sentimentally.
→ "It's an owl," Peter said, his voice trembling with fear.
→ "It's an owl," Peter said, to tease his sister.
→ "It's an owl," Peter said, to comfort his sister.

Although the content of the utterance is identical, the narrator's discourse in connection with the utterance presents the character in totally different manners because of the illocutionary and perlocutionary functions of speech.

In indirect speech, we do not hear the actual voice of the character but the mediated statement uttered by the narrator. We cannot be sure that the statement conveys the exact words of the character. Indeed, a sentence like "He said that he had seen an owl the day before" can be a very compressed summary of what the character actually said, omitting the adjectives, judgments, attitudes, and other features that might characterize the speaker. Compare with "He spoke, passionately and at some length, about the owl he had seen the day before," where the narrator's comments add substantially to our picture of the speaker.

Finally, direct speech presents no doubt as to whether the utterance is spoken or thought (at this point I shall refrain from considering interior monologue). Indirect speech may seem to be equally unequivocal, whereby the following simple transformations can be performed:

Indirect statement: Piglet said that Tigger *was* very Bouncy. (*The House at Pooh Corner*, 106; author's emphasis)
→ Direct statement: Piglet said, "Tigger is very bouncy."
Indirect question: Matthew . . . asked [the stationmaster] if the five-thirty train would be soon along. (*Anne of Green Gables*, 10)
→ Direct question: Matthew asked the stationmaster, "Will the five-thirty train be soon along?"

However, on closer examination, indirect speech can present some problems, especially when the simple tags "say" and "think" are replaced by "wish," "hope," "believe," "suppose," "assume," and so on. In *Pippi Longstocking*, Pippi tells Annika that she need not be afraid of ghosts in the attic because they have gone to a meeting of the Ghost and Goblin Society. "Annika sighed with relief and hoped that the meeting would last a long time" (156). It is not clear whether the utterance is spoken or not—that is, whether we should transform it into → "'I hope that the meeting lasts a long time,' Annika *said*" or → "'I hope that the meeting lasts a long time,' Annika *thought*." The first case characterizes Annika as a bore and an overt coward, totally in compliance with the gender stereotype. The second case, where she is scared but does not show it, gives us a slightly different portrait.

"Peter wished it were an owl" (described as *represented speech or thought* [RTS][2]) may equal one of the two direct speech acts, either "He said: 'I wish it were an owl'" or "He thought: 'I wish it were an owl.'" The two phrases definitely characterize the speaker in different ways. By way of mental exercise, let us try to make similar substitutions for the following statements:

→ He wished it had been an owl.
→ He hoped it was an owl.
→ He assumed it was an owl.
→ He believed it was an owl.
→ He feared it was an owl.
→ He doubted it was an owl.
→ He doubted it had been an owl.

And so on (cf. Cohn 1978, 104*f*.).

These simple games of transformational grammar demonstrate the infinite possibilities that speech acts leave for characterization. The tags, being the narrator's statements, may not wholly (or not at all) reflect the character's true feelings. "He believed that it was an owl" can be transformed into the following three direct statements: (1) He said, "I believe that it's an owl"; (2) He said, uncertainly, "It's an owl"; (3) He said, "It's an owl," but he was wrong. Thus, modal verbs in indirect speech create ambiguity, and they certainly add to the tension between the character and the narrator.

Locutionary Summary

While narrative summary refers to the duration of narrative in which story time is longer than discourse time, we can propose the concept of locutionary summary, implying indirect speech summarizing a character's direct speech. This device is used in fiction more frequently than simple indirect speech of the type: "Piglet said that Tigger was bouncy" (which is more habitual in journalism—e.g., "The senator said that measures would be taken to prevent drug abuse").

Locutionary summaries can be *durative* (rendering a long monologue or dialogue in condensed form) and *iterative* (rendering recurrent conversations over a period of time). In *The Lion, the Witch and the Wardrobe*, Lucy visits Mr. Tumnus the Faun and has a conversation with him, which finally goes over into a durative summary:

> [T]he Faun began to talk. He had wonderful tales to tell of life in the forest. He told about the midnight dances and how the Nymphs who lived in the wells and the dryads who lived in the trees came out to dance with the Fauns; about long hunting parties after the milk-white stag who could give you wishes if you caught him; about feasting and treasure-seeking with the wild Red Dwarfs in deep mines and caverns far beneath the forest floor; and then about summer when the woods were green and old Silenus on his donkey would come to visit them, and sometimes Bacchus himself, and then the streams would run with wine instead of water and the whole forest would give itself up to jollification for weeks on end. (20)

There are several purposes for using summary instead of direct speech here. The Faun's full account would take too much space, while it is not essential for the plot: it is only needed to give us some background about the country in which Lucy has arrived. The summary leaves a great deal to the reader's imagination and evokes a mythology with which the reader may or may not be familiar, but at least leading our thoughts in a certain direction through the mention of nymphs, dryads, Silenus, and Bacchus. A particular fairy-tale atmosphere is created, even if the reader does not recognize the names. Finally, the summary makes us—together with Lucy—lose track of time. Dealing with a summary, we cannot say how long the storytelling has been going on. Suddenly Lucy discovers that several hours must have passed. The rest of the chapter is narrated in a quick, dynamic dialogue, creating a discrepancy between the Faun's sweet and eternal tales and the concrete situation in which he and Lucy are caught. In terms of characterization, the summary presents the Faun as a skillful storyteller who can spellbind the listener; however, the perlocutionary act is to betray Lucy to the White Witch.

When Edmund meets the witch, their confrontation is depicted in direct speech, except for when she interrogates him about his siblings:

> She got him to tell her that he had one brother and two sisters, and that one of his sisters had already been in Narnia and had met a Faun there, and that no one except himself and his brother and his sisters knew anything about Narnia. (37)

The function of this summary is different from that of the previous one. The reader already knows all the facts that Edmund is telling the witch; thus, there is no need to render his speech in full. Before and after the summary, Edmund is characterized by his direct speech as mean and greedy, so rendering his account in direct speech would not add much. This is an example of one of the many narrative choices an author may have.

Since summaries are part of the (adult) narrator's discourse, they allow ironic comment on the speaker, not always possible in a character's direct speech. Consider the following example:

> Tommy's and Annika's mother had invited a few ladies to a coffee party, and as she had done plenty of baking, she thought Tommy and Annika might invite Pippi over at the same time. The children would entertain each other and give no trouble to anyone. (*Pippi Longstocking*, 116)

Converted into direct speech, the statement is relatively neutral and presents the mother as kind and generous: → "'I have invited some ladies to a coffee party,' mother told Tommy and Annika. 'I have done plenty of baking. I think that you may invite Pippi over at the same time.'" The way summary is formed, in its conjunction ("as she had done plenty of baking"), the mother's somewhat hypocritical thoughts are exposed, which is also confirmed by the last sentence in this quotation, a nonspoken utterance.

The Interplay of Direct and Indirect Speech

Usually, direct and indirect speech alternate in a novel. In most cases it is merely a question of variation and rhythm. However, occasionally we can see a pattern in which certain characters are preferably described through direct or reported speech. In *Winnie-the-Pooh*, Pooh has a long dialogue with Owl about writing a lost property notice, and as Pooh gets more and more confused, direct speech is changed into indirect:

> [H]e . . . tried very hard to listen to what Owl was saying.
> But Owl went on and on, using longer and longer words, until at last he came back to where he started, and he explained that the person to write out this notice was Christopher Robin.
> "It was he who wrote the ones on my front door for me. Did you see them, Pooh?" (46)

The statement "went on and on" is a durative summary. It reveals an ironic narrator mocking Owl's love for long and unintelligible words, some examples of which have appeared in his direct speech and been misinterpreted by Pooh: "customary procedure," "Issue a Reward," and so on. The phrase "he explained" brings the dialogue closer to characters' discourse and makes a neat return to direct speech in the last sentence. Although most speech acts in the *Pooh* books are direct speech, occasionally there are summaries similar to the one discussed here, such as "Owl was telling Kanga an Interesting Anecdote full of long words like Encyclopaedia and Rhododendron" (110). As Pooh, Piglet, and Rabbit discuss the arrival of Kanga, some of Rabbit's speech is rendered in summary form: "Rabbit went on to say that Kangas were only Fierce during the winter months, being at other times of an Affectionate Disposition" (85).

The function of such summaries is double. Primarily, they allow a compression of what would otherwise be an unbearably boring narrative (it is not coincidental that all summaries are of either Owl's or Rabbit's speech, the two joy killers of the story). But, as shown earlier, a summary also provides an opportunity for an ironic comment from the narrator. So if Owl is directly characterized by his high-flown style and difficult words, the narrator makes an additional point of this through an ironic summary. Rabbit is another character whose direct speech is avoided, presumably because it is boring. In *The House at Pooh Corner*, Pooh and Piglet are listening to Rabbit, or rather, Pooh is trying hard to listen, but cannot concentrate. Thus we do not know what Rabbit is saying, until the narrative turns into direct speech:

> "In fact," said Rabbit, coming to the end of it at last, "Tigger's getting so Bouncy nowadays that it's time we taught him a lesson. Don't you think so, Piglet?"
>
> Piglet said that Tigger *was* very bouncy, and that if they could think of a way to unbounce him it would be a Very Good Idea.
>
> "Just what I feel," said Rabbit. (106)

Exactly what Rabbit might have been saying while Pooh was not listening is left for the reader to imagine. This adds an ironic twist to the character of Rabbit.

The "Dialogue Novel"

To illustrate the difference between the impact of direct and indirect speech on our understanding of characters, I will compare a key scene in *Oliver Twist* with an abridged retelling:

Child as he was, he was desperate with hunger, and reckless with misery. He rose from the table; and advancing to the master, basin and spoon in hand, said, somewhat alarmed at his own temerity:

"Please, sir, I want some more."

The master was a fat, healthy man; but he turned very pale. He gazed in stupefied astonishment on the small rebel for some seconds, and then clung for support to the copper. The assistants were paralysed with wonder; the boys with fear.

"What!" said the master at length, in a faint voice.

"Please, sir," replied Oliver, "I want some more."

The master aimed a blow at Oliver's head with the ladle; pinioned him in his arms; and shrieked aloud for the beadle. (25)

In a Swedish abridged edition, the same scene goes as follows:

Oliver plucked his courage and went forward. But when he came over with his empty plate and asked for more food, the master went pale. He was furious over such impudence and hit Oliver on the head with the ladle.

Obviously, the retelling has preserved the event, but the characterization revealed in the original is lost. Children's books are often retold and abridged, whereupon scenes with dialogue are rendered as summaries. Apparently the retellers believe that young readers are interested in events rather than in characters, so that direct speech, contributing to characterization, can be omitted. Strangely enough, this tendency contradicts one of the most common prejudices about children's literature. It is often argued that young readers prefer direct speech to reported (some metapoetic comments from writers confirm this assumption, for instance, Alice thinks her sister's book boring because it has "no conversations"). Several pedagogical studies of children's literature apply as one of the criteria for "readability" the ratio between narration and direct speech, claiming that the abundance of dialogue makes texts more reader-friendly. This may be true in terms of pure reading skills. Direct speech utterances, especially coming from child characters and imitating their syntax and vocabulary, are usually shorter and simpler than authorial discourse, and a more everyday, colloquial idiom is used. A swift interchange of lines in a dialogue makes for a fast progression of the plot.

However, in terms of characterization, direct speech is an extremely demanding and confusing form, since the absence of narrative agency leaves readers without guidance. Are the characters honest and frank in their utterances? How can we know whether they are? Why do we trust some characters, but perceive others as liars and hypocrites? For instance, would we know that the White Witch is evil if we only had the dialogue between her and Edmund to judge, without the narrator's comments?

In extreme cases, when most of the text consists of dialogue, the readers must work hard to comprehend what is going on. For some reason, Hemingway's short story "Hills Like White Elephants" is frequently included in high school anthologies, and in my experience, students find it totally incomprehensible. The dialogue in the story hides more than it reveals. The man and the woman do not mean what they are saying, the actual subject of their discussion is never explicitly mentioned, and their real thoughts and feelings remain beyond the text. Their speech only characterizes them implicitly, by omission.

Red Shift is an example of a young adult novel in which the story is narrated almost wholly in direct speech, without tags (a form sometimes called *abruptive dialogue*). This is the beginning of the novel:

> "Shall I tell you?"
> "What?"
> "Shall I?"
> "Tell me what?" said Jan.
> "What do you want to know?" (7)

Except for the short tag "said Jan," we have no clues as to who is speaking, what the speakers are referring to, where they are, or who they are. Although the situation becomes somewhat more clear by the next page, we are still left without guidance as to the coherence of the conversation:

> "'Grotty' is excessively ugly," said Tom. "A corruption of 'grotesque.' It won't last."
>
> "I love you."
>
> "I'm not sure about the mean galactic velocity. We're with M31, M32, M33 and a couple of dozen other galaxies. They're the nearest. What did you say?"
>
> "I love you."
>
> "Yes." He stopped walking. "That's all we can be sure of. We are, at this moment, somewhere between the M6 going to Birmingham and M33 going nowhere. Don't leave me."
>
> "Hush," said Jan. "It's all right."
>
> "It's not. How did we meet? How could it be? Between the M6 and M33. Think of the odds. In all space and time. I'm scared."
>
> "Don't be."
>
> "Scared of losing—"
>
> "You're not—"
>
> "I always win." (8f.)

What is going on between these two young people? To understand, we must look at what they do *not* say rather than what they say, reading between lines and filling the gaps between their utterances with what might be taking place in their minds. From a careful reading of the novel, we can reconstruct what creates the tension in this scene. Jan has been away in Germany for two weeks. She does not tell Tom that she has had a relationship with the father of the family with whom she was staying and that she may be pregnant, but Tom certainly senses that she has changed in some way. In fact, as she will tell him much later, this brief relationship with an adult man made her emotionally geared to commit herself to Tom. Jan is going away to London the next week to start her training as a nurse. The two young people will not be able to meet more than once a month. Tom is very immature and not ready for a serious relationship; Jan's self-confidence scares him (see "I'm scared" above—a vague statement, since he is not aware exactly of what he is scared of). He is trying to hide his feelings behind irrelevant conversation, and, later on, behind numerous and highbrow quotations. Jan, on the other hand, is trying to reach him emotionally but fails. The dialogue does not reveal anything essential about the characters; rather, it is used to camouflage them.

The absence or sparse use of tags certainly impedes our understanding, since at times we are not even sure who says what. However, when tags are indeed used, they may indicate a hypothetical ellipsis:

"It's hurting you too much," said Jan. "I'll get rid of it."
"Have you caught up?" said Jan. (130)

Presumably, between these two utterances Tom and Jan have had intercourse.

The "dialogue novel" is a postmodern narrative form; in Garner's case, his novel is a deliberate intellectual puzzle. Its purpose is to confuse rather than clarify, and most of its characterization lies beyond the text itself. There are few similar novels, and *Red Shift* naturally implies mature readers, as does *I Am the Cheese*, partly written in dialogue representing tape-recorded conversations. One might argue that this extreme form is generally not relevant for children's fiction; however, we can also find "dialogue narrative" in picturebooks, which allegedly address very young children. One such example is John Burningham's *Granpa*, in which it is not always clear what the source of utterances is, whether the speech is external or internal. There is often no coherence between utterances, and the true events and relationships lie beyond the text. For instance, in one of the central doublespreads, the grandfather and the little girl are depicted with their backs turned against each other, while the text says: "That was not a nice thing to say to Granpa." The words hide more than they reveal, and the readers have to figure out by themselves what is going on between the characters (see further Nikolajeva and Scott 2001, 111–15).

The Content of Utterances as Characterization Device

So far I have been talking about *how* characters talk; however, of utter importance for characterization is what they say about the events and actions they are involved in, about themselves, and about other characters.

Child characters seldom come with any statements of belief or opinion. They may express their likes and dislikes, but it seems that children's authors do not trust their young characters to convey any serious views. Frequently, the implied author's ideology can be heard behind characters' opinions. For instance, Father Christmas gives Lucy and Susan magical gifts, warning them that those are not to be used in battle, and when Lucy protests, he adds: "battles are ugly when women fight" (100). Whether the author is referring to the ancient myth of Amazons or expressing a general attitude, his voice is definitely heard behind the character's. In the same novel, the Faun says to Lucy, "if only I had worked harder at geography when I was a little Faun, I should no doubt know all those strange countries" (17). The Faun may be self-ironic; however, the irony turns into didacticism since young readers are supposed to get the message.

By contrast, what we often do find, especially in supporting child characters' speech, are judgments and preconceived opinions. Not infrequently, these statements are sexist—for instance, "Girls aren't supposed to play on the lower field" (*Bridge to Terabithia*, 27). The boy who says this expresses the general opinion and the unwritten rules of his community.

Characters' reactions to events and happenings can be easily expressed through their speech. If several characters comment on the same event, their reactions are contrasted to each other and thus indirectly demonstrate the different characters' traits. Here is what the characters say when Roo has fallen into the river during the expedition to the North Pole:

> Piglet . . . was jumping up and down and making "Oo, I say" noises; Owl was explaining that in a case of Sudden and Temporary Immersion the Important Thing was to keep the Head Above Water; Kanga was jumping along the bank, saying "Are you *sure* you're all right, Roo dear?" to which Roo, from whatever pool he was in at the moment, was answering "Look at me swim-

ming!" Eeyore . . . was grumbling quietly to himself, and saying, "All this washing . . ."

. . . "All right, Roo, I am coming," called Christopher Robin.

"Get something across the stream lower down, some of you fellows," called Rabbit. (111*f*.; author's emphasis)

Characters are identified in this scene by what they say and how they say it. Piglet is making inarticulate noises, Owl starts one of his long, incomprehensible monologues, Kanga expresses her usual overprotective anxiety, Roo is totally self-centered, Eeyore as always questions everything in the world, Rabbit is bossy but inactive, while Christopher Robin promises the help he has always provided. Interestingly enough, Pooh—the poet and the dreamer of the group—is the one who is silent; instead he acts. Note that Owl's speech is once again presented in summary form. Capitalized words emphasize the supposed significance of his utterances.

Characters' statements about other characters have a dual purpose: they describe the speaker as well as the object of speech. In adult fiction, this device is widely used; for instance, in *Pride and Prejudice*, people constantly pass judgments on other people: "[Our daughters] are all silly and ignorant like other girls" (52); "Mary . . . you are a young lady of deep reflection" (55); "I think him very disagreeable" (121); "she is too much like her brother,— very, very proud" (125); "He is the best landlord, and the best master . . . that ever lived" (270); and so on. The opinions of various people clash and contradict each other, and the readers have to draw their own conclusions. When we find out that Wickham's statements about other people are lies, this immediately changes our understanding of his character. Interestingly enough, we seldom find similar judgments in children's fiction, at least not originating from child characters, apparently because children are not supposed to be able to judge other people. By contrast, as I have shown in my discussion of characterization in *Pippi Longstocking* and *Anne of Green Gables*, adults frequently scorn and condemn children.

In the characters' judgments of other people we are faced with the dilemma of whom to trust and why. A good example is the contradictory presentations of the White Witch in *The Lion, the Witch and the Wardrobe*. Since we have heard the Faun's version first, we are prepared to believe that the witch is evil. Lucy reports to her siblings what the Faun has told her: "She isn't a real queen at all . . . she's a horrible witch, the White Witch. Everyone—all the wood people—hate her" (57). Edmund is the only one who has firsthand information about the witch, and he shares his view with Peter: "How do we know that the Fauns are in the right and the Queen (yes, I know we've been *told* she's a witch) is in the wrong?" (59*f*.; author's emphasis). To Peter's remark that the Faun saved Lucy, Edmund retorts, "He *said* he did. But how do we know?" (60; author's emphasis). The degree of truth in each character's statements is left for the reader to decide. Why do we trust some characters, but not others? Often it has to do with our subject position. Following the literary conventions, we cannot adopt a witch's subjectivity and therefore we perceive her statements as deceitful. The word *witch* itself used by her adversaries makes us suspicious of her; she and her retinue refer to her as "queen."

The characters' statements about other characters have thus a double function in characterization. First, they reveal something about the object of the statement, in which case we have to consider whether we trust the speaker's judgment. The speaker may have various reasons for not telling the truth about other characters. In Edmund's case he is spiteful. But he has been deceived by the witch, so he may sincerely believe that she is good and that the Faun's story is false (the author does, however, tell us that deep inside Edmund knew he was wrong). If we clearly see a character slander another character, we should consider possible motivations. We tend to judge adult characters who blame children as being vicious, because in children's books we are on the child's side. Child characters, on the other hand, may have a deficient capability of judging people adequately. They may ascribe positive traits to people who have acted kindly (e.g., given them candy) and believe other people to be evil if they deny them their wishes. The author may let the reader decide whether the character's judgments of other characters are accurate. The majority of authors, however, prefer to let an (adult) narrative agency "correct" the character's judgments.

Finally, self-judgments compel us even more to weigh their honesty. Is what the characters say about themselves a truthful, candid opinion? Are they capable of evaluating themselves, are they overestimating or underestimating their own qualities? Are they deliberately lying, trying either to present themselves in a more favorable light or to ensure sympathy? Also in this case, other characterization devices are likely to be used, either narrative statements (which are more didactic) or actions. Karlson-on-the-roof is a very good example. He constantly boasts about himself being "the world's best steam-engine driver" or "the world's best builder," while his actions show exactly the opposite, so that the reader has no doubt about Karlson's overdimensioned self-esteem.

Individual Style

We have already noticed that Owl in *Winnie-the-Pooh* is characterized by sesquipedalianism, even though he can use plain language:

"The atmospheric conditions have been very unfavourable lately," said Owl.
"The what?"
"It has been raining," explained Owl.
"Yes," said Christopher Robin. "It has."
"The flood-level has reached an unprecedented height."
"The who?"
"There is a lot of water around," explained Owl.
"Yes," said Christopher Robin, "there is."
"However, the prospects are rapidly becoming more favourable." (127)

Incidentally, Pooh comments on his friends' speech habits as their main personal features:

"Rabbit," Pooh said to himself. "I like talking to Rabbit. He talks about sensible things. He doesn't use long, difficult words, like Owl. He uses short, easy words, like 'What about lunch?' and 'Help yourself, Pooh.'" (*The House at Pooh Corner*, 55)

We remember quite a number of characters by their favorite recurrent phrases. Several generations of Swedes have adopted the sayings of Karlson-on-the-roof: "a handsome, intelligent and reasonably stout man in my prime," "Easy, take it easy," or "That's a mere trifle." The sentence "There is scope for imagination" is used over a dozen times throughout *Anne of Green Gables* as Anne's representative statement. As shown in chapter 7, language is one of the most prominent characterization devices used for Anne Shirley. It is poetic, albeit imitative of the romantic literature Anne has been reading; it is rather advanced for her age, especially given the irregular education she has received.

Language idiosyncrasies are widely used to create peripheral and backdrop characters. The two tiny creatures in *Finn Family Moomintroll*, Thingumy and Bob, are primarily characterized by their peculiar speech: "Shall we dock on the knoor?"; "I can fell smood"; "Don't nake any totice"; and so on (125f.). The funny language is used for comic effect. In *Walk Two Moons*, one of Sal's classmates goes around saying strange things out of the blue, such as "Omnipotent!" or "Beef brain!" (11). A colorful backdrop character is portrayed with just this minute detail.

Style of direct speech can contribute to character development if there is some reason for a substantial change. In the end of *The Lion, the Witch and the Wardrobe*, the children "talked in quite a different way now, having been Kings and Queens for so long" (167). Their speech is marked by vocabulary such as "Fair Consorts" and "by my council"; by archaic grammatical forms such as "thee," "worketh" and "stirreth"; and by syntax such as "even so let us do." Imitating the Narnia stories, Leslie in *Bridge to Terabithia* speaks in a high-flown style that Jess finds hard to manage: "When Leslie spoke, the words rolling out so regally, you knew that was a proper queen. He could hardly manage English, much less the poetic language of a king" (40). Although the narrative, focalized through Jess, does not say so explicitly, Leslie's rhetoric reflects her upper-class education. However, with Leslie's instruction, and having read a number of children's books she has lent him, Jess soon comes on par with her, as shown in one of the scenes from the Terabithia games:

> "O God," she began. . . . O Spirits of the Grove."
> "Thy right arm hast given us the victory." He couldn't remember where he'd heard that one, but it seemed to fit. Leslie gave him a look of approval.
> She took up the words. "Now grant protection to Terabithia, to all its people, and to us its rules." (71)

Jess's linguistic development, although a tiny detail, is part of his overall change under Leslie's influence. While "precision of language" in *The Giver* characterizes the depicted society rather than its individual members, Jonas's successive breaking through the restrictions laid upon him by the limited vocabulary is part of his enormous change throughout the novel.

Dialect, Sociolect, Genderlect

Quite a number of children's writers employ various deviations from standard educated speech as a characterization device. The servants in *The Secret Garden* speak the broad Yorkshire dialect, which contributes strongly to the creation of plausible characters. By the end of the novel, Mary starts speaking dialect, to show that she belongs to this place now. Lyddie speaks as the uneducated girl she is. In *Roll of Thunder, Hear My Cry*, the local dialect of the community is conveyed in direct speech, which adds authenticity to the story. In the *Harry Potter* novels, Hagrid the giant speaks with a Scottish accent, apparently for comic effect and also because this is the dialect the author knows best.

The difference between dialect and sociolect is that the latter signals a social group or class rather than the idiom of a geographic location. The high school jargon used in *The Catcher in the Rye* marks the protagonist/narrator's belonging to a particular social group. Most contemporary young adult novels employ the same device. Babytalk, used to characterize very young children, is another form of sociolect.

Genderlect is a relatively new concept suggested by feminist criticism, denoting the differentiated idiom of men and women. Just as gender is a social construction, a genderlect reflects our abstract ideas of how men and women talk. Some rather vague criteria are, for instance, that men are reasonable, while women are imaginative; that masculine language is ordered and structured, while feminine language is impulsive and fragmentary; or that women use more figurative speech. So far there have been no consistent studies of genderlects in children's fiction. However, we may observe that boys and girls speak differently in books. It is sufficient to compare Tom Sawyer's and Anne Shirley's language to see the difference. Jo March is constantly reproached for her colloquial speech. We do not normally expect girls to use rough language, while it seems acceptable for boy characters. If a girl uses bad language, we will perceive her as deviating from social norms. It is assumed that girls up to certain age are more verbal than boys; therefore, female characters in children's fiction are more likely to use advanced vocabulary and syntax. There are many examples of boys failing to understand verbal jokes or puns, in books as different as *Ramona the Pest* and *Jacob Have I Loved*. Apparently the authors believe that boys' language acquisition is slower. Another widely spread assumption is that girls generally tend to talk more than boys, to share their thoughts with other girls, and so on. Without having done any statistical examinations, I would say that this is clearly reflected in the amount and the form of direct speech in children's novels.

Certain children's books have been subject to serious controversy because of characters' language. However, it is essential to understand that the author lets Tom Sawyer and Huck Finn use what today is perceived as offensive language for the sake of authenticity. It would be rather unnatural if street urchins in a little American town in the 1840s used politically correct language of the twenty-first century; certainly, it has nothing to do with racism.

Concluding Remarks:
The Power of Language

As demonstrated in this chapter, direct speech is a powerful characterization device. In assessing it, we should pay attention to who is allowed to speak, what the form and content of utterances are, and how speech contributes to our understanding of characters. Do boys speak more than girls and are they allowed to get away with what they say? Are children allowed to raise their voices against adults or are they silenced? Do characters have firm opinions which they convey in their utterances? Are they sincere in their statements?

More important, however, is the relationship between direct speech and narration. Narrator's comments and reported speech manipulate the reader to interpret the characters' utterances in a certain way. Assuming, as I have done throughout my study, that the narrator is an adult, we may notice that even when a child character is given a voice, there is always an adult voice accompanying direct speech, adjusting it to guide the reader toward "correct" understanding. Naturally, this is not always the case; however, I have provided enough examples to illustrate the mechanism. Although direct speech may seem a characterization device that presents characters in the most immediate manner, we should not forget that there is usually a narrative agency nearby to amend whatever impression we as readers might gain.

As stated earlier, one of the functions of direct speech is to carry the plot. It seems that in children's fiction, this function generally prevails over speech as a characterization device as far as content is concerned. Furthermore, our interpretation of character through direct speech is based on conventions. We assume that characters who speak a lot are extrovert, open-minded, candid, sometimes perhaps gullible. Anne Shirley certainly matches this description. We assume that a person who does not speak much is secretive and even dishonest. Seeing a character tell a lie—for instance, Edmund in *The Lion, the Witch and the Wardrobe*—we become suspicious of this character. We feel uncomfortable about Mary Lennox's rudeness. We do not condemn Pippi for lying since she is in fact just telling tall tales; however, we see that Karlson's speech is constantly aimed at cheating Midge. In judging characters by their speech, we apply our knowledge of human nature from real-life experience.

Notes

1. Speech act theory also includes various types of mental representation, such as interior monologue and free indirect discourse. I will discuss these in the next chapter. For a brief overview of speech acts, see Rimmon-Kenan (1983, 109–16).

2. The term was introduced by Ann Banfield (1982) and has been widely used by her followers (see, e.g., Erhlich 1990).

CHAPTER TWELVE

~

Figural Discourse
Internal Representation

Some General Remarks on Internal Representation

Although the issues of narrative point of view and the interaction between the narrator's discourse and the character's discourse have been discussed by literary critics since the late nineteenth century (e.g., by Henry James), only in the 1970s and 1980s did important studies putting the depiction of human consciousness under scrutiny appear (Hamburger 1973; Cohn 1978; Banfield 1982). Most surveys give Käte Hamburger priority in the examination of the transparency of literary characters and of mental representation, as she prefers to call this narrative mode.

"Narrative fiction is the only literary genre, as well as the only kind of narrative, in which the unspoken thoughts, feelings, perceptions of a person other than the speaker can be portrayed," says Dorrit Cohn (1978) in her study *Transparent Minds* (7). As mentioned before, the transparency of literary characters as opposed to real people has been often emphasized as the main appeal of fiction: as readers, we are allowed to penetrate other people in a way that is absolutely impossible in reality. We can share their views and opinions, their fears and hopes, their most secret dreams and desires (see Docherty 1983; Forster 1985; Hochman 1985).

The drive to reflect the characters' internal life is, however, a relatively recent development in Western literature, often connected with Henry James on the one hand and Virginia Woolf on the other. In children's literature, this tendency has only become prominent during the last twenty or thirty years. This development can be clearly described in Mikhail Bakhtin's terminology, as a shift from epic toward polyphone discourse, from depicting primarily an external flow of events toward attempts to convey the complex nature of human consciousness (see Bakhtin 1981, 1984, 1990). Among the premises for this mode of writing is the blending of the narrator's and the character's discourse, which results in a variety of narrative techniques classified as stream of consciousness (James 1890), free indirect speech (a direct translation of *"le style indirect libre,"* proposed by Charles Bally, 1912), *Erlebte Rede* (Lorck 1921), interior monologue (Dujardin 1931), narrated monologue (Hamburger 1973; Cohn 1978), dual-voice discourse (Bakhtin 1984, 1990), and so on (for an overview of terminology and theoretical approaches, see Pascal 1977, 8–32; Martin 1986, 130–51). All these techniques presuppose that, through their narrators, authors penetrate the minds of their characters and are able to convey their state of mind to readers by means of language. This statement in itself presents a problem, since language does not always have adequate means to express vague, inarticulate thoughts and emotions.

There are no special studies of the portrayal of internal life in children's fiction, apart from a few articles (see Kuznets 1989; see also some essays in Goodenough 1994). A general consensus about children's literature seems to be that adult writers can easily penetrate a child character's mind, while logically such a task should be infinitely more difficult than entering the mind of another adult. By analogy, it is often questioned, especially by feminist, postcolonial, and queer theories, whether male writers can successfully depict female characters; white writers, black characters; or heterosexual writers, homosexual characters. This skepticism is based on the unequal power positions, in which the "oppressors" presumably have limited possibilities for understanding the mentality of the "oppressed." Even though *all* adult writers have been children once, the profound difference in life experience as well as linguistic skills creates an inevitable discrepancy between the (adult) narrative voice and both the focalized child character's and the young reader's levels of comprehension. Children's literature critics refer to this dilemma as the "double address" (Wall 1991). The many successful attempts to breach this discrepancy—for instance, by using strong internal focalization of a child character or the first-person (autodiegetic) child perspective—do not eliminate the dilemma as such.

Käte Hamburger makes a prompt distinction between personal and impersonal narration, which some other narratologists, notably Gérard Genette, have tried to eliminate. Hamburger denies the first-person narration fictionality inherent to narrative fiction, which for her exclusively denotes third-person—that is, epic—or mimetic narration. Partially this may be accounted for by the year of original publication of Hamburger's study, 1957, when a wide variety of personal narrative techniques—for instance, in the French *roman nouveau*—had not yet been thoroughly investigated.

Hamburger acknowledges three kinds of first-person narratives: autobiography (which she rightly excludes from the scope of narrative fiction), the epistolary novel, and the memoir novel. She thus ignores such techniques, widely used in contemporary children's and young adult fiction, as fictitious autobiography (*The True Confessions of Charlotte Doyle*), fictitious diary (*The Secret Diary of Adrian Mole, Aged 13 3/4*), retrospective self-narration (*Jacob Have I Loved*), and introspective, self-reflexive first-person narration (*Johnny My Friend; Walk Two Moons*). By neglecting personal narration, Hamburger significantly limits the range of narrative forms for conveying consciousness. Since an ever-growing number of children's novels use first-person child perspective, taking this narrative option into consideration is all the more important. Dorrit Cohn, on the other hand, acknowledges the important distinction between the narrating self (extradiegetic-homodiegetic in Genette's terminology) and the experiencing self (intradiegetic-homodiegetic).[1] I find Genette's elimination of differences between personal and impersonal narration extremely helpful, as he instead operates with various patterns of distance and focalization. In children's literature especially, there is little difference between an omniscient adult narrator focalizing a child character (heterodiegetic) and a retrospective adult first-person narrator focalizing himself as a child (homodiegetic); both narrators are extradiegetic in Genette's terminology. Both occupy an unequal power position toward the child, possessing greater knowledge, life experience, and linguistic skills. On the other hand, the difference between personal and impersonal introspective narration—that is, between an autodiegetic child narrator and an adult narrator focalizing a child character—is indeed profound, due to the difference in cognitive level. Furthermore, far from all first-person narratives are concerned with the narrators' consciousness, even though they may contribute to characterization through the narrators' rendering of events and comments about themselves or other characters (e.g., Cassie in *Roll of Thunder, Hear My Cry*). Such a narrator is homodiegetic in Genette's terminology, but not autodiegetic. However, as a first-person narrator, he cannot penetrate other characters' consciousness. Such "outsider" narrators (or narrator-witnesses) are unusual in mainstream fiction; an example commonly referred to is Dr. Watson in the Sherlock Holmes stories. In children's fiction, such narrators are widely used. We may call this mode *quasi-self-narration*.

In this chapter, I will apply categories proposed by Dorrit Cohn in her *Transparent Minds*, adapting them to the variety of narrative forms occurring in children's fiction. Instead of separating personal and impersonal narration, I start with the simplest forms, in which the character's consciousness appears the most transparent and clear, and proceed toward the most complex and ambiguous forms, approximating the unconscious. As Cohn points out, historically, authorial techniques, in which the narrator's discourse prevails over the characters', precede figural techniques, in which the relation is the reverse. This is especially true of children's fiction and will be reflected in the texts I discuss.

Quoted Monologue

Quoted monologue implies a direct rendering of a character's mental discourse, with or without tags ("he thought"; "she wondered"). This is the most primitive and also the most direct way of conveying internal life. Established in the mid–nineteenth century, it is considered outdated and unnatural. Since the development of narrative techniques is usually delayed in children's fiction as compared with the mainstream, quoted monologue is still frequently used in children's novels today.

Quoted monologue conveys inner speech, endophasy, and not the unconscious, because it is dependent on language. In fact, it conceals more than it reveals, because of its verbal, structured nature; therefore, Cohn interrogates the term *stream-of-consciousness*. However, the unconscious can be individualized by employing such stylistic features as dialect, sociolect, babytalk, or other particular speech idiosyncrasies. Cohn (1978) mentions a possibility that child language is "a neglected source of *Ulysses*" (95). She further connects quoted monologue to Vygotsky's concept of "egocentric speech," the thinking aloud of small children. This device is widely used in children's fiction, and occasionally we may encounter problems deciding whether statements are uttered or not. This is especially relevant when there are no tags. On the other hand, if we have the tag "he said to himself," does it mean that the character is indeed talking aloud to himself? Yet in most cases the distinction between audible and inner speech does not change our understanding of the character's mind. However, we should pay attention to the psychological credibility of quoted monologue. In children's literature, it excludes advanced vocabulary, abstractions, a high level of knowledge and life experience, which would make the child character implausible.

In contemporary children's fiction, it is not unusual to omit quotation marks that otherwise indicate quoted monologue:

> Once I walk in that gate, I ain't free anymore, she thought. No matter how handsome the house, once I enter I'm a servant girl—no more than a black slave. (*Lyddie*, 18)

Tags can be omitted as well:

> Well, I'm eleven now, folks, and, in case you haven't heard, I don't wet my bed anymore. But I am not nice, I am brilliant. I am famous across this entire county. Nobody wants to tangle with the great Galadriel Hopkins. I am too clever and too hard to manage. Gruesome Gilly, they call me. She leaned back comfortably. Here I come, Maime baby, ready or not. (*The Great Gilly Hopkins*, 3)

In this passage, the only indication of the source of speech is the sentence "She leaned back comfortably." Apart from the character's highly personal style and conceited self-evaluation, tense and deictics enable the reader to identify the text as the character's discourse. This passage is an example of what is normally referred to as interior monologue, ostensibly the invention of Edouard Dujardin, further elaborated by James Joyce.[2] While children's fiction has not as yet produced a counterpart to Molly Bloom's interior monologue, the example above is by no means unique. However, in most cases interior monologue in children's novels is marked by italics, to help the reader.

Ironically Quoted Monologue (Authorial)
Winnie-the-Pooh is a text in which the character's mind is primarily revealed through quoted monologue.

> Winnie-the-Pooh sat down at the foot of the tree, put his head between his paws, and began to think.
> First of all he said to himself: "That buzzing-noise means something . . . ."
> Then he thought another long time, and said: "And the only reason for being a bee that I know of is making honey."
> And then he got up and said: "And the only reason for making honey is so as *I* can eat it." (4; author's emphasis)

Already in the first sentence, the author/narrator makes fun of the character who has to take special steps to start thinking. The mental process itself seems to be nonverbal ("thought another long time"), but the results are articulated in the typical "thinking-aloud" manner. The verb *said* emphasizes that the character is indeed talking aloud to himself. Pooh's mental activity can, however, be overtly expressed as thought:

> Winnie-the-Pooh took his head out of the hole, and thought for a little, and he thought to himself, "There must be somebody there, because somebody must have *said* 'Nobody.'" (21; author's emphasis)

Once again, the thinking as such is mute, as if the author were suggesting that the character is unable to verbalize his response to the puzzling events unless he talks to himself. We meet this didactic way of conveying thoughts throughout the book. Pooh's slow and painful mental efforts are frequently emphasized by the amount of tags interspersing quoted monologue:

> "And if anyone knows anything about anything," said Bear to himself, "it's Owl who knows something about something," he said, "or my name's not Winnie-the-Pooh," he said. "Which it is," he added. "So there you are." (42)

Not only Pooh but the other characters also are constantly thinking aloud:

> Eeyore . . . thought about things. Sometimes he thought sadly to himself, "Why?" and sometimes he thought, "Wherefore?" and sometimes he thought, "Inasmuch as which?"—and sometimes he didn't quite know what he *was* thinking about. (39f.; author's emphasis)

The irony of this sentence is obvious, but most likely lost on young readers.

> "Well, that's funny," [Piglet] thought. "I wonder what that bang was. I couldn't have made such a noise just falling down. And where is my balloon? And what's that small piece of damp rag doing?" (76)

Such structured thoughts are quite unlikely from a character in an agitated state, as Piglet is in this scene. The recurrent use of the tag "I wonder" in the characters' egocentric speech may feel unnatural, but it is necessary for didactic purposes: the characters' thoughts must sound as if they were uttered aloud. Piglet's long soliloquy when he is "entirely surrounded by water" is perhaps more plausible as it conveys the character's lengthy contemplation of his endangered situation.

We are only allowed one glimpse of Kanga's thoughts, in the chapter in which she is introduced:

Just for a moment, [Kanga] thought she was frightened, and then she knew she wasn't; for she felt sure that Christopher Robin would never let any harm happen to Roo. So she said to herself, "If they are having a joke with me, I will have a joke with them." (93)

Rabbit's monologue in *The House at Pooh Corner*, stretching over half a page, characterizes him as extremely conceited: "'After all,' Rabbit said to himself, 'Christopher Robin depends on Me. He's fond of Pooh and Piglet and Eeyore, and so am I, but they haven't any Brain'" (72).

On the whole, there is very little internal representation in the *Pooh* books. There is one instance of narrated monologue, for some reason originating from Piglet—to be precise, his contemplation about the Heffalump:

What was a Heffalump like?
Was it fierce?
Did it come when you whistled? And *how* did it come?
Was it Fond of Pigs at all? If it was Fond of Pigs, did it make any difference *what sort of Pig?*
Supposing it was Fierce with Pig, would it make any difference *if the Pig had a grandfather called TRESPASSERS WILLIAM?* . . .
Of course Pooh would be with him, and it was much more Friendly with two.
But suppose Heffalumps were Very Fierce with Pigs *and* Bears? Wouldn't it be better to pretend that he had a headache. (60f.; author's emphasis)

This is figural discourse, since the italicized and capitalized words very clearly convey the character's thoughts. It is illuminating in terms of characterization that authorial narration is used for Pooh, Rabbit, Eeyore, and Kanga (and summarized speech for Rabbit and Owl, as shown in the previous chapter), while figural narration is reserved for Piglet. It is quite remarkable, but not inconsistent with the books' buildup, that we never encounter any mental representation of Christopher Robin, the actual protagonist of the *Pooh* books. As suggested in chapter 3, the other characters are projections of Christopher Robin's persona, so his state of mind must be assembled from what we learn about the other characters' consciousness.

Unsignaled Quoted Monologue (Figural)
In *The Lion, the Witch and the Wardrobe*, the characters' thoughts are rare and usually expressed in quoted monologue.

"This must be a simply enormous wardrobe!" thought Lucy . . . . Then she noticed that there was something crunching under her feet. "I wonder is that

more moth-balls?" she thought. . . . "This is very queer," she said. . . . "why, it
is like branches of trees!" exclaimed Lucy. (13)

The grammatically incorrect phrase "I wonder is that more moth-balls" is
an example of individual style that enables the author to come closer to
figural narration. However, the whole scene is psychologically implausible,
since Lucy seems to be talking to herself in a rather unnatural way. Unlike
Milne's text, we do not find any ironic comments from the narrator.

Lucy and Edmund are the only characters in the novel whose minds we
are allowed to enter (which naturally emphasizes their prominent roles
within the collective protagonist). Lucy only appears on her own once, during her first exploration of the wardrobe, and since she cannot share her
thoughts with anyone else, she is talking to herself. Edmund is separated
from the rest of the group for a considerable part of the story, first as he
enters the wardrobe, following Lucy, and again he has nobody else to talk
to. In his mental discourse, all three interchangeable tags are used: "said,"
"thought" and "said to himself."

> "Thank goodness," said Edmund, "the door must have swung open of its own
> accord." . . .
> "She's angry about all the things I've been saying lately," thought Ed-
> mund. . . .
> "Just like a girl," said Edmund to himself, "sulking somewhere, and won't
> accept an apology." (31)

Further on, when he leaves his siblings, his thoughts are the only source of
information for the reader about his feelings, since he for obvious reasons
does not share them with the witch or any of her companions:

> "Because," [Edmund] said to himself, "all these people who say nasty things
> about her are her enemies and probably half of it isn't true. She was jolly nice
> to me, anyway, much nicer than they are. I expect she is the rightful Queen
> really. Anyway, she'll be better than that awful Aslan." At least, that was the
> excuse he made in his own mind for what he was doing. It wasn't a very good
> excuse, however, for deep down inside him he knew that the White Witch
> was bad and cruel. (83)

The narrator's comment is not ironic but didactic; it is as if he does not trust
the reader to make the correct inferences on the basis of Edmund's thoughts.

From the examples discussed, we may draw the conclusion that quoted
monologue is frequently used in action-oriented narratives, in which the
characters' internal life is of less importance and in which thoughts, like
speech, are primarily used to advance the plot.

Soliloquy

Although it is considered unnatural for people to talk aloud to themselves, they frequently do so in fiction. Apparently this is a remnant of dramatic representation, in which an actor's monologue on the stage represents internal rather than external speech (see Chatman 1978, 178–81).

Aunt Polly's almost page-long soliloquy in the beginning of *The Adventures of Tom Sawyer* has no other tags than "stood surprised for a moment, and then broke into a gentle laugh" (8). Her quoted thoughts may be apprehended as figural discourse, but several lines further on she is characterized as a "simple-hearted soul" (9), which immediately shifts the source of utterance from the character to the ironic narrator. Yet, the colloquial style of Aunt Polly's speech gives it strong authenticity.

Mrs. Rachel Lynde's soliloquy, in the first chapter of *Anne of Green Gables*, after her conversation with Marilla, is another similar example:

> "Well, of all things that ever were or will be!" ejaculated Mrs. Rachel when she was safely out of the lane. "It does really seem as if I must be dreaming. Well, I'm sorry for that poor young one and no mistake." (8)

This fifteen-line-long soliloquy does not mean that Mrs. Lynde is actually saying all this out loud while walking home from Green Gables. Although the *verbum dicende* is the emotional "ejaculated," it is apparent that the direct speech is a rendering of her thoughts, which are hardly as articulated as this direct speech makes them. The soliloquy is used for a didactic purpose, to dress a character's thoughts in clear-cut and coherent language. However, the choice of vocabulary, the incomplete sentences, and the emotional charge accentuate the spontaneous nature of thought: "I wouldn't be in that orphan's shoes for anything. My, but I pity him, that's what" (9).

Soliloquy in children's fiction is hardly ever longer than these two examples, and it is not accidental that they both originate from adult characters. Soliloquy slows down the plot and, especially in the case of adult secondary characters, we are not so much interested in what they have to say. A lengthy soliloquy from a child protagonist would certainly feel unnatural.

Autonomous Monologue

Autonomous monologue implies that the character's discourse is uninterrupted by a narrator's discourse. Conventional first-person novels may have a form of either written memoirs or spoken discourse, both of which present a clear narrative situation. Autonomous monologue cancels this clarity by the ambiguity of situation. We see this distinctly in *The Catcher in the Rye*, in which the narrative situation is undetermined. Holden may be telling his story to a psychiatrist in the clinic where he is treated; however, we do not know whether he tells the whole story at one go or whether there are temporal ellipses between chapters. He may also be telling the story, as self-therapy, in a letter, for instance, to his older brother, which is not very plausible, since he mentions the brother in the third person; besides, the brother would be familiar with the "David Copperfield kind of crap" which Holden rejects in the beginning of his story. He may, however, simply be writing the story down, either as self-therapy or as an exercise in creative writing. Depending on how we as readers determine the narrative situation, our interpretation of the story will be slightly different. The degree of reliability of the narrative changes if Holden is talking to a psychiatrist or to himself. In spoken discourse, we do not necessarily expect the narrator to remember all details, while in written discourse we allow for the possibility of after-the-fact adjustments. This is the narrative situation presented in *Dance on My Grave*, where the character/narrator Hal tells us that he is writing down his story and how much trouble he is having in this endeavor.

Cohn suggests as possible subdivisions of autonomous monologue autobiographical monologues, memory narratives, and memory monologues. I find the distinction too subtle to be of any practical interest, but it is clearly based on the narrative situation. Reciting one's own autobiography to oneself is not psychologically plausible, unless it is a public confession, or self-justification, which has a communicative purpose (Cohn 1978, 181). This is probably why we are inclined either to search for a covert narratee in *The Catcher in the Rye* or to view the narrative as a written account.

The narrative situation of a written memoir may be signaled in the beginning—for instance: "I, Penelope Taberner Cameron, tell this story of happenings when I was a young girl" (*A Traveller in Time*, 13). From this statement we know that the narrator is detached from the protagonist, even though they happen to be the same person; we are dealing with retrospective self-narration. On a deeper psychological level we can conclude that, since Penelope still has her maiden name, her involvement with the past has had a negative impact on her, and she has not been capable of developing a normal relationship in her primary world.

The act of written narration can also be stipulated in a fictive foreword—for instance, by claiming that the novel is an authentic manuscript found and published by the author. This metafictive device, widely used in classic (*Don Quixote; The Three Musketeers*) as well as contemporary novels (*The Name of the Rose*), has confused many readers of the Swedish historical novel *The Master*. Narratives based on spoken discourse are frequently embedded within other narratives; several novels and novelettes by Turgenev have this structure. Narratologists' favorite example is *Heart of Darkness* (see Brooks 1984, chap. 9). The initial establishment of the narrative situation, whether spoken or written, is often forgotten by the reader as it is dropped later in the story. An excellent example of this is *Lolita*, which is the protagonist's written account of his experience, performed while he is in jail waiting for trial. If we remember this and realize that the narrator is telling the story in self-defense (cf. Chatman's concept of the interest point of view) and most likely in a state of psychic disturbance, the events Humbert Humbert describes appear to be products of a sick imagination rather than a true account of facts. In juvenile literature, it seems that the authors feel obliged to remind the readers of the narrative situation. In *Dance on My Grave*, Hal's narration is written in self-justification, while he awaits a court trial, much like Humbert Humbert's. However, unlike *Lolita*, we are constantly reminded of the purpose of Hal's writing. In the beginning of *Johnny My Friend*, we see the protagonist/narrator confronted by a police officer interrogating him about his friend Johnny. The situation is reinforced throughout the novel. However, the complexity of the narrative is achieved by the constant cracks between what reasonably is Chris's spoken account of the facts and his confused, incoherent mental discourse. The alternation between the story as such and the narrative situation does not primarily have a didactic purpose but rather an aesthetic one.

We can further note the difference between chronological and nonchronological (associative) memory in autonomous monologues. In *Johnny My Friend*, Chris's reminiscences of his year with Johnny are chronological. Chronology seems to be among the last conventions that children's authors are prepared to abandon; *Johnny My Friend* is intricate enough without adding another complication. In *Dance on My Grave*, Hal occasionally jumps forward in his narration (prolepsis), but basically his account is also chronological.

However, we should not exclude the possibility of a nonchronological autonomous monologue. In *Walk Two Moons*, the narrator's memories alternate between the six-day car journey with her grandparents (which is more or less chronological), and the family story of Phoebe Winterbottom, told by the narrator to her grandparents as they are traveling by car. This story is embedded in the first memory narrative and has overt narratees. For the narrator, the thirteen-year-old Sal, telling her friend Phoebe's story works as a therapy; as she confesses in the beginning of the novel, "beneath Phoebe's story was another one. It was about me and my own mother" (3). The memory of the first time after she has moved to Ohio with her father—

what she refers to as the story of Phoebe and her lunatic—is repeatedly interrupted by the memories of the car travel, and the narrator also frequently leaps forward in her memories, in short prolepses, such as "But this was later, during the whole thing with Phoebe's lunatic, that I realized this" (13). There are also a number of side memories going beyond both primary stories, to the time when Sal's mother was alive, including the most traumatic reminiscence of the stillborn sibling. Presumably these memories are not part of the story she is telling her grandparents, although they are embedded within it.

There is no strict chronology in the memories; instead they are built wholly on associations, as memories usually are. For instance, the blackberry pie she eats at Phoebe's brings back the memory of picking berries with her mother (cf. the function of the madeleine cookie in Proust). Sal is trying to tell a coherent story to her grandparents, and at the same time she is telling the story about her travel with her parents to another, covert narratee. Thus, the memories acquire a structure, the absence of which would make the novel totally unreadable. At the time of narration, Sal knows the outcome of the story but pretends she does not, saying, for instance, "We found out that she wasn't coming back" (49), meaning "We found out that she was dead." In this novel, we encounter many varieties between narration and autonomous monologue described by Cohn: monologue in the present tense (signaling digression or comment), evocation by the present tense and synchronization (describing not a completed past but an ongoing present). Partly we can also see Phoebe's story as told by Sal as an example of Cohn's concept of pseudo-monologue ("then I went home and told him everything that has happened").

While *The Catcher in the Rye* and *Dance on My Grave* are more or less consistent autonomous monologues, *Johnny My Friend* and *Walk Two Moons* contain a number of autonomous monologues within the overall frame of retrospective self-narration, which naturally makes the narrative structure still more complex.

The Diary Novel
The difference between diary and autonomous monologue is that the diary is fragmented and discontinuous. Unlike autonomous monologue, a diary is focused on the present. It creates the illusion of immediacy, since it presupposes that at each given moment in the narrative, the narrator does not know what is going to happen next; neither can he judge the events and his own response to them from a distance. The pretended immediacy allows improbable narrative situations—for instance, the character keeping a diary

during his last minutes of life, especially when he is to be executed, or writing the last entries aboard a sinking ship.

The fictitious diary is a popular type of narrative in children's fiction.[3] The best-known contemporary example in the English language is *The Secret Diary of Adrian Mole, Aged 13 3/4* and its sequels. One would assume that a diary is the closest way of conveying a character's consciousness. However, fictitious diaries can be radically different in their degree of mental representation. Some diary novels merely attempt to render external events, imitating a child's limited vocabulary and unsophisticated worldview, and inserting the phrase "Nothing interesting happened today" every now and then for the sake of authenticity (*Skinny Melon and Me*). The success of the attempt is once again encumbered by the cognitive difference between the adult author and the child narrator (see Cadden 2000, 148f.). Not infrequently, the adult author's efforts to use grammatically corrupt and syntactically primitive sentences, naive judgments, and immature opinions produce an unnatural effect. It may seem that the adult author makes fun of the young character's inaptitude. More relevant for the present argument, characterization in such cases is restricted since the focus of attention lies outside the character. On the other hand, a fictitious diary writer may wholly concentrate on his inner world. A diary can also be palimpsestic—that is, pretend to be rendering external events while simultaneously having a deeper, underlying self-reflection (see my reading of such a text in Nikolajeva 1996, 107–8).

The Epistolary Novel

The difference between the fictitious diary and the epistolary novel is that the latter is supposed to have an addressee. Presumably, a letter writer is less likely to reveal his innermost thoughts to an external correspondent; however, since both situations are fictional, the degree of candor depends wholly on the author's intentions and skills. Otherwise, the difference is marginal: in both cases we see either external events described through a young person's eyes or a deeper self-reflection. In fact, part of the letters in *Dear Mr. Henshaw* are supposedly not mailed but written as a diary.

The classic epistolary novel for young readers, *Daddy-Long-Legs*, is noteworthy for its suspense plot. It invites feminist re-visions, as a depiction of a young woman's total submission to a man (see, e.g., Trites 2000, 61–65). In terms of characterization, however, the novel is of no interest at all. The narrator, Jerusha Abbott, describes an external flow of events during her four years in college, with a total lack of imagination or self-reflection, all the more remarkable since she aspires to be a writer. There is no change in style, which would mark a transition from a poor orphan to a well-educated young woman; there is no change in mentality, as if all the letters were written at one go. In fact, the character appears rather one-dimensional, her interest in clothes being her most prominent stereotypical feature. This is a good example of a novel in which the appeal is something other than characterization.

Dear Mr. Henshaw may appear to be a rendering of external events. On closer examination, we see that the letter writer, Leigh Botts, changes profoundly as time goes by. He develops better writing skills (spelling mistakes in the beginning supposedly add to authenticity) and style, becomes a more mature personality, acquires a good deal of imagination, and gradually becomes more self-reflective, stimulated by the sarcastic replies of his correspondent (to which the reader never has access). The epistolary form is used for extremely subtle characterization, in which character development is never stated explicitly, since the character is too young to judge himself. We can further read the novel as a Künstlerroman, about a young person's aspirations to become a writer. Among other things, Leigh contemplates characterization: "A character in a story should solve a problem or change in some way" (91)—the author's metacomment on her own character.

The Antiphonic and the Polyphonic
Epistolary Novel

Epistolary novels can be presented as a one-way correspondence (like *Daddy-Long-Legs* or *Dear Mr. Henshaw*), close to the diary form, or a two-way correspondence, in which the final meaning, including character construction, has to be assembled from the two sources of information the reader receives. In some contemporary juvenile novels, the epistolary form reaches considerably high levels of sophistication. In *Letters from the Inside*, we are allowed to take part in both sides of the correspondence, and this interaction of voices—antiphony—contributes to our understanding of both characters. At least we think so up to a certain point. To begin with, the two pen pals, who have never met, tell each other some basic facts about themselves. Mandy seems to be quite an ordinary fifteen-year-old, while Tracey presents her life as glamorous, with horseback-riding, water-skiing and other exciting activities. In Mandy's words, "your life sounds perfect. Great family, great boyfriend, stacks of money. I'm jealous!" (10). The correspondence is not especially exhilarating, dealing mostly with school, parties, boyfriends, pop concerts, and other events in a typical teenager's life. From the questions, trivial as well as existential, we learn a lot about the characters—however, more about their external life than their state of mind.

Reading Tracey's letters very carefully, we may discover some inconsistencies, but, like Mandy, we have no reason to suspect anything until it turns out that Tracey does not go to the school she has claimed she attends. Eventually Tracey admits that she is in fact an inmate in a high-security prison for juvenile delinquents. Her whole character has thus been a fake, a construction, apparently based on images from popular magazines. Then, a new character starts slowly emerging from Tracey's letters. She becomes increasingly open and self-reflective and seems to be changing for the better, emotionally and spiritually. When Mandy's letters suddenly discontinue, and Tracey's letters are returned, a new question is posed. We can simply assume than something has happened to Mandy: she has been hinting throughout the correspondence that her older brother has violent tendencies. However, is it plausible that Mandy's parents, who know about Tracey, fail to inform her? Viewing the novel as a depiction of an inner world rather than of external events, we may suggest that the whole correspondence is the product of one person's imagination. Perhaps Tracey is suffering from an identity split and has written letters to herself, or even merely imagined them, in a desperate attempt to make prison life endurable. On the other hand, the source can be Mandy's fancies, caused by her anxiety about her brother. Since there is no authorial discourse to guide the reader, only the two figural discourses, the reliability of both voices is dubious. If the whole correspondence has just one source, we are dealing with an extremely intricate case of intersubjectivity, in which the two minds literally merge and it is impossible to decide which character is real and which is merely a phantom. The fake Tracey in the beginning of the novel anticipates this interplay of identities.

Dear Nobody has a primary narrative, which in our classification would be a memory monologue, told by an autodiegetic narrator, the eighteen-year-old Chris. Into it a number of letters are woven, written by his girlfriend Helen and addressed to their unborn child, which practically means a diary. The letters complement Helen's portrait as recounted by Chris; he can only describe her externally, while in the letters we can enter her mind. At the same time, her descriptions of Chris certainly throw some light on his character. The events are identical, but described from two points of view, one immediate, the other at a distance of several months. Chris's memory narrative is evoked by Helen's letters, which he reads three days before he starts his own written account: "[T]oday is October 2nd, and this is where I begin to write, where I open a door into the past" (unpaginated preface). His account of the events are thus not immediate responses to individual letters, as would be the case in an ordinary correspondence (antiphonic). Rather, the two voices tell their own stories in counterpoint (polyphonic). I would not call this narrative intersubjective, since we are in fact dealing with two clearly separate subject positions.

It is not accidental that the two texts discussed in this section have adolescent characters and presumably address adolescent readers, since the complicated form is rather demanding.

Narrated Monologue

Narrated monologue implies a character's mental discourse in the guise of the narrator's discourse.[4] Narrated monologue is close to quoted monologue and can usually be converted into it by changing deictics and tense. Since these are connected with the character and not the narrator, narrated monologue originates from the character; that is, it is figural rather than authorial. However, the conversion does not always work, since narrated monologue is more complicated and ambiguous. This ambiguity, when we can never be quite certain whether the statements we read come from the narrator or from the character, allows for irony and satire. This is perhaps less desirable but not uncommon in children's literature.

Ironically Narrated Monologue (Authorial)
Let us consider the following passage from Mary Poppins:

> So Mary Poppins put on her white gloves and tucked her umbrella under her arm—not because it was raining, but because it had such a beautiful handle that she couldn't possibly leave it at home. How could you leave your umbrella behind if it had a parrot's head for a handle? Besides, Mary Poppins was very vain and liked to look her best. Indeed, she was quite sure that she never looked anything else. (22)

The first part of the first sentence, up to the dash, is either the narrator's or Jane and Michael's shared point of view. The second part, however, may equally be Mary Poppins's view of herself. The narrated monologue of the second sentence is either Mary Poppins or the Jane-and-Michael entity. To check whether the phrase is indeed narrated monologue, we can transform it into quoted monologue, changing tense and deictics:

→ 1. "How can I leave my umbrella behind if it has a parrot's head for a handle?" Mary Poppins thought.

→ 2. "How can she leave her umbrella behind if it has a parrot's head for a handle?" Jane and Michael thought.

The third sentence in the passage is obviously the authoritative narrator's comment (the word *vain* is hardly part of the children's vocabulary, while Mary Poppins would not describe herself as vain), unless we choose to interpret it as Mrs. Banks's thoughts expressed in narrated monologue. It could be transformed into quoted monologue as → "'Mary Poppins is very vain and likes to look her best,' Mrs. Banks thought." The fourth sentence can express the narrator's, the children's, Mrs. Banks's or Mary Poppins's evaluation, transformed as

→ 1. "She is quite sure that she never looks anything else," the children thought (admiration).

→ 2. "She is quite sure that she never looks anything else," Mrs. Banks thought (disapproval).

→ 3. "I am quite sure that I never look anything else," Mary thought (conceit).

Depending on which point of view we assume in each sentence, we get a slightly different portrait of the character Mary Poppins as well of the other characters. However, in any case, the individual sentences in narrated monologue are included in the otherwise authorial narration, which makes us perceive the whole passage as coming from the narrator rather than any of the characters.

Empathically Narrated Monologue (Figural)

In *Anne of Green Gables*, we find quite a few examples of narrated monologue. Here is one, appearing in the depiction of Anne's first morning at Avonlea:

Anne dropped on her knees and gazed out into the June morning, her eyes glistening with delight. Oh, wasn't it beautiful? Wasn't it a lovely place? Suppose she wasn't really going to stay here! She would imagine she was. There was scope for imagination here. (31)

Except for the first introductory sentence, the whole passage is Anne's narrated monologue, which can be transformed into:

→ "Oh, isn't it beautiful?" she thought. "Isn't it a lovely place? Suppose I wasn't really going to stay here! I will imagine I am. There is scope for imagination here."

There are several reasons for assuming that we are dealing with the character's discourse. The interjection "Oh" and the exclamation mark reflect Anne's exalted style, already familiar to us from the previous chapters. "There is scope for imagination" is her recurrent idiom, already used often enough for us to associate it with the character's way of expression. Finally, there is no indication of the authorial discourse in this passage. In fact, the chapter goes on for another three lengthy paragraphs, describing the view from the window, clearly seen through Anne's eyes (literal point of view). Then the figural discourse stops quite abruptly:

Anne's beauty-loving eyes lingered on it all, taking everything greedily in; she had looked on so many unlovely places in her life, poor child; but this was as lovely as anything she had ever dreamed. (32)

Here, the authoritative narrator takes over, evaluating the character's "beauty-loving eyes" (hardly a self-evaluation from an eleven-year-old), and especially in the condescending "poor child." Yet, the very last phrase can be a return to figural discourse: → "This is as lovely as anything I have ever dreamed," she thought. *Anne of Green Gables* on the whole uses figural representation; however—perhaps as a tribute to the tradition of didactic children's literature—every now and then it lapses into authorial discourse.

Psychonarration

Psychonarration is the most indirect technique, the narrator's discourse about a character's consciousness. In children's literature, since the third-person narrator is always an adult, while the character is a child, psychonarration is unavoidably affected by the adult narrator's experience and commonly makes use of a far more advanced language than the character would logically master. This has advantages as well as problems.

We can distinguish between two types of psychonarration: dissonant and consonant. In *dissonant* psychonarration, the narrator is detached from the psyche he describes; he may make comments, use abstract, analytical vocabulary, which is hardly used by characters in their thoughts, and so on. In *consonant* psychonarration, the narrator's mind fuses with the character's, and the narrator's knowledge coincides with the character's self-knowledge. In children's literature, it would seem that psychonarration is by definition dissonant, because of the cognitive disparity between narrator and character, as well as the pedagogical and ethical dimensions, since authors will try to make use of the narrators to pass judgment on characters. Classic novels avoid psychonarration in favor of external description: "The more conspicuous and idiosyncratic the narrator, the less apt he is to reveal the depth of his characters' psyches or, for that matter, to create psyches that have depth to reveal" (Cohn 1978, 25). Conspicuous, didactic, authoritarian narrators of traditional children's fiction seldom have the ability or interest to penetrate the secrets of a child's mind. However, in contemporary children's novels, there are many successful examples of consonant psychonarration.

Cohn mentions as an important option of psychonarration the rendering of subverbal states, taking her examples, as many other scholars, from *What Maisie Knew* (Cohn 1978, 46*ff*.). In this novel, we share both Maisie's literal and transferred point of view, and since she is unable to judge the events around her, her responses remain unuttered. As adult readers, we can liberate ourselves from the imposed point of view of the text and understand that things are not really as Maisie sees them. In children's literature, this situation is a rule rather than an exception. On the other hand, young readers are mostly just as naive and inexperienced as the child protagonists. The interaction of the various points of view becomes extremely intricate. The child characters' inability to verbalize their emotional responses to the events around them has always been the challenge of psychological children's fiction.

Dissonant Psychonarration (Authorial)

Let us consider the following passage:

> She was not an affectionate child and had never cared much for anyone. The noises and hurrying about and wailing over the cholera had frightened her, and she had been angry because no one seemed to remember that she was alive. Everyone was too panic-stricken to think of a little girl no one was fond of. When people had the cholera it seemed that they remembered nothing but themselves. But if everyone had got well again, surely some one would remember and come to look for her. (*The Secret Garden*, 11)

The first sentence is pure narration: it is a very strong judgment on Mary and cannot be her vision of herself. The second sentence begins in the narrative mode; "frightened" and "angry" are part of the narrator's judgment. However, the last clause is a representation of Mary's feelings, which is stressed by the verb *seemed*. Transformation into direct speech would give us → "'Nobody seems to remember I am alive,' she thought."

The next sentence is narration again, for two reasons. The word *panic-stricken* is not likely to be part of a poorly educated nine-year-old's vocabulary. "A little girl no one was fond of" is hardly an expression of Mary's thoughts. The verb *seemed* in the next sentence reestablishes representational mode. The word *people* reflects Mary's contemptuous attitude toward everybody around her. "Remembered nothing but themselves" is a young, selfish, self-centered child's indignation at the fact that someone else than she may think themselves important, expressed, typically, as an accusation of selfishness.

Finally, the last sentence is, by all standards, a clear case of free indirect discourse, or narrated monologue. "Everyone" is a typical childish hyperbole, "surely" indicates Mary's subjective feelings, and the whole sentence is focused on herself. The analysis of this paragraph shows a fluctuation between narration and representation that creates ambiguity and tension, since the readers are never wholly sure whose voice they hear. This blending of the narrator's and the character's point of view is consistent throughout *The Secret Garden*. I will give just a few more examples to show how complex psychonarration can appear:

> Four good things had happened to her, in fact, since she came to Misselthwaite Manor. She had felt as if she had understood a robin and that he had understood her; she had run in the wind until her blood had grown warm; she as been healthily hungry for the first time in her life; and she had found out what it was to be sorry for some one. (49)

In this passage, differentiation between the narrator's and the character's points of view is almost impossible. By this time, Mary may have become self-reflexive enough to make the observations about the change in her personality. By contrast, the following passage unmistakably comes from the didactic narrator:

> Living, as it were, all by herself in a house with a hundred mysteriously closed rooms and having nothing whatever to do to amuse herself, had set her inactive brain to working and was actually awakening her imagination. (66f.)

The judgment "her inactive brain" and the statement "awakening her imagination" are hardly Mary's self-evaluations. Generally, mental representation is not a prominent feature of *The Secret Garden*, in which external characterization is the foremost device. Whenever it is used, the authorial presence is highly tangible. Characteristically, as soon as Mary meets Colin, the narrative employs considerably more dialogue than the previous chapters. Instead of rendering the changes in Mary through the didactic narrator, the author allows the reader to follow Mary's self-discovery through direct speech. However, there are constant lapses back into authoritative narration, combined with narrated monologue:

> Mary had not known that she herself had been spoiled, but she could see quite plainly that this mysterious boy had been. He thought that the whole world belonged to him. How peculiar he was and how coolly he spoke of not living. (123)

The first sentence is the narrator's discourse; the following two employ narrated monologue, which we can easily test by transforming them into → "'He thinks that the whole world belongs to him. How peculiar he is and how coolly he speaks of not living,' Mary thought."

Consonant Psychonarration (Figural)

Many contemporary psychological novels for children use consonant psychonarration as a single and consistent narrative and characterization device. The challenge of this form is the delicate balance between the young character's mental capacity and the adult narrator's vocabulary and life experience, enabling mental representation to become considerably more sophisticated than quoted or narrated monologue would allow. Katherine Paterson is one of many writers who excel in consonant psychonarration, in order to convey the young characters' disturbed state of mind, what Cohn calls "a subverbal state." Here is a passage from *Bridge to Terabithia*, describing Jess's attempt to come to terms with Leslie's death:

> It came into his mind that someone had told him that Leslie was dead. But he knew now that that had been part of the dreadful dream. Leslie could not die any more than he himself could die. But the words turned over uneasily in his mind like leaves stirred up by a cold wind. If he got up now and went down to the old Perkins place, Leslie would come to open it, P. T. jumping at her heels like a star around the moon. It was a beautiful night. Perhaps they could run over the hill and across the fields to the stream and swing themselves into Terabithia. (106)

To separate authorial and figural discourse here is virtually impossible. Formally, the passage is in the third person. Several sentences are written in narrated monologue ("Leslie could not die"). "[L]ike leaves stirred up by a cold wind" or "like a star around the moon" are similes, poetical language which Jess, a nonreading and nonverbal boy, would not have as a part of his idiom. Yet the passage is a poignant rendering of the boy's thoughts and feelings. The narrator is articulating them for him, because he lacks the language to do so himself. Needless to say, this technique is more advanced than quoted or narrated monologue, and brings us closer to the character's mind than dissonant psychonarration.

Apart from the direct speech, the whole of *Bridge to Terabithia* is written in psychonarration, merging authorial and figural discourse into a highly intricate narrative. Here is another example:

> Now it occurred to him that perhaps Terabithia was like a castle where you came to be knighted. After you stayed for a while and grew strong you had to move on. For hadn't Leslie, even in Terabithia, tried to push back the walls of his mind and make him see beyond to the shining world—huge and terrible and beautiful and very fragile? (126)

Obviously, the language and the level of self-reflection are too advanced for Jess; however, the spirit of his feelings is adequately conveyed.

Most of Katherine Paterson's contemporary novels display the same techniques. In *The Great Gilly Hopkins*, Gilly's feelings are often dressed in much more mature expressions than she can possibly master, often involving refined intertextuality—for instance: "Like Bluebeard's wife, she opened the forbidden door and someday she would have to look inside" (115); or "To be herself, to be the swan, to be the ugly duckling no longer—Cap O'Rushes, her disguise thrown off—Cinderella with both slippers on her feet—Snow White beyond the dwarfs—Galadriel Hopkins, come into her own" (124). The second example especially reflects the unstructured, chaotic mode of a young person's thinking, "unspeakable sentences," to use Ann Banfield's phrase. Vinnie's crush on her schoolteacher in *Flip-Flop Girl*, like Jess's fear of death in *Bridge to Terabithia*, is described exclusively by means of psychonarration. Vinnie in *Flip-Flop Girl* cannot verbalize her feelings, so it is the reader's task to set them into words, following small clues such as: "Vinnie's face burned with pleasure. The teacher liked her" (18f.); "she had hardly paid any attention to anyone except Mr. Clayton" (20); "Mr. Clayton made up for not having any real friends. He was the best teacher she'd ever had" (25); "She had the whole walk home to think about clouds and Mr. Clayton" (28); and so on, finally articulated as "She'd already decided that she would marry him" (32). James's feelings toward his mother in *Come Sing, Jimmy Jo*, with a strong flavor of guilt, cannot be fully articulated either, so psychonarration helps hide his true thoughts behind the seemingly authorial discourse:

He wanted to be loyal to Olive. He really did. She was his mother, and though she wasn't like other people's mothers, she loved him in her way, even when she was so set on being Keri Su and making him into Jimmy Jo. (*Come Sing, Jimmy Jo*, 93)

Of all the modes of mental representation, consonant psychonarration is the most challenging for a children's author and the most demanding on the young reader. As a result of its ambiguity, it is seldom, if ever, used in traditional children's literature, and it has so far only been used by a limited number of children's writers, notably Maria Gripe in Sweden and Lois Lowry and Patricia MacLachlan in the United States.

Retrospective Self-Narration

The narrative situation of retrospective self-narration is similar to psychonarration. Self-narration is less omniscient and more self-reflexive than impersonal narration. Unlike the omniscient narrator, a first-person narrator is obliged to account in some way for his sources of information. A famous example from juvenile fiction is the chapter in *Treasure Island* in which Jim "happens" to hide in the barrel when he overhears the villains plotting. However, this is also true about impersonal narratives in which one character is focalized internally. The characters must either be told about the facts they have not witnessed or, just as Jim, "happen" to be in a situation where they overhear important facts, as Lyra does in the beginning of *Northern Lights*.

Like the impersonal narratives, self-narration can be either empathic or detached, consonant or dissonant. There are two further possibilities. Self-quoted monologue, taking the form of "I said to myself . . . ," creates great ambiguity, especially since it allows transition from past to present tense. Self-narrated monologue refers to something the narrator at the time of narrating knows, but pretends he does not. For instance, in *Mio, My Son*, the narrator, telling the story a year after it happened, naturally knows the outcome, and occasionally reveals that he does, but he usually narrates as if the events were unfolding in front of his eyes. As mentioned earlier, this is also the case in *Walk Two Moons*.

Like consonant psychonarration, retrospective consonant self-narration using a child focalizer meets the dilemma of the child's lack of vocabulary, experience, and understanding (see Cadden 2000). It is naturally an extremely difficult narrative form. In the mainstream, one of the possible strategies for achieving the same effect is to use a mentally retarded person:

I'm probly a lot brighter that folks think, cause what goes on in my mind is a sight different than folks see. For instance, I can *think* things pretty good, but when I got to try sayin or writin them, it kinda come out like jello or somethin. (*Forrest Gump*, 1–2; author's emphasis)

Like a young child, Forrest naturally has thoughts and emotions, but he cannot articulate them properly. The challenge of this narration is to keep the balance between the authenticity of his style and the coherence necessary for the reader to understand what is going on. Like so many children's novels, *Forrest Gump* demands that the readers liberate themselves from the character's subjectivity.

Retrospective Dissonant Self-Narration

In *Jacob Have I Loved*, the first-person narrator is homodiegetic, identical with the character. However, although both the narrator and the character are called Louise, they are not exactly the same person. There is a substantial gap between the actual time of the story and the time when the story is narrated. Louise's rendering of her adolescent years on the island is an analepsis which takes place while she, now an adult, is returning back to her childhood home. The narrator is extradiegetic. There is, in other words, a discrepancy between the naive perspective of a young person and the experience of an adult. This makes the narrator highly unreliable. Louise the narrator tells us exactly as much as she chooses to. She may omit facts or pass wrong judgments, or her memory may fail. Louise the character, who is thirteen in the beginning of the analepsis, may seem a classic tomboy, like Jo March or Anne Shirley. At least, Louise the narrator tries to present her this way. What the readers may see is a susceptible young girl, practicing self-defense against jealousy, bordering on hate, toward her pretty, talented, and admired twin Caroline, who has always received more attention because she was born weak and almost died. Louise the narrator tells us that Louise the character feels that she is treated unjustly. However, it is hardly possible for the reader to decide whether this is an objective fact (the narrator states that the character felt that way), a subjective memory (the narrator believes, many years later, that the character probably felt that way) or a deliberate lie (the narrator wants us to believe that the character was maltreated; "interest point of view" in Chatman's terminology). In the first place, we see that Louise the character is compensating for this feeling by being twice as diligent, by contributing to the family's economy, specifically to Caroline's music lessons. Louise the character pretends (or Louise the narrator portrays her as pretending) to be uninterested in clothes or her looks. We see her survival strategy, her frantic attempts to be different from Caroline, even if it means being inferior.

If as readers we penetrate Louise's unnecessary sacrifice and see the motivation for it as a rather hypocritical and self-righteous compensation, does the grown-up Louise penetrate herself? It seems that the author wants us to be skeptical of the narrator. Here we observe the contradiction between the point of view of the character and the narrator, who happen to be the same person, as well as the point of view of the reader. Louise the character has presumably patterned her life according to the Bible quotation, making herself the unloved twin. In telling her story, Louise the narrator deliberately constructs her character as an object in relation to her sister, her parents, and all other agents of the narrative. However, as readers we are inclined to perceive her as a subject and share her point of view. Unless we liberate ourselves from this compulsion to adopt the first-person narrator's subjectivity, we cannot judge Louise—or her story—properly.

Retrospective Consonant Self-Narration

It may seem that "retrospective consonant self-narration" in children's literature is a contradiction in terms, since the temporal gap between the described events and the narrative act prevents the necessary consolidation of the narrating self and the experiencing self. However, just as consonant psychonarration provides a way to breach the cognitive level between the narrator and the character, some successful attempts have been made to allow the narrator to reenter his own mind in the past. Often such narratives involve a relatively short lapse of time between the events and the narrative act, so that the narrator is still cognitively closer to the character than to the adult writer (e.g., in *Mio, My Son* or *Johnny My Friend*).

In *Baby*, the first-person narrator is used to emphasize the ambiguity of the narrative. The temporal pattern of the novel is extremely complicated. It may be an analepsis, similar to that in *Jacob Have I Loved* where the grown-up Larkin contemplates the events of the past. But it may equally be a "simultaneous" narrative combined with recurrent analepses (italicized in the book) with a different focalizer, Sophie, told ten years after Larkin's narrative act takes place.

Larkin's parents are immature and insecure, they cannot talk with her about the dead baby brother, and suppress their own sorrow instead of trying to come to terms with it. The name giving, one of many echoes from MacLachlan's earlier texts, becomes the metaphorical articulation of a suppressed relationship. However, the metafictive layers of the novel may suggest further reflections, if we interpret the short italicized parts as Sophie's memories ten years after the events, vague images that she lacked words to express at the time. Sophie's successive mastery of the language corresponds to the family verbalizing their sorrow. When the family accepts that Sophie must return to her biological mother, they have come still further toward reconciliation. The author here accentuates the significance of language in understanding the most complicated emotions. Without setting words to feelings it is impossible to cope with them. When the family starts calling the foundling "Sophie" instead of the superficially neutral but emotionally charged "baby," they become better prepared to handle their sorrow. The act of naming is duplicated.

Baby is an extremely sophisticated narrative, demanding great attention and empathy from the reader. It literally draws us into the characters' minds and forces us to re-live their memories in an intensive and painful manner. Unlike *Jacob Have I Loved*, there is no adult, mature narrative self providing distance to the experiencing self. The reader is left completely without guidance.

Subjectivity and Authorial Control

As repeatedly pointed out in this chapter, the most profound consequence of the different modes of mental representation in children's fiction is the discrepancy between the (adult) narrator and the child character. Naturally, this can also be the case in the mainstream first-person novels depicting the protagonist's childhood, such as *David Copperfield* and *Great Expectations* (cf. Galbraith 1994).

As observed, quoted monologue is the most primitive way of conveying a character's state of mind, because the narrator's and the character's discourse are kept clearly distinct, and the authoritative narrator can always correct whatever erroneous views young characters may express in their own thoughts. Assessing quoted monologue in its narrative context is always essential, since it is frequently interspersed with the narrator's comments, which creates either an ironic or didactic discrepancy between the narrator's discourse and the character's discourse, emphasizing the cognitive difference between the two. In blended narration, readers may be confronted with the difficulty of adopting a subject position, since at any given moment, the source of internal discourse and the textual point of view are ambiguous. Whether intentionally or not, the author loses control over the reader's subjectivity, which gives the reader greater freedom of interpretation and places higher demands on the reader in text decoding. While internal representation in itself is the most complex characterization device, the development in children's fiction toward psychonarration has contributed to the overall complexity of contemporary novels for young readers.

The different narrative modes for conveying consciousness are seldom employed consistently throughout a text but are mixed and combined, the transition often being very vague, almost indiscernible. Contemporary children's and juvenile fiction has also given us examples of experimental multiple techniques—for instance, a combination of personal and impersonal narration (*Breaktime*), of self-narration and witness narration (*Dance on My Grave*), of dialogue and self-narration (*I Am the Cheese*), and so on. In these novels, authorial presence is almost eliminated, while the subjectivity is obscure and ambivalent. Such experiments aim at still more elaborate ways of expressing the complex inner world of a young protagonist.

Notes

1. Cohn notes that she is familiar with Genette's terminology but abstains from introducing it into English-language scholarship. Since Genette's terminology has now become universal, I have used it in this book.

2. As a side comment, I may add that Vladimir Nabokov has pointed out examples of interior monologue in *Anna Karenina*, thus moving this "invention" several decades back in time. See Nabokov 1981.

3. Since I am only interested in fictional characters, I will not discuss the most famous example of a young person's authentic diary, Anne Frank's *The Diary of a Young Girl*, even though it poses some extremely interesting questions in connection with the writer's subsequent editing of her earlier entries with future publication in mind.

4. The term itself comes from the English edition of Käte Hamburger's study, as a direct translation of the German *Erlebte Rede*. The established term today is *free indirect discourse*, or FID (see Pascal 1977). I employ Cohn's terminology in this chapter for the sake of consistency.

CHAPTER THIRTEEN

~

Implicit Characterization

In this final chapter, I will briefly discuss some indirect, or implicit, characterization techniques. Implicit characterization is widely used in general fiction. However, in children's literature many implicit characterization devices are limited. We cannot expect characterization through the child protagonist's relation to alcohol or smoking; children are seldom free to express their taste in the choice of clothes or interior design (although they may to a limited extent); they seldom have money of their own; and so on. Adult characters may be implicitly characterized by their political views or religious beliefs, preference in alcoholic beverages, the newspaper they subscribe to, the department store where they buy their clothes, the area in which they have chosen to live (downtown; suburban; countryside), the car they drive, the art they have on their walls, the place they go to for vacation, and so on. For a child character, most of these means of characterization are significantly restrained. Anne Shirley's ugly clothes are made by Marilla. The fact that Ramona Quimby says her prayers before going to bed does not characterize her, but rather her parents. Equally, the fact that Leslie Burke's family has moved from a big city to the countryside and does not have a television set is not her decision.

Proper Names

The authors' choice of personal names is seldom accidental, and names, as well as characters' attitudes toward their names, can considerably enhance our understanding of characters. In children's literature, proper names have a number of special functions (see Aschenberg 1991; Tuten-Puckett 1993). Proper names are important for characterization, since they distinguish characters from one another; they have the nominative function (see Searle 1969, 172; Docherty 1983, 41–86; Pavel 1986, 31–42; Lamarque 1996, 33*ff.*). Characters' names are perhaps the first thing we learn about them.

An illuminating example of the nominative function of names can be gathered from *Winnie-the-Pooh*. The chapter in which Piglet is introduced starts, "The Piglet lived" (30), thus presenting the word *piglet* as a common rather than proper noun. The definite article is repeated twice—"the Piglet lived in the middle of the house. . . . When Christopher Robin asked the Piglet . . ." (30)—but dropped after that, so that Piglet is from now on apprehended as a personal name. Similarly, in the Moomin novels, some characters are first introduced as a species, which subsequently turn into personal names: "out of the tent came a Snufkin. . . . shouted Snufkin, hopping eagerly up and down" (*Comet in Moominland*, 54*f.*). Snufkins, hemulens, fillyjunks, and snorks seem to be species in these novels, while Sniff is obviously a personal name. All the names are created by the author, giving the reader specific, if somewhat vague, associations.

There is a long tradition in the mainstream of giving associative names, especially to secondary characters, which creates a comic or sometimes satirical effect; we can find many examples in Dickens, Thackeray, Gogol, and Waugh (cf. Rimmon-Kenan 1983, 68*f.*). Since satire is practically absent in children's fiction, this device is unusual. However, it is not impossible. For instance, the protagonist's name in *The Neverending Story* is Bastian Balthazar Bux, and another character's name is Carl Conrad Coreander. More recent examples are the names in the Harry Potter series: Dumbledore, Malfoy, and especially Voldemort (see further Schafer 2000, 56–61; Zipes 2001, 181). Against these inventive names, the hero's name sounds plain and ordinary.

Names are closely connected with identity, and since the identity quest is such a prominent part of children's fiction, the characters' names are not infrequently part of this quest. We remember that Anne Shirley is deeply dissatisfied with her name and would prefer to be called something more romantic, like Cordelia. She is envious of her friend Diana's name. In the Swedish Elvis Karlsson series, the protagonist has been named after his mother's great idol and must live up to her high expectations (the combination of the illustrious first name and one of the most common Swedish last names creates a comic effect in itself). It takes little Elvis a long time to come to terms with his name. Park in *Park's Quest* has the same name as his dead father, which makes the boy feel a special affinity with the father, but also sets expectations. In the previously mentioned *The Neverending Story*, the character finally loses his name as his identity gradually disintegrates, and in the last chapters he is referred to as "the boy without a name." This is a very concrete illustration of the interconnection of name and personality. In some time-shift fantasy novels, characters from different time periods are associated through their names (Nikolajeva 1988, 109).

A great number of literary characters are so closely associated with their qualities that their names are sometimes used to denote these qualities. We can, for instance, speak of a Peter Pan complex (just as we speak of an Oedipus complex) referring to a child character's reluctance to grow up. We can further allude to characters' specific traits in order to describe real people; for example, we can call somebody "an Eeyore," meaning a killjoy.

Literary characters' names can occasionally become such strong trademarks that it is impossible to use them again. It is feasible to have protagonists named Chris, Jane, Mary, Michael, or Peter, but it is hardly possible to avoid unnecessary connotations when using such names as Alice or Dorothy. A protagonist can be called James White, or Tom Smith, or Harry Brown, but not James Bond or Tom Sawyer, and, after 1997, not Harry Potter. Unusual names, created specifically for a particular text, are unlikely to be used again. Wendy, a name coined for the character in *Peter Pan*, has become a regular first name in English and has even been used in several minor literary works. Ronia, a name invented by Astrid Lindgren, became a regular first name but has so far not been used in literature. Some names have strong connotations in a specific language or culture and cannot be reused. The Swedish Emil became Mickel in the German translation, because the name Emil was already "occupied" by the character of *Emil and the Detectives*. Max, the young hero of a popular Swedish picturebook series, became Sam in English, apparently not to be confused with Max of *Where the Wild Things Are*.

On the other hand, a name may be intentionally chosen to give associations and guide the reader toward a better understanding of the character. Roland in *Elidor* bears an intertextual name, alluding to Childe Roland of the medieval ballad.

Age

The character's exact age, which is perhaps less important in adult fiction, is essential in children's literature. It is seldom crucial whether a character in a mainstream novel is forty-seven and a half or forty-eight, while the difference between seven and a half and eight in a children's novel can be decisive. A title such as *The Secret Diary of Adrian Mole, Aged 13 3/4* is illuminating in this respect. Most likely, authors will indicate the protagonists' age when introducing them, either directly or indirectly:

> Once upon a time there were three children and their names were Carey, Charles and Paul. Carey was about your age, Charles a little younger, and Paul was only six. (*Bedknob and Broomstick,* 9)

The indication of a character's age has several functions. First, it helps the reader to adopt a subject position. In the prior example, the three characters are interchangeable (a collective protagonist), and readers can choose subjectivity based on their own age. Empirical research shows that young readers can share subjectivities most easily with characters who are the same age or slightly older. Furthermore, an indication of age immediately allows a reader to make inferences about shared experiences, even though these may not be mentioned in the text or be irrelevant to it. Age will be connected with being in a particular grade at school and therefore possessing certain knowledge and skills. We cannot infer from the fact that a character in an adult novel is forty-five that he has a Ph.D. For a child character, age will be connected with the level of education and certain practical skills, unless there are very good reasons (e.g., in a historical novel). In addition, each year in a child's life brings about crucial physical changes. Thus, a character of eight or nine years old is expected to be able to read and write, to have basic table manners, and to have lost his baby teeth, but probably not to have smoked, drunk alcohol, or had sexual intercourse. Knowing that Jo March is fifteen, we assume that she has begun to menstruate, although this fact was one of the unmentionables at the time the novel was written. Among the many curious facts of children's literature, Nancy Drew's age was subsequently changed from sixteen to eighteen, the only reason being that she would not be able to drive legally in all states at sixteen.

Amazingly many children's novels portray characters of eleven or twelve. I do not think this is a coincidence. This is the age of initiation in many archaic cultures, and although this connotation has been lost in Western society, some remnants may be left in the authors' imagination. Children in *The Giver* are assigned their jobs, and therewith their place in society, at the age of twelve. Here is what another character says about this age: "Twelve is the magical dividing line, we all know that. I don't care what grown-ups say, but that's when your childhood comes to an end" (*Johnny My Friend,* 89). Formally, of course, after twelve you are a "teenager," not a child.

Setting

Setting as such cannot be considered part of characterization. However, setting can enhance characterization—for instance, if a character primarily appears indoors (Laura in the Little House series) or outdoors (Tom Sawyer); whether characters prefer home and safety or dangerous places away from home (see some further argument in Chatman 1978, 138–45). Characters portrayed against idyllic rural landscapes, such as Mary Lennox, are perceived differently from characters who act within urban, menacing environments. Although the character in *Slake's Limbo* feels confident and safe in the New York subway, this setting creates a sense of threat and anxiety, since it is not a natural place for a child to be. By contrast, Ronia is described as a "child of nature;" she feels at home in the forest, and her exploration of the joys and dangers of nature goes parallel with her exploration of self. The fact that most of Ramona's adventures and misadventures take place in school makes us believe that for this character school is the most important part of her life.

A character's room can contribute to characterization, as I have shown in my discussion of Anne Shirley in chapter 7. Setting is frequently used to symbolize the character's moods as well as power position. The bright sunny morning in the beginning of *Anne of Green Gables* corresponds to her hopeful expectations. A change of setting can parallel the change in the character's frame of mind. A storm can symbolize the turmoil in the character's psyche. The close interdependence of character and setting in *The Secret Garden* has already been discussed. Mary's mental and spiritual awakening echoes the garden starting to bloom again after ten years of lying fallow. Colin's coming out from his voluntary isolation in his bedroom signifies his physical and mental healing. In many other books, the change of seasons marks the character's evolution. On the most primitive level, winter symbolizes death; spring, resurrection; summer, heyday; fall, decay. Hundreds of children's books taking place in summer emphasize childhood as a happy, but also static, unchanging period. There is an interesting change in weather conditions in the sequel to *Winnie-the-Pooh*. Although in the first book we have witnessed a flood, the season has constantly been summer. In *The House at Pooh Corner*, the seasons alternate between winter, summer, and fall, with a severe storm. The change of seasons emphasizes the flow of time and the imminent changes in the protagonist's life situation. The fog in which Rabbit tries to lose Tigger in order to "unbounce" him may symbolize the character's confused mind. The storm marks the first radical change in the hierarchy of the Forest: Owl's house is blown down, Piglet is coaxed into ceding his house to Owl, Pooh generously invites Piglet to live with him—some profound changes in the previously static characters are initiated.

By placing a character in an extreme setting—varying from war or natural catastrophe to a slightly deviating situation in a relative's home—writers can initiate and accelerate a maturation process in a character, which would not be plausible in an everyday surrounding. A good example is *The True Confessions of Charlotte Doyle*. The female protagonist, a thirteen-year-old upper-class girl fresh from "Barrington School for Better Girls," is placed on a ship crossing the Atlantic from England to the United States in the 1830s. Her self-discovery, not least her overtly androgynous behavior, would not be possible in her usual setting. Thus, setting can function as catalyst for character evolution.

We should further distinguish between the physical environment and the human environment, such as family or class (cf. Rimmon-Kenan 1983, 66). Although the latter is less essential for characterization as compared with the mainstream, once again because child characters cannot choose their own social environment, we can expect some additional characterization from the fact that the character comes from a Catholic, Jewish, Muslim, or atheist family, is a newly arrived immigrant, or lives in the same place his ancestors have lived in for many generations, and so on.

All these elements of setting are based on conventions, and they are culturally dependent. Rain as a symbol for a character's state of mind will be interpreted differently in a northern country, where it prevents the children from playing outside, and in an African country or in southern California, where it is welcome after a period of drought.

Attributes

Fairy-tale characters are often connected with their special attributes, which become extensions of their inner qualities. A hero will have a sword and a horse symbolizing his invincible bravery. Some characters in children's fiction also have permanent attributes. Emil in *Emil's Pranks* has his cap and his toy rifle. Johnny's attribute is his bicycle, which naturally is merely a transformation of the archetypal hero's horse. A bicycle is, unlike a horse, a kenotype rather than archetype, a recurrent image without any direct connection with archaic thought (see Nikolajeva 1996, 145–51). In *Dance on My Grave*, Barry's motorbike is a similar attribute, symbolizing power and freedom, but ultimately causing the character's death. Mary Poppins is characterized by her umbrella, as well as the things she carries in her bag: "a large cake of Sunlight Soap, a tooth-brush, a packet of hairpins, a bottle of scent, a small folding arm-chair and a box of throat lozenges" (17); "seven flannel night-gowns, four cotton ones, a pair of boots, a set of dominoes, two bathing-caps and a postcard album" (19). Like Moominmamma's handbag, Mary Poppins's carpetbag is a cornucopia from which anything necessary is easily available. Many characters have pets as attributes. For instance, Pippi has her horse and her monkey.

Clothes

Clothes speak a very powerful and eloquent language in society (see Lurie 1981), which is naturally reflected in literature. Unlike adult characters, children in children's novels can only be characterized by their clothes indirectly, since they usually cannot choose their clothes themselves. Conversely, their clothes can tell the reader something about the child character's parents or guardians. I have discussed the discrepancy between Anne's dream of puffed sleeves and the sensible, dull clothes Marilla provides her with; the clothes Anne is wearing characterize Marilla rather than Anne. Similarly, Anne's first dress with puffed sleeves does not reflect her fulfilled desire but rather Matthew's insight about young girl's need for fancy clothes.

Clothes can characterize characters in a variety of ways. Gender differences are very prominent: girls dream of pretty clothes (in addition to Anne, e.g., Meg in *Little Women*), while boys hate proper clothes viewing them as restrictive, like Tom Sawyer. Heidi, however, shares Tom's suspicion of nice clothes. As Heidi returns from Frankfurt to her grandfather, she takes off her city clothes to show the grandfather that she is unchanged underneath.

Wearing the wrong clothes often leads to child characters being ostracized by their peers. Inheriting clothes from an older sibling is perceived by children as oppressive, as if somebody else's personality is imposed together with the clothes. This is a frequent motif in children's books—for instance, *Karlson on the Roof* and *Ramona the Brave*. The protagonist of the Elvis series inherits all his clothes from his long-dead uncle, which is a serious dilemma for the young boy: he wonders whether he is a person in his own right, with a borrowed name and borrowed clothes. For Lyddie, fine clothes are a token of slavery:

> Mistress Cutler provided her with a store-bought calico gown. It was softer than her rough brown homespun and fit her much better, but somehow it suited her less. How could she enjoy the garments of her servitude? (*Lyddie*, 23)

Leslie's cutoff jeans and faded T-shirts reflect her casual attitude toward material wealth as well as her deliberate deviation from the norms of the society she lives in. Once again, this attitude is something imposed on her by her parents. Since we do not share Leslie's point of view, we do not know whether she longs to be like other girls deep inside, wear dresses, and have long braided hair. We assume that her perseverance in wearing shabby clothes, even after she has noticed her difference from her classmates, is a deliberate choice, which naturally characterizes her as a strong personality. However, she knows that certain situations demand formal clothes, so she does wear a dress when going to church with Jess's family.

Cross-dressing is a powerful characterization device as it clearly shows the characters' attitude toward their gender. For Johnny, cross-dressing is a necessity, not an amusement. The protagonist of *The True Confessions of Charlotte Doyle* finds herself in a situation in which cross-dressing is the only possible survival strategy. Stranded as the only passenger on a transatlantic ship with a morally dubious captain and crew, and having involuntarily caused a man's death, she sheds her female clothes as well as her well-bred manners and joins the crew to make up for the ill she has brought about. Well before this event, Charlotte is given a set of sailor's clothes by the benevolent black cook, which she takes as a kind of warning: she has been walking freely around the ship and even attempted climbing the riggings:

> I took the gift as a warning that I had been forgetting my station. I told him—rather stiffly, I fear—that I thought it not proper for me, a girl—a lady—to wear such apparel. But, so as not to offend him deeply, I took the blouse and the trousers to my cabin.
>
> Later on, I admit—I tried the garments on, finding them surprisingly comfortable until, shocked, I remembered myself. Hurriedly, I took them off, resolving not to stoop so low again. (71)

The fact that Charlotte finds men's clothes "surprisingly comfortable" is illuminating. Although the text does not mention it, we may assume that she is subject to the torture of Western female clothing in the 1830s: stays, tight shoes, and so on. Trying on practical, loosely fitting sailor's clothes, she is symbolically confronted with gender inequality and is prepared to take the first step toward liberation. However, when the course of events forces Charlotte to wear men's clothes, the experience is less joyful: "Slowly, fearfully, I made myself take off my shoes, my stockings, my apron, at last my dress and linen. . . . The trousers and shirt felt stiff, heavy, like some skin not my own" (113). In adopting an androgynous image, Charlotte also finally performs the symbolic action many of her literary sisters have done before her: she cuts off her hair.

Upon arrival in Providence, Charlotte, who has managed the hard trial of being a deck hand under an inhuman captain, must once again change her identity by means of clothes:

> I went to my cabin and excitedly dressed myself in the clothes I had kept for the occasion: bonnet over my mangled hair. Full if somewhat ragged skirts. Shoes rather less than intact. Gloves more gray than white. To my surprise I felt so pinched and confined I found it difficult to breathe. I glanced at my trunk where I had secreted my sailor's garb as a tattered memento. For a moment I considered changing back to that, but quickly reminded myself that it must—from then on—remain a memento. (213)

However, the inner change in Charlotte is so profound that it cannot be camouflaged merely by a change of clothes. Having experienced freedom and independence, she cannot accept the oppression her father imposes on her. Since she has kept her men's clothes as a reminder of her new self, she can easily slip back into this role. Clothes are, for most cross-dressing characters, a tangible expression of identity.

Food Preferences and Other Habits

Characterization through food preferences may provide many valuable additional insights into characters. Certainly, vegetarianism says a good deal about a character, especially if the child is the only vegetarian in the family, challenging the parents. However, Laura's exorbitant appetite for meat in *Little House in the Big Woods* does not characterize her negatively, although she feels no sympathy for the wild and domestic animals her father constantly kills in front of her. Her taste reflects the time and environment in which she lives (although today's reader may be disturbed by this).

Pooh's passion for honey and his irresistible urge for "a little something" around eleven o'clock in the morning is one of his most prominent traits. In general, the figures in the *Pooh* stories are characterized by what they eat (see further Nikolajeva 2000, 99–103). If conspicuous, characters' tastes may produce a comic effect. Lloyd Alexander creates an unforgettable little character, Gurgi, in his Prydain Chronicles, whose main trait is his constant craving for "crunchings and munchings." Karlson-on-the-roof has a sweet tooth and is exceptionally greedy. Another well-loved Swedish character, the famous detective Ture Sventon, has a weakness for marzipan rolls. Even without the comic tone, food habits add considerably to characterization. The protagonist in *A Reason for Janey* has a passion for oranges. Although there are no special consequences of this fact, it makes the character colorful and unique.

Other indirect habits that can contribute to characterization are the books characters read (or simply the fact that they read), the music they listen to, their favorite TV shows, and so on. Basically, these devices do not differ from how they work in the mainstream, with some reservations. The young characters' intellectual habits are once again imposed or at least supported by the parents or other adults. We cannot accuse Anne Shirley of being hopelessly romantic if cheap romances are the only reading to which she has ever been exposed; and we cannot give Leslie all the credit for being familiar with *Hamlet* and *Moby Dick* since she has received intellectual stimulation from her parents.

Contrastive Characterization

Fairy-tale characters are frequently presented through contrasts: a lazy and a diligent sister, or a greedy and a generous brother. Similarly, characters in children's books can be contrasted according to their looks, with or without evaluation (dark—blond, tall—short, fat—slim, ugly—pretty), according to their moral qualities (good—bad), their manners (well behaved—naughty), their age (young—old), their gender, social status, and so on. We may not pay much attention to these juxtapositions, but they certainly contribute to our overall impression of characters. In formulaic fiction, characters are often contrasted in their physical appearance—for instance, a dark and a blonde girl. Quite a number of classic novels have a supporting character contrasting the protagonist in looks and temperament: Don Quixote and Sancho Panza, Fileas Fogg and Passepartout. In *The Adventures of Tom Sawyer*, Tom is contrasted to his well-behaved brother Sid. Tommy and Annika are opposed to Pippi:

> They were good, well brought up, and obedient children. Tommy would never think of biting his nails, and he always did exactly what his mother told him to do. Annika never fussed when she didn't get her own way, and she always looked pretty in her little well-ironed cotton dresses; she took the greatest care not to get them dirty. (14)

In *Anne of Green Gables*, Diana is presented as an opposite to Anne in her looks: she "was a very pretty little girl, with her mother's black eyes and hair, and rosy cheeks, and the merry expression which was an inheritance from her father" (85). Diana is further contrasted to Anne when she is not allowed to study at Queen's, since she is supposed to marry and lead what her mother views as a normal life.

The most explicit contrastive device for characterization is the use of twins (see McCallum 1999, 75–97). The annotated bibliography *Twins in Children's and Adolescent Literature* (Storey 1993) features over 350 books portraying twins. A large portion of these are peripheral characters, used for comic purposes. In the vast majority of books, the appearance of twins is not crucial. Twins as protagonists are widely used in formulaic fiction, from the Bobbsey Twins to the Sweet Valley Twins. In the former case, the twins are used as a simple duplication of the protagonist, in entertaining adventure and mystery plots. This also occurs in a number of other mystery series, apparently on the principle "two heads are better than one," as well as in the "comedy-of-error" plots (cf. Shakespeare or *The Iron Mask*). In the Sweet Valley series, the twins are indeed opposed. Elizabeth is nice and intelligent, while Jessica is selfish and conceited. Apart from these superficial qualities, there is not much characterization in these books, as is common in formulaic literature.

In the classic story *The Prince and the Pauper*, the characters are not actually twins, but so much alike that they can easily switch places. They are revealed by the superficial contrast of rich and poor; however, since the story is plot oriented, there is not much room or interest for characterization. In *Lisa and Lottie*, the two girls are identical twins separated at a very young age who grow up without knowledge of each other. Their meeting creates a good deal of confusion. Similarly, in quite a number of books, the comedy of mistaken identity is the main reason for using twins. *The Horse and His Boy* is just another of many examples.

In *Jacob Have I Loved*, Louise's twin sister is used primarily to characterize the protagonist. Caroline is everything that Louise is not, but would like to be: pretty, talented, and admired. In Jungian terminology, Caroline is Louise's shadow, the dark and unfamiliar part of herself that she must learn to accept before she can become a whole individual. To underscore the motif, the author makes Louise, who has become a midwife, deliver a woman of twins in the end of the book, as a symbolic liberation from her obsessive jealousy of Caroline.

Sylleptic Characterization

Syllepsis is a narrative pattern that implies a connection between two narratives by any means other than temporal—for instance, thematic. We can call characterization sylleptic when characters in a syllepsis are used to amplify or contrast character traits of the protagonist in the primary narrative. Since syllepsis is an extremely unusual device in juvenile fiction, I can give only one example of sylleptic characterization. In *Red Shift*, the three male characters in the primary story and the two sylleptic stories are connected by their names, the place of action, and the pattern of behavior. The purpose of the syllepses is to illuminate the primary story, and the purpose of Thomas and Macey is to contrast the immaturity and emotional deficiency of Tom in the primary narrative (see further Nikolajeva 1988; 1996, 177–80).

Intertextual Characterization

A number of characters in children's fiction allude to other fictional characters, explicitly or implicitly, intentionally or unintentionally. One of the most vivid examples of intertextual characterization is the use of Pippi Longstocking to characterize Johnny in *Johnny My Friend*. When Chris first sees the strange, red-haired girl on a bike, he has a feeling that he has seen her before:

> Pippi Longstocking, I reckoned. Pippi Longstocking, that was it, suddenly come to life, by magic. Her hair wasn't in plaits, but the colour was right. The grin white and dazzling among a few million freckles. (10)

What is the purpose of a reference to Pippi in a novel written in a totally different genre and tone? The first superficial similarity seems to be a false thread: Chris's new friend turns out to be not a Pippi-like girl but a boy, Johnny. So the first lesson we learn is that appearances are deceptive. Yet references to Pippi keep coming back throughout the novel, as if to remind us that the parallel is by no means accidental. Johnny has far more profound similarities with Pippi than red hair and freckles. Like Pippi, Johnny appears from nowhere, demonstrates a number of remarkable, although not supernatural skills, wears deviant and challenging clothes, does not have to keep hours and go home for supper, does not go to school—in other words, Johnny is an individual outside societal norms. Like Pippi, Johnny is a liminal, androgynous figure, a mixture of masculine and feminine traits. Both characters transgress gender stereotypes in their personalities and in their behavior. More importantly, Johnny plays the same catalyst role toward Chris that Pippi has toward Tommy and Annika: bringing a change into their lives. Naturally, the change in Chris is more crucial, and Johnny's fate more dramatic. However, Pippi and Johnny share the mystery and the tragedy of the lonely child. The allusion to Pippi, a figure with whom the reader is assumed to be familiar, guides the reader toward a better understanding of the character. For unlike Pippi, Johnny does not live in the sugar-sweet, idyllic world of a small sleepy town where burglars happily dance to the music of Pippi's comb. Johnny lives in a dangerous, criminal world, totally exposed to abuse from adults. By first focusing on the similarities, the author highlights the differences all the more.

Pippi herself has implicit, but highly intentional intertextual links to Anne Shirley. Not only is she red-haired and freckled, but she defies society and the norms of behavior much in the same way as Anne (see Åhmansson 1994). In many respects, Pippi is a deconstruction of Anne. The special conditions provided by the genre allow Pippi to be the tomboy Anne must give up being. One of the maxims Anne has to face repeatedly, "Children should be seen, but not heard," is marvelously parodied in the *Pippi* books.

Red-haired heroines in children's fiction have become such a prominent stereotype (hot-tempered, strong-minded, independent) that practically any female character with red hair will be involuntarily associated with one of its literary predecessors. Like any stereotype, it substantially constrains authors' use of red hair.

Characterization by Omission

Omission, or *paralipsis*, is a narrative device in which a piece of essential information is withheld from the reader, either permanently or temporarily. Characterization by omission implies that some cardinal fact about the character or some important trait is not mentioned so that the reader is misled in making inferences about the character. A notorious example of omission is found in Agatha Christie's crime novel *The Murder of Roger Ackroyd*, in which the first-person narrator "forgets" to inform the reader that he is the murderer. Omission is a rather demanding device and is used sparsely in juvenile fiction. In *Anarkai* we do not realize for a long time that the first-person narrator is in a wheelchair. Once we are aware of this, much of his strange behavior becomes understandable. Similarly, in *Winter Bay*, we are not told one of the most important facts about the protagonist, that he is black. Such omissions are possible in fiction only because everything we learn about the characters is conveyed by words. Indeed, in the film version of *Winter Bay*, this important characterization device was lost.

Picturebooks, with their twofold visual-verbal characterization, can use omission as a counterpoint between words and images. For instance, in

Where the Wild Things Are, the mother is presented in the text, but not portrayed in the pictures. By contrast, a vast number of picturebooks have secondary characters in the pictures, who are not mentioned by words.

As compared with all the previously discussed characterization devices, implicit characterization naturally presupposes the most active participation on the reader's part, since the implicit connections between textual elements and characters have to be made by readers. Some of these elements may be too complex or too subtle for every reader to notice. Some of them, such as intertextual characterization, require a substantial amount of previous reading experience. Yet these devices should not be neglected in our assessment of characters; many of them may work on the subconscious level—that is, without the readers being aware of them.

CONCLUSION

~

Returning to the Text

This whole study has been about the various aspects of literary characters and about the mechanisms of extracting them from texts and sorting them into the many proposed categories. However, characters are not isolated elements that can be enjoyed for their own sake, apart from the narrative. Among other scholars, Baruch Hochman argues that after having retrieved the characters from texts, we must necessarily resolve them back into the texts where they belong and view them as part of a whole. I would therefore like to conclude my book by returning to the text to see how the results of our investigation of characters may help us to appreciate them.

First, we have learned that our understanding of character is highly dependent on our general approach to fiction. In children's fiction, our understanding will depend on whether we perceive the text as an educational implement or an aesthetic object. During my long career as a scholar of children's literature, I have always given priority to the aesthetic aspects of children's books. Therefore, for me personally, the semiotic approach to literary characters seems more natural than the mimetic. However, I do not deny children's literature its educational or ideological value, and I am highly aware of the pragmatic applications of children's books, for the purposes of literacy as well as socialization. At least in the latter case, characters are the primary vehicles for conveying social values. In other words, in approaching characters in children's fiction, we must take into consideration the overall context of our discussion, basically either literary or educational. Recently, children's literature scholars have started interrogating the "literary-didactic split." By viewing characters, and by extension even texts, as allowing both mimetic and semiotic interpretations, we can enrich our understanding, making the approaches complementary instead of mutually exclusive.

Second, our assessment of characters is genre bound. We cannot judge characters outside the narrative to which they belong; we cannot expect characters in formulaic fiction to be as complex as characters in psychological novels; we cannot expect characters in historical novels to be politically correct; we cannot expect protagonists in feminine narratives to behave contrary to the conventions of the genre. This means that we necessarily must consider the nature of narrative before we pass judgments about "inadequate characterization" or "sexist tendencies." Children's literature studies are normally more inclusive than general literary criticism. Since children's literature is marginalized within the mainstream, it has incorporated genres and modes that are today exiled to culture studies. Fantasy, in particular, which has such a strong and important tradition within children's literature, has certainly been examined more seriously by children's literature scholars than by general criticism. The reverse side is that children's fiction has been treated as a homogeneous group of texts, and in comparison with the mainstream, R. L. Stine has been used as a yardstick rather than Katherine Paterson. As I have demonstrated repeatedly, in both the present study and my previous research, it is not a fair and legitimate scholarly method to compare R. L. Stine with James Joyce, just as it is fruitless to compare Katherine Paterson with Sidney Sheldon. R. L. Stine's and Sidney Sheldon's characters are not artistically inferior to Katherine Paterson's or James Joyce's; they are different, and it is only within the context of their respective narratives that we can judge them rightfully. Furthermore, it is perhaps not quite fair (or fruitful) to compare Katherine Paterson's and James Joyce's characters, because the narratives represent different stages of literary development. It would, however, be possible and, I believe, illuminating to compare Katherine Paterson's and Henry James's characters; or James Joyce's and Aidan Chambers's. Personally, I find Ramona Quimby inferior to Gilly Hopkins as a character; but placing both characters in their respective narratives, I must admit that they both fit perfectly. Our demands for characters' complexity, dynamism, integrity, wholeness, and so on, must be matched against the narrative in which they appear.

Finally, we have seen how the various characterization devices work to reveal characters. These devices, however, are not given to us at the beginning of the text as a ready-made tool kit to use whenever we encounter a character in the text. As readers, we assemble the information we receive from the text into a coherent and credible portrait. When we as students or critics write a "character sketch," we operate with the available information (occasionally complemented by our extratextual experience), discussing the characters in their entirety—that is, as an already assembled whole. However, when we read and enjoy fiction, we meet with characters in a linear progression, inside the text, not outside it. We do not meet them as whole, complete, coherent personalities the way they appear in critical essays. They are part of the text, of its space and time; they are distorted by the narrative perspective, they are obscured by the writer's design. Outside the narrative, they are dead; but put back into the narrative, they start living and appealing to us. Paraphrasing Henry James, we cannot have a narrative without characters, and we certainly cannot have characters without a narrative.

I have in this study outlined some principal questions pertinent to the nature and function of characters in children's fiction. It cannot be more than an outline because of the unlimited scope of the material as well as the highly dynamic nature of children's fiction.

~

Bibliography

Primary Sources

Adams, Richard. *Watership Down*. Harmondsworth: Penguin, 1973.

Alcott, Louisa May. *Little Women* (1868). Harmondsworth: Penguin, 1994.

Alexander, Lloyd. *The Book of Three*. New York: Holt, 1964. (The first of the five chronicles of Prydain.)

————. *The Illyrian Adventure*. New York: Dutton, 1986. (The first book in the Vesper series.)

Andersen, Hans Christian. *The Complete Fairy Tales and Stories*. New York: Doubleday, 1974.

Applegate, K. A. *The Invasion*. Jefferson City: Scholastic, 1996. (The first of over forty books in the Animorphs series.)

Austen, Jane. *Pride and Prejudice* (1813). London: Penguin, 1985

————. *Mansfield Park* (1814). London: Penguin, 1994.

Avi. *The True Confessions of Charlotte Doyle* (1990). New York: Avon, 1992.

Babbitt, Natalie. *Tuck Everlasting*. New York: Farrar, Straus, Giroux, 1975.

Banks, Lynne Reid. *The Indian in the Cupboard*. Garden City, N.Y.: Doubleday, 1980.

Barrie, James M. *Peter Pan in Kensington Gardens* (1906). In *Peter Pan in Kensington Gardens; Peter and Wendy*. Oxford: Oxford University Press, 1991.

————. *Peter Pan and Wendy* (1911). London: Hodder & Stoughton, 1951.

Baum, L. Frank. *The Wonderful Wizard of Oz* (1900). New York: HarperCollins, 2000.

Bawden, Nina. *Carrie's War*. Philadelphia: Lippincott, 1973.

Beckman, Gunnel: *Admission to the Feast*. New York: Holt, 1971 (*Tillträde till festen*, 1969).

Beskow, Elsa. *The Tale of the Little, Little Old Woman*. Edinburgh: Floris, 1988 (*Sagan om den lilla, lilla gumman*, 1897).

Blyton, Enid. *Five on a Treasure Island*. London: Hodder & Stoughton, 1942. (The first book in the Famous Five series.)

————. *The Secret Seven and the Mystery of the Empty House* (1949). Chicago: Children's Press, 1972. (The first of the Secret Seven series.)

Boccaccio, Giovanni. *Decameron*. Berkeley: University of California Press, 1982 (*Il Decamerone*, 1348–53).

Bond, Michael. *A Bear Called Paddington*. London: Collins, 1958. (The first title in the Paddington series.)

Boston, Lucy M. *The Children of Green Knowe* (1954). Harmondsworth: Penguin, 1975. (The first book in the Green Knowe suite.)

Brontë, Charlotte. *Jane Eyre* (1847). London: Penguin, 1985.

Browne, Anthony. *Gorilla*. London: Julia MacRae Books, 1983.

Bunting, Eve. *Terrible Things*. New York: Harper & Row, 1980. Reprinted as *Terrible Things: An Allegory of the Holocaust*. Philadelphia: Jewish Publication Society, 1989.

Bunyan, John. *The Pilgrim's Progress* (1678). Oxford: Oxford University Press,1984.

Burnett, Frances Hodgson. *Little Lord Fauntleroy* (1886). London: Penguin, 1995.

————. *The Secret Garden* (1911). London: Penguin, 1995.

Burningham, John. *Granpa*. London: Cape, 1984.

Carroll, Lewis. *Alice's Adventures in Wonderland* (1865). In *The Penguin Complete Lewis Carroll*. Harmondsworth: Penguin, 1982.

Cervantes, Miguel. *The Adventures of Don Quixote de la Mancha* (1606–15). New York: Knopf, 1951.

Chambers, Aidan. *Breaktime* (1978). London: Random House, 1995.

————. *Dance on My Grave* (1982). London: Random House, 1995.

Christie, Agatha. *The Murder of Roger Ackroyd* (1927). New York: HarperCollins, 1987.

Cleary, Beverly. *Ramona the Pest* (1968). New York: Avon, 1992.

————. *Ramona the Brave* (1975). New York: Avon, 1995.

————. *Dear Mr. Henshaw* (1983). Harmondsworth: Penguin, 1985.

Collodi, Carlo. *The Adventures of Pinocchio*. Oxford: Oxford University Press, 1996 (*Le avventure di Pinocchio*, 1881).

Conrad, Joseph. *Heart of Darkness* (1902). New York: Columbia University Press, 1999.

Coolidge, Susan. *What Katy Did* (1872). Harmondsworth: Penguin, 1997.

Cooper, Susan. *Over Sea, Under Stone* (1965). Harmondsworth: Penguin, 1968.

————. *The Dark Is Rising* (1973). Harmondsworth: Penguin, 1976.

————. *Greenwitch* (1974). Harmondsworth: Penguin, 1977.

————. *The Grey King* (1975). Harmondsworth: Penguin, 1994.

————. *Silver on the Tree* (1977). Harmondsworth: Penguin, 1979.

————. *Seaward* (1983). Harmondsworth: Penguin, 1985.

————. *The Boggart*. New York: Margaret K. McElderrly Books, 1993.

————. *The Boggart and the Monster*. New York: Margaret K. McElderrly Books, 1997.

Cormier, Robert. *I Am the Cheese* (1977). New York: Dell, 1997.

Creech, Sharon. *Walk Two Moons*. London: Macmillan, 1994.

Crompton, Richmal. *Just William*. London: Newnes, 1922. (The first in a series of more than forty books about William.)

Dahl, Roald. *Charlie and the Chocolate Factory* (1964). Harmondsworth: Penguin, 1973.

Defoe, Daniel. *Robinson Crusoe* (1719). New York: Norton, 1975.

———. *Robinson Crusoe*. Retold by James Baldwin. New York: Aladdin, 1951.

Dickens, Charles. *Oliver Twist* (1837–39). Oxford: Oxford University Press, 1999.

———. *David Copperfield* (1849–50). London: Penguin, 1994.

———. *Bleak House* (1852–53). London: Penguin, 1994.

———. *Great Expectations* (1860–61). New York: Columbia University Press, 2000.

Doherty, Berlie. *Dear Nobody* (1991). London: Collins, 1995.

Doyle, Arthur Conan. *The Adventures of Sherlock Holmes* (1892). Oxford: Oxford University Press, 1994.

Dumas, Alexandre. *The Three Musketeers*. New York: Pan, 1974 (*Les trois mousquetaires*, 1844).

———. *The Man in the Iron Mask*. Oxford: Oxford University Press, 1991 (*Homme au masque de fer*, 1848–50).

Eager, Edward. *Half Magic*. New York: Harcourt, 1954.

———. *Knight's Castle*. New York: Harcourt, 1956.

———. *Magic by the Lake*. New York: Harcourt, 1957.

———. *Time Garden*. New York: Harcourt, 1958.

———. *Magic or Not?* New York: Harcourt, 1959.

———. *The Well-Wishers*. New York: Harcourt, 1960.

———. *Seven Day Magic*. New York: Harcourt, 1962.

Eco, Umberto. *The Name of the Rose*. San Diego: Harcourt Brace, 1994 (*Nome della rosa*, 1980).

Ellis, Bret Easton. *American Psycho*. New York: Vantage, 1991.

Ende, Michael. *The Neverending Story*. New York: Penguin, 1984 (*Die unendliche Geschichte*, 1979).

———. *Momo*. New York: Doubleday, 1985 (*Momo*, 1973).

Farmer, Penelope. *Charlotte Sometimes* (1969). Harmondsworth: Penguin, 1972.

Faulkner, William. *The Sound and the Fury* (1929). Bromall, Pa.: Chelsea House, 1999.

———. *As I Lay Dying* (1930). New York: Random House, 1990.

Fitzgerald, F. Scott. *The Great Gatsby* (1925). New York: Simon & Schuster, 1995.

Fitzhugh, Louise. *Harriet the Spy*. New York: Harper, 1964.

———. *The Long Secret*. New York: Dell, 1965.

Fleming, Ian. *Casino Royale*. London: Cape, 1953. (The first of the James Bond novels.)

Fowles, John. *The French Lieutenant's Woman*. Boston: Little, Brown, 1969.

Frank, Anne. *The Diary of a Young Girl*. London: Penguin, 1997.

Gaarder, Jostein. *The Solitaire Mystery*. New York: Farrar, Straus & Giroux, 1996 (*Kabalmysteriet*, 1990).

———. *Sophie's World*. New York: Farrar, Straus & Giroux, 1994 (*Sofies Verden*, 1991).

García Marquez, Gabriel. *One Hundred Years of Solitude*. Boston: Hall, 1993 (*Cien años de soledad*, 1967).

Garner, Alan. *The Weirdstone of Brisingamen* (1960). New York: Philomel, 1979.

———. *The Moon of Gomrath* (1963). New York: Philomel, 1981.

———. *Elidor* (1965). London: Collins, 1974.

———. *Red Shift* (1973). London: Collins, 1975.

Gibson, William. *Neuromancer*. New York: Ace Books, 1984.

Grahame, Kenneth. *The Wind in the Willows* (1908). New York: Scribner's, 1983.

Grimm, Jacob and Wilhelm. *The Complete Fairy Tales of the Brothers Grimm* (1812). Vols. I–II. New York: Bantam, 1988.

Gripe, Maria. *Josephine*. New York: Delacorte, 1973 (*Josefin*, 1961).

———. *Hugo and Josephine*. New York: Delacorte, 1969 (*Hugo och Josefin*, 1962).

———. *Papa Pellerin's Daughter*. London: Chatto & Windus, 1966 (*Pappa Pellerins dotter*, 1963).

———. *Hugo*. New York: Delacorte, 1970 (*Hugo*, 1966).

———. *The Night Daddy*. New York: Delacorte, 1971 (*Nattpappan*, 1968).

———. *Elvis and His Secret*. New York: Delacorte, 1976 (*Elvis Karlsson*, 1972).

———. *Elvis and His Friends*. New York: Delacorte, 1976 (*Elvis! Elvis!* 1973).

———. *Agnes Cecilia*. New York: Harper, 1990 (*Agnes Cecilia—en sällsam historia*, 1981).

Groom, Winston. *Forrest Gump*. New York: Doubleday, 1986.

Hamilton, Virginia. *The Planet of Junior Brown*. New York: Macmillan, 1971.

Hemingway, Ernest. "Hills Like White Elephants." pp. 211–14 in *The Complete Short Stories of Ernest Hemingway*. New York: Scribner's, 1987.

Hoban, Russel. *The Mouse and His Child*. New York: Harper, 1967.

Hoffman, E. T. A. *The Nutcracker*. New York: Ariel, 1987.

Hoffmann, Heinrich. *Slovenly Peter, or Cheerful Stories and Funny Pictures for Good Little Folks*. Philadelphia: Winson, 1915 (*Struwwelpeter*, 1845).

Holman, Felice. *Slake's Limbo*. New York: Scribner's, 1974.

Hope, Laura Lee. *The Bobbsey Twins, or Merry Days Indoors and Out* (1904). New York: Grosset & Dunlap, 1950. (The first in the Bobbsey Twins series.)

Horwood, William. *The Willows in Winter*. New York: St. Martin's, 1994.

Hughes, Thomas. *Tom Brown's Schooldays* (1856). Harmondsworth: Penguin, 1994.

Huxley, Aldous. *Brave New World* (1932). New York: Chelsea House, 1996.

James, Henry. *What Maisie Knew* (1897). Oxford: Oxford University Press, 1998.

Jansson, Tove. *A Comet in Moominland*. New York: Walck, 1968 (*Kometjakten*, 1946).

———. *Finn Family Moomintroll*. New York: Walck, 1965 (*Trollkarlens hatt*, 1949).

———. *Exploits of Moominpappa*. New York: Walck, 1966 (*Muminpappans bravader*, 1950).

———. *Moominsummer Madness*. New York: Walck, 1961 (*Farlig midsommar*, 1954).

————. *Moominpappa at Sea.* New York: Walck, 1967 (*Pappan och havet,* 1965).

————. *Moominvalley in November.* New York: Walck, 1971 (*Sent i november,* 1970).

Johns, W. E. *The Camels Are Coming.* London: John Hamilton, 1932 (The first book in the Biggles series.)

Jones, Diana Wynne. *The Homeward Bounders.* New York: Greenwillow, 1981.

————. *The Lives of Christopher Chant.* New York: Greenwillow, 1988.

Joyce, James. *Ulysses* (1922). New York: Signet, 1998.

Juster, Norton. *The Phantom Tollbooth* (1961). New York: Random House, 1996.

Kästner, Erich. *Emil and the Detectives.* New York: Doubleday, 1930 (*Emil und die Detektive,* 1928).

————. *Lottie and Lisa.* Boston: Little, Brown, 1951 (*Das doppelte Lottchen,* 1949).

Keene, Carolyn. *The Secret of the Old Clock* (1930). Bedford, Mass.: Applewood, 1991. (The first book in the Nancy Drew series.)

————. *The Haunted Bridge* (1937). Nancy Drew Mystery Stories 15. New York: Grosset & Dunlap, 2000.

Kingsley, Charles. *The Water Babies* (1863). New York: Morrow, 1997.

Kipling, Rudyard. *The Jungle Book* (1894). New York: Viking, 1996.

————. *Just So Stories* (1902). In *The Complete Just So Stories.* New York: Viking, 1993.

————. *Puck of Pook's Hill* (1906). In *Puck of Pook's Hill; and Rewards and Fairies.* Oxford: Oxford University Press, 1993.

Kirkegaard, Ole Lund. *Gummi-Tarzan.* Copenhagen: Gyldendal, 1975.

Konigsburg, Elaine. *From the Mixed-up Files of Mrs. Basil E. Frankweiler.* New York: Atheneum, 1967.

Krüss, James. *Timm Thaler, oder das verkaufte Lachen.* Ravensburg, Germany: Ravensburg, 1997.

Lagerlöf, Selma. *The Wonderful Adventures of Nils.* New York: Dover, 1995 (*Nils Holgerssons underbara resa,* 1906–7).

Le Guin, Ursula. *A Wizard of Earthsea.* New York: Parnassus, 1968 (The first book in the Earthsea series.)

————. *Tehanu.* New York: Atheneum, 1990.

Lewis, C. S. *The Lion, the Witch and the Wardrobe* (1950). Harmondsworth: Penguin, 1959.

————. *Prince Caspian.* New York: Macmillan, 1951.

————. *The Voyage of the Dawn Treader.* New York: Macmillan, 1952.

————. *The Silver Chair.* New York: Macmillan, 1953.

————. *The Horse and His Boy.* New York: Macmillan, 1954.

————. *The Magician's Nephew.* New York: Macmillan, 1955.

————. *The Last Battle.* New York: Macmillan, 1956.

Linde, Gunnel. *The White Stone.* New York: Harcourt, 1966 (*Den vita stenen,* 1964).

Lindgren, Astrid. *Pippi Longstocking.* New York: Viking, 1950 (*Pippi Långstrump,* 1945).

————. *Pippi Goes on Board.* New York: Viking, 1957 (*Pippi Långstrump går ombord,* 1946).

————. *The Children of Noisy Village*. New York: Viking, 1962 (*Alla vi barn i Buller-byn*, 1947).

————. *Pippi in the South Seas*. New York: Viking, 1959 (*Pippi Långstrump i Söder-havet*, 1948).

————. *Mio, My Son*. New York: Viking, 1956 (*Mio, min Mio*, 1954).

————. *Karlson on the Roof*. London: Methuen, 1975 (*Karlson på taket*, 1955).

————. *Emil's Pranks*. Chicago: Folett, 1971 (*Emil i Lönneberga*, 1963).

————. *The Brothers Lionheart*. New York: Viking, 1975 (*Bröderna Lejonhjärta*, 1973).

————. *Ronia, the Robber's Daughter*. New York: Viking, 1983 (*Ronja Rövardotter*, 1981).

————. *I Don't Want to Go to Bed*. New York: Farrar/R&S, 1988.

Linklater, Eric. *The Wind in the Moon*. London: Macmillan, 1948.

Lofting, Hugh. *The Story of Doctor Dolittle* (1920). New York: Delacorte, 1988. (The first of the Doctor Dolittle stories.)

Lowry, Lois. *The Giver*. New York: Doubleday, 1993.

————. *Gathering Blue*. Boston: Houghton Mifflin, 2000.

MacDonald, George. *At the Back of the North Wind* (1871). Harmondsworth: Penguin, 1984.

MacLachlan, Patricia. *Cassie Binegar*. New York: Harper, 1982.

————. *Sarah, Plain and Tall*. New York: Harper, 1985.

————. *The Facts and Fictions of Minna Pratt*. New York: Harper, 1988.

————. *Baby*. New York: Doubleday, 1993.

Magorian, Michelle. *Back Home*. New York: Harper, 1984.

Major, Kevin. *Dear Bruce Springsteen*. Toronto: Doubleday, 1987.

Malot, Hector. *The Foundling*. New York: Harmony, 1986 (*Sans famille*, 1878).

Marsden, John. *Letters from the Inside* (1991). Sydney: Pan Macmillan, 1994.

————. *Tomorrow When the War Began*. Boston: Houghton Mifflin, 1995.

Milne, A. A. *Winnie-the-Pooh* (1926). London: Methuen, 1965.

————. *The House at Pooh Corner* (1928). London: Methuen, 1965.

Montgomery, L. M. *Anne of Green Gables* (1908). New York: Bantam, 1992.

————. *Emily of the New Moon*. New York: Stokes, 1923 (The first of three books about Emily.)

Nabokov, Vladimir. *Lolita* (1955). New York: Chelsea House, 1993.

Naipaul, V. S. *Miguel Street* (1959). New York: Vintage, 1984.

Nesbit, Edith. *The Story of the Treasure Seekers* (1899). Harmondsworth: Penguin, 1995. (The first book in the Treasure Seekers series.)

————. *Five Children and It* (1901). Harmondsworth: Penguin, 1984.

————. *The Phoenix and the Carpet* (1904). Harmondsworth: Penguin, 1984.

————. *The Railway Children* (1906). London: Penguin, 1995.

————. *The Story of the Amulet* (1906). Harmondsworth: Penguin, 1959.

————. *The Enchanted Castle* (1907). Harmondsworth: Penguin, 1979.

————. *The House of Arden* (1908). Harmondsworth: Penguin, 1986.

————. *Harding's Luck* (1910). London: Benn, 1949.

————. *The Wonderful Garden* (1911). New York: Coward McCann, 1935.

Nilsson, Per. *Anarkai*. Stockholm: Rabén & Sjögren, 1996.

Norton, Mary. *Bedknob and Broomstick* (1945, 1947). Harmondsworth: Perrault, 1981.

———. *The Borrowers* (1952). San Diego: Harcourt, Brace, Jovanovich, 1991.

Nöstlinger, Christine. *Konrad*. New York: Avon, 1982 (*Konrad oder das Kind aus der Konservenbüchse*, 1975).

O'Shea, Pat. *The Hounds of the Morrigan* (1986). New York: HarperCollins, 1999.

Orwell, George. *Animal Farm* (1945). Harmondsworth: Penguin, 1951.

———. *1984* (1948). Harmondsworth: Penguin, 1989.

Park, Ruth. *Playing Beatie Bow* (1980). New York: Atheneum, 1982.

Pascal, Francine. *Best Friends*. New York: Bantam, 1986 (The first book in the Sweet Valley twins series.)

Paterson, Katherine. *Bridge to Terabithia* (1977). New York: HarperCollins, 1987.

———. *The Great Gilly Hopkins* (1978). New York: HarperCollins, 1987.

———. *Jacob Have I Loved* (1980). New York: HarperCollins, 1990.

———. *Come Sing, Jimmy Jo* (1985). New York: Penguin, 1995.

———. *Park's Quest*. New York: Dutton, 1988.

———. *Lyddie*. New York: Dutton, 1991.

———. *Flip-Flop Girl* (1994). New York: Penguin, 1996.

———. *Jip: His Story*. New York: Dutton, 1996.

Paulsen, Gary. *Hatchet*. Scarsdale, N.Y.: Bradbury, 1987.

Pearce, Philippa. *Tom's Midnight Garden* (1958). Harmondsworth: Penguin, 1976.

Perrault, Charles. *The Fairy Tales*. New York: Avon, 1977.

Pierce, Meredith Ann. *The Darkangel*. New York: Atlantic, 1982.

Pohl, Peter. *Johnny My Friend*. London: Turton & Chambers, 1991 (*Janne min vän*, 1985).

Potter, Beatrix. *The Tale of Peter Rabbit*. London: Warne, 1902.

Preussler, Ottfrid. *The Satanic Mill*. New York: Macmillan, 1976 (*Krabat*, 1971)

Prévost, Antoine François. *Manon Lescaut*. Chester Springs, Pa.: Dufour, 1987 (*L'Histoire du Chevalier Des Grieux et de Manon Lescaut*, 1731).

Proust, Marcel. *Swann's Way*. London: Penguin, 1988 (*Du côté de chez Swann*, 1913). (The first novel *The Remembrance of Things Past*.)

Pullman, Philip. *Northern Lights*. London: Scholastic, 1995 (published in the United States as *The Golden Compass*).

———. *The Subtle Knife*. London: Scholastic, 1997.

———. *The Amber Spyglass*. London: Scholastic. 2000.

Ransome, Arthur. *Swallows and Amazons* (1930). Harmondsworth: Penguin, 1968.

Rey, H. A. *Curious George*. Boston: Houghton Mifflin, 1941; rev. ed. 1969.

Richler, Mordechai. *Jacob Two-Two Meets the Hooded Fang*. New York: Knopf, 1975.

Rowling, J. K. *Harry Potter and the Philosopher's Stone*. London: Bloomsbury, 1997. (The first of the Harry Potter series.)

Sachar, Louis. *Holes* (1998). New York: Dell Yearling, 2000.

Saint-Exupéry, Antoine de. *The Little Prince*. Harmondsworth: Penguin, 1962 (*Le petit prince*, 1943).

Salinger, Jerome D. *The Catcher in the Rye* (1951). Philadelphia: Chelsea House, 2000.

Salten, Felix. *Bambi*. New York: Simon & Schuster, 1992 (*Bambi*, 1923)

Sendak, Maurice. *Where the Wild Things Are*. New York: Harper, 1963.

Seuss, Dr. *The Cat in the Hat*. New York: Random House, 1957.

———. *How the Grinch Stole Christmas*. New York: Random House, 1957.

Shakespeare, William. *Hamlet* (1600–1). New York: Chelsea House, 1996.

———. *King Lear* (1605). New York: Chelsea House, 1992.

Spyri, Johanna. *Heidi*. Ware: Wordsworth, 1993 (*Heidi*, 1881).

Stendhal. *The Red and the Black*. New York: Chelsea House, 1988 (*Le rouge et le noir*, 1830).

Sterne, Laurence. *Tristram Shandy* (1759–67). New York: Knopf, 1991.

Stevenson, Robert Louis. *Treasure Island* (1883). New York: Signet, 1998.

Stine, R. L. *Welcome to Dead House*. Milwaukee, Wisc.: Gareth Stevens, 1997 (The first title in the Goosebumps series.)

Stoker, Bram. *Dracula* (1897). New York: Modern Library, 1996.

Storr, Catherine. *Marianne Dreams* (1958). Harmondsworth: Penguin, 1964.

Streatfeild, Noel. *Ballet Shoes* (1936). New York: Random House, 1993.

Stretton, Hesba. *Jessica's First Prayer* (1867). In *Jessica's First Prayer; Little Meg's Children; Alone in London; Pilgrim Street*. New York: Garland, 1976.

Swift, Jonathan. *Gulliver's Travels into Several Remote Nations of the World* (1726). New York: Chelsea House, 1996.

———. *Gulliver's Travels*. Adapted for young readers by Vincent Buranelli. Morristown, N.J.: Silver Burdett, 1984.

Tatar, Maria, ed. *The Classic Fairy Tales*. New York: Norton, 1999.

Taylor, Mildred D. *Roll of Thunder, Hear My Cry* (1976). New York: Penguin, 1991.

Tetzner, Lisa. *Schwarzen Brüder* (1941). Ravensburg, Germany: Maier, 1980.

Tolkien, J. R. R. *The Hobbit* (1937). Boston: Houghton Mifflin, 1997.

———. *Lord of the Rings* (1954–55). Philadelphia: Chelsea House, 1999.

Tolstoy, Leo. *War and Peace* (1867–69). New York: Knopf, 1992.

———. *Anna Karenina* (1873–77). New York: Viking, 2001.

Townsend, Sue. *The Secret Diary of Adrian Mole, Aged 13 3/4* (1982). London: Mandarin, 1989.

Travers, Pamela. *Mary Poppins* (1934). London: Collins, 1971.

———. *Mary Poppins Comes Back* (1935) London: Collins, 1998.

———. *Mary Poppins Opens the Door* (1944). London: Collins, 1994.

Twain, Mark. *The Adventures of Tom Sawyer* (1876). Harmondsworth: Penguin, 1985.

———. *The Prince and the Pauper* (1881). New York: Penguin, 1997.

———. *The Adventures of Huckleberry Finn* (1884). New York: Penguin, 1995.

Ure, Jean. *Skinny Melon and Me* (1996). New York: Holt, 2000.

Uttley, Alison. *A Traveller in Time* (1939). Harmondsworth: Penguin, 1977.

Verne, Jules. *Around the World in Eighty Days*. New York: Simon & Schuster, 1957 (*Le tour du monde en quatre-vingts jours*, 1872).

Voigt, Cynthia. *Homecoming*. New York: Atheneum, 1981.

Wahl, Mats. *Husbonden*. Stockholm: Bonnier, 1985.

———. *Anna-Carolinas krig*. Stockholm: Bonnier, 1986.

———. *Vinterviken*. Stockholm: Bonniers Junior, 1993.

Webster, Jean. *Daddy-Long-Legs* (1912). Harmondsworth: Penguin, 1995.

White, E. B. *Stuart Little* (1945). New York: HarperCollins, 1999.

———. *Charlotte's Web* (1952). New York: HarperCollins, 1999.

Wilder, Laura Ingalls. *Little House in the Big Woods* (1932). New York: HarperCollins 1971. (The first book in the Little House series.)

Wilson, Nancy Hope. *The Reason for Janey*. New York: Macmillan, 1994.

Wilson, Yates. *More Alice* (1959). New York: Roy, 1963.

Woolf, Virginia. *The Waves* (1931). San Diego: Harcourt Brace Jovanovich, 1978.

Yolen, Jane. *The Devil's Arithmetic* (1988). New York: Penguin, 1990.

Zipes, Jack, ed. *The Great Fairy Tale Tradition. From Straparola and Basile to the Brothers Grimm*. New York: Norton, 2001.

Secondary Sources

Abrams, M. H. *The Mirror and the Lamp: Romantic Theory and Critical Tradition*. Oxford: Oxford University Press, 1953.

Adams, Gillian. "Medieval Children's Literature: Its Possibility and Actuality." *Children's Literature* (1998): 1–24.

Åhmansson, Gabriella. *A Life and Its Mirrors: A Feminist Reading of L. M. Montgomery's Fiction*. Uppsala, Sweden: Acta Universitatis Upsaliensis, 1991.

———. "Mayflowers Grow in Sweden Too: L. M. Montgomery, Astrid Lindgren and the Swedish Literary Consciousness." pp. 14–22 in *Harvesting Thistles: The Textual Garden of L. M. Montgomery*, ed. Mary Rubio. Guelph: Canadian Children's Press, 1994.

Alberghene, Janice M., and Beverly Lyon Clark, eds. *Little Women and the Feminist Imagination: Criticism, Controversy, Personal Essays*. New York: Garland, 1998.

Allison, Alida, ed. *Russell Hoban: Forty Years. Essays on His Writing for Children*. New York: Garland, 2000.

Ariès, Philippe. *Centuries of Childhood: A Social History of Family Life*. New York: Vintage, 1962.

Aristotle. "Poetics." In *Classical Literary Criticism*. Harmondsworth: Penguin, 1965.

Aschenberg, Heidi. *Eigennamen im Kinderbuch: Eine textlingvistische Studie*. Tübingen: Narr, 1991.

Auerbach, Erich. *Mimesis: The Presentation of Reality in Western Literature*. Princeton, N.J.: Princeton University Press, 1974.

Auerbach, Nina. *Communities of Women: An Idea in Fiction*. Cambridge, Mass.: Harvard University Press, 1978.

Austin, J. L. *How to Do Things with Words*. New York: Oxford University Press, 1962.

Avery, Gillian. *Nineteenth-Century Children: Heroes and Heroines in English Children's Stories 1780–1900*. London: Hodder & Stoughton, 1965.

————. *Childhood's Pattern: A Study of the Heroes and Heroines of Children's Fiction 1770–1950*. London: Hodder & Stoughton, 1975.

Avery, Gillian, and Kimberley Reynolds, eds. *Representations of Childhood Death*. New York: St. Martin's, 2000.

Bakhtin, Mikhail. *Rabelais and His World*. Cambridge, Mass.: MIT Press, 1968.

————. *The Dialogic Imagination*. Austin: University of Texas Press, 1981.

————. *Problems of Dostoyevsky's Poetics*. Minneapolis: University of Minnesota Press, 1984.

————. *Speech Genres and Other Late Essays*. Austin: University of Texas Press, 1986.

————. "Author and Hero in Aesthetic Activity." pp. 4–256 in his *Art and Answerability: Early Philosophical Essays*. Austin: University of Texas Press, 1990.

Banerjee, Jacqueline. *Through the Northern Gate: Childhood and Growing Up in British Fiction 1719–1901*. Studies in Nineteenth-Century British Literature, vol. 6. New York: Lang, 1996.

Bal, Mieke. *Narratology: Introduction to the Theory of Narrative*. 2d ed. Toronto: University of Toronto Press, 1997.

Bally, Charles. "Le style indirect libre en français moderne." *Germanisch-romanische Monatsschrift* 4 (1912): 549–56, 597–606.

Banfield, Ann. *Unspeakable Sentences: Narration and Representation in the Language of Fiction*. Boston: Routledge & Kegan Paul, 1982.

Barthes, Roland. *S/Z*. New York: Hill & Wang, 1974.

————. *Image, Music, Text*. London: Fontana, 1977.

Beckett, Sandra L., ed. *Transcending Boundaries: Writing for a Dual Audience of Children and Adults*. New York: Garland, 1999.

Bergsten, Staffan. *Mary Poppins and Myth*. Studies published by the Swedish Institute for Children's Books, no. 8. Stockholm: Almqvist & Wiksell International, 1978.

Bergstrand, Ulla, and Maria Nikolajeva. *Läckergommarnas kungarike. Om matens funktion i barnlitteraturen*. Stockholm: Centre for the Study of Childhood Culture, 1999.

Birkhäuser-Oeri, Sibylle. *The Mother: Archetypal Image in Fairy Tales*. Toronto: Inner City Books, 1988.

Bloom, Harold. *Shakespeare: The Invention of the Human*. New York: Riverhead, 1998.

Blount, Margaret J. *Animal Land: The Creatures of Children's Fiction*. New York: Morrow, 1974.

Booth, Wayne C. *The Rhetoric of Fiction*. Chicago: University of Chicago Press, 1961.

Bosmajian, Hamida. *Sparing the Child: Children's Literature about Nazism and the Holocaust*. New York: Garland.

Bradford, Clare, ed. *Writing the Australian Child: Texts and Contexts in Fiction for Children*. Nedlands: University of Western Australia Press, 1996.

Bradley, A. C. *Shakespearean Tragedy* (1904). 3d ed. London: Macmillan, 1993.

Brombert, Victor, ed. *The Hero in Literature: Major Essays on the Changing Concepts of Heroism from Classical Times to the Present*. Greenwich, Conn.: Fawcett, 1969.

Brooks, Peter. *Reading for the Plot: Design and Intention in Narrative*. Cambridge, Mass.: Harvard University Press, 1984.

Butler, Francelia. "Death in Children's Literature." pp. 72–90 in *Reflections on Literature for Children*, ed. Francelia Butler and Richard Rotert. Hamden, Conn.: Library Professional Publications, 1984.

Byrnes, Alice. *The Child: An Archetypal Symbol in Literature for Children and Adults*. New York: Peter Lang, 1995.

Cadden, Mike. "The Irony of Narration in the Young Adult Novel." *Children's Literature Association Quarterly* 25, no. 3 (2000): 146–54.

Campbell, Joseph. *The Hero with a Thousand Faces* (1949). 2d ed. Princeton, N.J.: Princeton University Press, 1968.

Card, Orson Scott. *Character and Viewpoint*. Cincinnati, Ohio: Writer's Digest Books, 1988.

Carlson, Maj. Asplund. "Gummy Tarzan in the School Library." *Para*doxa* 2, nos. 3/4 (1996): 393–98.

Cawelti, John G. *Adventure, Mystery and Romance: Formula Stories as Art and Popular Fiction*. Chicago: University of Chicago Press, 1976.

Chamberlain, Daniel Frank. *Narrative Perspective in Fiction: A Phenomenological Mediation of Reader, Text, and World*. Toronto: University of Toronto Press, 1990.

Chambers, Aidan. "The Implied Reader." In his *Booktalk: Occasional Writing on Literature and Children*. London: Bodley Head, 1985.

Chatman, Seymour. *Story and Discourse: Narrative Structure in Fiction and Film*. Ithaca, N.Y.: Cornell University Press, 1978.

———. *Coming to Terms: The Rhetoric of Narrative in Fiction and Film*. Ithaca, N.Y.: Cornell University Press, 1990.

Clark, Beverly Lyon. "A Portrait of the Artist as a Little Woman." *Children's Literature* 17 (1989): 81–97.

Clark, Beverly Lyon, and Margaret R. Higonnet, eds. *Girls, Boys, Books, Toys: Gender in Children's Literature and Culture*. Baltimore: Johns Hopkins University Press, 1999.

Coats, Karen. "The Reason for Disability: Causes and Effects in the Construction of Identity in Contemporary American Children's Books." *Bookbird* 39, no. 1 (2001): 11–16.

Cohn, Dorrit. *Transparent Minds: Narrative Modes for Presenting Consciousness in Fiction*. Princeton, N.J.: Princeton University Press, 1978.

Connolly, Paula. *Winnie-the-Pooh and The House at Pooh Corner: Recovering Arcadia*. Twayne's Masterworks Studies no. 156. New York: Twayne, 1995.

Coveney, Peter. *The Image of Childhood. The Individual and Society: A Study of the Theme in English Literature*. Harmondsworth: Penguin, 1967.

Cowden, Tami, Caro LaFever, and Sue Viders. *The Complete Writer's Guide to Heroes and Heroines: Sixteen Master Archetypes*. Hollywood, Calif.: Lone Eagle, 2000.

Crew, Hilary S. *Is It Really "Mommie Dearest"? Daughter–Mother Narratives in Young Adult Fiction.* Lanham, Md.: Scarecrow, 2000.

Crouch, Marcus. *The Nesbit Tradition: The Children's Novel 1945–1970.* London: Benn, 1972.

Culler, Jonathan: *Structuralist Poetics: Structuralism, Linguistics and the Study of Literature.* London: Routledge, 1975.

———. *On Deconstruction: Theory and Criticism after Structuralism.* Ithaca, N.Y.: Cornell University Press, 1982.

———. *The Pursuit of Signs: Semiotics, Literature, Deconstruction.* Ithaca, N.Y.: Cornell University Press, 1983.

Cunningham, Hugh. *The Children of the Poor: Representation of Childhood since the Seventeenth Century.* Oxford: Blackwell, 1991.

Cuseo, Allan A. *Homosexual Characters in YA Novels: A Literary Analysis, 1969–1982.* Metuchen, N.J.: Scarecrow, 1992.

Day, Frances Ann. *Lesbian and Gay Voices: An Annotated Bibliography and Guide to Literature for Children and Young Adults.* Westport, Conn.: Greenwood, 2000.

Dierks, Margarete, et al., eds. *Kinderwelten: Kinder und Kindheit in der neueren Literatur.* Festschrift für Klaus Doderer. Weinheim, Germany: Beltz, 1985.

Docherty, Thomas. *Reading (Absent) Character: Toward a Theory of Characterization in Fiction.* Oxford: Clarendon, 1983.

Dujardin, Edouard. *Le monologue intérieur.* Paris: Messein, 1931.

Eco, Umberto. *A Theory of Semiotics.* Bloomington: Indiana University Press, 1976.

———. *The Role of the Reader: Explorations in the Semiotics of Texts.* Bloomington: Indiana University Press, 1979.

Edelstein, Linda N. *The Writer's Guide to Character Traits.* Cincinnati, Ohio: Writer's Digest Books, 1999.

Edström, Vivi. *Barnbokens form. En studie i konsten att berätta* (1980). 3d ed. Studies published by the Swedish Institute for Children's Books, no. 11. Stockholm: Rabén & Sjögren, 1992. (With a summary in English: "Form in Children's Books: A Study in Narrative Art.")

Ehrlich, Susan. *Point of View: A Linguistic Analysis of Literary Style.* London: Routledge, 1990.

Erlich, Victor. *Russian Formalism: History, Doctrine.* 2d ed. The Hague: Mouton, 1965.

Fish, Stanley. *Is There a Text in This Class? The Authority of Interpretative Communities.* Cambridge, Mass.: Harvard University Press, 1982.

Fisher, Margery. *Who's Who in Children's Fiction: A Treasury of Familiar Characters of Childhood.* New York: Holt, Rinehart & Winston, 1975.

———. *The Bright Face of Danger: An Exploration of the Adventure Story.* London: Hodder & Stoughton, 1986.

Flanagan, Victoria. "Cross-dressing as Transvestism in Children's Literature: An Analysis of 'Gender-performative' Model." *Papers* 9, no. 3 (1999): 5–14.

Forster, E. M. *Aspects of the Novel* (1927). San Diego: Harcourt, Brace, 1985.

Foster, Robert. *The Complete Guide to Middle Earth.* New York: Ballantine, 1978.

Foster, Shirley, and Judy Simons. *What Katy Read: Feminist Re-readings of "Classic" Stories for Girls.* London: Macmillan, 1995.

Franz, Marie Louise von. *Puer Aeternus: A Psychological Study of the Adult Struggle with the Paradise of Childhood.* 2d ed. Santa Monica, Calif.: Sigo, 1981.

French, Warren. *J. D. Salinger, Revisited.* Boston: Twayne, 1988.

Frye, Northrop. *Anatomy of Criticism: Four Essays.* Princeton, N.J.: Princeton University Press, 1957.

———. *Fables of Identity: Studies in Poetic Mythology.* New York: Harcourt, Brace & World, 1963.

———. *The Secular Scripture: A Study of the Structure of Romance.* Cambridge, Mass.: Harvard University Press, 1976.

Gaarden, Bonnie. "The Inner Family of *The Wind in the Willows.*" *Children's Literature* 22 (1994): 43–57.

Galbraith, Mary. "Pip as 'Infant Tongue' and as Adult Narrator in Chapter One of *Great Expectations.*" pp. 123–41 in *Infant Tongues: The Voices of the Child in Literature,* ed. Elizabeth Goodenough et al. Detroit: Wayne State University Press, 1994.

———. "Deictic Shift Theory and the Poetics of Involvement in Narrative." pp. 19–59 in *Deixis in Narrative: A Cognitive Science Perspective,* ed. Judith F. Duchan et al. Hillsdale, N.J.: Erlbaum, 1995.

"Gay and Lesbian Literature," *Children's Literature Association Quarterly* 23, no. 3 (1998).

Genette, Gérard. *Narrative Discourse: An Essay in Method.* Ithaca, N.Y.: Cornell University Press, 1980.

———. *Narrative Discourse Revisited.* Ithaca, N.Y.: Cornell University Press, 1988.

———. *Palimpsests: Literature in the Second Degree.* Lincoln: University of Nebraska Press, 1997a.

———. *Paratexts: Thresholds of Interpretation.* Cambridge: Cambridge University Press, 1997b.

Gilbert, Sandra. "Costumes of the Mind: Transvestism in Modern Literature." *Critical Inquiry* 7 (1980): 391–417.

Gilbert, Sandra M., and Susan Gubar. *The Madwoman in the Attic: The Woman Writer and the Nineteenth-Century Literary Imagination.* New Haven, Conn.: Yale University Press, 1977.

Gillie, Christopher. *Character in English Literature.* London: Chatto & Windus, 1967.

Golden, Joanne M. *The Narrative Symbol in Childhood Literature: Exploration in the Construction of Text.* Berlin: Mouton, 1990.

Goodenough, Elizabeth, et al., eds. *Infant Tongues: The Voices of the Child in Literature.* Detroit: Wayne State University Press, 1994.

Greimas, Algirdas Julien. *Structural Semantics: An Attempt at a Method.* Lincoln: University of Nebraska Press, 1983.

Griswold, Jerry. *The Classic American Children's Story: Novels of the Golden Age.* New York: Penguin, 1996.

Hamburger, Käte. *The Logic of Literature.* 2d rev. ed. Bloomington: Indiana University Press, 1973.

Harvey, W. J. *Character and the Novel*. Ithaca, N.Y.: Cornell University Press, 1965.

Hochman, Baruch. *The Test of Character: From the Victorian Novel to the Modern*. Rutherford, N.J.: Fairleigh Dickinson University Press, 1983.

————. *Character in Literature*. Ithaca, N.Y.: Cornell University Press, 1985.

Hollander, Anne. "Reflections on *Little Women*." pp. 191–200 in *Reflections on Literature for Children*, ed. Francelia Butler and Richard Rotert. Hamden, Conn.: Library Professional Publications, 1984.

Hollindale, Peter. *Signs of Childness in Children's Books*. Stroud, England: Thimble Press, 1997.

Holub, Robert C. *Reception Theory: A Critical Introduction*. London: Methuen, 1984.

Hood, Anne. *Creating Character Emotions: Writing Compelling, Fresh Approaches That Express Your Characters' True Feelings*. Cincinnati, Ohio: Story Press, 1998.

Hourihan, Margery. *Deconstructing the Hero: Literary Theory and Children's Literature*. London: Routledge, 1997.

Hunt, Peter. "Winnie-the-Pooh and Domestic Fantasy." pp. 112–24 in *Stories and Society: Children's Literature in Its Social Context*, ed. Dennis Butts. London: Macmillan, 1992.

————. *The Wind in the Willows: A Fragmented Arcadia*. New York: Twayne, 1994.

Hutcheon, Linda. *A Poetics of Postmodernism: History, Theory, Fiction*. New York: Routledge, 1988.

Iser, Wolfgang. *The Implied Reader: Patterns of Communication in Prose Fiction from Bunyan to Beckett*. Baltimore: Johns Hopkins University Press, 1974.

————. *The Act of Reading: A Theory of Aesthetic Response*. Baltimore: Johns Hopkins University Press, 1978.

James, Henry. *The Art of the Novel: Critical Prefaces*. New York: Scribner's, 1934.

————. *Theory of Fiction* (1884). Edited with an introduction by James E. Miller Jr. Lincoln: University of Nebraska Press, 1972.

James, William. *The Principles of Psychology*. Vols. 1–2. New York: Holt, 1890.

Jauss, Hans Robert. *Toward an Aesthetic of Reception*. Minneapolis: University of Minnesota Press, 1982.

Jones, Dudley, and Tony Watkins, eds. *A Necessary Fantasy? The Heroic Figure in Children's Popular Culture*. New York: Garland, 2000.

Jones, Raymond E. *Characters in Children's Literature*. Detroit: Gale Research, 1997.

Jung, C. G., ed. *Man and His Symbols*. London: Aldus, 1964.

Jurich, Marilyn. *Scheherazade's Sisters: Trickster Heroines and Their Stories in World Literature*. Westport, Conn.: Greenwood, 1998.

Kermode, Frank. *The Sense of an Ending: Studies in the Theory of Fiction*. London: Oxford University Press, 1968.

Keyser, Elizabeth Lennox. *Little Women: A Family Romance*. Athens: University of Georgia Press, 1999.

Knapp, John, ed. *Literary Character*. Lanham, Md.: University Press of America, 1990.

Knights, L. C. "How Many Children Had Lady Macbeth?" *Explorations* (1965): 1–39.

Kress, Nancy. *Dynamic Characters: How to Create Personalities That Keep Readers Captivated*. Cincinnati, Ohio: Writer's Digest, 1998.

Krips, Valerie. *The Presence of the Past. Memory, Heritage and Childhood in Postwar Britain.* New York: Garland, 2000.

Kuznets, Lois. *Kenneth Grahame.* Boston: Hall, 1987.

———. "Henry James and the Storyteller: The Development of a Central Consciousness in Realistic Fiction for Children." pp. 188–98 in *The Voice of the Narrator in Children's Literature: Insights from Writers and Critics,* ed. Charlotte von Otten and Gary D. Smith. New York: Greenwood, 1989.

———. *When Toys Come Alive: Narratives of Animation, Metamorphosis and Development.* New Haven, Conn.: Yale University Press, 1994.

Lamarque, Peter. *Fictional Points of View.* Ithaca, N.Y.: Cornell University Press, 1996.

Lanser, Susan Sniader. *The Narrative Act: Point of View in Prose Fiction.* Princeton, N.J.: Princeton University Press, 1981.

Lassén-Seger, Maria. "The Fictive Child in Disguise: Disempowering Transformations of the Child Character." pp. 186–96 in *Text, Culture and National Identity in Children's Literature,* ed. Jean Webb. Helsinki: Nordinfo, 2000.

Lathey, Gillian. *The Impossible Legacy: Identity and Purpose in Autobiographical Children's Literature Set in the Third Reich and the Second World War.* Bern: Lang, 1999.

Lauther, Howard. *Creating Characters: A Writer's Reference to the Personality Traits That Bring Fictional People to Life.* Jefferson, N.C.: McFarland, 1998.

Lehnert, Gertrud. *Maskeraden und Metamorphosen: Als Männer verkleidete Frauen in der Literatur.* Würzburg, Germany: Königshausen & Neumann, 1994.

Lessing, Gotthold Ephraim. *Laocoön: An Essay on the Limits of Painting and Poetry.* Baltimore: Johns Hopkins University Press, 1984.

Littlefield, Henry M. "The Wizard of Oz: Parable of Populism." *American Quarterly* 16 (1964): 47–58.

Lorck, Jean Etienne. *Die Erlebte Rede: Eine sprachliche Untersuchung.* Heidelberg: Winter 1921.

Lotman, Jurij. *The Structure of the Artistic Text.* Michigan Slavic Contributions 7. Ann Arbor: University of Michigan Press, 1977.

Lowery, Ruth McCoy. *Immigrants in Children's Literature.* Rethinking Childhood 13. New York: Lang, 2000.

Lubbock, Percy. *The Craft of Fiction* (1921). New York: Viking, 1957.

Lukens, Rebecca J. *A Critical Handbook of Children's Literature.* 4th ed. New York: HarperCollins, 1990.

Lundell, Torborg. *Fairy Tale Mothers.* New York: Peter Lang, 1990.

Lurie, Alison. *The Language of Clothes.* New York: Random House, 1981.

———. *Don't Tell the Grownups: Subversive Children's Literature.* Boston: Little, Brown, 1990.

Lynn, David H. *The Hero's Tale: Narrators in the Early Modern Novel.* New York: St. Martin's, 1989.

MacCann, Donnarae. *White Supremacy in Children's Literature: Characterizations of African Americans, 1830–1900.* New York: Garland, 1998.

MacCann, Donnarae, and Gloria Woodard, eds. *The Black American in Books for Children: Readings in Racism*. Metuchen, N.J.: Scarecrow, 1972.

Marshall, Cynthia. "Bodies and Pleasures in *The Wind in the Willows*." *Children's Literature* 22 (1994): 58–69.

Martin, Wallace. *Recent Theories of Narrative*. Ithaca, N.Y.: Cornell University Press, 1986.

Matejka, Ladislav, and Krystyna Pomorska, eds. *Readings in Russian Poetics: Formalist and Structuralist Views*. Cambridge, Mass.: MIT Press, 1971.

May, Keith M. *Characters of Women in Narrative Literature*. New York: St. Martin's, 1981.

McCallum, Robyn. *Ideologies of Identity in Adolescent Fiction: The Dialogic Construction of Subjectivity*. New York: Garland, 1999.

McElroe, Janice S. "Images of Grandparents in Children's Literature." *The New Advocate* 12, no. 3 (1999): 249–58.

McGavran, James Holt, ed. *Romanticism and Children's Literature in Nineteenth-Century England*. Athens: University of Georgia Press, 1991.

————. *Literature and the Child: Romantic Continuations, Postmodern Contestations*. Iowa City: University of Iowa Press, 1999.

McGillis, Roderick. *The Nimble Reader*. New York: Twayne, 1996.

Miller, Dean A. *The Epic Hero*. Baltimore: Johns Hopkins University Press, 2000.

Miller, J. Hillis, ed. *Aspects of Narrative: Selected Papers from the English Institute*. New York: Columbia University Press, 1971.

Mitchell, W. J. T., ed. *On Narrative*. Chicago: University of Chicago Press, 1981.

Moi, Toril. *Sexual/Textual Politics. Feminist Literary Theory*. London: Methuen, 1985.

Morris, Pam, ed. *The Bakhtin Reader: Selected Writings of Bakhtin, Medvedev, Voloshinov*. London: Arnold, 1994.

Morson, Gary Saul. *Narrative and Freedom: The Shadows of Time*. New Haven, Conn.: Yale University Press, 1994.

Morson, Gary Saul, and Caryl Emerson. *Mikhail Bakhtin: Creation of a Prosaics*. Stanford, Calif.: Stanford University Press, 1990.

Mortimore, Arthur D. *Index to Characters in Children's Literature*. Bristol: Mortimore, 1977.

Mueller Nienstadt, Irma. *Die Mumins für Erwachsene: Bilder zur Selbstwerdung*. Düsseldorf: Walter, 1994.

Murray, Heather. "Frances Hodgson Burnett's *The Secret Garden*: The Organ(ic)ized World." pp. 20–43 in vol. 1, *Touchstones: Reflections of the Best in Children's Literature*, ed. Perry Nodelman. West Lafayette, Ind.: Children's Literature Association, 1985.

Nabokov, Vladimir. *Lectures on Russian Literature*. New York: Harcourt Brace Jovanovich, 1981.

Nikolajeva, Maria. *The Magic Code: The Use of Magical Patterns in Fantasy for Children*. Studies published by the Swedish Institute for Children's Books, no. 31. Stockholm: Almqvist & Wiksell International, 1988.

————. "Stages of Transformation: Folklore Elements in Children's Novels." *Canadian Children's Literature* 73 (1994): 48–54.

————. *Children's Literature Comes of Age: Towards a New Aesthetic.* New York: Garland, 1996.

————. "The Child as Self-Deceiver: Narrative Strategies in Katherine Paterson's and Patricia MacLachlan's Novels." *Papers* 7 (1997a) 1: 5–15.

————. *Introduction to the Theory of Children's Literature.* 2d ed. Tallinn: Tallinn University Press, 1997b.

————. "Reflections of Change in Children's Books Titles." pp. 85–89 in *Reflections of Change,* ed. Sandra L. Beckett. Westport, Conn.: Greenwood, 1997c.

————. "Two National Heroes: Jacob Two-Two and Pippi Longstocking." *Canadian Children's Literature* 86 (1997d): 7–16.

————. *Barnbokens byggklossar.* Lund, Sweden: Studentlitteratur, 1998a.

————. "Exit Children's Literature?" *The Lion and the Unicorn* 22 (1998b) 2: 221–36.

————. *From Mythic to Linear: Time in Children's Literature.* Lanham, Md.: Scarecrow, 2000.

Nikolajeva, Maria, and Carole Scott. *How Picturebooks Work.* New York: Garland, 2001.

Nodelman, Perry. "Interpretation and the Apparent Sameness of Children's Literature." *Studies in the Literary Imagination* 18 (1985a) 2: 5–20.

————. "Text as Teacher: The Beginning of Charlotte's Web." *Children's Literature* 13 (1985b): 109–27.

————. *The Pleasures of Children's Literature.* New York: Longman, 1992; 2d ed., 1996.

Onega, Susana, and José Angel García Landa, eds. *Narratology.* London: Longman, 1996.

Orwell, George. "Charles Dickens." pp. 55–111 in his *A Collection of Essays.* Garden City, N.Y.: Doubleday, 1954.

Österlund, Mia. "Girls in Disguise: Gender Transgression in Swedish Young Adult Fiction of the 1980s." pp. 175–85 in *Text, Culture and National Identity in Children's Literature,* ed. Jean Webb. Helsinki: Nordinfo, 2000.

Otten, Charlotte von, and Gary D. Smith, eds. *The Voice of the Narrator in Children's Literature: Insights from Writers and Critics.* New York: Greenwood, 1989.

Pascal, Roy. *The Dual Voice: Free Indirect Speech and Its Functioning in the Nineteenth-Century Novel.* Manchester: Manchester University Press, 1977.

Pasternak, Lena, ed. *Female/Male: Gender in Children's Literature.* Visby, Sweden: Baltic Centre for Writers and Translators, 1999.

Paterson, Katherine. *A Sense of Wonder: On Reading and Writing Books for Children.* New York: Penguin, 1995.

Paul, Lissa. "Enigma Variations: What Feminist Criticism Knows about Children's Literature." pp. 148–66 in *Children's Literature: The Development of Criticism,* ed. Peter Hunt. London: Routledge & Kegan Paul, 1990.

————. *Reading Otherways*. Stroud, England: Thimble, 1998.

Pavel, Thomas G. *Fictional Worlds*. Cambridge, Mass.: Harvard University Press, 1986.

Pearson, Carol, and Katherine Pope. *The Female Hero in American and British Literature*. New York: Bowker, 1981.

Petruso, Thomas F. *Life Made Real: Characterization in the Novel since Proust and Joyce*. Ann Arbor: University of Michigan Press, 1991.

Petzold, Dieter. "Taking Games Seriously: Romantic Irony in Modern Fantasy for Children of All Ages." pp. 87–104 in *Literature and the Child: Romantic Continuations, Postmodern Contestations*, ed. James Holt McGavran. Iowa City: University of Iowa Press, 1999.

Pfeffer, Susan Beth. *Who Were They Really? The True Stories behind Famous Characters*. Brookfield, Conn.: Millbrook, 1999.

Phelan, James. *Worlds from Words: A Theory of Language in Fiction*. Chicago: University of Chicago Press, 1981.

————. *Reading People, Reading Plots: Character, Progression, and the Interpretations of Narrative*. Chicago: University of Chicago Press, 1989.

Pinsent, Pat. "Paradise Restored: The Significance of Coincidence in Some Children's Books." *Children's Literature in Education* 20 (1989) 2: 103–10.

Plotz, Judith. " Literary Ways of Killing a Child: The 19th Century Practice." pp. 1–24 in *Aspects and Issues in the History of Children's Literature*, ed. Maria Nikolajeva. Westport, Conn.: Greenwood, 1995:1–24.

Pratt, Annis, with Barbara White, Andrea Loewenstein, and Mary Wyer. *Archetypal Patterns in Women's Fiction*. Bloomington: Indiana University Press, 1981.

Pratt, Mary Louise. *Toward a Speech Act Theory of Literary Discourse*. Bloomington: Indiana University Press, 1977.

Price, Martin. "The Other Self: Thoughts about Characters in the Novel." pp. 279–99 in *Imagined Worlds*, ed. Mack Maynard and Ian Gregor. London: Methuen, 1968.

————. *Forms of Life: Character and Moral Imagination in the Novel*. New Haven, Conn.: Yale University Press, 1983.

Prince, Gerald. *A Grammar of Stories*. The Hague: Mouton, 1973.

————. *Narratology: The Form and Functioning of Narrative*. Berlin: Mouton, 1982.

————. *A Dictionary of Narratology*. Lincoln: University of Nebraska Press, 1987.

Propp, Vladimir. *Morphology of the Folktale*. Austin: University of Texas Press, 1968.

————. *Theory and History of Folklore*. Manchester: Manchester University Press, 1984.

Rabine, Leslie W. *Reading the Romantic Heroine: Text, History, Ideology*. Ann Arbor: University of Michigan Press, 1985.

Reynolds, Kimberley, and Paul Yates. "Too Soon: Representations of Childhood Death in Literature for Children." pp. 151–77 in *Childhood in Culture: Approaches to Childhood*, ed. Karín Lesnik-Oberstein. New York: Macmillan, 1998.

Ricoeur, Paul. *Time and Narrative*. Vols. 1–2. Chicago: University of Chicago Press, 1984–85.

Rimmon-Kenan, Shlomith. *Narrative Fiction: Contemporary Poetics*. London: Methuen, 1983.

Robinson, Debra. *Portraying Persons with Disabilities: An Annotated Bibliography of Fiction for Children and Teenagers*. New Providence, N.J.: Bowker, 1992.

Romberg, Bertil. *Studies in the Narrative Technique of the First-Person Novel*. Stockholm: Almqvist & Wiksell, 1962.

Rose, Jacqueline. *The Case of Peter Pan, or The Impossibility of Children's Fiction*. London: Macmillan, 1984.

Rudman, Masha Kabakow. *Children's Literature: An Issues Approach*. 3d ed. White Plains, N.Y.: Longman, 1995.

Ryan, Marie-Laure. "The Pragmatics of Personal and Impersonal Fiction." *Poetics* 10 (1981) 517–39.

Sale, Roger. *Fairy Tales and After*. Cambridge: Cambridge University Press, 1978.

Sammonds, Martha C. *A Guide through Narnia*. London: Hodder & Stoughton, 1979.

———. *"A Better Country": The Worlds of Religious Fantasy and Science Fiction*. New York: Greenwood, 1988.

Schafer, Elizabeth D. *Exploring Harry Potter*. Osprey, Fla.: Beacham, 2000.

Schakel, Peter J. *Reading with the Heart: The Way into Narnia*. Grand Rapids, Mich.: Eerdman, 1979.

Scholes, Robert. *Structuralism in Literature: An Introduction*. New Haven, Conn.: Yale University Press, 1974.

Scholes, Robert, and Robert Kellogg. *The Nature of Narrative*. London: Oxford University Press, 1966.

Schwarcz, Joseph, and Chava Schwarcz. *The Picture Book Comes of Age*. Chicago: American Library Association, 1991.

Scott, Carole. "Between Me and the World: Clothes as Mediator between Self and Society in the Works of Beatrix Potter." *The Lion & the Unicorn* 16, no. 2 (1992): 192–98.

———. "A Century of Dislocated Time: Time Travel, Magic and the Search for Self." *Papers* 6, no. 2 (1996): 14–20.

Scutter, Heather. *Displaced Fictions: Contemporary Australian Books for Teenagers and Young Adults*. Melbourne: Melbourne University Press, 1999.

Searle, John R. *Speech Acts: An Essay in the Philosophy of Language*. Cambridge: Cambridge University Press, 1969.

Segal, Robert A., ed. *Jung on Mythology*. Princeton, N.J.: Princeton University Press, 1998.

Skalin, Lars-Åke. *Karaktär och perspektiv: Att tolka litterära gestalter i det mimetiska språkspelet*. Uppsala, Sweden: Uppsala University Press, 1991. (With a summary in English: "Character and Perspective: Reading Fictional Figures in the Mimetic Language Game.")

Snodgrass, Mary Ellen. *Characters from Young Adult Literature*. Englewood, Colo.: Libraries Unlimited, 1991.

Springer, Mary Doyle. *A Rhetoric of Literary Character: Some Women of Henry James*. Chicago: University of Chicago Press, 1978.

Stephens, John. *Language and Ideology in Children's Fiction*. London: Longman, 1992.

————. "Gender, Genre and Children's Literature." *Signal* 79 (1996): 17–30.

Stephens, John, and Robyn McCallum. *Retelling Stories, Framing Culture: Traditional Story and Metanarratives in Children's Literature*. New York: Garland, 1998.

Storey, Dee. *Twins in Children's and Adolescent Literature: An Annotated Bibliography*. Metuchen, N.J.: Scarecrow, 1993.

Suleiman, Susan R., and Inge Crosman, eds. *The Reader in the Text: Essays on Audience and Interpretation*. Princeton, N.J.: Princeton University Press, 1980.

Swain, Dwight V. *Creating Character: How to Build Story People*. Cincinnati, Ohio: Writer's Digest Books, 1990.

Todorov, Tzvetan. *The Poetics of Prose*. Ithaca, N.Y.: Cornell University Press, 1977.

————. *Bakhtin: The Dialogic Principle*. Minneapolis: University of Minnesota Press, 1984.

Torrance, Robert M. *The Comic Hero*. Cambridge, Mass.: Harvard University Press, 1978.

Trites, Roberta Seelinger. *Waking Sleeping Beauty: Feminist Voices in Children's Novels*. Iowa City: University of Iowa Press, 1997.

————. "'Queer Performances': Lesbian Politics in *Little Women*." pp. 139–60 in *Little Women and the Feminist Imagination: Criticism, Controversy, Personal Essays*, ed. Janice M. Alberghene and Beverly Lyon Clark. New York: Garland, 1998.

————. *Disturbing the Universe: Power and Repression in Adolescent Literature*. Iowa City: University of Iowa Press, 2000.

Tunnell, Michael O. *The Prydain Companion: A Reference Guide to Lloyd Alexander's Prydain Chronicles*. New York: Greenwood, 1989.

Tuten-Puckett, Katharyn E. *My Name in Books: A Guide to Characters' Names in Children's Literature*. Englewood, Colo.: Libraries Unlimited, 1993.

Uspensky, Boris. *A Poetics of Composition: The Structure of the Artistic Text and Typology of a Compositional Form*. Berkeley: University of California Press, 1973.

Usrey, Malcolm. "Johanna Spyri's *Heidi*: The Conversion of a Byronic Hero." pp. 232–42 in vol. 3, *Touchstones: Reflections on the Best in Children's Literature*, ed. Perry Nodelman. West Lafayette, Ind.: Children's Literature Association, 1985.

Veglahn, Nancy. "Images of Evil: Male and Female Monsters in Heroic Fantasy." *Children's Literature* 15 (1987): 106–19.

Vygotsky, Lev. *Thought and Language*. Cambridge, Mass.: MIT Press, 1986.

Wall, Barbara. *The Narrator's Voice: The Dilemma of Children's Fiction*. London: Macmillan, 1991.

Warner, Marina. *From the Beast to the Blonde: On Fairy Tales and Their Tellers*. New York: Farrar, Straus & Giroux, 1994a.

————. *Managing Monsters: Six Myths of Our Time*. London: Vintage, 1994b.

————. *No Go the Bogeyman: Scaring, Lulling, and Making Mock*. New York: Farrar, Straus & Giroux, 1998.

Watt, Ian. *Myths of Modern Individualism. Faust, Don Quixote, Don Juan, Robinson Crusoe*. Cambridge: Cambridge University Press, 1996.

Waugh, Patricia. *Metafiction: The Theory and Practice of Self-Conscious Fiction*. London: Methuen, 1984.

Westfall, Gary, and George Edgar Slusser. *Nursery Realms: Children in the Worlds of Science Fiction, Fantasy, and Horror*. Athens: University of Georgia Press, 1999.

Westin, Boel. "The Androgynous Female (or Orlando Inverted)—Examples from Gripe, Stark, Wahl, Pohl." Pp. 91–102 in *Female/Male: Gender in Children's Literature*, ed. Lena Pasternak. Visby, Sweden: Baltic Centre for Writers and Translators, 1999.

Wullschläger, Jackie. *Inventing Wonderland: The Lives and Fantasies of Lewis Carroll, Edward Lear, J. M. Barrie, Kenneth Grahame and A. A. Milne*. London: Methuen, 1995.

Zipes, Jack. *Happily Ever After: Fairy Tales, Children and the Culture Industry*. New York: Routledge, 1997.

———. *When Dreams Came True: Classical Fairy Tales and Their Tradition*. New York: Routledge, 1999.

———. *Sticks and Stones: The Troublesome Success of Children's Literature from Slovenly Peter to Harry Potter*. New York: Routledge, 2001.

Zipes, Jack, ed. *The Oxford Companion to Fairy Tales*. Oxford: Oxford University Press, 2000.

Zornado, John. *Inventing the Child: Culture, Ideology, and the Rise of Childhood*. New York: Garland, 2000.

Name Index

Title Index

Character Index

Subject Index

About the Author

Maria Nikolajeva is a professor of comparative literature at Stockholm University in Sweden, and associate professor of comparative literature at Åbo Akademi University in Finland, where she teaches children's literature and literary theory. A graduate of Moscow Linguistic University, she received her doctorate from Stockholm University in 1988, for *The Magic Code: The Use of Magical Patterns in Fantasy for Children*.

She is the author and editor of several books on children's literature, among them *Children's Literature Comes of Age: Toward the New Aesthetic* (Garland, 1996), a ChLA Honor Book, *From Mythic to Linear: Time in Children's Literature* (Scarecrow, 2000), and, in collaboration with Carole Scott, *How Picturebooks Work* (Garland, 2001). She has also published a large number of articles in professional journals and essay collections. Her academic honors include a Fulbright Grant at the University of Massachusetts, Amherst, a research fellowship at the International Youth Library, Munich, and Donner Visiting Chair at Åbo Akademi University. She was the president of the International Research Society for Children's Literature in 1993–97. She is one of the senior editors of the forthcoming *Oxford Encyclopedia of Children's Literature*.